Shooting the Stickbow
A Practical Approach to Classical Archery

By
Anthony Camera

"Shooting the Stickbow," by Anthony Camera. ISBN 978-1-60264-244-7.

Published 2008 by Virtualbookworm.com Publishing Inc., P.O. Box 9949, College Station, TX 77842, US. ©2008, Anthony Camera.

Manufactured in the United States of America.

Dedicated to my wife Susan, without whose love, understanding and patience, none of this would be possible or worthwhile.

I would also like to thank the following people for reviewing this book and making suggestions to improve its content and readability: Harold Rowland, David A. Sosa, Ryan Kowalick and Kirk Batten.

Special thanks to Ed Cerchione, John Treutlein and Matt DeStefano and the owners and staff of American Outdoor Sports in Farmingdale, NY, for use of their range which was used for some of the photographs in this book.

I am an Archer.

I am not a traditional archer, bowhunter, compound shooter, or target archer.

I draw a bow with the first three fingers of my hand. The bow's limbs bend in direct proportion to my strength and to the length of my draw. My fingers are callused and my back is strong from years of shooting.

I focus completely on the one target I wish to hit. I use no device to direct my arrow toward its mark, save my eyes and my will.

As long as I have the strength to bend a bow, the eyesight to direct my arrow, and the mental faculty to understand what that means,

I am an Archer.

Those simple statements are applied to how I try to live my life. I do and I am many things, as we all do and are, but the loosing of a well-aimed arrow defines how I try to do all those things.

For those of you who understand these simple words, there is no doubt as to what we do, or who we are.

Contents

Introduction i
About the author – iii
Part 1   Basics of Shooting the Stickbow 1
   Chapter 1   Equipment Fundamentals 3
   Chapter 2   Basic Equipment Setup 29
   Chapter 3   Elementary Shooting Form 35
   Chapter 4   Common Errors and How to Correct Them 49
   Chapter 5   Tuning the Bow and Arrow - The First Steps 65
   Chapter 6   Tuning the Bow and Arrow - Beyond the Basics 75
   Chapter 7   Tuning with Gadgets – An Introduction to Olympic Style
Shooting 95
Part 2   Equipment - A Detailed View 121
   Chapter 8   Bow Design – Building a Virtual Bow 123
   Chapter 9   Arrows 151
   Chapter 10   Fletching, the Art of Building an Arrow 179
   Chapter 11   Bowstrings 193
Part 3   Making the Shot – Theories and Practice 219
   Chapter 12   Aiming 221
   Chapter 13   Back Tension, Breathing and Related Topics 245
   Chapter 14   Variations in Technique 255
   Chapter 15   Physical Fitness 271
   Chapter 16   Archery – the Mental Game 285
Part 4   Memories and Musings 307
   Chapter 17   The Golden Age of Archery 309
   Chapter 18   The Life and Legacy of Earl Hoyt Jr., the Father of Modern
Olympic Archery 331
Appendices 341
   Appendix A   Math, measurements and standards 343
   Appendix B   Bowstring and arrow references 353
   Appendix C   Resources 365
   Appendix D   Frequently Asked Questions 370
   Appendix E   Glossary 373

Introduction

Archery - the use, or rather the skill, of shooting the bow and arrow is as old as recorded history. Its historical accounts have filled hundreds, if not thousands, of volumes throughout the ages with documented findings, conjecture and folklore. The use of the bow and arrow as a means of putting food on the table or waging war has its roots in nearly all cultures and civilizations. Truly, the history of archery is the history of mankind.

This book is designed to teach the fundamentals of archery, shooting the bow and arrow, and to give the reader a better understanding of the actual processes involved. It assumes nothing but that the would-be archer has reasonable physical capacity, mental keenness, and the desire to learn to shoot a stickbow and shoot one to the best of his ability.

We will first create a solid foundation emphasizing correct shooting form and a basic understanding of the equipment we will be using, as well as its configuration and tuning. Then we will build on that foundation to allow the new archer to refine his shooting form and tune his equipment so he may go on to whatever aspect of archery he finds most intriguing or challenging. That aspect may be target or Olympic style target archery, bowhunting, or just walking through the forest with bow in hand, shooting at leaves or tree stumps, and being able to hit them. It is my hope that after reading this book, the archer will be able to pass on what he has learned to others and help keep the spirit of archery alive.

OK, you've just seen _The Lord of the Rings_ movie (in my day it was _The Adventures of Robin Hood_ with Errol Flynn) and think you have the "bug". Maybe you've tried archery as a youth in school or summer camp and something rekindled an old interest. Perhaps you've been shooting a compound bow for a few years and have grown tired of the hi-tech mechanics and tinkering that are involved and you just want more of a challenge from archery.

In a book written over a century ago, called simply _Archery_, by C.J. Longman and Col. H. Walrond, the Rev. Eyre W. Hussey wrote:

"Simple and innocent, however, as it (the bow) appears, and capable as it is of being a trusty friend and ally, a bow is at the same time a watchful enemy, ready to take advantage of the smallest slight."

Perhaps that is the strongest reason that so many of us are drawn to this particular style of archery. **No matter how sophisticated the materials may become, nor how efficiently they perform, the shot or rather the shot placement is due to, and only to, the skill of the archer.** Here we succeed or fail based on our own ability to choose and configure our equipment and to learn to use it properly. It is a journey that begins with our first attempt to draw a bow and loose an arrow and the dream of making that arrow reach a mark off in the distance that captures the hearts and souls of budding archers today as it did thousands of years ago. It is that journey we now begin.

I will frequently reference the "Golden Age of Archery", a period that began in the late 1950's and lasted through the middle 1980's. Archery at that time was the most rapidly growing sport in America and it was during those years that I first learned to shoot the bow and arrow. Most of the theories and practices presented in this book were solidified during that period as well. While some materials used for building bows and arrows may have changed over the years, the principles governing their use have not.

One of the most compelling reasons for writing this book is that today the practice of archery, even "stickbow" archery, has diverged into two very separate camps. There are the highly competitive Olympic-style target archers who approach the technological level of the compound archers and back their beliefs with scores that rival the best compound archers. Then there are the purists or "traditionalists" that have in some sense shunned the world of the hi-tech equipment of target archery in favor of a simpler venue. Some traditionalists have gone beyond traditional and become what can be described as primitive. They handcraft their bows, arrows and related equipment in the same way and sometimes from the same materials that were used hundreds or thousands of years ago. There are numerous volumes currently on the market that cater to both camps. What has been missing is a work that deals with the person in the middle, the man or woman who is simply interested in learning archery, the skill of shooting the bow and arrow, and being able to do it to the best of his or her ability. In addition to the simple enjoyment of shooting a bow and arrow, they want to have an understanding of how and why certain things work. It is for this last group of archers this book is intended. Hopefully with the information contained in the following pages, that archer will have the tools necessary to build a solid foundation and excel at whichever aspect of archery he chooses.

Let's get started – just don't be surprised if it's not exactly what you expected. Hang on!

This work begins at the most basic level and progresses to more advanced topics. Salient features will be repeated when necessary for continuity, but each chapter builds on the previous ones. While it may be used a reference, if this is your first exposure to archery or to shooting the stickbow it is strongly recommended that you start from the beginning and work your way through each section.

The first section deals with buying and setting up your first bow, arrows and related equipment. After that I give an explanation of rudimentary shooting techniques or "form". Later we'll see how to tune your equipment for increased efficiency or "performance". The second section delves into the archery "hardware". We'll take a closer look at how and why bows and arrows do what they do. There are also sections on building your own arrows and bowstrings, if you're so inclined. The third section gives an in-depth look at the process of making the shot, not only what is required during the shooting sequence, but steps that can be taken to prepare for the shooting session. The final section goes under the category of "author's prerogative" and is presented to give the new archer a feeling for how archery was practiced during its heyday in America. It may also serve to clear up some of the current myths about "traditional" archery.

The learning process can be greatly enhanced if you have access to experienced shooters who can watch and critique what you're doing. If you don't at the very least work with a friend, spouse, or someone who can see what you're doing and offer comment or criticisms, based on what has been presented here. The problem with this or any written work is that I can't see what you're doing from here, and neither can you. A second set of eyes can be the most valuable tool in your new arsenal.

About the author –

In the summer of 1968 the author was 11 years of age and as luck would have it, he saw *The Adventures of Robinhood* with Errol Flynn on television one Saturday afternoon. Something clicked, and later that year he acquired a solid fiberglass bow, three wooden arrows and related archery accessories by selling Christmas cards to family, friends and neighbors. Without any formal training, the three arrows didn't last very long, especially since he was shooting into a concrete garage; this was Brooklyn after all, not exactly the wide open spaces. Happily, several sporting goods stores in the area carried archery equipment, and "kid's" arrows weren't expensive, so replenishment wasn't too difficult. By the next year he was able to purchase a "real" laminated recurve bow, well, an entry-level semi-recurve, anyway. Weather permitting, archery practice was every day after school and almost all day, every day, during the summer months.

This continued for a few years, and with no signs of losing interest, he finally had the bright idea to ask one of the sporting goods storeowners whether there were any archery ranges in the area. Yes, it took him nearly four years to think of that. He convinced his father to drive him to the range one very snowy night. (The Comanche Bowmen Inc. Archery Club in the Bay Ridge section of Brooklyn, about five miles from his house.) His father wasn't happy about driving to an archery range in near blizzard conditions but the kid was determined! One look at the place, and he was hooked!

He soon after joined the club as a junior member and made the half-hour bus trip two, sometimes three, times a week. With proper instruction, his skill developed and he began competing in the adult classes at age 16. Thereafter he became the youngest Range Officer the club had to date, and began teaching with the club's JOAD (Junior Olympic Archery Development) program, and instructed local Scout troops and the PAL (Police Athletic League) members that regularly used the range.

In his twenties, he (out of necessity) became an expert fletcher and string maker, and was competing at state and regional levels, with an NFAA "AA" barebow (without the use of bow sights) rating. He became one of the range's senior range officers and a certified New York State Bowhunting Safety Instructor. He also gave archery demonstrations in the 1970's and 80's at the New York Renaissance Faire at Sterling Forest (as Robinhood, of course) and did trick shooting on the CBS daytime soap opera "As the World Turns" and the children's cable TV show "The Great Space Coaster".

Taking a small hiatus from archery in the late 1980's and early 90's, to learn rifle marksmanship, the author achieved Masters' ratings in both International and Conventional Hi-Power rifle styles of shooting. The two disciplines (archery and rifle marksmanship) worked well together, and lessons learned from one were easily transferred to the other.

The author completed his undergraduate studies at New York University, with a BA in Biology and continued his graduate studies there in Physiology. That knowledge helped him to understand the mechanics of shooting and the processes of many of the theories presented in this book.

Although no longer competing, he shoots three to four times a week at local ranges and has moderated an archery forum on the Internet. After nearly 40 years in the sport, he says, "It's nice to be able to relax at the range, shoot and maybe pass along some of the things I've learned over the years to others."

Part 1

Basics of shooting the stickbow

Chapter 1

Equipment Fundamentals

The title of this work is _Shooting the Stickbow_. So, what is a stickbow? For the sake of simplicity a stickbow is a longbow (diag 1-1), recurve (diag 1-2), or any other bow without cables or pulleys which is drawn and released with the unaided fingers. The term "stickbow" has had many connotations throughout the years based on design, appearance, and even manner of use. We'll just keep it simple and use the above definition for the time being.

Before we start talking about buying your first bow and learning how to shoot it, there are a few terms and definitions we should discuss.

Longbow – This used to be a pretty simple idea, but times have changed. For our present discussion, it is a bow that when strung (or braced), the limbs arc in a single direction and the bowstring touches the limb only at the string grooves (or nocks) (diag 1-1).

Longbow

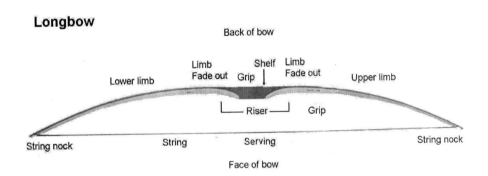

1-1 Generic longbow nomenclature

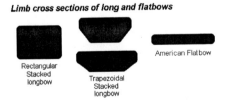

Diag 1-1a Various types of longbow cross-sections.

Longbows initially had a "stacked" design, meaning the limbs were relatively thick from face to back and thin from side to side. A variation of the longbow sometimes called an American Flatbow followed the same basic rules as a longbow, but its limbs were thinner face to back and wider side to side (diag 1-1a). As we'll see in section 2, that simple change improved performance.

Recurve – A bow that when braced has its limb tips pointing away from the shooter, and the string contacts not only the string nocks, but rests along the limbs for several inches (diag 1-2).

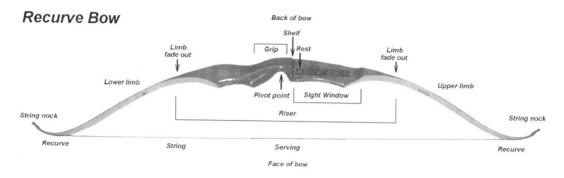

1-2 Generic recurve nomenclature

Limbs – The primary working parts of the bow. They bend and store energy as the bow is drawn and transfer that energy to the arrow when the string is released.

Riser – The middle part of the bow to which the limbs are attached. The riser contains the grip area that the archer holds while shooting.

Limb Fade outs or Feather area – The sections on the bow where the riser tapers into the limbs.

Sight window – Cutout section of the riser allowing the arrow to be closer to the center of the bow which affords a better view of the target when the bow is held vertically.

Grip – The part of the riser held in your hand.

Pivot point – The deepest part of the grip.

Arrow shelf – The part of the riser at right angles to the long axis of the bow and directly above the grip.

Arrow rest – Stick-on or screw-in device on which the arrow rests during the draw and anchor.

String – The thing that turns a stick into a bow! (Strings and components will be discussed in detail later in the book.)

String nocks – The cutout area on each limb tip that keeps the string in place when the bow is braced.

String groove (recurves only)– A channel cut into the face of the limbs, a few inches in length, in which the string rests (diag 1-2a)

Back of bow – The part of the bow that faces away from the shooter when the bow is held in the shooting position.

Face (or belly) of bow - The part of the bow that faces the shooter when the bow is held in the shooting position.

If you think of the bow as a person, when you engage someone, you face his face (or belly) and cannot see his back. That's the derivation of the face and back of a bow.

Bow length – Historically, recurves and longbows have been measured from string nock to string nock along the back of the bow following all curvatures.

Brace Height – The distance from a point perpendicular to the bowstring to the pivot point (deepest cut of the grip) (diag 1-2b). Note: some custom bowyers measure the brace height from the string to the face of the arrow shelf or sight window.

Brace Height

1-2a String grooves on the back of a recurve limb
1-2b Standard brace height measurement

ATA (AMO) length – (Archery Trade Association, formerly the Archery Manufacturers' Organization, a standardizing organization for the archery industry) states only that the AMO length of a bow, either longbow or recurve, is 3" longer than the length of a string that when used will provide the manufacturer's recommended brace height. For example, if you obtain a 66" AMO string, it will be 63" in length, and provide the correct brace height for an AMO 66" bow.

Draw weight – The amount of force required to bend the limbs by drawing the string to the archer's draw length. Bows are typically rated at a draw length of 28".

These days, both recurves and longbows are generally "laminated" bows. That means that the limbs are made up of several layers of materials such as wood (usually maple), carbon, carbon foam or even an epoxy/ceramic matrix laminated or sandwiched between two outer layers of fiberglass or carbon (diag 1- 3).

Basic laminated limb

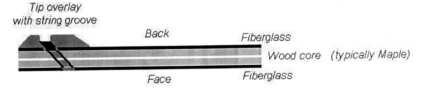

Tip overlay
with string groove

Back   Fiberglass

Wood core   (typically Maple)

Face   Fiberglass

1-3 Schematic of a generic limb lamination (right).

Many people today have rekindled the primitive side of archery, and choose to make their own bows. More often than not these are self-bows, with the limbs and riser made from a single piece of wood or "stave". *(Stave is the term for a piece of wood suitable and destined to become a bow.)* While great satisfaction can be gained from crafting your own bow and using it to compete in tournaments or harvest game, they are by-and-large at a performance disadvantage compared to modern laminated bows. This is not to say that selfbows cannot be used successfully, but they will not cast an arrow as fast or as far as laminated bows and generally will not shoot as sweetly as their laminated counterparts. A bow that is said to shoot sweetly draws smoothly, is comfortable in the hand, and casts an arrow well. Also, given that they are crafted from a single piece of wood, they are more prone to failure than laminated bows (diag 1-4).

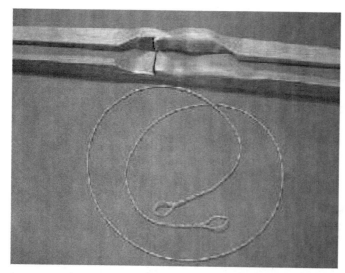

1-4 A Pair of wooden selfbows and a hand laid Flemish Splice string made by Bruce Minnick, a friend of the author

Both recurves and longbows can be simple one-piece designs, or "takedown" models. The takedowns or T/D bows can come apart in either two or three pieces. The two piece bows split in the middle of the riser by means of a sleeve or knuckle, and the three-piece bows consist of a riser (handle section) and separate limbs. The latter is more popular as an archer can have one riser and several sets of limbs, varying in length and draw weight. Either variant makes transporting the bow much easier (diag 1-5).

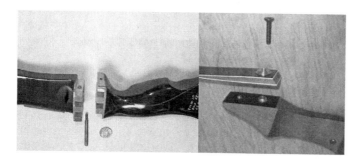

1-5 Ben Pearson two piece T/D bow showing a "knuckle and bolt" coupling (left) and a more common bolt and pin three piece arrangement on a PSE Impala (right).

Arrow – the long, thin stick with a point on one end and feathers on the other (diag 1-6).

Typical arrow nomenclature

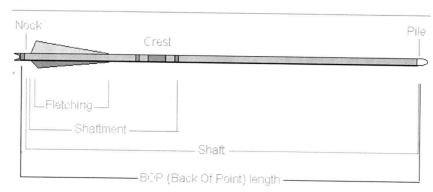

1-6 Typical arrow nomenclature

Shaft – the rod or tube from which the arrow is made.

Shaftment – the last 8" – 12" of the arrow shaft.

BOP (Back Of Point) length – The length of the arrow measured from the throat of the nock to the back of the arrowhead.

Head, tip or pile – the pointy business end of the arrow.

Nock – the grooved, usually plastic, piece that attaches to the rear of the arrow and engages the string.

Fletching – the feathers, typically from a turkey or goose, attached to the shaftment that steer the arrow. Plastic fletching, called vanes, is also used and will be discussed later.

Cresting – optional colored bands painted on the shaftment for decorative or identification purposes.

So far pretty simple, no?

Ready to buy your first bow? Not so fast!

Before you do, open the phone book and find the nearest Archery Range or Club. Visit them and look around; see if there are any stickbow shooters there. There might not be. If not, ask if there's a "traditional" night, or a time when stickbow (either traditional or Olympic style) shooters come around. If not, you might also want to check with local sporting goods stores to see if they sell stickbows (you might want to call them recurves or longbows, though). If they do, they might know where their customers are shooting them. If all else fails, you can try some of the archery web sites listed in appendix C. There's usually a lot of good information there and you might also be able to find other archers in your area and find out where they're shooting. Some sites also have schedules of archery events by state or region.

Let's assume that you've found a range, (if you really can't, see the last section of this chapter for tips on setting up a safe practice area at home), and if you're lucky, there'll be some decent stickbow shooters there. First thing to do is just watch. Especially watch the good or best shooters – it's usually pretty easy to figure out who the best are; generally, they are the ones pulling their arrows from the center of the target. You can also tell a lot about a shooter without even seeing where his arrows are going. A good shooter will be very relaxed and the shot will look effortless. Every shot execution will look like every other. The archer will be nearly still when he releases the arrow except for the release hand, which moves slightly rearward. The odds are that's the guy who'll be pulling his arrows from the center of the target! While it's probably not a good idea to walk up and introduce yourself while the guy or gal is trying to make a shot (double that, if there's a match going on), most good shooters will be more than happy to talk to you. They'll actually want to talk to you about archery and get you involved. If they didn't like doing it, they wouldn't be there; you'll find that most archers are quite passionate about their sport. Talk to as many people as you can, get their opinions, then think about them and try to formulate your own opinion of how you'd like to start. Just don't buy anything – yet.

Still interested? Good, let's get started!

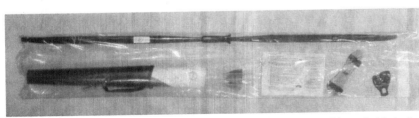

1-7 Most of us who've been at this longer than we'd care to mention, myself included, probably started out with an "Archery Set" similar to this with a solid fiberglass bow, a few wooden arrows and the basic accessories. While still an option, it's probably better left to younger archers.

The Bow

You've been to an archery range, a sporting goods shop, you've talked to a few people, you've probably done a few Internet searches on "archery" or "bow manufacturers", you might have stopped by a few online archery forums. You might even have taken a few shots from a borrowed bow. You probably have a pretty good idea of what type of bow you'd like and what style of archery you want to get into. Sorry – no, you don't.

Right or left handed?

The first thing you'll have to consider is whether you'll need a right or left-handed bow. A right-handed archer holds the bow in his left hand and draws the string with his right. If you're right-handed with most other activities, the odds are you'll be shooting a right-handed bow. While generally true, there is one possible exception. In addition to your "handedness" humans are also right or left eye dominant. That means that you favor one eye over the other; typically your stronger eye is your dominant eye. While there are some advantages to having handedness match eye dominance, unless the eye dominance is so great that it prevents you from aiming, it's best to choose a right- or left-handed bow based on your natural inclinations. In other words, if you're generally right-handed, start with a right-handed bow! Eye dominance will be discussed in greater detail in the chapter on aiming. If you're uncertain about what you should do, you may want to jump ahead to that chapter.

Basic bow requirements

What you require in your first bow is that it be relatively inexpensive and have a draw weight that you can comfortably handle. In other words, your first bow needs to be cheap and light; here's why:

Watching others shoot, handling a few bows and even shooting a few arrows won't let you know with any certainty what will be an optimal bow for you. As much fun as archery is, and it is fun, it's also a lot of work. Being human, we learn things by doing them. Your first bow will always be a guess, hopefully an educated one, but still a guess. That's why I'm suggesting you begin with an inexpensive bow. As you start shooting, you'll learn more and more about what you like or dislike in a bow, not just the color or shape, but the style of bow, the length, draw weight, physical (or mass) weight, type of grip, etc. You might even decide you'd rather shoot a compound bow, or give it up entirely; yes, it does happen! If you do stick with it odds are, within six months you'll be getting another bow. The difference is that the educated guess will be more "educated". You'll also have built up some archery muscles that will allow you to shoot a heavier bow if you decide that's what you want. You should also have a better idea of what you want out of archery. Hopefully your technique or form will have developed to a point where you can take advantage of the features a new bow can offer.

Let's talk about those archery muscles a bit. As we'll discuss in greater detail later, the bow is drawn and held at anchor by the deep center muscles of the back. These muscles aren't used much for anything else, and even if you're a seasoned weight lifter and you developed a weight training program to build those muscles, lifting weights will not condition them to work the same way they do when drawing a bow and releasing the string. *(The only way to develop archery muscles properly is to practice archery.)* That's not to say that weight training or aerobic exercise won't help you shoot better; anything that makes you stronger and healthier, including a solid diet and adequate sleep will help you to shoot better, because you'll be in better shape overall. It's been said that archery is about 10% physical and 90% mental, but you really do need that 10%, without it, the other 90% won't be possible.

A few notes for those coming from a compound bow background:

Some people turn to stickbows after years of shooting a compound bow. While the basic principles of shooting are the same, the mechanics of the shot are quite different. Those differences need to be addressed when considering a first stickbow.

On the positive side, having shot a compound for a while, the odds are you've developed an understanding of proper form and that you may have had some exposure to stickbows from your local range or matches. Therefore you might already have an idea of what you want to do and what to expect. That's a great start, but there are a few caveats that need to be discussed and considered.

Draw weight – The first and biggest mistake that a compound convert can make is to equate the draw weight of a compound bow to that of a stickbow. A 70# (the # sign after a number indicates pounds) compound bow with a nominal 65% let-off has a holding weight of approximately 25#; a 70# compound bow with an 80% let-off has a holding weight of only 14#! The 70# peak weight is never really held for any length of time, it is actually only "passed" during the draw, on the way to the anchor. A 70# stickbow has a holding weight of 70#. Please think about that for a moment. If you were to buy a 70# stickbow, you'd be holding three to five times more weight than you're used to holding on the compound. While most compound shooters really wouldn't buy a stickbow of the same draw weight as their compound's peak weight, they might think that a modest reduction to 50# would be acceptable. While it might be possible to make the transition with that weight, it's really stacking the odds against you. As we'll discuss later, fighting or struggling with the bow is something that needs to be avoided, not only during the beginning stages, but throughout your archery career. A good rule of thumb is to take your holding weight and add about 50-75%. For most situations that would mean a 30# to 40# bow for men and 20# to 30# for women.

Draw length – Most compound shooters use a release aid or trigger and so pull further back to anchor on their faces or necks than they would when shooting a stickbow with fingers. Typically, most people lose 1" to 2" when switching from a compound bow to a stickbow. In addition to the anchor being farther forward, the increased holding weight will result in some shoulder compression. While usually not harmful, it can also shorten your draw (diag 1-8).

1-8 Comparison of compound to stickbow anchors. Notice that with a release aid, the anchor position is farther back on the face than with a finger release.

Fingers – In addition to losing a few inches of draw length, the clean snap of the mechanical release is replaced by the not-so-clean release of the first three fingers of the drawing hand. At first, it usually appears that each finger has a mind of its own and refuses to work in concert with the other two. It takes more than a few arrows downrange for the three to learn to work correctly with each other. The other issue is that the fingers are now directly bearing the weight of the bow at full draw; they will eventually callus to some degree, but in the beginning some soreness is to be expected.

Sight vs. no sight – While a stickbow can be shot with sights most people who make the transition try to shoot "barebow", without a sight at first. I'll discuss later why and when a bow sight should be added. Shooting a stickbow will take time to get used to, either with or without a sight. Fighting a heavy bow while trying to focus on the target or your form makes the learning process that much more difficult. It's another reason why a light bow is always the best option for a new shooter.

Your first bow - a few suggestions:

Remember, when buying your first bow there are only two requirements that need to be met and they are that the bow needs to be inexpensive and of a light draw weight.

A good starting bow for most people would be a new or used recurve, between 62" and 66" in length and a maximum of 35# in draw weight, for most men, and 25# for most women, at their respective draw lengths.

You are looking for a bow that's going to be comfortable to shoot; therefore we want one that's within the aforementioned 62" to 66" range. At longer lengths there's increased stability and reduced finger pinch (diag 1-9). (As the string is drawn back, it forms an angle around the drawing fingers; the shorter the bow, the more acute the angle, and the less comfortable the bow is to shoot and the harder it is to release the string smoothly.)

1-9 Comparison of finger pinch on a 60" bow (left) and a 70" bow (right). Notice how much more acute the string angle is on the shorter bow? The more acute the angle, the less comfortable the shot and the more difficult it is to get a clean release.

When self bows were the norm, charts where published recommending specific bow lengths relative to the archer's draw length and even to his height! This was necessary, not only to allow for a smooth draw, but to prevent the bow from being overstressed and failing due to being drawn beyond its breaking point. With the designs and materials used in laminated bows manufactured in the last 40 years, those charts are no longer relevant. However, if you are short of stature, implying a shorter draw length, it might be advantageous to look at bows closer to 62", as shorter bows will usually have a slight performance edge for people with a shorter draw. Conversely, if you are on the tall side, or are a "knuckle dragger", you should be looking at bows closer to 66" or even longer. People with draw lengths exceeding 33" will need to work with an Archery Pro Shop, not so much for the bows, but for the arrows, as standard or full-length arrows are approximately 32" to 33" or less (some aluminum arrows are now available in 34").

The draw weights I recommend work best for most beginners *(even if the ultimate goal is to bow hunt big game, which would require considerably heavier poundage)*. Learning to shoot well takes quite a few arrows loosed downrange, and trying to remember correct form and later focusing on the target, is easier when you're not fighting the bow's draw weight. A 50# bow may feel comfortable or even "easy" for the first shot or two, but after ten, twenty or a hundred shots, the extra weight starts taking a toll. Once fatigue sets in and you start fighting the bow, any real attempts at productive training are lost. **If you draw a bow and believe the weight feels like "nothing", that's probably the bow you need to begin with.** If you really need a 50# bow, fine, let it be the bow you get six months down the line.

If you have access to a larger archery range or club that rents equipment on a daily or hourly basis, consider renting a 10# - 20# bow and practicing basic form on that before you go on to your real bow. By doing that, there's no effort required to draw the bow and hold at anchor. You'll get a better feel for what proper form is, or should feel like. **It's my very firm belief that two hours with a 10# bow will do most new shooters more good than two years with a bow that feels slightly heavy.** *With a "slightly" heavy bow it's possible that a new shooter will be unable to distinguish the difference between what a good shot should feel like and what an error feels like.*

Recurves have a few advantages over longbows in the beginning stages for most shooters. Most recurves have pistol grips (diag 1-10). These fit more comfortably in the hand than the straight grips common on many longbows and allow for more consistent hand placement. Consistency is a word we'll be using a lot as we get into training, so you should get used to hearing it now. They also usually have more physical or *mass* weight than a longbow, and so will feel steadier in the hand.

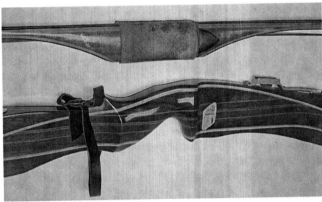

1-10 Comparison of a straight long bow grip (Ben Pearson "Pro Staff 5000" left) vs. a recurve pistol grip (Hoyt Pro Medalist, right)

As far as finding a bow, a local range or pro shop might be a good place to start. At least they should be able to give you an idea of what's out there and what it's going to cost. Even your first bow should be something that you like and will enjoy shooting. The actual requirements are simply the draw weight and length; everything else is up to you. A very popular option for new shooters, or those new to stickbows, is to look into the used bow market. There are many good used bows out there, including vintage bows from the 60's and 70's that shoot every bit as well as their modern counterparts, some even better. Best part is, they can be purchased for a fraction of the cost of a new bow. Suggestions on what to look for when buying a used bow are discussed in Chapter 17.

We'll assume the bow came with a string and an arrow rest. If it didn't, that's your next order of business. New bows usually come with strings; they may not be the best strings for that bow, but they're usually adequate to start with. If you did get a used bow, then you'll most likely need a new string for it. If you're not sure of the age of the bow, get a string made from B-50 Dacron. B-50 has been around for over half a century and is one of the "softer" materials for bowstrings. "Softer" means it has a little stretch to it and so acts as a protective cushion for the bow at shock (when the string abruptly stops the forward motion of the limbs). B-50 can be used on any bow; I even prefer it on my Olympic-style bows, which typically call for low-stretch stings. While it results in a slightly slower arrow, it's safe and quiet.

Here's a quote from the AMO Standards dated 5/2000. *"AMO Bow Length Standard is designated to be three inches longer than AMO Bow String Master that braces bow at proper String or Brace Height. Bow String Master will carry only the bow length designation. Example: A Bow String Master designated as AMO 66" (bow length) will have an actual length under tension of 63".*

Current AMO standards state that a bow carrying a given AMO length will accept a bowstring 3" shorter than that length. They also specify that the string length is measured under either 50# (for 8 or 10 strand B-50 strings) or 100# (for greater than 10 strand B-50 strings) of tension.

However, if your bow has an AMO length written on it, for example AMO 66", you may simply order an AMO 66" string with the correct number of strands and that should work. Note, in my experience, most recurve bows take strings that are 3.5" to 4" shorter than the stated AMO length of the bow; longbows take strings that are 3" shorter. *For the remainder of this book, we'll assume that recurves will use strings 4" shorter than their AMO length and longbows use 3" shorter.*

The following is basic rule of thumb for the number of strands of B-50 for a given draw weight.

20# - 30# 10 or 12 strands
30# - 45# 12 strands
45# - 65# 14 strands
65# - 90# 16 strands

By our previous discussion, you'll probably be using a 12 strand string on that 35# bow. These are only basic recommendations. A 28# bow could do quite well with a 12 strand, and a 43# bow might just like a 10 or 14 strand string! (I generally don't go below 12 strands of dacron for any weight bow, not for strength, but for better arrow nock fit.)

We will discuss other string materials and string making in chapter 11.

There are two types of bowstrings currently being used; the most common is called an "Endless Loop" string. It's one very long strand of string material looped around posts and bound together with serving material to form the loops. The other is called a "Flemish Splice", and is made up of individual strands in two or three bundles, twisted or braided at the ends to form one or two loops for the bow nocks (diag 1-11). If there is only one loop, then the loop-less end is simply tied to the lower bow nock. Flemish strings have a more rustic appearance and can be a little easier on the bow, as the braided ends have a little more give or stretch than an Endless Loop string. On the downside, the Flemish strings tend to stretch more than the Endless Loop strings. Again, while either is acceptable, I'd recommend that your first string be an Endless Loop string. We'll assume that's what you're using for our discussion in the next chapter.

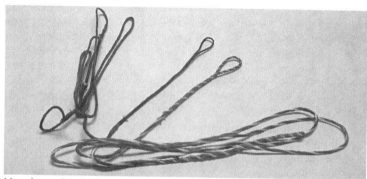

1-11 Endless loop (top) and Flemish Splice (bottom) bowstrings. Notice the served loops on the Endless Loop string and the braided loops on the Flemish.

Note about draw weights: Most factory or non-custom bows are weighted at a draw length (see next section) of 28", but you may draw more or less than that amount. Here's a simple formula to figure out how much weight you are pulling on a particular bow that's marked for a 28" draw.

Stated draw weight @ 28" divided by 20 equals the number of pounds to add or subtract from the weight @ 28" for every inch above or below 28".

Therefore:
A 20# bow will gain or lose 1# per inch
A 30# bow will gain or lose 1.5# per inch
A 40# bow will gain or lose 2# per inch
A 50# bow will gain or lose 2.5# per inch
A 60# bow will gain or lose 3# per inch
A 70#bow will gain or lose 3.5# per inch
An 80# bow will gain or lose 4# per inch

Here's an example: your bow is 40# @ 28", but you draw only 26".
40/20# = 2# per inch. 2# x 2 inches = 4#, so 40# - #4 = 36# @ 26".

Likewise, if you have a 50# bow @ 28, but draw 30.5", 50#/20 = 2.5# per inch. 2.5# x 2.5 inches = 6.25#, so you're actually holding 56.25#. Again, all bows are different, so your mileage may vary, but at least you'll be in the right ballpark.

Before we leave the topic of draw weight, it must be remembered that not all bows are accurately labeled from the factory as to draw weight. If a bow feels considerably heavier or lighter than its specified weight, it should be checked on a calibrated bow scale.

An arrow rest, the plastic or metal device that the arrow sits on, is necessary for best performance, but need not be expensive or complicated. Usually a $3.00 Bear Weather rest or J-2 rest will work just fine and both are quite durable. Some people do shoot off the shelf covered with a piece of fur, leather, or even Velcro (diag 1-12). While it's a common practice, it's an unnecessary disadvantage. The string will also need a nocking point and we'll discuss setting one up shortly.

1-12 Bear J2 and Weather arrow rests (left) Typical shelf arrow rest or "rug" on a mid 1990's SKY Sky Hawk bow (right)

The Arrows

Most people who are new to archery believe that the bow is the most important piece of equipment in their quest for accuracy. ***Actually, it's not – the arrows are.*** *A very mediocre bow, with well-matched arrows (matched both to the bow and to each other) will perform infinitely better than a top-of-the-line bow with poorly matched arrows.* Think of it this way: a laminated bow, even a mediocre one, will pretty much loose an arrow the same way every time provided its string is drawn back the same distance and released the same way. However, all of the arrows need to react to the bow exactly the same way every time; that not only means the arrows have to be straight, but be configured the same, be of equal weight, and have the same stiffness (or spine).

It would probably be best for you to get your first set made for you at a Pro Shop or sporting goods store that routinely does that sort of work, as opposed to mail ordering them. There's nothing wrong with mail ordering arrows, but you'll need to have at hand all the information we're about to discuss.

These days, we have several choices of arrow shaft material. Aluminum is still the most popular for beginners, followed closely by carbon, then wood.

Aluminum arrows are pretty tough, very straight, and come in enough sizes to fit almost any bow and archer. Except for the very high-end carbon arrows, they offer the greatest degree of precision and uniformity. If you accidentally bend one, it can usually be straightened to very useable tolerances. They are the easiest to refletch if, or rather when, that becomes necessary. Many different grades are available for practice, target shooting and hunting. I would very strongly recommend aluminum for your first arrows. They are the only kind I shoot.

Note: As we'll discuss later, there are several grades of aluminum currently being used for arrow shafting. I would suggest an xx75 grade arrow, such as Easton's GameGetter II or Platinum plus arrows, as they withstand the abuse a new shooter will inflict on his arrows. As the shooter's skill increases, the softer arrows such as Easton's Fall Stalker shafts make adequate utility arrows for archers on a budget.

Carbon and carbon composite arrows are also very straight and durable, but in rare instances can shatter or crack on impact with hard objects or each other. Minor damage may not initially be noticed and that may result in an arrow that breaks on release causing damage to the bow and/or injury to the shooter. They, like aluminum arrows, come in several grades and can be slightly more expensive than comparable grade aluminum arrows. Carbon arrows are generally lighter in weight compared to anything else, and so will tend to shoot faster, but some people find them more difficult to tune properly.

Wood arrows are very popular with traditional archers. They can be very inexpensive or cost as much as the best carbon or aluminum arrows. They require a lot more maintenance to keep straight and must be carefully and frequently inspected for signs of damage.

Fiberglass arrows have not been manufactured in several decades or at least not in great quantities. They are very heavy shafts, and stay straight until they break, which is rare. Like carbon, they're either straight or broken.

The arrow is stabilized and kept on course in flight primarily by its "fletching". Classically turkey or goose feathers are used, but several types of plastic fletching, called "vanes", are also common. Feathers tend to be more forgiving to shooter error, as they can stabilize the arrow faster. They are also lighter than vanes and since they flex under pressure they cause fewer clearance problems than vanes. Both feathers and vanes come in sizes from 1" to 5-1/2" in length. For beginning shooters, three 4" or 5" feathers would be a good choice.

When choosing arrows, the first consideration is the length. It's typically measured from the deepest part of the nock's groove to the back of the point, and is called the length to BOP (back of point), or simply the BOP length. To get the right length arrow, the first thing you need to do is determine your draw length. Bow shops have a special draw length check bow to do this (diag 1-13). It's a very lightweight bow, with an arrow attached to the string. The arrow is graduated or marked near the pointy end, in inches. As you draw the string back, several times, the point where the arrow crosses the back of the bow will be noted. To get a reasonably accurate draw length you need to come to an "anchor", by placing the index finger of your drawing hand to the corner of your mouth. If you are not familiar with that term, the salesman should be able to show you how to do it, for the sake of determining draw length; else you might want to skip ahead to Chapter 3 on Basic Shooting Form, where it's fully explained. That measurement should be somewhere around 28" for most adult men, a little shorter for women. That draw length is a factor of the length of your arms, the width of your chest and where you anchor.

1-13 Using a light weight draw-check bow. The arrow is graduated in inches and the draw length is noted at the point where the arrow crosses the back of the bow.

Other methods have been devised to determine draw lengths, for example, measuring the distance from fingertip to fingertip with the archer's arms outstretched at shoulder level, and dividing by two or some "fudge factor". Most of these alternate methods prove less than accurate, as we are all built a little differently. The only way to know your actual draw length is to draw the bow. The draw length is normally close to the length of the arrow you will need. However, since these are your first arrows, add about 2". So, if you draw 27.5", you should order 29" to 29.5" arrows. As your form develops, your draw length will probably increase. By how much is impossible to say, but it's always easier to shorten an arrow that's too long, than it is to lengthen an arrow that's too short.

If a draw check bow isn't available, you can check your draw length in several other ways. The easiest is to draw a bow with an arrow on the rest and have someone mark the arrow shaft where it passes the back of the bow. You then measure the distance from that mark to the groove in the arrow nock. Alternatively, you can take a piece of paper a few inches square, and pierce the center with the arrow and slide it about half way down the shaft. Put the arrow on the rest and come to full draw. The paper will make contact with the back of the bow and be pushed down the shaft. The distance from where it rests to the nock groove is your draw length (diag 1-14). Again, repeat this a few times for consistency and consider making your first set of arrows a few inches longer.

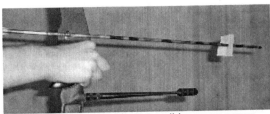

1-14 Draw check using a paper slider on an arrow

The next thing we have to consider about arrows is something called spine. We'll go into this in more detail later when we start tuning the bow, but basically the arrow has to flex around the bow when it's being fired. The spine is a measurement of how much that arrow will bend or flex and is measured in fractions of an inch. The correct term for describing the spine of an arrow is deflection, meaning how much the arrow bends or deflects when a given weight is applied to its center.

Let's assume you're following my advice and going with aluminum. Easton Archery has been the sole manufacturer of aluminum arrows and arrow materials for decades, so they are a pretty safe bet (diag 1-15).

1-15 Easton aluminum arrow size markings. From top to bottom: Gamegetter II 1916, X7 Eclipse 2014 and Maxim 2117.

The nomenclature for aluminum arrow sizing is "XXYY", defined as follows:

XX = XX/64" = the outside shaft diameter
YY = YY/1000" = the shaft wall thickness

For example an 1816 shaft will be 18/64" or 9/32" in OD, and have a wall thickness of 16/1000". A 2018 will be 20/64" or 5/16" in OD and have a wall thickness of 18/1000". Generally, as the numbers get bigger the spine and weight of the arrows get stiffer and heavier. Easton currently produces arrows with outside diameters from 12/64" (1214s) to 27/64" (2712s) and wall thicknesses from 11/1000" (2311s) to 20/1000" (2020s). The gamut runs from a 1214 (the softest) to a 2712 (the stiffest). That'll cover just about anything from 15# to well over 100# draw weight bows!

Here's a table of recommended shaft sizes for beginners. The draw weights are at your draw length, and are related to the BOP arrow length.

Draw weight at your draw length	Arrow length 25"	Arrow length 26"	Arrow length 27"	Arrow length 28"	Arrow length 29"	Arrow length 30"	Arrow length 31"
25 lb	1716	1716	1716	1716	1716	1716	1816
30 lb	1716	1716	1716	1716	1716	1816	1816
35 lb	1716	1716	1816	1816	1816	1816	1916
40 lb	1716	1816	1816	1816	1816	1916	1916
45 lb	1816	1816	1816	1916	1916	1916	2016

These are only initial recommendations; certain bows will allow or require weaker or stiffer arrows. There will always be some trial and error involved. If you go with a 35# bow and fall within the 27" – 29" arrow length, then an 1816 will certainly work.

For this part of the exercise we are only concerned with the arrow leaving the bow relatively straight. As we develop our shooting form and accuracy, we'll be able to fine-tune our equipment for near perfect arrow flight. If you do find you have a very short draw and are using a very light bow, I'd still stay with a 1716, as indicated in the above chart. Anything smaller may be too fragile to hold up to the pounding that most beginners inflict on their arrows. As you progress, and more of your arrows stay centered in the target, it's safer and less expensive to use lighter, thinner-walled shafts.

There's usually some question about the weight of the arrowhead or "pile". For your first arrows, 100-grain heads will work well, but you can also use 125 grain or 75 grain heads. We can use the head weight to help fine tune the arrow flight later on.

Please note that modifying the arrow length or the point weight will affect the spine of the arrow, but at this stage they will still be within a usable range.

The last thing to consider is nock orientation. Stickbow shooters generally shoot with the odd colored feather perpendicular to the bow's long axis and pointed away from the riser. For that to happen the nock groove has to be perpendicular to the odd colored feather. Before compound bows began using specialized arrow rests, this was never a problem, as that was the only way arrows were made. Today, stickbow shooters still orient their nocks and feathers that way, but compound bow shooters typically have their odd colored feathers in line with the bow's long axis and pointed downward. Therefore, when ordering arrows you have to make sure the dealer understands that you will be shooting a stickbow (diag 1-16).

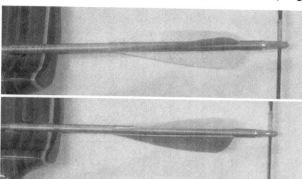

1-16 Nock orientation: The arrow in the top picture is set for a stick bow with the cock feather perpendicular to the string and facing away from the riser. The arrow in the bottom picture is set for a compound bow with a release and has the cock feather parallel to the string.

A note concerning arrows for children and youngsters with lightweight bows and short draw lengths. This is going to sound almost blasphemous, but arrow selection really doesn't matter. At shorter draw lengths (less than 25") and lighter weights (less than 20#), the bow isn't exerting enough energy to make spine critical. The current Easton "kids" aluminum arrows are 1820s, and that means they are 18/64" OD and 20/1000" wall thickness. That would be, by normal conventions, a very stiff arrow, actually spined for approximately 50#. It's safest just to use inexpensive aluminum or carbon "kids" arrows and let them have some fun shooting, while they're learning the basics. When they get older and graduate to bigger bows, then you can worry about perfectly matched arrows.

Necessary Accessories

Tabs and gloves

The reason for finger protection will become quite apparent after a few shots. In addition to protecting the fingers of the shooting hand, a well-made and cared-for tab or glove will actually improve your release, and thus your shooting.

A tab is a piece or several pieces of leather or similar material that covers the first three fingers of the shooting hand (diag 1-17). There are numerous types on the market, the one right for you depends on fit and personal preference. They come in small, medium and large, sometimes extra large sizes. Find one that fits a little larger than you need and trim for a perfect fit. Again, at this stage of the game, close is close enough. We'll talk more about trimming tabs in the tuning section.

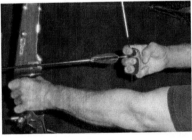

1-17 Tabs Archery Mitt (top left), Wilson tab (bottom left) and CANT Pinch tab with finger spacer to prevent pinching the arrow between the index and middle fingers (right). The second picture shows the position of string when being drawn with a tab. The fingers are nearly perpendicular to the string.

An archery glove is a set of three individual leather finger stalls for the index, middle and ring fingers with strips of leather connecting them to a wristband (diag 1-18). Basically it's a glove's skeleton for the three shooting fingers. They also come in various styles and sizes. If you choose to use a glove, find one that is snug but not tight on the fingers and held in place with slight tension by the straps that connect the stalls to the wristband. Both tabs and gloves require some break-in time and routine maintenance. You can care for them as you would any leather material. An occasional application of baby powder to leather tabs or gloves where they contact the string not only protects the leather but also provides a smoother release.

An alternative to a tab and glove is a *"No-Glov"*; rubber sleeves that slide over the center of the bowstring widening its diameter and serving as a guide for arrow placement. The increased diameter distributes the pressure of the string against the fingers over a wider (and softer) area and eliminates the need for a tab or glove. (diag 1-19) The No-Glov is a good idea for young children as it is quite intuitive to use and is one less item for them to lose. It may also be beneficial in some situations where a tab or glove may not be practical. For serious shooting, they pose several problems - they add weight to the center of the bowstring, which acts as adding weight to the arrow and therefore hurts performance. Second, as we'll see later on, the bowstring rotates as it rolls off the fingers and the increased diameter of the No-Glov increases that rotation making a clean release difficult. Lastly, they may slip or move on the string changing the arrow's position.

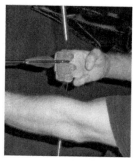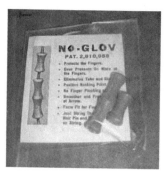

1-18 *Three archery shooting gloves from Bear Archery (left) and position of string when being drawn with a glove (middle)*
1-19 *The No-glov can eliminate the need for a glove or tab, but may adversely affect accuracy (right)*

Arm guards

Arm guards do just as the name suggests. They go on the forearm of the bow arm and protect it from the occasional string slap. They too can be made from leather, plastic, or almost any relatively firm material. I'll deviate from classic thought here: with proper form, *(I firmly believe that an arm guard is not only unnecessary, but it can be a hindrance to good shooting.)* Quite simply, every time the string hits the arm guard, it means you did something wrong, and the result will be poor shot placement. On the other hand, one or two string slaps are usually sufficient to convince most people that not using an arm guard isn't an option. For a new shooter, using one is probably a good idea. You can think about taking it off later (diag 1-20).

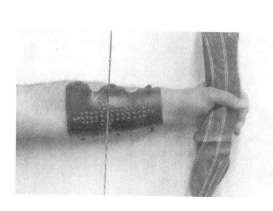
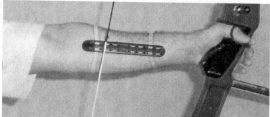

1-20 *Several popular types of arm guards: the classic full bracer with laced ties (left), the skeleton type with elastic bands (top right) and a thin plastic arm guard current used by target archers (bottom right)*

Chest protectors

Some target archers find it useful to wear a chest protector (diag 1-21). They are usually made from nylon or plastic mesh and used to prevent abrasion from contact with a rapidly accelerating bowstring, or the bowstring snagging your clothing as it leaves the fingers, resulting in an errant shot. While popular with target archers, unless your physical make up or shooting style requires it, don't bother. (*I use one when shooting my Olympic-style target bows.*)

1-21 Solid type chest protector (left) and mesh type (right) (Neet Archery)

Quivers

You'll need some place to keep your arrows while you're shooting. An arrow quiver can be anything from a pipe stuck in the ground to a fancy belt quiver with arrow dividers and accessory pockets, to a leather back quiver with fur lining. It's really your preference as each has its advantages and disadvantages, but having one does make one's day at the range easier and more enjoyable. Bowhunters typically use bow quivers that attach to the riser and hold three to six or even eight arrows. While very practical in hunting situations, they might not be the most convenient at the archery range.

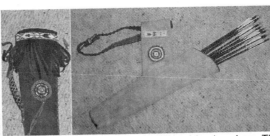

1-22 Quivers from left to right: Target style quiver with separate arrow tubes, traditional back quiver. The bow quiver attaches to the riser or limbs and keeps the arrows at hand for hunting situations. Decorating quivers with additional leather trim or beads can add a distinctive flair

Bow stringer

This item is often overlooked by beginners, but it's probably the most important thing you can own for your protection and that of your family and friends, as well as for proper care of the bow. Fact: a modern laminated bow can remain strung for decades without undue harm to the bow, or loss of draw weight. That's very true, but unfortunately leaving a bow strung when not in use is the same as leaving a loaded gun out in the open. A strung bow is nothing more than a spring under tension, waiting to be released. While the bow itself, and more than likely the string, may be perfectly happy if left alone, there's always a chance that a failure of either component can result in damage to the bow, your other nearby property, or injury to a family member or friend. Further, a strung bow in plain sight is an open invitation to a new guest to see if he can pull it, or just "try it out". This is especially true if you have young or not so young children around. While pets may not be able to draw a bow, a dog or cat might smell the bees wax on the string and want to taste it. It may be a long shot, but not one you should risk. Some bow manufacturers insist that more damage is done to a bow by improperly stringing and unstringing it, than by leaving it strung. I agree; that's why I own several bow stringers, and know how to use each of them properly. I would not deal with a bowyer who suggests leaving a bow strung between shooting sessions.

Cord type bow stringers are the most common and come in two forms. Both are basically a length of parachute cord longer than the bow string, and have either leather cups on each end that go over the limb tips or pieces of rubber that are held against the back of the bow limbs by friction. By stepping on the cord and pulling up on the bow, the limbs bend, allowing the bowstring loops to be seated in the nock grooves. We'll discuss more about this in the next chapter (diag 1-23).

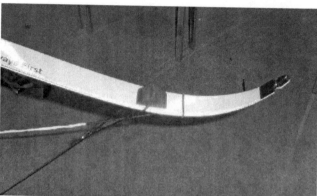

1-23 Cord and pocket type bow stringer (left). Friction type bow stringer, with friction pad on upper limb (right)

Bow tip protectors and string keepers

Bow (limb) tip protectors are plastic, rubber or leather cups that go over the lower limb tip to protect it from scratches and dings if the bow will be stood on end on a vertical bow rack. These types of racks were popular in the 60's and 70's due to their efficient use of space. The tip protectors shouldn't impede performance, but unless your local range still uses vertical bow racks, they really aren't necessary.

String keepers, usually made from leather or nylon, fit over the upper limb and attach to the upper string loop, keeping some tension on the string and holding it in place. If your bowstring was correctly made to fit your bow the diameter of the upper loop should hold sufficient tension on the string to keep it from falling off. If you find you need a string keeper, an inexpensive alternative is a rubber band with one end looped around the upper string loop and the other around the limb nocks (diag 1-23a).

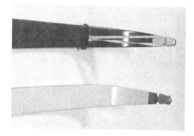

1-23a Rubber band string keeper (top) and plastic tip protector (bottom).

Bow Cases

You could probably use the cardboard box the bow came in for a while with no problem, but sooner or later you'll want something a little more protective, if not more fashionable. Bow cases can be simple "socks" that you slip the bow into and tie shut, or soft plastic or leather cases with fleece padding and a zipper on one end, or hard plastic cases with thick foam padding and locks. Aluminum or metal/plastic cases that lock are also available and are required for airline transport.

Most cases have pockets to carry accessories, like spare strings, a stringer, etc., and those can come in very handy (diag 1-24).

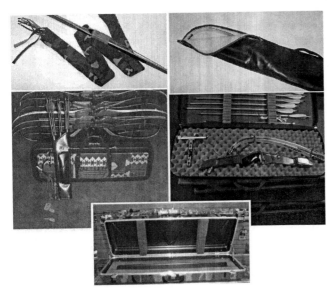

1-24 Bow cases: "Sock" type (top left) Lined vinyl case (top right) Takedown bow case and quiver from Neet Archery Products (middle left) Inside T/D bow case (middle right) there is ample room for a riser, limbs, arrows and accessories. This case has tie-downs to secure components. Hard sided camo pattern T/D bow case from Hoppe's (bottom).

Target faces

If you already have a place to shoot with an adequate backstop, then all you will need is something to aim at. The target face doesn't have to be anything elaborate; I'm fond of the indoor NFAA "blue" face (diag 1-25), and we'll actually be using it later on, but right now, a pie plate, a piece of masking tape or almost anything will do.

1-25 Official NFAA indoor 20 yard target face. For practice any standardized face will do.

Clothing

Yes, clothing. You probably didn't think that clothing would be part of your equipment, but it is, especially if you want to make shooting as safe and comfortable as possible. As with any sport, you want to wear clothing that won't restrict your movements, but with archery, you have moving objects to contend with, namely, the bow's limbs, the bowstring, and the arrow. A loose fitting sweatshirt or sweater might not be the best attire for archery practice, and anything that gets in the path of the bowstring will at the very least result in a miss, and in the worst case, result in injury. Snug fitting Tee shirts are probably best, but if the weather is brisk, a sweatshirt can be used, but it too should be fairly close fitting. Loose fitting jewelry, like earrings and neck chains, should also be left home. Baseball caps with large brims may also prove problematic if the bowstring touches the brim at anchor.

A word about eye glasses.

Even with all the talk about laser vision correction and disposable contact lenses these days, a lot of us still wear glasses. While not necessarily a problem for an archer, there are a few considerations. As with clothing, the closer the lenses are to your face the less chance of them coming in contact with the bowstring at anchor. More importantly, the optical center of the lens is typically near the center of the lens, so you'll get the best correction when looking straight ahead. If your head is fully rotated toward the target, then you're looking through the corrective area of the lens and you should be fine. If, however, you can't or don't rotate your head nearly square to the target, then you're looking through the side of the lens, and depending on the prescription, you might get some distortion. Bifocals, especially progressive lenses have a very narrow vertical "keyhole" where the correction is centered and so can be problematic for an archer. If you have any difficulty seeing the target or maintaining focus on it, discuss it with your eye care professional. Most will work with you to find an acceptable solution.

1-26 When shooting with eye glasses, it is imperative that your line of sight be as close to the optical center of the lens as possible. Although not terrible, this archer may need to rotate his head a bit more towards the target

A note to new "target" archers *(those who are certain that target archery will be their main interest).*

Target archery at its highest level is the most demanding and complex form of archery practiced today. The equipment is therefore specialized for that purpose. It would behoove the new target archer to start with a specialized target bow. If you are certain that your only interest will be "target" or competitive Olympic style archery, it might be necessary to slightly modify the initial requirements.

While obtaining a vintage wood risered target bow would be an adequate starting point, a better choice would be a current (model) entry level competition bow such as the Hoyt Gold Medalist or similar riser paired with light draw weight, wood core limbs. Here's why:

1. Olympic risers are draw weight adjustable (within 5 to 10%)

2. Olympic risers have accessory bushings for any option a new or veteran target archer could need, including sights, stabilizers, arrow rests and clickers (which will be discussed in detail in Chapter 7).

3. The bow's takedown feature will allow limb changes or upgrades so the archer can change draw weights, bow length and limb material as necessary.

4. Wood core limbs are inexpensive and available in draw weights from 24# to 50# and short, medium and long lengths. Therefore bows can be configured with AMO lengths of 66", 68" and 70" with 25" risers and 64", 66" and 68" with 23" risers. *(The Gold Medalist riser is only available in a 25" length; others are available in both 23" and 25" versions.)* When an archer is ready for a heavier bow, he need only replace the limbs, not the entire bow or accessories.

5. Both risers and limbs are readily available on both the new and used market, at very reasonable prices.

6. Given the interchangeability of Olympic style limbs, almost any manufacturer's limbs will work with almost any riser.

Determining what length bow to use:

Archer's draw length	recommended riser length	recommended limb length	AMO bow length
Less than 26"	23"	Short	64"
26" to 27.5"	23"/25"	Medium/Short	66"
27.5" to 29.5"	23"/25"	Long/Medium	68"
Greater than 29.5"	25"	Long	70"

The initial draw weight recommendations still hold, but I would strongly suggest you lean toward the light end of the draw weight spectrum, rather than the heavy. There are no indoor matches that require a bow of more than 25# to 30#. Given the number of arrows required and the extended time holding at anchor, the greater the draw weight the sooner fatigue will set in and effective training will end.

- Aluminum arrows are still a good choice.

- A tab is preferable to a shooting glove.

- An arrow rest is required, but need not be complicated or expensive. A simple flipper rest and plunger is recommended and both can be purchased for under $20.

With Olympic style shooting, the use of a bow sight is strongly recommended. While not necessary in the early stages, the sooner the sight is introduced, the better. *(I strongly suggest building a foundation without a sight first and then progressing to a sight once that foundation is established.)*

A stabilizer is a necessity on most Olympic bows (see chapter 7). A simple 30" tubular aluminum rod with a small weight at the end will suffice.

A finger, wrist or bow sling will allow the archer to keep his bow hand relaxed during the shot sequence and allow for a clean follow-through (see chapter 7).

The most important piece of equipment for a new target archer is an instructor.

As I said, this type of archery is very demanding. Small mistakes in the beginning can lead to big problems later on. If you believe Olympic archery is for you, seek out a qualified instructor or coach as early as possible. The initial investment in time and money can save you a great deal of grief later on.

Finding a "target" instructor:

A good teacher for a new target archer need not have a 5-star rating to be an effective mentor. He or she needs to understand the particular type of archery you wish to learn and be able to explain it in a way you can understand. (I like to think of that as a common sense approach.) It is vital that an instructor or "coach" not only be able to see what you're doing right and wrong, but be able to see the cause and prescribe the appropriate corrective exercises when necessary. He also needs to demonstrate patience with a new shooter who may not pick up certain things as quickly as he would like. Usually, but not always, the better local shooters are more than adequate as first instructors. Talk to a few, ask questions and find one with whom you believe you can successfully work. A simple test to see if someone knows how to teach is to ask, "Why?" when they tell you to do something. If they can't or won't answer that question, or answer it in a way that doesn't make sense to you, you might need to look elsewhere. While it may not necessarily mean they can't teach, there might be a personality conflict that will hinder your progress.

Finally, remember shooting a stickbow accurately is not a skill that can be learned overnight. This type of shooting takes considerable time to learn and many years to master, if mastery is even possible. One Olympic coach stated that it takes at least seven years to develop an Olympic class archer. Relax and enjoy the ride.

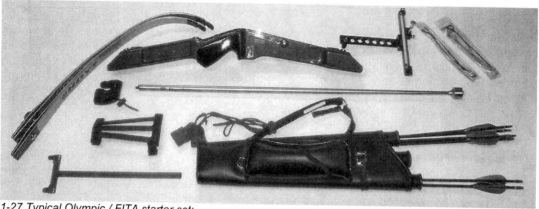

1-27 Typical Olympic / FITA starter set:

Hoyt Gold Medalist riser with flipper rest, cushion plunger and clicker (clicker may be added later)
Hoyt Epic wood core limbs
Side mount sight with aperture (This is an old model the author purchased for about $20)
Tubular Aluminum stabilizer
One dozen aluminum arrows matched to the archer's draw length and bow weight
Bowstrings (two identical strings are preferable)
Tab, arm guard, bow stringer, quiver and bow square
It's also advisable to purchase a case as shown earlier in this chapter
Similar rigs can be purchased in the $300 – $400 range with a little shopping effort.

Can't find a range, tips for shooting at home.

The first things you may want to consider are your local ordinances. This may not be a problem if you live in a rural setting and you have plenty of land surrounding your home. However, many suburban and city dwellers are only permitted to discharge a weapon (and a bow is considered a weapon) in specified areas, such as designated shooting ranges. It's always best to consult with your local police department before you start flinging arrows in your backyard. In a lot of areas, the local police officers might even have archers or bowhunters in their ranks and they might be able to suggest a better alternative.

If it's legally permissible to shoot in your backyard, there are several common sense rules that should be followed. Not only is an acceptable arrow receptacle, also known as a "target", required, but so is an adequate backstop. A backstop is anything positioned behind the target to prevent an errant arrow from travelling too far. The side of an unoccupied barn, small hill, or worst case, a brick wall can suffice; naturally the last option would not bode well for any arrows missing the target. It may however, provide an adequate incentive to keep your arrows in or near the center of the target!

A true story: there was a gentleman who used to practice for bowhunting season by shooting into his garage. The walls of the garage provided an adequate backstop and his driveway was fenced in, so he had a safe line of fire. While "discharging a weapon" was frowned upon in his town, the local Police gave him a courtesy as he had taken adequate precautions. One season, he planned on using a tree stand (a device that is carried a distance up a tree and secured there so the bowhunter has a more advantageous shooting position). As we will discuss in detail later, shooting at downward angles can cause aiming problems; this bowhunter was well aware of this, and decided he needed to get some practice shooting downhill. Unfortunately, the route he chose was to shoot from the roof of his house into his garage. Needless to say, after a few phone calls to the Police Department from neighbors about "some nut" on the roof with a bow and arrow, his at-home shooting career was unceremoniously ended.

(Note that this type of activity may be perfectly acceptable in some parts of the country; however, before trying it, I would strongly recommend checking local ordinances or talking to your local police department. Once a complaint is filed, the Police must act on it.)

In the same vein, care must be taken that the neighbors, adults as well as their children and pets, are prevented from inadvertently wandering into the line of fire, more precisely, anywhere from a plane perpendicular to your shooting position to the plane of the backstop. Not only must you consider left and right misses, but also arrows that may fly above the target. It does happen.

There is a fitting line from <u>Hamlet</u> (*act V, scene ii*) by William Shakespeare that we might remember when thinking about backstops and arrow trajectories. It begins with:

"Give me your pardon, Sir, I have done you wrong…"

And ends with *"… for I have shot mine arrow o'er the house, and hurt my brother."*

Granted, Hamlet was speaking figuratively, but a literal occurrence could have had equally dire consequences.

OK, you have a safe and adequate shooting area; now you'll need that arrow receptacle. Targets can be anything from "bosses" or "mates" specially made from tightly bound hay or straw, varying in size from less than 24" up to 48", with a target face attached, to foam or layered cardboard cubes designed to stop arrows safely, including arrows with broadheads. They can also be hard foam animal targets as used in 3D competitions. These types of targets have been around for years, the former, for centuries, but have the drawback of being fairly expensive and typically quite heavy. If you live a rural area, hay bales make excellent arrow receptacles and are fairly inexpensive. Excelsior bales, made from wood shavings, are heavier, and afford more arrow stopping power, but are more expensive and may not be as readily available (diag 1-28).

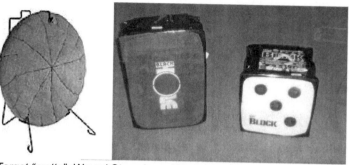

1-28 Target "matts": Wound Straw boss (Saunders 48" Target Matt, left) Block foam targets (Black Hole and BLOCK, middle) 3D Animal foam target (Mckenzie, right)

If you have access to a large number of corrugated cardboard sheets that can be cut to strips of 6 to 10 or 12 inches wide and a few feet long, they can be glued together with ordinary wall paper paste and will serve as an excellent target. The layered cardboard strips can also be tightly bound together with wire or cord and serve perfectly well. A number of commercially available targets are made the same way. Note that you should be shooting into the edges of the cardboard, and not perpendicular to the surface, as that orientation provides longer effective target life (diag 1-29).

Compressed cardboard target frame

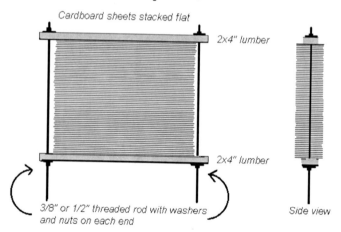

With this type of portable target frame you can create any size target you need. The threaded rods may be left long on one side to anchor the frame in the ground.

1-29 Stacked cardboard target matt

A more elaborate target can be made using two, two to three foot pieces of standard 2x4 lumber and several feet of 1/2" threaded rod, washers and nuts (diag 1-17).

Drill a hole at each end of the 2x4s large enough to accept the threaded rods.

Place a washer and nut on one end of each rod.

Slide one rod through each hole on one piece of lumber.

Stack strips of cardboard over the two-by-four and between the threaded rods to a height of two to three feet (or to whatever size you deem necessary). Old telephone books or magazines may be used in place of cardboard, but given their greater density, they should not be compressed as tightly, nor may they be appropriate for very light children's bows, due the to possibility of glancing shots or bounce-outs. Slide the other two-by-four onto the threaded rods. Place a washer and nut on each rod and tighten to compress the cardboard.

This version of a portable target, while heavier than the previous one made with wallpaper paste, has the advantage of allowing you to shift the cardboard strips around as areas become shot out. Our old archery club used that type of target in a four by four-foot configuration for our outdoor shoots.

Perfectly useable targets can also be made from adequately sized cardboard boxes stuffed with old rags, tightly crumpled plastic grocery bags or newspaper. Naturally with any type of target, even with commercially manufactured ones, it is the user's responsibly to verify that it is able to withstand repeated arrow strikes and not allow a pass-through or glance-off.

It may sound obvious, but you should be shooting only at distances that you are fairly certain will have most of your arrows actually hitting the target and be certain that there is an adequate backstop behind the target!

Chapter 2

Basic Equipment Setup

Before we get started shooting we need to do a little work on the bow. This is easier with help from a more experienced archer and will usually be done for you if you bought the bow at an archery range or Pro Shop. If you mail-ordered the bow, or found a used one at a yard sale you might be on your own. Relax, you can do it yourself by following a few basic instructions.

Take the bow out of the box. Even a new bow should be given a careful inspection. If it's a used or vintage bow clean it thoroughly. Check for any cracking in the fiberglass, separations in the laminations or glue joints, any twists in the limbs or anything that doesn't look right. You might even want to check the string nocks and grooves for any sharp edges or irregularities. While rare, it's better to see them before you try to string it (diag 2-1).

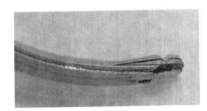
2-1 The beginnings of a limb delamination (fiberglass on the face of the limb just below the string nock is separating from the wood core). This one may be repairable we'll see how later in the book!

If anything appears questionable have it checked by another archer or if that's not possible discuss it with the seller, and if you're still uneasy about it – return it. Even if there's nothing really wrong with it, if you believe there is, and can't be convinced to the contrary, you'll never trust the bow enough to be comfortable shooting it.

The arrow rest

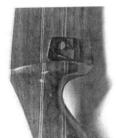

2-2 Types of basic rests (left to right): shelf or "rug" rest, Bear J-2 rest, old Style Hoyt Pro rest, and ARE target style flipper rest.

If the bow already has an intact arrow rest on it, great! If not, now's the time to get one. The Bear Weather Rest and J-2 Rest are good first choices, easy to put on and virtually indestructible. Other options are the Hoyt Super Rest, and various types of flipper rests (diag 2-2). These are available at most sporting goods stores that carry archery equipment or from the mail-order dealers listed in appendix C.

Why are we using a rest?

The rug rest, usually called "shooting off the shelf" has become popular in recent years due to a presumed increased reliability. However, the rug and strike plate (typically a piece of thin leather affixed to the sight window to protect the riser from the arrow) system results in the greatest arrow to bow contact, and as we'll see later, makes tuning the bow more difficult. The plastic or rubber finger type rests such as the Bear Weather or J-2 rests reduce the arrow-to-bow contact and therefore facilitate tuning and result in improved arrow flight. The old style Hoyt Pro rest is shown, as it has been a standard on both target and hunting style bows for decades. While no longer in production, several other rests are using the same principle of a soft, flexible arrow finger and a flexible piece of plastic to act as a dampener for the arrow as it leaves the bow. The final step is the use of a spring or magnetically loaded flipper rest. With that type of rest, the arrow is supported by a thin wire that moves out of the way as the arrow is launched, resulting in minimal contact and maximum clearance.

Remove the bow's old rest or "strike" plate, usually a piece of leather or some kind of fur from the bow's sight window. It's just held on with adhesive, so you can peel it off. Clean any glue residue with a general-purpose cleaner, like Fantastik or a good wood cleaner. Isopropyl alcohol can be used as well. *Don't use anything that leaves a wax film as that will prevent the new adhesive from sticking (diag 2-3).*

If there's a "rug" or some sort of material on the arrow shelf, you can leave it on or take it off; it really doesn't matter. Just make sure the area to which you are going to attach the rest is squeaky clean. Remove the backing from the rest and place it on the sight window, with its bottom edge close to the shelf and the base of the "arrow holder" part of the rest directly above the deepest part of the grip (diag 2-4). That's the conventional location, as in that location it theoretically diminishes any ill effects on arrow flight due to the archer twisting (torqueing) the grip during the shot. In practice the exact placement really isn't that critical, so if you're off by a bit, don't worry. Press it on, and you're set.

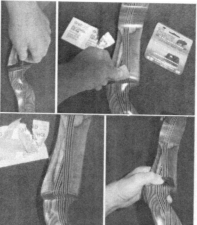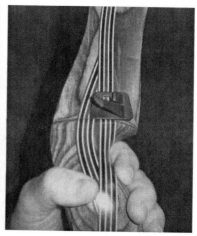

2-3a *Materials required to replace an arrow rest (left)*
2-3b *Steps in replacing a "rug" rest with an elevated rest. 1. Peel off the old strike-plate. 2. Remove any glue residue with an alcohol pad. 3. A squeaky clean riser. 4. Press the new rest in place (middle pictures).*
2-4 *Another picture of the Bear Weather rest. Notice the base of the arrow holder "finger" is directly in line with the deepest cut of the grip. This should help reduce the effects of hand torque on arrow flight.*

Time to string the bow. The bow string, probably an endless loop type string, will have a loop at each end. While that really shouldn't surprise you, what you should notice is that one loop is larger than the other (diag 2-5).

Take the larger loop and slide it over the upper limb of the bow, approximately 6"- 8" down. Now, take the smaller loop and settle it in the nock grooves of the lower limb (diag 2-6). Make sure the lower loop is seated. Take the bow stringer, and follow the instructions that came with it for stringing the bow. If there weren't any instructions, here's the basic principle. If you have a two-pocket stringer, the larger pocket will go over the lower limb tip, and the smaller one on the upper tip. Notice that the stringer may be almost parallel with the real string. (If it's not, you may have to adjust the length of the cord.) Grab the bow by the handle, with the back of the bow facing up. Step on the stringer's cord, with both feet, about shoulder width apart, and pull up on the bow, by straightening your back (diag 2-8). Notice the limbs are bending? They should bend enough to slip the bowstring's upper loop into the nocks of the upper limb. Use your fingers to feel that the loop is indeed seated in both grooves. Remove the stringer's cups from the limbs and double check to make sure both upper and lower string loops are evenly seated in their respective nocks/grooves (diag 2-9). To unstring the bow, you do exactly the same thing in reverse order, but don't unstring it just yet.

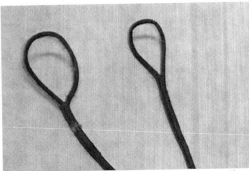

2-5 Notice that the upper string loop is larger than the lower one.
2-6 (left two pictures) Slide the upper (larger loop) 6" – 8" down the upper limb and place the lower (smaller) loop on the lower limb nocks.
2-7 (right two pictures) Placement of bow stringer cups on limb tips, the larger cup on the lower limb tip and the smaller cup on the upper limb tip.

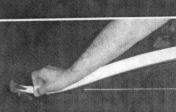

2-8 Proper position for using the bow stringer (top two pictures).
2-9. Bowstring being slid toward the string nocks and proper seating of the bowstring in the nocks (bottom two pictures)

Another type of bow stringer uses either a limb tip cup with a friction block, or two friction blocks. The string is initially placed on the bow the same way as we did with the two-cup stringer, but the friction block is positioned on the limb proximal to the upper loop (diag 2-10).

Draw the bow up as before and slip the string loop onto the nocks.

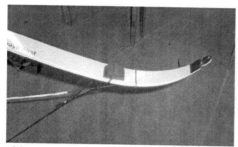

2-10 Position of friction block on upper limb: the upper loop is slid into the string nocks as in the previous example.

At this point, there's a natural tendency to draw the bow. By all means do so. We'll get into the proper technique for drawing the bow shortly. The only thing to remember is that **under no circumstances should you draw a bow and release the string without a nocked arrow.** For reasons we'll describe in detail later on, this "dry firing" will release a considerable amount of energy, and without the arrow to accept that energy, damage to the bow, injury to the shooter, or both may result. Even if both the bow and the shooter survive, it's an unpleasant experience and should really be avoided. Needless to say, loosing an arrow without an appropriate target or backstop should also be avoided.

Now you have to set the nocking point or "nockset". As I said earlier, we're going to be using the word **consistency** a lot. The first thing toward that end is to ensure the arrow is placed on the string the same way each and every time. Lay the bow flat on a table, sight window up. Put an arrow on the rest and engage the arrow's nock on the string, so the shaft of the arrow is perfectly perpendicular to the bowstring. Now slide the arrow's nock toward the upper limb about 1/8" (diag 2-11). That's where we want the arrow to be. To make sure it is always there, we need a physical reference point on the string. There are several types of nocking points currently being used. The crimp-on nocksets (diag 2-12) are very common, come in three sizes to fit most string diameters, and are easy to put on, adjust, and take off. They're what most Pro Shops use, for exactly those reasons. Assuming you're doing this for the first time at home, you probably won't have any crimp-on nocks or special pliers to crimp them.

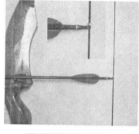

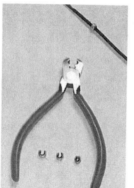

2-11 The nocking point or "nockset" is positioned so that the arrow is slightly above perpendicular in relation to the string (top left).
2-12 Crimp-on nocks (in various degrees of closure) and nocking pliers (right) Brass crimp-on nocks are available in three color coded sizes (the plastic under the brass ring is color coded). Blue/green for small diameter strings (2-3 grains in weight), black for medium diameter strings (4-6 grains in weight) and red for large diameter strings (6-8 grains in weight), (bottom left)

As we may have to adjust or tune our nocking point to some degree after we start shooting, the simplest approach is to wrap a layer of masking tape around the string. With the arrow nock positioned as above, place the edge of the masking tape so that its edge is butting against the arrow nock. We now have a quick but temporary nocking point (diag 2-13). I have used this trick in emergency situations quite successfully.

After shooting a bit when the string has had a chance to stretch, we'll be able to decide where the nocking point should be and we'll need something a little more permanent. You probably have some dental floss, sewing thread and some household cement; that's all we will need. Place the arrow in its correct position on the string, and begin tying loops of dental floss or thread on the string above the arrow nock, toward the upper limb. Make several loops and then tie it off; repeat until there is a slight bead (diag 2-14). Remove the arrow, add a drop of household cement, e.g. Duco Cement or Crazy glue, and let it dry for a bit. Some people prefer two nocking points, one above the arrow nock and one below. While not necessary in most cases, if you decide to use two, make sure they are at least 1/8" farther apart than the width of the arrow nock. If the nocking points squeeze the arrow nock, arrow flight will be affected.

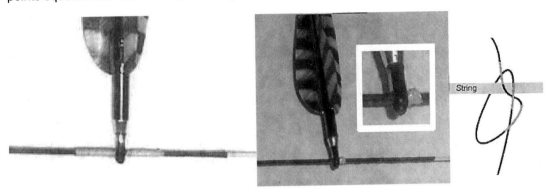

2-13 Masking tape nocking point. This nocking point is made from two pieces of 3/4" masking tape, one above and one below the arrow nock (left).
2-14 To make a tie-on nocking point, begin by tying half hitches and repeat until there's a slight "bead" formed. Complete the nocking point by tying a triple hitch or two and then add a drop of household cement or crazy glue. Cut off any loose pigtails and you're done (middle). Tying a half hitch (right)

If you want to draw it a few more times - go ahead. Wrap the first three fingers around the string with the index finger above the new nocking point, and the middle and ring fingers below; get the string to sit in the crease of the first joint of each finger. You can place an arrow on the string with its nock below the nocking point and draw the bow with the arrow (diag 2-15). **Enjoy – just don't let go of the string, with or without an arrow!**

Before you unstring the bow there is one last thing you might check. Look at an arrow and notice that there are three feathers, two of one color and one of a different color. The odd colored one is called the cock or index feather and the other two are called hen feathers. When you nock an arrow on the string, the cock feather should be perpendicular to and pointing away from the bow's riser (diag 2-16). The color of the feathers is entirely up to the archer (or his supplier) and the cock feather need not be a different color than the hen feathers (diag 2-17).

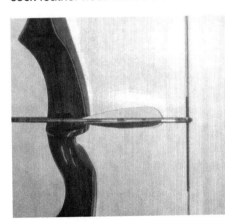

2-16 Correct positioning of the arrow on the bow; the odd colored feather, called the cock or index feather, is pointing away from the riser (left).
2-17 Some archers prefer not to use an odd colored cock feather for aesthetic reasons. It's still fairly easy to figure out the correct orientation (right).

If the cock feather is pointing toward the bow, just rotate it 180 degrees; if it's pointing straight up or straight down (toward the ceiling or floor), the arrows were set up for a compound bow, not a stickbow. Some nocks can be rotated in their bushings (see chapter 9); just turn them 90 degrees. If the arrows have their nocks glued on, your only real options are to return them, or replace the nocks. At this point, it's easier to return them and get the right ones.

You are almost ready to start shooting!

Before you head out to the range: Understand that a strung bow with a nocked arrow is a weapon, not a toy; within its range it is as deadly as any firearm. Never point a nocked arrow at anything you do not wish to hit. That means nocked arrows are always pointed downrange and an arrow is never nocked while people are between you and your target. Most public ranges insist on that rule, and some go as far as not allowing anyone even to touch a bow when people are down range. This sounds pretty simple, but the one time you forget will be the one time an accident will happen.

Chapter 3

Elementary Shooting Form

W ith most endeavors it's usually better to take the first steps in a comfortable, relaxed environment. We've already set up the bow as best we could without actually firing it; the next step is to gain an understanding of basic form, or simply how to shoot the bow. This part can be done at home, without the bow. Ready? Let's get started!

The following is for a right-handed shooter; if you're left-handed you'll need to reverse the hand/arm designations.

- Stand up straight, feet about shoulder-width apart, relax and make yourself comfortable (diag 3-1).

- Raise both arms to the side, to shoulder level. Make sure your palms are facing forward and the tips of your elbows are pointing backward (diag 3-2).

- Keeping both the forearms and the upper arms parallel to the floor, bend both arms only at the elbows as far as they will go. Your palms should now be facing your shoulders and be at shoulder level (diag 3-3).

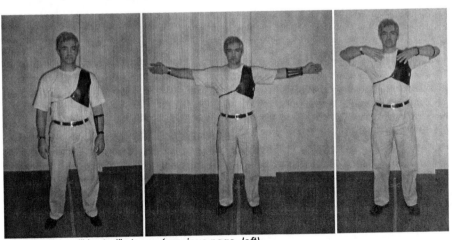

3-1 Natural or "Neutral" stance (previous page, left).
3-2 Neutral stance with arms extended. Your palms are facing forward and elbows are pointing backward. (previous page, middle).
3-3 Neutral stance with arms bent at the elbows (previous page, right).

- Open and close your arms a few times to establish the feeling. Good, and no, we're not going to be auditioning for Big Bird on Sesame Street!

- Now, this time bend only the right elbow leaving the left arm straight (diag 3-4).

- Keeping your arms in that position, turn your head to look over your left shoulder (diag 3-5).

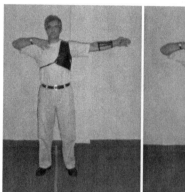

3-4 Neutral stance with left arm extended and right arm bent at the elbow (left).
3-5 Neutral stance with left arm extended, right arm bent at the elbow and head turned over left shoulder (middle).
*3-6 Neutral stance with left arm extended and right hand in the anchor position. Notice that the index finger touches the corner of the mouth and the web of the thumb and forefinger is **anchored** under the jaw bone (right).*

Get used to that position. If you can commit that position to memory, muscle memory actually, you'll never miss a shot due to bad form. Compare it again to diagram 3-5. Practice getting into that position a few more times. That is very close to the position you should be in after the shot (the position you'll be in after you release the string) and is called the follow-through position. If you end up there, your form at least, was perfect.

Obviously there's a slight problem; you can't shoot from that position, as the drawing hand is somewhere out in space, and so, gives us an inconsistency, which we can't have. The drawing hand needs to be anchored somewhere.

So, let's go back into the follow-through position and creep the right hand forward, until the index finger touches the corner of your mouth. If you move your hand around a bit, probably closer to your face, you'll notice that the web of your thumb and index finger should fit under the edge of your jawbone. The index finger in the corner of the mouth and the web under the jaw is called an anchor; actually it's called a Mediterranean anchor (diag 3-6). It is the most common, solid and reproducible anchor for most serious stickbow shooters (diag 3-7). **The index finger actually becomes a reference point (it places the hand in the same position every time) and the web of the thumb and index finger under the jaw makes it solid, or "anchors" it there. *Get used to that position!*** The combination of the reference point and the anchor will supply the consistency necessary to make reproducible shots. The release of the string, the actual "making of the shot" then becomes a non-event. If the shot is set up properly, then the "release" doesn't exist as a separate entity; it's what happens between the anchor and the follow-through positions. If you look at it that way, it's kind of hard to make a mistake!

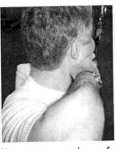

3-7 Correct anchor position (from left to right) from the side, 3/4 rear, rear and rear from below.

There are obviously other ways of anchoring, and we'll discuss them later, but it's been my experience that most people are more consistent with this method in the beginning.

If you're comfortable with the anchor, great! There's one other step we can add that might refine the follow-through position just a little more.

Assume the anchor position once more, but this time as you move it back to the follow-though position, keep the hand in contact with your face. As your hand moves back, the ridge of your index finger should lightly rub against your cheek and continue back across the side of your neck. It should end up somewhere on your neck or almost behind your head (diags 3-8, and 3-9). Not only does this ensure rearward motion on follow-through, but it will keep the hand from moving away from your face. Roy Matthews, in his book <u>Archery in Earnest,</u> recommends that the drawing hand end up in a lightly clenched fist behind the head, near the nape of the neck. I have found that gives many new archers an easily reproducible end-point.

3-8 View of a correct release and follow-through. Notice how the drawing hand stays in contact with the face as it snaps straight back.

Last thing you might want to do, if possible, is to repeat this exercise in front of a full-length mirror. What you want to look for is a straight line from your left hand through your shoulders and continuing through the right forearm to the right elbow, when looking at the anchored position from the side. When getting a target's eye view you want to be sure that the point of the right elbow has rotated so that the forearm is almost in line with the bow arm and perpendicular to the target. (It's physically impossible to have the bow arm and drawing forearm perfectly in line.) With an arrow on the bow, the right forearm needs to be in line with the arrow when viewed from above. This is easier to see than to describe, so pay particular attention to diagrams 3-9 through 3-12.

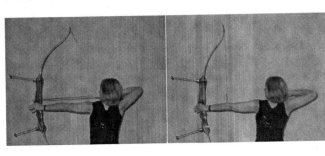

3-9 Release to follow-through as seen from the back. The follow-through must be done in a clean and consistent manner Correct shoulder alignment, side view.

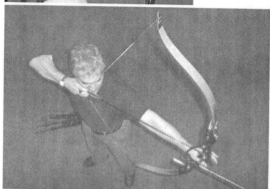

3-10 Correct shoulder alignment side view (left top)

3-11 View from above (left bottom)

3-12 From above rear, showing proper alignment (right)

Here's an alternative method for finding your anchor position. Assume the same position in diagram 3-6, but this time take your right hand, place it over your mouth, and kiss the back of your index finger (diag 3-13 and 3-14). Now turn your head to the left and notice where your hand ended up. The tip of your index finger should be near the corner of your mouth and the web of your thumb and index finger under your jaw (diag 3-6). If the web of your thumb and index finger is not solidly under your jaw, adjust the position so that it is.

3-13 Same as diagram 3-6, but with your head facing forward and your index finger touching your lips (left).

3-14 Starting from the position shown in diagram 3-13. turning your head to the left places your hand very close to the anchor position (right).

The above is probably the most important thing you can learn from this book, and believe it or not, if you can do that with a bow in your hand you're well on your way to becoming an archer!

At the range

A couple of things you need to remember if you're using a club or commercial range facility, you'll probably need to sign in, pay a fee, or join the club or establishment. Ask questions about range protocol, policy and procedure – the basic dos and don'ts. The range rules should be clearly posted, but sometimes they aren't. You might want to see if they have a practice or short-range area; 5 or 10 yards would be a good start. You really don't want to worry too much about missing the target at this point, and 10 yards is about all most folks can, and should, handle on their first few times out.

Go to a 10 yard point (shooting position), and when the range is cleared (everyone has stopped shooting) hang a target face on the butt or bale, if one is not already in place. If you have a choice, I would recommend the indoor 40 cm NFAA blue target with a single white bull's eye (diag 3-15). The color is easy on the eyes compared to the more familiar four-color "FITA" target (diag 3-16), and is pretty universal when comparing notes or scores.

The four-color target is used for various types of matches and its history can be traced back to the Middle Ages. Unfortunately, the longer and more intently you focus on it, the more the colors have a tendency to blur and blend into each other, making focus difficult. The NFAA blue indoor target is much easier on the eyes, and the white "hot spot" serves to draw your attention.

3-15 20 yard, 40cm NFAA blue indoor target face is the easiest on the eyes and readily available (left).
3-16 The 20 yard indoor NFAA five spot face (middle) and 18m 40cm indoor FITA face (right) can be more difficult for a new shooter (see text).

It's now time to string your bow with the stringer as we did in the last chapter, and place your arrows within reach, preferably in a quiver. Put on your arm guard and tab or glove. Make sure it's clear to shoot. Stand as we discussed, with your feet roughly shoulder-width apart. If there's a shooting line on the ground, it is accepted procedure to place one foot in front of the line and one behind it (diag 3-17). Imagine a line perpendicular to the shooting line and running through your heels and through the center of the target; that's called a neutral stance and is the easiest to reproduce (diag 3-18). Go through the same exercise as you did at home without the bow, extend your arms out and look over your left shoulder. This time look at the target, bend your right elbow in to the follow-through position and bring your right hand forward to anchor. Got it? Great! Repeat it a few times to get comfortable; don't worry if people look at you strangely; that happens to me all the time!

Line to Center of target

3-17 Straddling the line: one foot in front and one behind the shooting line ensures that all archers are in a safe position relative to each other (left).

3-18 The neutral stance in relation to the tar-get. Imagine a line going through both your heels and continuing down-range until it cuts the bullseye in half (right).

When the line has opened, meaning every one is behind the shooting line and it's safe to shoot, get your bow and move up to the shooting line. Take the same position as before, grab the nock of an arrow between your thumb and index finger and place it on the string below the nocking point, cock feather away from the bow (diag 3-19). Wearing a tab or glove, put two fingers on the string below the arrow, with the middle finger lightly touching the arrow's nock, and place the index finger about 1/4" above the arrow. The string should be at the level of the first finger joint or deeper and all fingers should be nearly perpendicular to the string (diag 3-20). Do not draw the bowstring with your fingertips; besides having less holding power, a fingertip release will actually make your release slower! That's because it increases tension in the drawing hand, which really needs to remain relaxed to let the string escape cleanly.

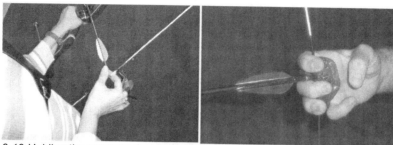

3-19 Holding the arrow nock between the thumb and forefinger, snap the nock onto the string so that the cock feather points away from the riser. (Finger tab reversed for clarity.)
3-20 Place your fingers on string, so the string rests in the first groove, the middle finger lightly touching the arrow nock and the index finger about 1/4" away from the nock. This archer's tab has a spacer between the index and middle fingers, making the separation easy. Also note that the archer's fingers are nearly perpendicular to the string.

Bring the bow arm up so it's pointing at the target (diag 3-21), keep the bow vertical, and draw the string back to your anchor point (diag 3-22). Once the anchor feels solid, look at the center of the target, and think about the first position we worked on - the left arm straight out and the right arm bent. The fingers should have relaxed by now, and the arrow should be somewhere in or near the target (diag 3-23). Relax. Did you end up in the right position? If so, hopefully the arrow is somewhere close to where you were looking. If the line is still open, try another shot.

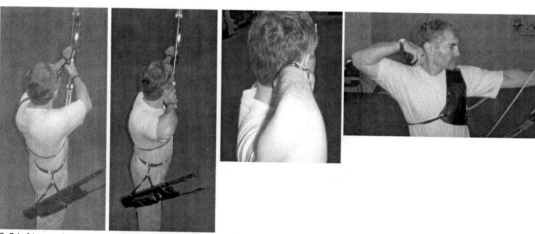

3-21 At pre-draw, note that the bow is held vertically and not tilted to one side or the other (left)
3-22 Full draw and anchor (right)
3-23 Follow-through as viewed from the rear and side. Notice how the drawing hand almost forms a fist behind the head.

Things to remember

- In the beginning, limit the number of arrows to four or five at a time; the more arrows you shoot at one time, the faster you'll get tired.

- Once you start shooting, don't change your foot placement or aspect to the target until you've finished shooting your four or five arrows and are ready to retrieve them.

- Slow down! It's common for new archers to shoot too quickly. Pace yourself, be deliberate in each step of shot execution and give yourself adequate time to rest between shots. Some coaches believe there needs to be a minimum of 20 seconds between shots and possibly longer for new shooters.

- Once you start to fatigue, all effective training has ceased.

- When looking at the target, assuming you're using the NFAA blue face, look only at the "X" in the center of the target, and not the whole target paper.

- Do not look at the arrow or the tip of the arrow or your bow arm, or anything besides the target's center.

By now, you're probably asking, "How do I aim this thing?" Honest answer is, you just do. If I walked up to you and stuck out my hand, you would do the same, and we'd shake hands. We just knew where our respective hands were, and they connected. The neural mechanism for shooting a bow is actually the same! At 10 yards, the mind perceives the shot as flat, meaning it has no trajectory or arc. That's not exactly true, but that's how we interpret it. Given enough shots and some mental trial and error, your brain and your left hand will make the connection. (*I firmly believe that the most overrated aspect in archery is "aiming".*) It may take months or years for it to become automatic or "subconscious" for any individual person, but it does happen. If you can follow the simple form exercises we talked about, you'll start making mental corrections by yourself, without having to think about them. You'll subconsciously correct for up and down, left and right. As that happens, you'll be on your way. Note: if you try to use the tip of the arrow as a pointer or sight and put it on the bullseye, you will shoot high – very high. Anchoring as we discussed, puts the arrow about 3" below your eye, so raising the tip of the arrow to the target's center, actually aims the arrow over the target (diag 3-24)! Most new shooters shoot too high their first time out, for that very reason. If you're shooting with an instructor, he/she should tell you to aim higher or lower, before you release. If you have a friend with you, have them stand to the side, and see where the arrow is pointing; have them indicate higher or lower. Another good idea is to use a word like "stop" to indicate that your observer sees something wrong or unsafe, and you should relax the draw and not shoot. It should go without saying, that any time a shot sequence needs to be aborted, and the arrow let down, that action needs to be done slowly and deliberately. If you let down abruptly, not only may you create an unsafe condition for yourself and those around you, but you may add undue stress to your shoulders and injure yourself that way.

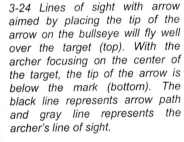
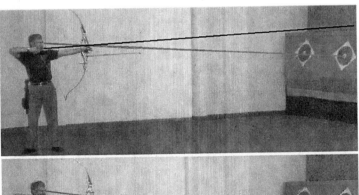
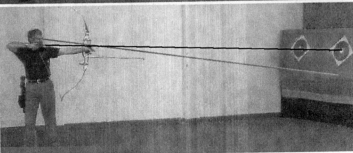

3-24 Lines of sight with arrow aimed by placing the tip of the arrow on the bullseye will fly well over the target (top). With the archer focusing on the center of the target, the tip of the arrow is below the mark (bottom). The black line represents arrow path and gray line represents the archer's line of sight.

Unless your arrows are very far off-target, keep shooting. We are not looking for an occasional arrow or two in the bullseye. Although that may be exciting, it doesn't mean very much. What we are really looking for is the formation of a group, a clustering of arrows somewhere on the target; almost anywhere will do (diag 3-25). Grouping means that you're doing the same thing every time, or at least almost every time. That consistency is the first step. Let me repeat, if all of your arrows are going high and left or low and left, or low and right of center, even off the target, that's great! If your form is consistent, in time your brain will make the necessary corrections and bring that group to center. Happily, we can help it along a little. Later on, we'll work on the bow to make sure it's doing its part; right now, you the archer, have to do the work. Keep shooting at a comfortable pace until you start to feel tired, then take a break or stop for the day.

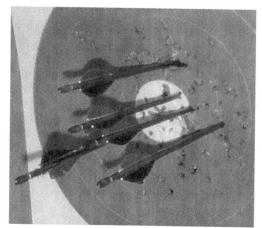

3-25 Example of a good 10 yard group for a new archer.

A brief note about retrieving arrows.

In addition to being certain that everyone has stopped shooting before walking downrange, you might be surprised to learn that there is a right and wrong way to pull arrows from a target. If you're right handed, grab the arrow shaft with your right hand near where it enters the target, and place the left hand flat against the target near the shaft. Making sure that neither you nor anyone else is standing directly behind the arrow, pull it straight out while exerting slight pressure on the target (diag 3-26). If you have several shafts grouped closely together, they may, of course, be extracted at the same time. That way, there's no chance of bending or breaking the arrows, or stabbing yourself with the nock end of the arrow. As strange as that sounds, one of the few accidents I witnessed at my old archery range was a new shooter trying to extract an arrow from a wooden target frame and embedding the nock end of the arrow about 1/2" into his thigh. After that experience my guess is that archer will always remember the correct way to extract arrows.

If you are shooting where there is a high possibility of embedding arrows into solid objects, such as wooden target frames like our friend in the last paragraph, a commercial arrow puller (diag 3-27) or a rubber kitchen jar opener may come in handy. Some archers shooting in the field carry a small knife to assist in extracting stubborn arrows.

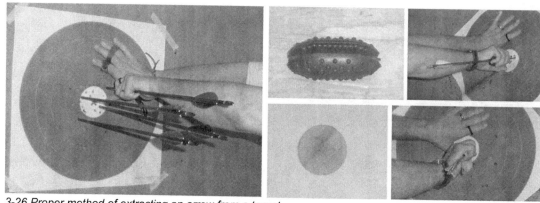

3-26 Proper method of extracting an arrow from a target.
3-27 Rubber commercial arrow puller (top) and a kitchen jar opener being used as an arrow puller (bottom).

The Hanger

3-28 A hanger is a good indication to stop shooting!

Depending on the type of target backstop you use, it's very possible that sooner or later you'll get a hanger. A hanger is an arrow that either hasn't sufficiently penetrated the target or more likely the target has deteriorated to a point where it can't support the weight of the arrow. Either way, you have an arrow hanging from its point with the shaft lying across the scoring area (diag 3-28). If this happens during a practice session, stop shooting! Your next shot will invariably hit the hanging arrow and either dent it, cut it right in half or otherwise render it useless. If it happens during a match, contact the range officer or a match official for an explanation of the rules governing "hangers".

How often should you shoot?

Another very common question or concern is, "How often should I practice?" Work schedules or family responsibilities may dictate the answer to that question for a lot of people. If that's the case, then the answer is simple, *as often as you can!* To develop your skill at a reasonable pace, most people require two shooting sessions per week at a minimum and not on consecutive days. Less than that and it is very possible that your body will have some difficulty remembering what it did last, as some of the muscle memory may not be well established. Some people are fortunate enough to be able to shoot every day. In the beginning, that may not be the greatest thing to do. As we'll see later, archery has some similarities to weight lifting. After a shooting session, some time is required for your body to recover; therefore, shooting every other day may be more beneficial. As you've probably noticed, archery can be quite addictive, so the desire to shoot every day for extended periods can be very strong. While it would be hard to discourage such dedication, the best advice would be, if you are going to shoot every day, limit the number of shots per session to possibly 100, and the time to an hour or so. You body will be happier and you'll become a better archer, faster. As your strength and stamina increase the number of shots and duration of the session can be extended.

If things don't go well...

If things are going well – great! Keep doing whatever it is you're doing! If not, meaning your arrows aren't anywhere near the target, or aren't grouping at all, we need to make sure your form matches the pictures in the previous section. First, check your anchor point placement. A very common mistake with new shooters is to keep the drawing hand away from the face or not reaching a consistent anchor (diag 3-29). Called a floating anchor; it means that the rear "sight" of the aiming system has become a variable, therefore the resultant shot placement becomes equally variable. Make sure the anchor is exactly that – an anchor. If you or your shooting partner sees that it's floating, stop and correct it.

Closely akin to a floating anchor is a failure to reach anchor (diag 3-39a). This can happen for several reasons including using a bow that's too heavy to draw comfortably. If that's the case, a lighter bow must be obtained as soon as possible. If the archer can physically draw the bow to anchor, but still comes up short, the following exercise needs to be performed before the "short draw" becomes the norm.

3-29 "Anchoring" away from face. This will result in severe inconsistencies from shot to shot (left)
The short draw – this archer is approaching his anchor but is still about an inch short of getting his index finger to the corner or his mouth and his thumb locked under his jaw (right).

An exercise that we'll be referring back too is called the non-releasing or *DON'T SHOOT* or *DON'T FIRE* exercise. Set up for the shot, stand perpendicular to the target, put the fingers around the bow string, in or deep to the first joint and raise the bow arm towards the center of the target. Draw and anchor, but DON'T RELEASE. Lock into your anchor and for the few seconds you're there, make a mental note of how your hand fits into your face. Note what's in your peripheral vision and feel how you're actually holding the weight of the bow with your deep back muscles. Try to ensure that the bow arm is relatively straight, but not locked or rigid. The exercise should be taking no more than five or six seconds. Let down slowly – don't release the arrow; bring the string back to its resting position. Rest a minute or two and repeat. It should now become apparent why I suggested a bow with a light draw weight. Do this exercise as many times as you have to, to get used to that feeling at full draw. When ready, repeat the exercise, but this time center your focus on the center of the bullseye, and release. What happened? No – not where did the arrow go, but rather did you end up in a position similar to the follow-through position in diagram 3-23? Remember – the follow-though position not only means a rearward movement of the drawing hand, but a relatively non-moving bow arm. It also tells you if you were lined up correctly before the shot. If so, excellent, rest and try it again. If you are anchoring solidly and following through, the arrows should be fairly near each other. Take a few more shots. You should be able to tell before the arrow hits the target whether it left the bow correctly or not. As you practice, more and more of the arrows should be ending up in a group; if not, go back to the DON'T SHOOT exercise.

Flailing the bow arm

The other readily visible anomaly that can plague new shooters is the flailing bow arm (diag 3-30). Improper lines of force or *alignment* at the instant of release always cause this. While shoulder alignment is the most likely problem area, the culprit can be anywhere along the system.

3-30 Flailing the bow arm on release, exaggerated for clarity.

What we'll be looking at next are a few additional aspects of elementary form. We'll briefly discuss a lot of information in this section. If you followed the initial instructions you're already achieved pretty good form. The newer points should not all be tried at one time! As you get comfortable with the basics, then begin working on or confirming the items listed below.

Holding the bow vertically

That's probably the easiest way to shoot a bow. It's true that canting the bow slightly (tilting the top limb slightly to the right, for a right-handed shooter), might feel more natural and comfortable, but for now it's easier to reproduce a vertical bow than a 5 degree cant. Small changes in the degree of cant will change the point of impact on the target, so in our quest for consistency, a vertical position is preferred.

Gripping the bow

The questions are – how and how firmly? Most bow's grips fit well into the area of the palm, just deep/central to the mound of the thumb, along the lifeline (diag 3-31). This is a very natural grip and easy to reproduce. At this stage keep the force along the lifeline; we'll go into variations a bit later. Of even greater importance is how tightly you grip the bow. In the old days, we were all taught that the grip on the bow should be like a good handshake, firm but not tight or vise-like. That's still good advice, but not great advice; we need go a step further. Your hand should feel comfortable on the grip, but you should have only a light hold on the handle, if any at all (diag 3-32). Even an inexpensive bow has a fair amount of balance built into it. By placing a stranglehold on the handle, you are effectively nullifying any balance the bow has. By allowing the bow to react naturally to the release and "shock" (the effect of the bowstring stopping the forward movement of the limbs) the bow will cast a cleaner and faster arrow. In effect, you're not getting in the way of what the bow wants to do. ("Cast" is an old term for how well – how far and how fast – a bow will shoot an arrow.)

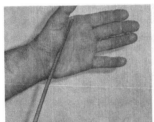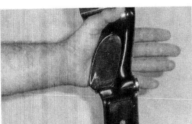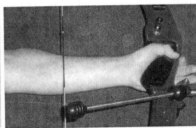

3-31 With a relaxed bow hand, the grip rests along the life line of the palm. The first picture shows the position of the lifeline and the second the grip resting against it (right two pictures).
3-32 Relaxed bow hand on riser grip (left).

The bow arm

The bow arm should be *relatively straight*, but *never locked* (diag 3-33). If the bow arm is held rigid the shoulder joint becomes the fulcrum or pivot point, of the system and lengthens the lever arm. Therefore, a stable bow arm becomes impossible. The elbow should be rotated as far outward (backward) as possible or rather as far as comfortable (3-34). The entire arm, especially the forearm, should be relaxed and as tension-free as possible. You basically want to do as little work as possible.

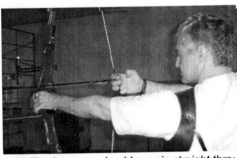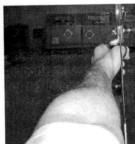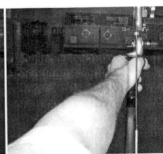

3-33 The bow arm should remain straight through the shot, but never locked.
3-34 The elbow of the bow arm should be rotated as far clockwise as comfortable. Notice the difference in string to arm clearance between the two pictures.

Head and Shoulders

The shoulders should be fairly level, with the head seeming to float high above them. The head should be rotated as far as comfortable to the left. Careful here, everybody is built differently. Some folks will be able to turn their heads a full 90 degrees to the left, some even more, some of us, a lot less. It has to be as far as is comfortable (diag 3-35). If you force it you'll strain your neck muscles, making a clean shot impossible and possibly resulting in neck pain or injury; if you don't rotate enough, the bowstring will hit your nose or lip on release. Lastly, and this may sound obvious, but unless you're shooting with a bow sight, both eyes should be open!'

Back muscles, back tension and a detailed discussion of shoulder alignment will be discussed in a later section.

The Drawing Arm

Like the bow arm, the drawing arm (both forearm and upper arm) needs to be as relaxed as possible. The string is placed in or deep to the first joint, and the rest of the hand and wrist is relaxed and straight. The drawing fingers can be likened to hooks holding a heavy weight, for that is exactly what they are, and that's the only thing they are doing. The forearm and elbow need to be in the same vertical and horizontal planes as the arrow (diag 3-36). This ensures that on release, the drawing hand can travel only straight back.

3-35 The basic "T" stance, with the head high above the shoulders and rotated as far to the left as comfortable. Careful examination will reveal that the bow shoulder is slightly higher than the drawing shoulder. This asymmetry will occur by itself, if the previous steps have been followed correctly (left)
3-36 Alignment of the drawing hand and arm should nearly coincide with the axis of the arrow (right).

Spine

Your spine, not the arrow's. The spine should retain its natural curvature, meaning you should be standing naturally upright. Some archers lean forward slightly, and the operative word is "slightly", at the waist to provide better bowstring clearance. The feet should be shoulder-width apart to balance the spine adequately and support the rest of the body as shown in diagram 3-35.

"Blank Bale" shooting and the "Watch the Arrow" exercise.

Before we leave this section, I'd like to introduce two exercises that have proven invaluable for developing and maintaining shooting form.

The first exercise is called "blank bale" shooting and as the name implies, the archer stands a few yards from the target board and practices his shooting form or technique without the distraction of having to aim at a target. A variation would be to simply shoot at close range with the eyes closed. Both scenarios allow the shooter to focus on the individual aspects of form such as the anchor, shoulder position, release and follow-through without worrying about where the arrows are going. In the past, this exercise was considered so important that many instructors would not allow their students to "aim" at a target until they had spent a number of weeks or months blank baling. With today's impatient society, blank baling may be a tough regimen for new shooters to adhere to because there's no visual feedback and most new shooters aren't quite sure what proper form should feel like.

Elementary Shooting Form

Blank bale shooting subsequently evolved into the "WATCH the ARROW" exercise. While similar in theory, it provides the shooter with visual feedback and as we'll see later in the book, has broader implications and uses. The shooter prepares to shoot at close range, acquires the target, draws and anchors normally, but while at anchor he shifts his focus from the target to the tip of the arrow, taking note of where the shaft contacts the rest or passes a given part of the riser. He then allows the string to slip from his fingers and watches the arrow as it leaves the bow.

This exercise accomplishes the following:

1. Ensures that the arrow is drawn the same amount each time (consistent draw length).
2. The draw length doesn't waver back and forth while at anchor (there's no creeping).
3. The release is clean (the drawing shoulder doesn't collapse, allowing the arrow to move forward just before the release).
4. The bow arm is steady throughout the shot (any movement of the bow arm on release will be readily apparent).

As we'll see later in the book this exercise will be called on to hone form, and diagnose and correct a number of form and shooting problems. This exercise is so critical that I practice it at the end of every shooting session.

3-36 The "blank baling" (left two pictures) and "watch the arrow" exercise (right).

Final thoughts on form:

Good "form" means exactly the same thing for every archer – using your body efficiently to execute the shot – or put another way, *making the shot by doing as little work as possible!*

That usually means:

1. Proper joint alignment
2. Proper body orientation to the target
3. Reproducible anchor
4. Reproducible bow grip
5. Maintenance of muscle tension throughout the shot
6. Maintenance of focus on the target at the time of release
7. Consistent follow-through

The last part is a natural evolution that all good archers experience. The individual steps described will turn into the parts of a larger whole. Each step will blend or flow into the next and will add to the foundation of the shot. Your orientation to the target and the way you place your hands on the grip and the string will affect the manner in which to draw the bow. Your draw will set up your anchor and shoulder alignment. The anchor and shoulder alignment will establish proper lines of tension, which will determine your ability to hold a steady aim and yield a good follow-through.

This is a time-proven method of getting you to lay the foundation of proper shot execution. How you handle the technical details is your business, and no two people will "look" exactly alike, but I'll bet you that all the top shooters have those seven principles in common.

Believe it or not – that's really all there is to shooting! Well, sort of…

Chapter 4

Common Errors and How to Correct Them

Most problems that both new and experienced shooters face have a fairly well known cause-and-effect relationship. While the problem may be troublesome or downright painful, there's usually a readily available remedy.

Bowstring hitting the forearm

Probably the most common and painful problem a beginning archer will face is the bowstring hitting his forearm. While wearing an arm guard will protect your arm from welts, it is really only masking the underlying problem, which is typically poor or incorrect form. There are three characteristic areas of injury. The most frequent is the inner part of the forearm, just distal to the elbow (diag 4-1). The cause is almost always the point of the elbow being rotated downward (towards the shooter's six o'clock position when viewed over the left shoulder), instead of being rotated outward (towards the shooter's eight or nine o'clock position). When the elbow is rotated downward, it brings the fleshy part of the forearm right into the path of the bowstring. Simply rotating the elbow back (clockwise, as you look over your left shoulder) solves the problem. You can prove this yourself by holding the bow in the shooting position and rotating the elbow clockwise and counterclockwise a few times, and seeing how the bowstring's clearance to the forearm changes (diag 4-2). Another option is to open the stance slightly. We began with both feet perpendicular to the target, and both heels in line with the bullseye. For some people, simply moving the rear foot forward a few inches and opening themselves to the target may mean the difference between a successful shooting session and a painful one (diag 4-3). Note that this may do more to mask a form or alignment problem, rather than cure it.

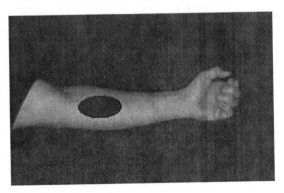

4-1 Typical location of a high forearm string slap

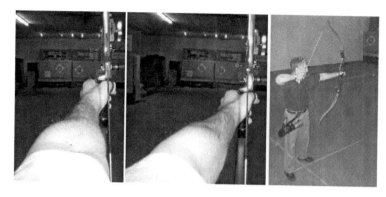

4-2 Elbow rotation in relation to string. Notice the increased clearance when the elbow is rearward (clockwise), as compared to when it's rotated downward (counter-clockwise) – (left and middle).

4-3 Slightly opening the stance (by bringing the rear foot slight forward of the front foot) may increase the bowstring to forearm clearance - right.

If the injury is lower (diag 4-4), it can mean that you are rotating your hand too far into (deep) the bow's grip (diag 4-5). Remember that it should be right along the lifeline, just central to the mound of the thumb. Another cause is pushing your shoulder forward in its socket, thereby placing the entire bow arm in harm's way (diag 4-6). If that's the case the most likely causes are either being over-bowed, fatigued, or both. If the former, and a lighter bow isn't available, resign yourself to taking fewer shots per end (an "end" is defined as the number of arrows fired before they are retrieved) and building up gradually; if the latter, then either take a break or call it quits for the day. Drawing the bow while a partner observes your form, or by looking in a mirror from different angles, should let you see if your shoulder is moving forward.

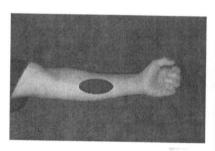

4-4 Typical location of a medium to low forearm or wrist string slap (left).
4-5 Placing the wrist too deep on the grip may result in a low forearm or wrist string slap (middle). Ouch, that's gonna hurt!
4-6 Thrusting the bow arm forward in the shoulder socket may place the entire arm in the path of the bow string. Notice the minimal clearance between the arrow/bowstring and shoulder/arm, not to mention that this archer's nose is in danger (right)!

If the bowstring strike is very low on the forearm, near the wrist (diag 4-7), it usually means that the brace height is too low. This happens more often with longbows as opposed to recurves, due to their inherent lower brace heights (diag 4-8). The only real solution is to raise the brace height, or get a different bow. Again, it's worthwhile to confirm that you're not going deeper than your lifeline on the bow's grip and turning your wrist into the path of the bowstring. We discussed earlier why just wearing a very heavy arm guard isn't the answer. In rare cases when the brace height is marginally low, the possibility of the arrow nocks being too tight on the string can exacerbate the problem by pulling the string forward than it should travel. We'll talk more about that in the tuning section.

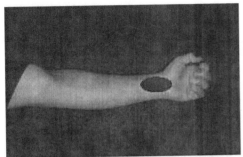

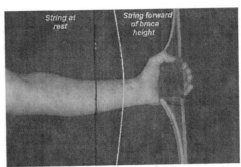

4-7 Typical location of a very low forearm/wrist strike
4-8 Very low wrist string strikes are typical with some longbows that have very low brace heights. Notice how the bowstring travels beyond the resting brace height just before the arrow nock disengages. A tight nock may pull the string even further forward and result in a wrist slap.

Lastly, the archer's interface with the bow, also known as the bow grip, may simply not match the archer's anatomy. While most incompatibilities can be corrected with a slight change in form including the position of the bow hand on the grip, as your skill and understanding develops you may find that one style or shape grip just works better for you than another.

Hitting your nose or face with the bow string
The string hitting your nose on release just means that you are not turning your head far enough towards the target (diag 4-9 and 4-10). It should be rotated as far as is comfortable. Not everyone has the flexibility in his cervical spine to get his head square to the target, especially as one gets older. Conversely, new shooters, in an attempt to draw the bow fully will occasionally overextend the draw, and begin to turn their heads away from the target. With any luck, before they clip their noses too many times, they'll realize that they going a little too far! Again, a watchful friend may be quite helpful.

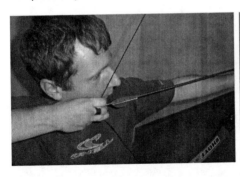

4-9 Incomplete head rotation towards target, the tip of the nose and part of the lips are directly in the path of the bowstring (left).

4-10 Correct head position at anchor in relation to the string and target (right).

Hitting the chest, stomach, or other extraneous body parts
While this may be a touchy topic (no pun intended) we are all built differently. So, while the basic form we described in the last chapter is best for most people, there are always exceptions, so modifications must be considered. There are two ways of increasing clearance for the bowstring's travel. The simplest is to "open the stance". As we described when discussing bow arm injuries, the neutral stance may not be the best choice for some shooters. Moving the rear foot (right foot, for a right-handed shooter) forward a few inches, and opening the stance should afford those that need it an added measure of safety. Second, and this should be a last resort, is bending slightly forward from the waist. While this does increase string clearance, the position is difficult to reproduce, and quite honestly isn't the greatest position for your spine. If this is a requirement,

then enter cautiously, and remember the operative word is SLIGHTLY (diag 4-11 and 4-12). Lastly, several versions of archery chest protectors are available for both ladies and gentlemen. The same caveat holds for chest protectors as for arm guards (diag 4-13).

4-11 and 4-12 Some people require more string clearance than others. Two possible solutions are opening the stance and/or leaning slightly forward by bending at the waist. Notice the ample clearance this large archer attains by using those two techniques.
4-13 Use of a chest protector prevents accidental string contact with your body or clothes.

Hand slipping on the bow

Although rare, some people, especially those with sweaty palms, have trouble keeping their hands from sliding around on the bow grip. The typical answer is to wrap the grip with leather or rubber wrapping similar to that used on tennis rackets or golf clubs (diag 4-14). While that may afford some relief, it doesn't get to the root of the problem. Either the hand is not being placed on the grip correctly or the grip simply doesn't fit the shooter. With the bow grip resting along the lifeline, the hand should be pushed into the throat of the grip, and not be able to move or slip. If the hand position is correct and there's still slippage, then it's very possible that the grip just isn't right for your hand. (That's why serious competitors may resort to custom-made bow grips for a perfect fit.) If that's the case, the aforementioned wraps may exacerbate the problem. While they prevent the hand from slipping on the grip, the added adhesion introduces torque, a twisting motion, to the bow and that usually makes matters worse by interfering with the arrow as it is launched. Diagrams 4-15 to 4-17 show proper hand positions for the high, medium and low grips.

4-14 Use of a leather or synthetic grip wrap may make the grip more comfortable, and while it may also help keep the hand localized on the grip, it doesn't address the root cause of the slippage. Top photo shows a leather tennis racquet wrap on a Bear "C" riser and the bottom photo shows a synthetic bicycle handlebar wrap on a Jeffery's Tradition longbow (left).

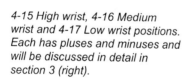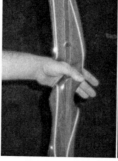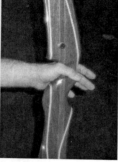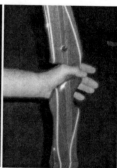

4-15 High wrist, 4-16 Medium wrist and 4-17 Low wrist positions. Each has pluses and minuses and will be discussed in detail in section 3 (right).

Sore Muscles

Archery practice is in some ways akin to weight lifting, except that with archery usually there are more repetitions and less weight. Therefore, in the beginning some soreness is expected, natural, and necessary. It's just your body's way of telling you that you're doing something new. The soreness typically develops the day after the practice session. With regular shooting, the soreness should dissipate after a few weeks as the muscles get used to the new and increased workload. It's also natural for the soreness to reappear, if you return to shooting after several weeks off, or get a new and heavier bow. If the soreness continues for months, and you've been practicing regularly, there may be something amiss. Before running off to the doctor there are a few things to consider.

Are you over-bowed?

The symptoms include:

- Difficulty drawing the bow
- Unsteadiness at anchor
- Rapid fatigue
- Rapid loss of accuracy
- You're 6'2" tall, wear a size 52 jacket and claim to have a 25" draw

If any or all of these symptoms are present, then a lighter bow may be in order. If that's not a viable option, then limiting the number of arrows per session and per end may help, as will taking more time between shots. The last symptom may require some re-programming in addition.

Is there something wrong with your form?

Even with a light bow, trying to draw the bow by using arm or shoulder muscles instead of the deep back muscles may lead to soreness and poor shooting. Review the form pictures in Chapter 3 and see how closely your form matches.

Are you just over doing it?

Archery can be quite addictive and most new shooters can't get enough of it. It's entirely possible that you're simply shooting more than your body can handle. Try shortening your practice sessions and building up gradually.

Of particular concern is prolonged pain in the front part of the shoulder joint. This usually affects the shoulder of the drawing arm, but can happen to the bow shoulder as well. The worst-case scenario for that symptom would be a rotator cuff injury. The rotator cuff is comprised of four muscles and tendons that socket the upper arm to the shoulder blade and collarbone. That type of injury requires rest and medical attention. See the chapter on Physical Fitness for additional information on the rotator cuff and related muscles.

Sore Fingers

Sore fingers, for the most part, are an occupational hazard, especially for beginning archers. Fingers get sore, and then callus over. There are several things that can lessen the pain. Most importantly, as we discussed in the Basic Shooting section, the string needs to be held in the first joint of the first three fingers, or deeper. That alone will alleviate most of the finger problems. Second, is the use of a good tab or glove. The glove should fit snugly, but not be constricting, and the tab will usually need to be trimmed to fit the archer's hand. It should only cover the fingers when they are fully wrapped around the string, and not when the fingers are extended. There are several styles, materials and sizes of both gloves and tabs and there will be some experimentation required to find the "right" one for you. The section on tuning will have more information on trimming the tab.

Most often, archers, both new and veteran, find that the ring finger takes a bit more of a beating that the other two, and is called shooting with a "heavy third finger". It can be caused by simply putting too much pressure on that finger (using it to pull more than its fair share). You might consider re-distributing the force on each finger, but be prepared to experiment. Another cause is raising the drawing elbow too high (diag 4-18). It is usually safer to keep the drawing forearm in line with the arrow, both during the draw and at full draw (diag 4-19).

4-18 High drawing elbow and resultant 3rd finger pressure (left).

4-19 Keeping the elbow level with the arrow may take some pressure off the 3rd finger (right).

Another area of discomfort can be the inner side of the index finger. This is usually caused by excessive pressure on the arrow nock, due to finger pinch (diag 4-20). Remember that the middle finger should lightly touch the lower edge of the nock and the index finger should begin about 1/4" above the nock; that way, as the draw progresses the force of the index finger on the nock will be minimized. Many tabs on the market today come with (optional) finger spacers, between the index and middle finger (diag 4-21). Archers at all levels, including top Olympic shooters, successfully use finger spacers.

4-20 Pinching the arrow nock by starting the draw with the index finger too close to the nock can result in soreness near the inner cuticle of that finger (left).

4-21 Use of a tab with a finger spacer may alleviate the problem (right).

While soreness, calluses and even blisters may be part and parcel of the neophyte archer's existence, tingling or numbing sensations should not. If that happens, and more so if it persists well after the shooting session, practice should be discontinued, and medical advice sought. Tingling, called paraesthesia, may be a symptom of a more serious problem. Hopefully it won't be, but it's always best to have it evaluated by a physician.

Closely akin to finger soreness is the arrow falling off the rest during the draw. While not painful, except to your ego, it can be a source of frustration for the new archer. This typically happens because either the index or middle finger is exerting too much pressure on the arrow's nock (diag 4-22a). Recall that we said the middle finger should slightly touch the nock and the index finger should be about 1/4" above at the beginning of the draw. If the middle finger is actually pressing against the nock, the force exerted will lift the arrow from the rest. Simply start the draw with the middle finger a little further away from the arrow. The natural uncurling of the fingers during the draw should help to keep the arrow on the rest.

Pinching the arrow may also result in unexplained misses anywhere on the or even off the target. By pinching the arrow, it is possible to exert enough pressure on the nock to bend the arrow downward between the drawing hand and the arrow rest (diag 4-22b). With the arrow bending while at anchor, upon release it may bounce off the rest, fly erratically and impact anywhere on the target.

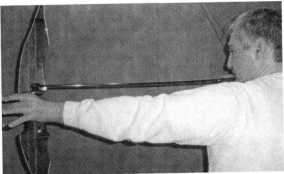

4-22a Pinching the arrow nock may also lead to the arrow falling off the rest. While not physically painful, it can lead to a bruised ego if it happens often enough (left).
4-22b If you look closely, you can see that the arrow is bending downward. There's nothing physically wrong with the arrow, but the archer is pinching the nock and forcing the arrow to bend (right). A finger spacer attached to the tab may solve the problem.

Analyzing arrow strike patterns

Hopefully by this point you're grouping arrows and the group is near the center of the target. Hint: if you do decide to use the NFAA blue indoor target, or any common target face, start off with a new one for each session, and don't throw it out when you're done. The paper has recorded every shot (except those that missed it completely and there shouldn't have been too many of those, right?) If you're grouping, the target will show a greater amount of hits in one area relative to the others (diag 4-23). The target paper has a perfect memory, and great diagnostic abilities.

4-23The target will record every shot and can be of diagnostic value. It this case we see a predominance of left and right hits or horizontal stringing

The following assumes a right-handed shooter:

Very High Groups (diag 4-24)

If your arrows are repeatedly hitting well above the paper, the first thing to confirm is that you are not using the arrow point as a sight, and placing it on the bullseye or near the target. Since the rear of the arrow is well below your eye when at anchor, raising the tip to the bullseye effectively has you aiming well above the target. There are aiming methods that employ similar practices, but for our current purposes, just focus on the target and not the arrow. Yes, until you consciously forget about the arrow, it will appear to be well below the target, when you're actually aiming at the center. That's normal. For now, just focus on the very center of the bullseye and make whatever adjustments are necessary, even if they don't seem "quite right".

Arrows stringing vertically (diag 4-25)

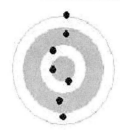

This means that your arrows are showing a vertical dispersion pattern without significant left or right deviation. Not to worry; either your brain hasn't made the connection to elevation/trajectory yet, or the bow requires additional tuning to have the arrow go where you're looking. For now, slightly high or slightly low is not a matter for concern.

Arrows grouping high or low (diag 4-26)

Nocking point too low or too high. See chapter 5 on tuning.

1. Inconsistent string finger tension. There are several methods or theories of tension or weight distribution on the three string fingers. Some practices are preferred, by certain groups of archers, over others. For example, most Olympic target shooters hold 50% of the draw weight with their middle finger, 35% with their ring finger and only 15% with their index finger. Some do the exact opposite, 80% with the index and middle fingers, and 20% with the ring finger. Some even advocate equal tension on all three fingers.

While I've had good success with the first method, cases can be made for each. As long as the technique stays the same, unexpected high and lows should not appear.

2. Inconsistent pressure from the bow hand. As we discussed, the bow should fit comfortably deep to the mound of the thumb, along the lifeline. Even with that position there are still an infinite number of variations. The wrist of the bow arm can be held in a high, medium, or low (heeled) position (refer to diagrams 4-15, 4-16 and 4-17). While a major factor may be the geometry of the physical grip of the bow (which grip is best for you can only be determined by experience) most bows do allow for some variation. Like the string fingers, each position has its devotees. As long as you can reproduce the position each time, the shot will be the same each time, provided, you were consistent in the other aspects of your form. I tend to start people off with a medium to low grip. In the beginning, the archery muscles are generally not well developed; after a few dozen arrows the wrist tends to fatigue, and the archer begins to "heel" the bow, meaning the grip naturally turns into a low grip. Some coaches believe that if you start off with a low grip, there'll be less variation as the shooting session progresses. There's merit to that theory. The only caveat is that heeling the bow may result in pushing the bow upward on release, and hence result in a vertical shot distribution. You'll have to experiment with the different positions and see which is most consistent for you.

3. Another common reason for arrows striking low or high is an inconsistent draw length. The drawing hand creeping and/or collapsing may cause this. Creeping means that you have come to your anchor and then crept forward, shortening your draw length (diag 4-27). If the draw length is shorter, the force the bow can impart to the arrow is less, and it falls short, or at close range, low. If you think this isn't a serious issue, Olympic archers shooting at 70 meters, and FITA shooters at 90 meters can miss the entire target if their draw length changes by as little as 1/4". These shooters use a device called a clicker to ensure consistent draw length every time. We'll talk about that too, in the section on Olympic tuning. There are several reasons for creeping or short drawing, but most will fall into two categories. Either the bow is too heavy for the archer to hold at anchor or the lines of tension haven't been correctly established.

4. Collapsing means that the drawing hand moves forward slightly at the moment of release, and typically results in a left or low left arrow, depending on the distance to the target.

5. Related to the above is the possibility that the drawing fingers may be uncurling too much at anchor (diag 4-28). While some uncurling of the drawing fingers is unavoidable, it's possible that they may uncurl so much that the arrow may creep forward and result in a shortened draw. The only way to combat this is to confirm that you are beginning the draw using a deep hook grip on the string (string into or past the first joint) and it stays there, as much as possible, until the follow-through.

An excellent exercise to correct both creeping and collapsing is to watch the tip of the arrow, as described in the last chapter. Stand relatively close to the target to minimize the possibility of missing and prepare to shoot normally. Draw, anchor and aim, but before you release, shift your focus from the target to the tip of the arrow, taking note of where the shaft contacts the rest or passes a given part of the riser. Do not let the arrow move forward of that point! With a tangible reference point most people correct the problem within a few sessions. This exercise has the added advantage of also letting the archer know exactly how steady his bow arm remains during the shot. In fact, we'll discuss it again when we talk about steadying the bow arm and in several other sections as well! I regularly use this exercise to reinforce a consistent hold and clean release.

Arrows grouping to the left (diag 4-29)

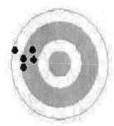

You may not have the right arrows. An over-spined arrow will shoot left. If you believe this is the case, as per the arrow/spine chart in Appendix B, then you may need weaker-spined arrows or need to tune the bow to handle the arrows (chapters 5 to 7). At this stage of your training, unless the arrows are so over-spined that they are striking the riser (you'll hear that as a definite slapping or cracking sound on release) you might not need to do anything. If the arrows are grouping well, and the flight appears decent, just accept the left arrows. As we're dealing with instinctive shooting here, after enough shots, your brain should compensate and bring the arrows toward center.

1. You're actually aiming left. A very simple way to check if you're doing this is to bore-sight or shotgun a few arrows. Draw and anchor normally, but instead of aiming as you normally do, look down the arrow shaft with your right eye (for a right-handed shooter). Make sure it's lined up with the center of the target (diag 4-30). If not, make whatever corrections are necessary. When you go back to focusing on the bullseye, your brain will correct the problem. If the arrow looks centered before the release, but still impacts left, then weaker-spined arrows or different tuning is required.

2. You're cross-eye dominant. Consciously or not, you may be looking at the arrow at full draw. If you're shooting right-handed, and left eye dominant, you will be holding left and hitting left. Bore-sight a few arrows, as previously described; making sure that you're bore-sighting with the eye that's over the arrow. Cross-eye dominance is discussed in the aiming section.

3. You're torqueing the bow. Even if you're shooting with a completely open hand, it's possible to do a slight grab on release. Even a little thumb pressure can cause torque, and that will be enough to give you a left arrow (diag 4-31). It can happen so quickly, that you may not know you're doing it, and only an experienced observer will be able to see it happening. To correct this, you'll simply need to practice shooting with a relaxed grip and not grab the bow. One thing a lot of target shooters use is some type of sling. There are finger slings, wrist slings, and slings that attach to the bow (diag 4-32a-c). These will allow you to keep an open hand and not have to worry about dropping the bow on release. Another trick is holding the bow

with only the thumb and index finger, or having the tips of the thumb and index finger touching each other and curling the other fingers into the palm (diag 4-33). (If you recall, we suggested placing the arrow rest directly over the deepest part of the grip, so if the hand does torque the grip, its effect on the arrow will be minimized.)

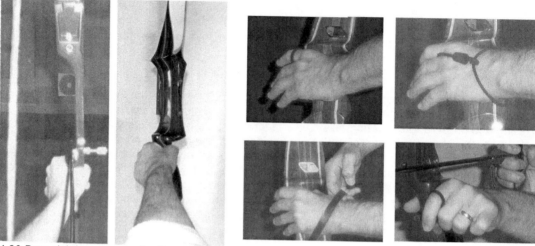

4-30 Bore sighting an arrow for diagnostic purposes (right).
4-31 Torqueing the bow grip is usually seen as the bow twisting to the left from the shooter's perspective (next right).
4-32 Slings: Finger sling (left top), Wrist Sling (left top-right), Bow Sling (left bottom left).
4-33 Bow grip with thumb/forefinger curled into the palm of the hand (left bottom-right).

4. You're collapsing on release. If your drawing hand is moving forward, even slightly, instead of back on release, there may be a number of problems happening at the same time. If they're very minor, like torqueing the bow, you might not be able to see or feel what you're doing. Again, you'll need someone to watch what you're doing and then to go back to the basics and work on the anchor position, alignment and the follow-through positions (diags 4-34 & 4-35).

4-34 & 4-35 Example of "collapsing" prior to release. Notice how the draw arm moves slightly forward just on the release.

A time-honored method for dealing with these types of form problems is "blank bale" shooting or the "watch the arrow" exercise, from the last chapter. Set yourself a few yards away from the target, and practice shooting without aiming, focusing only on the correct form and feel of the shot, or focus on the tip of the arrow as it leaves the bow.

5. You may be anchoring away from your face. By moving the rear of the arrow to the right, you are effectively moving the point of the arrow to the left. Review the diagrams in Chapter 3 and make sure your hand is solidly "anchored" against your face.

6. You may be "reverse-canting" the bow. If the top limb of the bow is tilted to the left (counter clockwise), the tip of the arrow will be displaced to the left.

Arrows grouping to the right (diag 4-36)

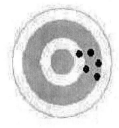

1. The arrows are under-spined. See comments above for over-spined arrows.
2. You're aiming to the right. See comment #2 above for aiming left.
3. You're plucking the string on release (diag 4-37). "Plucking" means that the drawing hand doesn't come straight back on release, but moves laterally away from the face, akin to plucking a guitar string. While that might work if you're a musician, it's not going to help your shooting! Go back and look at the follow-through pictures in Chapter 4. On release, the only hand movement must be directly away from the shot, meaning straight back. We'll go into the anatomy of the shot in Section 3, but for now, review and rehearse the follow-through position, and work on ending up there after the shot. An old target archer's trick is to have someone place an arrow in the crook of your elbow once you're at full draw (diag 4-38). If the arrow falls out on release, you've plucked.

4-37 Plucking – The drawing hand comes away from the face, causing the arrow to whip around the riser and strike to the right of its mark (left).
4-38 Placing an arrow in the crook of the drawing elbow will tell you very quickly if you're plucking or not! If the arrow stays in place – no pluck! (middle and left).

5. You're canting the bow (diag 4-39). Tilting the top limb clockwise will change the geometry of the shot and cause the arrow to go farther right than expected. At this stage of your training, I strongly suggest you use a vertical bow.

4-39 Canting the bow can also cause a right group, if done inconsistently.

Arrows grouping both left and right (diag 4-40)

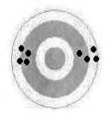

That might well be a combination of errors. I cannot repeat enough times, if you can follow the diagrams and ingrain the anchor and follow-through positions, most errors will never appear. But, let's say they have; here are two exercises to get back on track. These exercises are also useful for honing basic techniques, so even if you don't have the problems we've been talking about, you might want to try them.

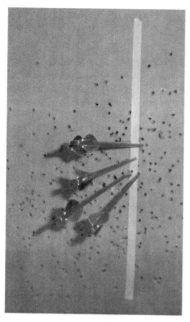

Wand shooting

This exercise, dating back to the time of the English longbowmen, was used to develop clean release and true arrow flight. In the Middle Ages, longbowmen shot en masse, meaning that dozens or hundreds of archers would draw and release arrows at the same time to barrage the enemy forces. While pinpoint accuracy wasn't required, the arrows needed to be directed toward the enemy masses several hundred yards away, and not to the left or right. The young archers were required to shoot at a vertical wand or reed at a distance of 100 yards, in order to perfect the shot. We'll stay at 10 yards, and instead of a real wand, we'll replace the target with a vertical strip of tape, one to two inches wide and two to three feet long. Your goal is to hit the tape and anywhere on the tape counts as a point. Try this for a while and you'll be surprised how quickly your release improves (diag 4-41)

4-41 Example of modern day wand shooting using a strip of masking tape.

Bow arm exercise. If you or your shooting partner notices that your bow arm is flailing on release, or that it really isn't staying in the follow-through position throughout the shot, we'll need to correct that and quickly. It's been said, probably not often enough, that a solid bow arm will hide a multitude of sins. While that's a very true statement, making the bow arm "solid" is quite another story. At the moment of release, lines of tension are broken, and the opposing forces released explode faster and are stronger than most people can control by sheer muscle strength alone. **The only way to keep the bow arm really solid or steady is to have the correct shoulder alignment in the first place.** That means a solid anchor and a well-defined picture in your mind of the follow-through position. It's impossible to control individual muscles, so we need to be able to do it on a different level.

Here's the exercise (a variation on the "follow the arrow" exercise). Use a regular target at 10 yards or closer as we did previously, set up as usual, draw and anchor, and focus on the center of the bullseye. This time before you shoot, change the focus from the bullseye to the face of the bow. Instead of focusing on the shot itself, focus on the position of the bow in relation to the target or backstop. Think about keeping the bow arm steady, not by exerting extra tension in the arms

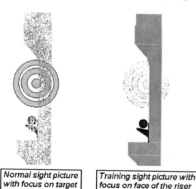

| Normal sight picture with focus on target | Training sight picture with focus on face of the riser |

or shoulders, but by keeping them as relaxed as possible, just as we discussed. Watch the bow, and "let" it stay still (diag 4-42). As simple as it sounds, most people notice a dramatic reduction in bow arm movement after just a few shots. The more you do the exercise, the steadier you'll become. Once the new muscle memory has been learned, you should be able to go back to focusing on the bullseye again, and the bow arm will stay where it belongs. It's also a good exercise to do from time to time to verify and reinforce bow arm stability. You can also maintain focus on the face of the bow and see whether your arrows still hit near center – a real test of how steady you can keep your bow arm!

4-42 Changing your focus from the center of the target to the face of the bow will help to reprogram your brain to steady your bow arm

Arrows striking the target at strange angles (diag 4-43)

These are usually tuning errors, but may also be caused by a sloppy or inconsistent release. Another factor may be something interfering with the arrow before it leaves the string. Contact with the arm guard, clothes or even excessively large feathers hitting riser or rest may affect arrow flight.

Arrows all over the target, with no definable grouping at all (diag 4-44)

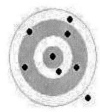

First we'll need to define a group. If you're shooting at 10 yards, and most of your arrows are around the center of the target within a 12" circle, that 12" group qualifies, as would a group containing most of the arrows hitting in the same relation/direction to the bullseye. If some arrows are going below the target, some above, some left and some right, then we have a problem. If you understand and can implement the shooting positions I've been describing and can establish a focus or "a lock" on the target's center, but still are not grouping, we'll need to try a bow sight. That will let us see if there is a form problem or you just haven't made the eye-hand connection yet.

Setting up a temporary bow sight

What we have been doing thus far is using a technique called instinctive shooting. Very simply it means focusing our attention on something we wish to hit and letting our brains subconsciously do all the work. We've been staying relatively close to the target, so trajectory hasn't really entered into the picture, at least not in any significant way. If you have the feeling that you don't have a handle on how to aim, you're not alone. It takes some folks longer than others to pick it up, and some folks never get it at all. This actually isn't a problem. Sights or aiming devices have been around almost as long as archery has. What we'll do is make a very simple, yet effective sight and see what happens. All you'll need is a toothpick or similar object and a piece of tape.

1. Measure the distance from the right corner of your mouth to the center of your right eye; as always, we're assuming you're right handed. Use the left corner of the mouth and left eye, if you're a lefty. It's usually about 3" for most adults.

2. Tape the toothpick so that the head or tip is that distance above the arrow rest and position it so the point is over where the arrow rests, or slightly to the left (diag 4-45). That's the sight!

3. Set up to shoot as usual, except this time, close your left eye and put the tip of the "sight" right on the bullseye (diag 4-46). Probably a good idea to have a friend watch to make sure that you're basically still pointing at the target. While this method has always worked for setting up a sight and getting the arrows near the center of the target, in my experience, nothing is foolproof and a little added insurance doesn't hurt.

4. Shoot, following through as always. If the arrow hits anywhere near the target, great. Shoot again; the second arrow should be near the first, if you followed-through correctly.

What we are looking for here isn't necessarily bullseyes, but rather a group. As the sight really can't move, any variation in arrow placement must be due to inconsistencies in form. Review the steps for shot execution, and work on getting the arrow off cleanly. Then the arrows will start grouping.

By the way, if you're interested in having the arrows hit center, not an uncommon thought, all you have to do is adjust the sight or "calibrate" the sight. That is easy to do, as it's only held on with tape. The tricky part, especially if you're used to rifle shooting, is that the bow sight is actually the front sight of the rifle, not the rear sight as we are usually accustomed to adjusting. So, to correct for a HIGH arrow, you move the sight UP; if the arrows are going LOW, move the sight DOWN; if RIGHT, then RIGHT, and LEFT, LEFT (diag 4-47). Give the sight an honest try; once you establish confidence in for your form and you know that's no longer an issue, you can remove the sight and try your hand at instinctive shooting again, or one of several other aiming methods we'll discuss in section 3. Just don't be surprised if you like using the sight; a lot of archers do and do quite well with it. There are also many shooters who can shoot with or without the sight, even with the same bow!

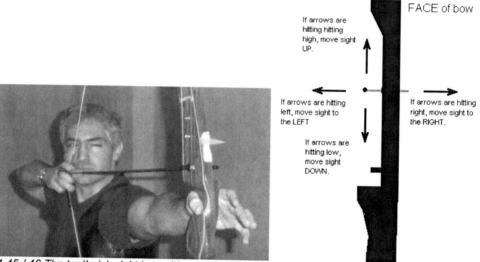

4-45 / 46 The toothpick sight in position on the back of a riser. This "toothpick" sight was made from part of a vane (plastic fletching) that was found on the floor of the range! When shooting with the toothpick sight, the left eye may be closed.
4-47 Adjusting the toothpick sight to center the group. The adjustments shown are from the archer's perspective while holding the bow.

Finally, if your arrows are still not flying as expected, you may need to question your equipment. Although rare, if you are certain that your equipment has been set up properly, that no changes have been made to **any** of it, and you are indeed performing each of the shooting tasks correctly, then you may have to consider the possibility of an equipment malfunction or failure. In addition to a close visual inspection it may be beneficial for another archer to examine and possibly shoot your equipment. Likewise, shooting a different bow, even a borrowed one may shed some light onto the cause of the problem or serve to rule some out. Some impending equipment failures may present themselves as unexplained shot placement. For example, a limb that is beginning to delaminate may show a change in the draw weight and tiller (relative balance of force between the upper and lower limbs) of a bow and result in erratic arrow flight or shot placement.

If you've been using that NFAA blue target, as soon as you have all your arrows in the four ring (the first blue concentric circle outside the bullseye), try moving back to 15 yards; when you can keep them in the four ring at 15, try 20 yards. Once you have the form down, distances up to about 40 yards aren't a real problem, as you'll see when we talk about aiming later on. Believe it or not, this really is all there is to shooting a bow. A very wise man once said about archery, "It's meant to be simple, not easy." After mastering the fundamentals, all that's left is refining the additional skills that can enhance or hone the experience.

Other indoor NFAA (National Field Archery Association) rounds.

We been discussing the NFAA "300" round consisting of 12 ends of 5 arrows each, shot from 10, 15 or the regulation 20 yards. These rounds are divided into three "games" of four ends each. While this might seem odd at first, it allows each game to total 100 points for a perfect score; I guess the NFAA likes nice round numbers. The "300" is a good benchmark of your shooting progress, but there are other rounds that may help your development.

In fact, there are a number of sanctioned "indoor" rounds that can be used to help hone your shooting ability. Each has its own target face, but for this exercise, the two I'll discuss can be shot using the same 40 cm, 20 yard blue face, scored 5, 4, 3, 2, 1.

The Freeman round

This round also consists of 12 ends of 5 arrows each.
- The first game consists of three ends at 10 yards and one end at 15 yards.
- The second game consists of thee ends at 15 yards and one end at 20 yards.
- The third game consists of four ends at 20 yards.

A perfect score is 300 points.

The indoor Mini-field round

Since urban archery clubs rarely had access to outdoor ranges, the NFAA scaled down a field type match to be shot at a standard 20-yard indoor range. For this match a large (8") target was used at longer distances and small (6") faces at the shorter distances; both 8 and 6 inch targets had only two scoring areas, a 5 for the bullseye and an outer 3 ring. We'll just use the "300" blue targets, as they are readily available.

The Mini-Field consists of 14 or 15 ends of four arrows each (target size included, in case you have access to regulation faces):

1. 4 arrows at 17 yards (large face)
2. 4 arrows at 20 feet (small face)
3. 4 arrows at 20 yards (large face)
4. 4 arrows at 15 yards (large face)
5. 4 arrows at 13 yards (small face)
6. 4 arrows at 10 yards (small face)
7. 1 arrow at 20 yards, 1 arrow at 17 yards, 1 arrow at 13 yards and 1 arrow at 10 yards (all on the large face).

Repeat ends one to seven.

Additionally, some clubs added a 15th end so the total possible score would equal 300.
The 15th end consisted of 2 arrows at 20 yards (large face) and 2 arrows at 10 yards (small face).

By regularly shooting these rounds, the new archer quickly becomes accustomed to varying, albeit close range, distances.

Additional items to bring to the range

If you need to travel to an archery range, in addition to the bow, bowstring, arrows, tab or glove, arm guard, quiver and a bow stringer, you may want to consider bringing several other items to make your time there as pleasant and profitable as possible.

- It's always a good idea to carry an extra string (with a nocking point in place) and spare arrow rest. While it's not likely these will fail without adequate warning, accidents can happen. Being able to replace a string or rest may save you from having to leave the range early.

- A spare tab or glove. (They can wear out or be misplaced too!)

- Some archers carry a bow square in their quivers, and while not a bad idea, as we've seen there are easier ways of checking brace heights.

- A small role of masking tape can be used to fabricate a temporary nocking point and to "fix" a host of other things that might need attention. It's probably the one item whose uses are limited only by your imagination.

- Extra arrow nocks and glue are old standards, but since I carry at least a dozen arrows, it's rare that I'll need to replace a nock at the range. I've stopped carrying them.

- If you're using a takedown bow, or bow with mechanical adjustments, having the appropriate tools (usually wrenches and screwdrivers) is a must.

- A Swiss-Army type knife.

- Depending on how long your shooting sessions are, you may want to consider bringing a snack or beverage, if refreshments aren't available.

After you've shot for a while, you'll have a better idea of what belongs in your personal archery "kit bag". It's not necessary to bring an entire tool chest, but knowing you can quickly and effectively deal with most emergencies can add to your confidence at the range. For serious competitive archers, having a second bow ready to shoot is not uncommon.

Chapter 5

Tuning the Bow and Arrow – The First Steps

Open most current archery books or magazines, or go to almost any archery web site, and you'll find volumes of information or theories on methods of tuning your equipment, and various interpretations of the data derived from those methods. A lot of that information is subjective and will serve no end but to waste time and frustrate the shooter. Yes, tuning is necessary for optimal performance, but it need not be difficult or time consuming. If you have chosen the correct arrows for your bow, and followed the instructions in the basic set-up section of this book, you're probably 90 – 95% "tuned" already.

Tuning serves two purposes, both equally important. First is to ensure that the arrow flight is as true as possible, and second, that the arrow goes where we are aiming/looking, assuming you are not using a sight.

Let's examine that a little more closely; a well-tuned bow and arrow combination will:

1. Yield the best possible arrow flight – *the truer an arrow flies, the better the chances of it hitting its intended target.*

2. Be more forgiving to shooter error – *since we are not shooting machines, form errors will always be something we'll have to contend with. Anything that minimizes the effects of those errors increases accuracy.*

3. Reduce energy loss due to erratic arrow flight – *as we'll see, the arrow needs to bend or "flex" around the riser; a properly tuned bow and arrow combination will stabilize faster and retain more energy.*

4. In a target scenario, extend effective range with greater accuracy. – *Since the arrow retains more energy it travels farther.*

5. In a hunting scenario, increase penetration – *As the arrow is flying straighter upon impact, there will be greater retained energy and therefore a cleaner penetration.*

Additionally, we can use "tuning" to slightly shift the point of impact. *This helps place the arrow precisely where we want it on the target.*

*** IMPORTANT ***

You must be shooting consistently before any additional tuning can be done! If you've been using the blue NFAA face as a practice target, when you can keep the majority of your arrows in the four ring, or at least in a group that size (approximately six inches) at 10 yards, then you're ready to start "tuning your bow".

Basic Tuning

Tuning means configuring certain parameters on the bow or arrow so it will shoot as efficiently as possible. That means that the bow will be relatively quiet, have minimal hand shock, cast an arrow quickly and allow the arrow to fly true (without horizontal or vertical oscillations).

Note: we'll be using the terms *static* and *dynamic* spine to describe the stiffness of the arrow. Static spine is the actual measurement of how much the arrow will bend under a given load and dynamic spine is the way the arrow reacts when shot from a bow.

The first thing we need to address is the brace height. If you followed the basic instructions on finding the right string for the bow, you're probably at or near the manufacturer's recommended brace height. We also said that might, or might not, be the best brace height for you. If the bow seems quiet and doesn't shock your hand on release, it's more than likely fine and should be left as it is for now. If the bow seems noisy, or there is excessive hand shock, you might be able to adjust the brace height to minimize those annoyances. You can increase the brace height by adding twists to shorten the string, and lower the brace height by removing twists to lengthen it until you find the bow's "sweet spot". The sweet spot is the brace height where the bow is quietest and has the least hand shock. Remember to add twists in the direction that tightens the serving or splice (diag 5-1 and 5-2). We'll discuss the effects of varying the brace height in greater detail later; it's mentioned here, as it's typically the first thing to consider when tuning a bow. *(Note that care should be taken when untwisting a Flemish Splice string, as the twists are in part what hold the string together.)*

5-1 and 5-2 Twisting a bow string in the direction that tightens the splice (left) or serving (right)

Other factors that can affect bow noise and hand shock are arrow weight, bowstring material and even the number of strands contained in the bowstring. Form errors such as plucking the string on release or torqueing the bow need also be considered. These factors will be discussed in later sections.

Arrow flight should describe a pure parabolic arc from the archer to the target. Once an arrow has stabilized, vertical and horizontal oscillations should be minimized or eliminated.

From a tuning perspective:

Vertical oscillations (or deflections) are caused by an error in nocking point location.

Horizontal oscillations (or deflections) are caused by the use of an arrow with incorrect spine.

In each of the following tuning scenarios I'll suggest either moving the nocking point up or down to correct vertical oscillations or altering the dynamic spine of the arrow. In the three methods I'll describe, you should be able to recognize a similar pattern of cause and effect.

Moving the nocking point is self-explanatory, and should be attempted in 1/16" or 1/8" intervals until improvement is seen. *(Recall that in the section on basic equipment setup, I recommended that your first nocking point be a piece of masking tape?)*

Changing the dynamic spine of an arrow requires a little more work.

To correct for a stiff arrow:

Try moving the rest closer to the bow, if possible. If you are using one of the Bear J-2 rests, the little piece of plastic that pushes the arrow away from the riser can be trimmed with a pair of scissors or a fingernail clipper. A simple way of testing this before you cut anything is to use a piece of tape to hold it closer to the riser. If you see an improvement, then it's safe to cut it down.

Increase the brace height by adding twists to the bowstring. This slightly increases the draw weight of the bow, typically one to three pounds per inch, and decreases the angle of offset as the arrow leaves the string, thus making the arrow act weaker.

If you're using screw-in heads, going to a heavier head might help, as that will weaken the dynamic spine (stiffness) of the arrow.

Unfortunately, it's been my experience that if the spine appears stiff on the tuning methods we'll describe shortly, you won't be able to add enough weight to the head to correct the problem without weighing down the arrow and worsening its trajectory.

If none of the above succeeds in correcting the problem, the only recourse might be new arrows of the correct spine.

To correct for a weak arrow:

Decrease the brace height by removing twists from the string. This slightly decreases the draw weight of the bow and increases the angle of offset as the arrow leaves the string, thus making the arrow act stiffer. Be careful not to remove too many twists from a Flemish Splice string, as it may weaken the loop braids and result in string failure.

Move the arrow rest away from the riser. If the arrow rest has no provision for adjustment, you may have to build out the rest (away from the riser). Test this by adding layers of masking tape to the side of the rest to move the arrow away from the riser and see if it resolves the problem. If it does, then remove the rest and reapply it with an additional layer or layers of backing adhesive or double stick tape. 3M foam double stick tape is typically used to attach most rests; it is about 1/16" thick, and multiple layers can be used.

If you've been shooting for a while and the arrows are still longer than your draw length, shortening the arrows will stiffen the dynamic spine. Usually 1" in shaft length equals about 5# in spine. Therefore a 29" arrow that spines to 40# with spine to about 35# if cut down to 28".

You could also try using a lighter weight head, lowering the brace height, or as in the above case, just get stiffer arrows.

Let's start tuning

If you're comfortable with the brace height, the next thing to do is simply to shoot four or five arrows into a target placed 10 yards away at approximately shoulder-height. If the arrows appeared to fly straight to your unaided eye, or to an observer standing behind you, then the odds are you're already fairly well tuned. Next examine the arrows in the target. If they are relatively straight in, meaning the shaft is perpendicular to the target in all directions and relative to your shooting position, you're probably good to go (diag 5-2). (That assumes that the target material is not unidirectional, meaning it will allow free entry of the arrow and not straighten it out by virtue of corrugations or layering of materials.) If not, we can determine what is going on by analyzing the data and making small changes to the nocking point and sometimes to the degree of center shot to correct the problem.

- If the Nock end is higher than the point (diag 5-3a), lower the nocking point.
- If the Nock end is lower than the point (diag 5-3b), raise the nocking point.
- If the Nock end is to the right of the point (diag 5-3c), soften the spine of the arrow.
- If the Nock end is to the left of the point (diag 5-3d), stiffen the spine of the arrow.

For most beginners, the above procedure is more than adequate. While the arrow angle in the target is useful, we can get a more exact record of what's happening by capturing a snapshot of the arrow in flight by "shooting through paper" or "paper tuning".

5-3 Arrows entering the target (from left to right): nock high, nock low, nock right and nock left. Angles are exaggerated for clarity.

Paper Tuning

If your range doesn't have a paper-tuning frame, they are fairly simple to design and make. All that's required is a wood or metal frame with a thin sheet of paper fastened to it through which an arrow can be shot (diag 5-5). A simple one can be made from a cardboard box and a clean paper (not cardboard) target face or piece of newspaper. Simply tape the target or newspaper in front of the opening of the box (diag 5-6). The back of the box should be removed so it won't interfere with the flight of the arrow as it passes through the paper. The box can be placed on a suitable stand or attached to one or two poles buried in the ground. If a single pole is used (as in the illustration), the box will have to be braced on the backside to prevent it from collapsing. In a pinch, two sticks of suitable height can be stuck in the ground and a piece of newspaper stapled to the top part of each.

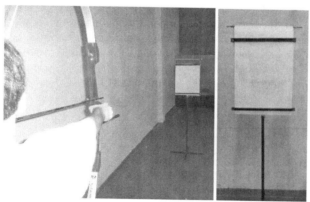

5-4 Typical positioning for paper tuning. This archer is paper tuning his bow with the paper frame at the prescribed distance of 15' (5 yards) (left).

5-5 Paper tuning frame consisting of a metal frame with provisions to hold a roll of paper and retainers to keep the paper flat (right).

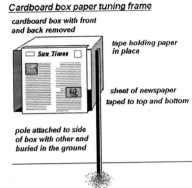

cardboard box with front
and back removed

tape holding paper
in place

sheet of newspaper
taped to top and bottom

pole attached to side
of box with other end
buried in the ground

5-6 Paper tuning using a cardboard box and a sheet of newspaper. The box may be placed on a suitable stand or attached to a piece of wood buried in the ground (right).

Set the frame or box approximately 15 feet (5 yards) from your shooting position, with its center about shoulder height. Shoot several arrows through the paper and observe the tears. Note that if each arrow is making a different tear, then there are still shooting form errors present, or something else is amiss and needs to be corrected before tuning can continue.

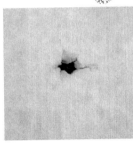

Diag 5-7a "Bullet hole" pattern. If you see this, then the bow is set up correctly. Note that a slight variation, anything less than 1" in any direction is perfectly acceptable for most stickbows. While it is possible to reduce a 1" tear to a bullet hole, the effort is usually unnecessary at this point, and will probably result in nothing more than frustration.

Diag 5-7b This usually means a high nocking point, Try placing the arrow below the nocking point by 1/16" to 1/8" intervals and note any change. If the tears get smaller, note the position of the arrow nock, and move the nockset to maintain that position.

Diag 5-7c This usually means a low nocking point. Try nocking above the nocking point and see whether there's any improvement. If so, then continue raising the nocking point, in 1/16" or 1/8" intervals, until the tear is less than 1".

Diag 5-7d
This indicates a stiff spine. Soften the spine as described above.

Diag 5-7e
This indicates a weak (under-spined) arrow. Stiffen the spine as described above.

If lateral tears are shorter than one inch and the arrow flight seems true, then the arrow's paradox may be causing the tear, and you need not be overly concerned.

*Diag 5-7f An angled tear indicates both a nocking point and spine problem. In this case, you'll need to correct for a **high** nocking point and a **weak** spine. Start by adjusting the nocking point until you get a horizontal tear similar to diagram 5-7e. Once the nocking point is correct, then start working on the spine issues. It's always safer to tackle one problem at a time.*

Thus far, we have been holding the bow vertically. While that's still preferable for new shooters, some people do tilt or cant their bow. If you do decide to cant the bow, then you must tune the bow from the canted position, as shooting form may change between the two styles. However, the paper tears will be skewed by the same degree of offset as the cant. For example, a right handed shooter canting to 15 degrees will need to understand that his paper tears will be offset clockwise by 15 degrees.

With any of these patterns, if making the appropriate changes doesn't fix or lessen the problem, there is a significant equipment mismatch, or there's something else throwing a wrench into the machinery. The most common cause is some type of arrow interference. We'll assume that you're not hitting your arm guard, sleeve, chest or face and that your release is relatively clean.

The next culprit is usually the fletching. Today there's a trend in some circles to use the biggest feathers with the highest profile possible (diag 5-8). The theory is that the more fletching surface area you have, the quicker the arrow will stabilize. While that may be true, it's not without a price; in addition to slowing the arrow sooner, there's increased risk of the fletching striking the rest or riser as it passes. We'll discuss arrow dynamics (the archer's paradox) in detail later, but simply, the arrow shaft should bend around the riser as it's being fired. Sometimes with the larger feathers it doesn't bend sufficiently and there's feather or shaft to riser contact and that can easily give you false readings. Several remedies have been suggested, including rotating the arrow nocks to lessen the angle of the feathers in relation to the bow. This might work, but unless you're using UNI-bushings (Universal Nock Insert Bushings) or some other type of arrow nock that rotates in relation to the shaft, rotating the nocks usually means cutting them off and gluing on new ones with the hope of finding the right position. Raising the nocking point, sometimes over 1" above perpendicular is another option often used on certain longbows. Honestly, it's easier just to get normal-sized fletching in the first place. Usually 5" standard height parabolic feathers are about as large as is needed for any shooting situation, including bow hunting, where large broadheads are used and need to be stabilized quickly in flight. For target shooting, 3" feathers are sufficient, and some experienced archers actually use feathers or vanes smaller than 1" without difficulty.

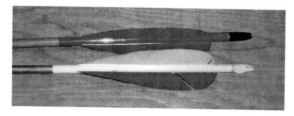

5-8 Very large, high-back feathers may stabilized the arrow faster, but may also adversely affect tuning due to interference with the riser or rest

Odds are, your bow was shooting pretty well before you even thought about tuning. If so, great! If not, hopefully this quick exercise helped.

Some archers today feel that paper tuning is not an adequate means of tuning a stickbow, or any bow shot with fingers (as opposed to being shot with a release aid). The reason is that the paradox may impart some lateral movement as the arrow goes through the paper, even with a well-tuned bow. That may be a problem, but that's why we generally don't worry about tears shorter than one inch, especially lateral ones. If an archer is shooting at a level where additional tuning is necessary, then bare-shaft tuning may be in order.

Bare-shaft tuning

Another method of bow tuning is called bare-shaft tuning. While visual inspection and confirmation by paper tuning are usually sufficient for most archers, especially when shooting at close range, bare-shaft tuning has gained popularity in recent years and requires serious consideration.

There have been various methods of performing bare-shaft tuning, but the planing method is the simplest and most reliable. It does however require that the archer is capable of shooting well-defined groups. As the name implies, it uses a bare or unfletched arrow's position in the target compared to the position of a normally fletched one. The theory is that a well-tuned bow and arrow combination will send an arrow to the same point on the target, whether it's fletched or not, providing of course that the archer is doing his part consistently.

Bare-shaft testing should be performed at 15 – 20 yards. You'll need a few fletched and a few unfletched arrows. Shoot a group of fletched arrows at a target followed by the unfletched arrows.

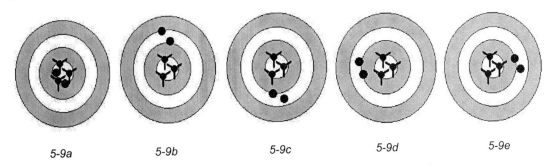

| 5-9a | 5-9b | 5-9c | 5-9d | 5-9e |

If both groups coincide (diag 5-9a), you're done.

If the bare shafts are grouping high (diag 5-9b), raise the nocking point, slightly, 1/16" – 1/8" at a time.

If the bare shafts are grouping low (diag 5-9c), lower the nocking point.

If the bare shafts are grouping to the left (diag 5-9d), (stiff spine), move the rest closer to center shot, or weaken the arrow. (As previously discussed.)

If the bare shafts are grouping to the right (diag 5-9e), (weak spine), move the rest away from center shot, or stiffen the arrow. (As previously discussed.)

Note that it's normal for a well-tuned bow to show bare-shaft arrows as being slightly weak. Adding weight to the rear of the arrow, even the weight of a few feathers, can slightly stiffen the spine of the arrow. Therefore, an arrow that appears slightly weak when bare shaft tested will probably be just right once fletched.

Another method of bare-shaft tuning, directly related to paper tuning, is shaft orientation in the target. If the fletched arrows are perpendicular to the target face, but the bare shafts are not, then the same analysis we used for paper tuning holds. Nock end high suggests a high nocking point; nock end low, a low nocking point; left indicates a weak arrow and right a stiff arrow (diag 5-10). While used by some archers, this method is not as reliable as the planing method, as the target must not hinder the penetration path of the arrow.

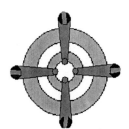

5-10 Bare shaft nock position patterns
When bare-shaft tuning, I begin with the planing method and if the bare and fletched shafts coincide, will usually stop there. If the nock angle is consistently off in the same direction, I may refine the tuning to correct the nock orientation.

The concern with presenting these methods to a new archer is that it may over-complicate the process and make it appear more confusing or cumbersome than it really needs to be. That may result in the new archer devoting too much time to tuning and fiddling with his equipment and not enough time to shooting! It's quite natural for you to want the best shooting, most finely tuned equipment possible; we all do. As we'll see with most things however, there comes a point of diminishing returns, and for most of us, "perfectly tuned", if that's even possible when shooting a stickbow, will not benefit our shooting accuracy any more than just "well tuned". As the old saying goes, it just needs to be "close enough for government work".

There is an exception to the "close enough for government work" rule. As an archer's skill increases, he or she will tend to begin shooting at farther and farther distances. A bow that is "close enough for government work" at 20 and 30 yards may not be at 40, 50 or 100 yards (90M). This will become evident at extended ranges by the arrow showing either an unexplained left or right drift or the arrows no longer entering the target perpendicular to the vertical plane. If that does occur, then bare-shaft tuning must be performed at the extended ranges and the appropriate changes made in either nock location and/or degree of center shot. An alternative method of fine-tuning for extended distances is called "walk-back" tuning and will be discussed following the introduction of the cushion plunger in the chapter on "Tuning with Gadgets". *As the archer's skill improves, the bow, or rather the arrows will tell him when additional tuning is necessary.*

The second part of tuning, making sure that the arrows are going where the shooter is looking, has actually already been covered. Hopefully with a clean arrow flight, the arrow will hit where the shooter is looking, or mentally aiming. This should be the case; if not, review Chapter 4 on basic troubleshooting for possible causes.

Some archers are guilty of having more than one bow!

While this may seem unlikely in the beginning, it's an unfortunate affliction from which many of us suffer. In addition to taking up considerable space in our homes and a fair amount of our spouses' patience, it can be frustrating to the archer when he wants to shoot more than one bow during a given session or consecutive sessions and the two bows have different points of impact. While bow configuration and arrow speed play a major role in the point of impact, judicious tuning may be able to narrow the gap. When a bow is tuned, it's usually not tuned to a knife-edge degree; there's a certain amount of "wiggle room" to adjust the point of impact without totally destroying the properties of the arrow's flight.

The following pertains primarily to barebow, or non-sight shooters. With a sight or physical sighting method, as described in the chapter on aiming, moving the aiming device will solve the problem, as long as the bow has been tuned for optimal arrow flight in the first place. When shooting instinctively, or a variation of that, we generally want the arrow to strike where we're focusing our attention.

Typically, moving the nockset up will slightly lower the point of impact and lowering the nockset will raise the point of impact. As long as the arrows do not porpoise (show visible up and down movement in flight), the paper tears are still within an inch, and/or bare-shaft tuning is still yielding acceptable results, you're still within the bow's tuning envelope. Moving the arrow's placement on the bow to the right by bringing it closer to center shot (by adjusting the position of the strike plate) should move the arrow's point of impact to the right. Moving the arrow's placement on the bow to the left, reducing the degree of center shot, should move the impact point to the left.

Stiffening the arrow spine, by shortening the arrow or switching to a lighter head, will move the impact point to the left, and weakening it by switching to a heavier head will move it to the right. In this case, as long as the arrows are not fishtailing (showing visible side to side movement in flight), and paper tears/bare-shaft tuning are still within parameters, you're OK. As you've guessed, a heavier arrow will impact lower and a lighter arrow will impact higher, usually!

You should be thinking – won't this negate all the tuning we've been doing to get the best arrow flight? The answer is – well, maybe. What we're doing is manipulating the arrow dynamics, and you may not have enough "wiggle room" to make the required adjustments, or you may not be happy with the change in flight characteristics or the results from paper or bare-shaft tuning. This is presented only as an option for your consideration. For some, a slightly less than perfect arrow flight (if perfect is even possible) is tolerable to gain the freedom of switching bows without having to spend time re-adjusting the aiming mechanism. Hopefully, after completing this and the next two chapters, you'll understand the physics behind bow tuning and be able to determine what variables are acceptable in your particular case.

Basic recipe for bow tuning

1. Confirm correct brace height

2. Visually confirm arrow flight at 10 and 20 yards

3. Paper or bare-shaft test several arrows

4. Adjust nocking point to eliminate (or reduce) vertical tears or spacing

5. Adjust "spine" to eliminate (or reduce) horizontal tears or spacing, using one or more of the techniques described in this and the next chapter

Don't worry about tuning again, unless something changes!

Cheat Sheet comparing the previously described tuning methods:

	NP too high	NP too low	Stiff Arrow	Weak Arrow
Visual	Arrow nock High	Arrow nock Low	Arrow Nock Right	Arrow Nock Left
Paper Tuning	Arrow nock High	Arrow nock Low	Arrow Nock Right	Arrow Nock Left
Bare Shaft Planing	BS below Fletched	BS over Fletched	BS to left of Fletched	BS to right of Fletched
Bare Shaft Nock Angle	Arrow nock High	Arrow nock Low	Arrow Nock Right	Arrow Nock Left

NP = Nocking point, BS = Bare Shafts

With the above table it's easy to see the relationship between the various tuning methods.

Chapter 6

Tuning the Bow and Arrow – Beyond the Basics

What follows might not make you a better shot, but will hopefully give you a better understanding of bow mechanics and bow/arrow system dynamics.

The first things we need to understand are the terms "center shot" and the "archer's paradox" (diag 6-1).

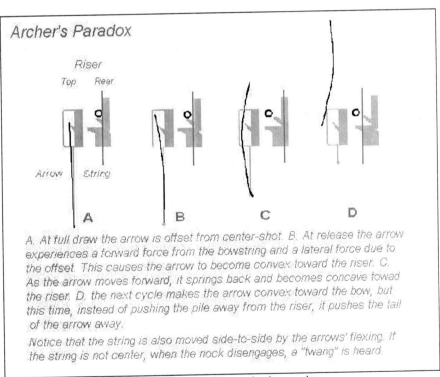

6-1 Schematic of the archer's paradox

Center shot or degree of center shot can be defined as the relationship between the long axis of the arrow and the long axis of the bow. A bow that is truly center shot would have the string bisecting both the limbs and the arrow (diag 6-2). If you were to hold a strung bow with a nocked arrow in the shooting position and move your head to align the string so it perfectly bisected the upper and lower limbs, you would notice that the arrow is not aligned perfectly with the string. Rather, the arrow is slightly off to the left on a right-handed bow (diag 6-3). As we discussed, the arrow rest was tuned to hold the arrow slightly to the left of center shot for a right-handed shooter, meaning it has a positive deflection. When the bowstring is drawn and released using the fingers, even though the string begins in the first joint or deeper, the force of the bow pulling the string will begin to uncurl the fingers and push the arrow in toward the riser. Unfortunately, we can't exert the same force every time. That offset allows for a buffer of sorts.

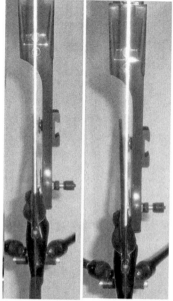

6-2 and 6-3 Arrow offset from center shot. In the left picture the string is bisecting both the centerline of the bow and the arrow, called zero offset or true center. In the right picture the arrow bisects the centerline of the bow, but the arrow (tip) is offset to the left, called positive offset. This degree of positive offset is the correct starting point.

Look again at diagram 6-1. When we first release the arrow, the string is moving forward, but given the arrow's offset, the shaft bends convex toward the riser. After the initial push, the shaft is no longer on the rest at all. The shaft material being elastic then springs back and becomes concave towards the riser. If the spine of the arrow is correct for the bow, the timing is such that the concave bending coincides with the arrow passing the riser. Its tail clears the rest/riser and never touches it. Once past the riser, there is a dampened oscillation sequence and the shaft bends in the same direction as it initially did, but with a diminished amplitude. These oscillations continue for some time until stopped by the internal molecular resistance of the shaft and ballistic rotation (spin) imparted by the fletching.

To further this, it should be noted that the arrow oscillates about two "nodes" or points of zero amplitude, as shown in diagram 6-4a.

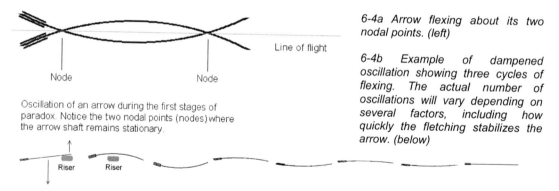

Line of flight

Node   Node

Oscillation of an arrow during the first stages of paradox. Notice the two nodal points (nodes) where the arrow shaft remains stationary.

Riser   Riser

6-4a Arrow flexing about its two nodal points. (left)

6-4b Example of dampened oscillation showing three cycles of flexing. The actual number of oscillations will vary depending on several factors, including how quickly the fletching stabilizes the arrow. (below)

Take a few minutes to digest that.

The "internal molecular resistance of the shaft", or "modulus", is the property of the material to resist or recover from repeated flexing after driving force has been removed.

The "ballistic rotation imparted by the fletching" means that as the fletching causes the arrow to spin in flight, the resultant spinning forces hasten the reduction of the arrow's oscillations.

If the arrow is too stiff, or over-spined, then the timing is late and the tail of the arrow may hit the riser, resulting in a smacking sound and an erratic flight, usually striking the target left of its intended point of impact. A slightly stiff arrow may not hit the riser, but may veer to the left of its mark. If too weak, the lateral forces will be too great for the shaft and the timing will be early. In that case the increased oscillations (possibly amplitude and frequency) will send the arrow to the right of target center (diag 6-5). In a worse case scenario, a severely under-spined arrow may fishtail wildly, and in the case of wooden arrows, may actually break.

Put another way – If the arrow is too stiff, it won't bend enough to return to the direction it was initially aimed and hit left of center; if it's too weak, it will flex too much, and may become erratic and/or hit right of center.

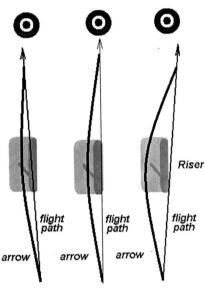

6-5 A slightly stiff arrow will not flex sufficiently to bend fully around the riser and will impact left of center. A slightly soft arrow will flex too severely and whip around the riser, impacting right of center. The arrow in the center of the illustration is correctly spined and will fly to center.

To make matters worse, recall that that nocking point is also placed off center (above perpendicular). There is a similar paradox in that direction as well (diag 6-6). Here, of course, we're dealing with vertical forces. Where unbalanced lateral forces result in side-to-side oscillations (called fishtailing) here vertical oscillations occur and are called porpoising. Again, both lateral and horizontal deflections help to buffer unequal finger pressure. (I'm not sure about the origins of all the marine references, though.)

Over-spined   *Correctly spined*   *Under-spined*

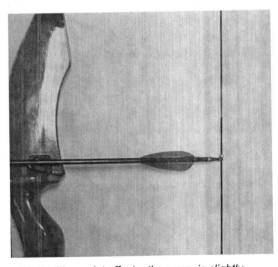

An understanding of this does serve a purpose. If we determine by paper tuning or by bare-shaft tuning, that our arrows are under-spined, then it would stand to reason that we have options for correcting the problem. Seeing as the arrow is bending more than it should, we should be able to compensate for this by simply making it "need" to bend more. We do this by decreasing the degree of center shot, or put another way, pushing the rest away from the riser. Now, the force exerted by the offset is equal to the flexibility or "spine" of the shaft. Of course, there is a practical limit to how far the rest can be extended, and when we approach that point we have no choice but make the arrow behave stiffer or go out and buy stiffer arrows, but there is some room to play.

6-6 Nocking point offset – the arrow is slightly above perpendicular relative to the string

If the arrows prove to be over-spined, then the converse is true and we'll need to bring the arrow closer to center shot. This may or may not be possible, depending on the design and features of the bow. We'll discuss other options shortly when we talk about arrow tuning, as opposed to bow tuning.

The same basic principles also apply to nocking point placement, but for vertical forces. What this means is that for any given system there will be an optimal position, or small range of positions, for degree of center shot and nocking point position on the string. We knew that already; hopefully now we understand why. If we experiment and find those optimal positions, we should see that optimal not only means yielding the best performance, but also the greatest tolerance for error, not only for human error, but system variations as well. That's what's referred to as the "forgiveness" of a bow. Forgiveness is a very desirable feature in a bow; it means that the bow will not be critical to a given shooter's specific idiosyncrasies, nor to small system changes, such as small amounts of string stretch or the effects of temperature or humidity on the bow material.

Another interesting effect of the archer's paradox is its relation to the sound a bow makes on release, or rather when the arrow leaves the string. As the arrow flexes, it pulls the string slightly to the right, then left. If the point at which the nock leaves the string coincides with the string being in or near its center position, the odds are the bow will be quiet. If the timing is off so that the string is far left or right, then a twang will be heard (diag 6-7).

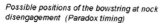

Possible positions of the bowstring at nock disengagement (Paradox timing)

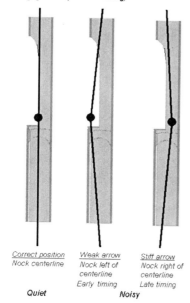

Correct position
Nock centerline

Quiet

Weak arrow
Nock left of centerline
Early timing

Noisy

Stiff arrow
Nock right of centerline
Late timing

6-7 If the arrow nock disengages the string while the string is shifted left or right due to the archer's paradox, a twang or bow noise will be heard. Schematic from the archer's view.

The next stop is the bowstring. Without that, a bow and arrow are little more than two sticks. When the bow is strung taut and an arrow nocked, magic happens. The string needs to be first matched to the bow in length. As we said earlier, if the bow has an AMO length written on it, then getting a string of the same AMO length should yield the manufacturer's recommended brace height. (The brace height, as you recall, is the distance from the deepest part of the grip to a point perpendicular on the string.) Typically, the length of a bow (both recurve and longbow) is measured from nock groove to nock groove along the backside of the bow. For our purposes, a bow with an AMO length marked on it will accept a string 4" shorter than the stated AMO length, in the case of a recurve; for a longbow, it will be 3" shorter. For example, an AMO 60" recurve will accept an AMO 60" string that will have an actual length of 56". Is this the best brace height for you to use? Maybe, maybe not, but it's probably a safe start. Still, as we'll see, we might be able to improve on it.

The type of string material (Dacron, Fast Flight, or anything in between, which we'll talk about in the chapter on bowstrings) as well as the thickness of the strands and number of strands will alter the optimal brace height. The type and weight of the arrow and any peculiarities of your shooting style will also play a role.

Brace Height

In the days of the English Longbow (circa 1100 - 1600), the brace height was called a fistmele, literally meaning a fist-measure(ment). The archer's clenched fist and outstretched thumb (diag 6-8) measured the distance from the bow to the string. Today, it's determined by the manufacturer's preferences in relation to the design and expected performance of the bow and measured with a bow square (diag 6-9).

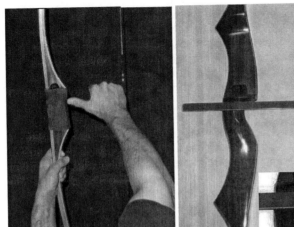

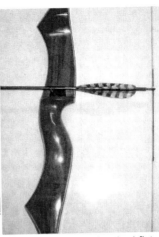

6-8 Brace height or "fistmele" was initially measured on English longbows by placing a clenched fist with an outstretched thumb between the riser and the bowstring.
6-9 Correct bow square placement to measure brace height. The brace height is measured from a point perpendicular to the bowstring to the deepest part of the grip's throat.
6-9a A variation on the bow square idea is shown here with an arrow being used as a reference. On this particular bow, the correct brace height corresponds to the leading edge of the fletching just touching the rear of the arrow shelf.

As can be imagined, the shorter the string, the higher the brace height and the heavier the draw weight at any given draw length. That is because with the shorter string, the limbs will need to bend into a tighter arc. It's been estimated that most bows can gain or lose between 1 and 3 pounds per inch of brace height change. Two things should be noted: first a 1" change in brace height is fairly significant, and second, most home and Pro Shop bow scales aren't accurate enough to show that amount of weight change. Most archers won't notice the change either. The lower the brace height (longer string length) the faster the arrow leaves the bow. This is due to the longer time the arrow is in contact with the motive force – the string. The distance covered before the arrow leaves the string is called the **power stroke**. The power stroke divided by the amount of time in which the arrow is being propelled by the string determines the speed of the "bow", and so the arrow. The longer the power stroke, the more energy is transferred to the arrow and the faster it goes.

Example 1 – given a bow with an 8" brace height drawn to 28", upon release, the arrow will be propelled by the string for approximately 22" (approximately 2" beyond the resting brace height) in a specified amount of time. If the brace height were reduced to 6", the arrow would be propelled by the string for approximately 24", and despite a slightly longer time period, would demonstrate a greater power stroke.

Examples 2 – on any given bow, the longer the draw length, the greater the power stroke (the amount of time the string is accelerating the arrow). Typically, an additional inch of draw length equates **in speed** to approximately 10# of draw weight. Therefore, a bow marked 50# @ 28", drawn to 29" would have a approximately speed equal to a bow marked 60# @ 28", and drawn to 28", even though the former would only have a draw weight of 52.5#.

Example 3 – given two bows with equal brace heights and drawn to the same draw length, the bow with the faster limbs will have a greater acceleration, even though the power strokes will be equal.

Let's repeat this: a taller brace height increases the poundage but decreases speed, and a lower brace height reduces the draw weight but increases speed or cast.

Less intuitive is that a taller brace height will WEAKEN the dynamic spine of an arrow and a shorter brace height will STIFFEN the dynamic spine. With a taller brace height, the weakening effect is due to the increased draw weight at full draw resulting in a faster initial push, and the decreased angle of offset as the arrow's nock leaves the string. The faster initial push of the bowstring causes greater flexing of the shaft and the decreased angle of offset lessens the amount the shaft needs to flex. Conversely the decreased draw weight and increased angle of offset will STIFFEN the arrow's dynamic spine. It's a tough concept to grasp, but may be proven using the tuning methods in the previous chapter while adjusting brace heights.

While lowering the brace height sounds like a good thing, there are limitations and caveats. A very low brace height can let the bowstring slap the archer's wrist on shock. High-speed photography has shown that the string actually goes beyond its resting position when launching an arrow, at times several inches past the resting position. This is a fairly common problem with classic "D" style longbows that usually sport brace heights (fistmeles) around 6".

A low brace height can make the bow more critical, meaning less forgiving to shooter error. This is not due to the speed increase, as was commonly believed, but because the angle the arrow makes with the string can be more severe or acute at the point when the arrow nock leaves the string. If you recall, because of the archer's paradox, the arrow is whipping around the riser after release. The more severe the angle, the less forgiving the bow can become. Another factor is that the arrow is in contact with the string for a (albeit slightly) longer period of time. Any mistakes or movements the archer makes while the string is pushing the arrow will affect shot placement.

As discussed in the section on the archer's paradox, one practical reason for determining an optimal brace height is noise reduction. The "twang" heard when some bows are fired, can be due to several factors. However, one often-overlooked factor is the position of the arrow's nock at the instant of disengagement from the string. The string is trying its best to move forward in a straight line, however the arrow is bending around the riser. If at the instant of disengagement, the nock is in a central position, the arrow leaves the string cleanly and quietly. If the nock is off-center due to its position in paradox, then the nock is effectively plucking the string to one side or the other, and like plucking a guitar string, you get a "twang".

Further, if the arrow isn't heavy enough to accept all the energy from the limbs, then the energy transfer is incomplete, and the excess must be accounted for elsewhere. Elsewhere usually manifests itself as string or bow noise, the characteristic "thwack" or "twang" described above, or excess vibration to the riser, which can be felt as hand shock. This is exactly why a higher brace height generally, but not always, quiets a noisy bow. The shortened power stroke reduces the amount of energy transferred to the arrow. Using a heavier string or heavier arrows accomplishes the same thing. String silencers (small pieces or rubber, plastic, fur or similar material) also add weight to the string, and so dampen the vibrations and the resultant sound by absorbing energy. The same holds true for stabilizers and Limb-savers. Limb-savers are rubber devices that adhere to the limbs and absorb energy (vibration) (diag 6-10).

6-10 String silencers: Variety of older silencers including "Brush Buttons", "Beads", "Beaver Tails" and "Deltas" or tri-pronged silencers (top left). Brush button/rubber bead being applied with a hairpin and pliers and "Beaver Tail" on string (top right). Fur (bottom left) and Cat Whisker silencers (bottom right).

If the brace height is too high (shorter string length), the converse is true. Less energy is imparted from the limbs to the arrow due to the shorter power stroke. There might be diminished or no string noise and reduction of hand shock (vibration felt by the archer at shock) because all the energy from the limbs is now being imparted to the arrow, but there will be a decrease in performance. I prefer my bows to perform as well as possible; however, each archer will need to find his own tolerance level for noise, hand shock and performance.

So what do we do? As we said, the correct AMO string for the bow should put you pretty close to where you need to be. If there's no excessive sound or hand shock, you might do well to leave well enough alone. If there is, you'll have to try shortening the string, or possibly try a longer one. Bowstrings, both Endless Loop strings and Flemish splices have, or should have, some twists in them. It helps to keep the strands together and prevent "ballooning" (the separation of strands that may happen after the release and before shock). Usually 10 to 20 twists are sufficient. To shorten the string, simply add more twists. To do this, look at the servings or the splice. You'll notice that if you twist the string one way, you'll be loosening the serving or splice, generally a bad idea; if you twist it the other way, you'll be tightening it. The latter is the way you want to twist the string. Add an additional 10 to 20 twists, take a few more shots, and see if there is any improvement. If there's some, add more twists until it's quiet or at least down to an acceptable level. This is a trial and error process, so don't be surprised if you have to do this several times and you may have to add or remove twists. Also note that if this is a new string, it will stretch and the process may have to be repeated. Some strings will stretch more than others will, but they will all stretch to one degree or another. If you think the string is too short, you may be able to remove a few twists, but usually there isn't enough to make a significant difference. In that case, you may need to try a longer string. Once you feel you've got it figured out, measure the brace height from a point perpendicular on the string to the deepest cut in the throat of the grip, and write that number down. That's your brace height.

We see a lot of shooters around the range pulling out a bow square and repeatedly measuring the brace height to see if it changed. Kind of silly really, when you actually have a bow square built right into the arrow. Once you know your brace height, nock an arrow and look at riser or rest. Usually a band or mark on the crest will be over the face or back of the riser, or where the rest touches the arrow (diag 6-11). (Most commercial arrows have some sort of cresting, even if it's just the manufacturer's logo.) Once you know that position, you can tell immediately if the brace height has changed, and it's one less piece of equipment you'll need to carry around.

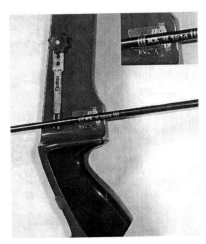

6-11 Using the factory crest on an X7 aluminum arrow to check the brace height.

A brief note on brace height in relation to required arrow spine: **a higher brace height will require a stiffer spined arrow and a lower brace height a softer one.**

The reasoning is that at full draw, while the offset from center shot imparted by the rest position remains constant, the additional draw weight forces the arrow forward faster at launch, and so requires increased arrow resistance to flexing (stiffer spine). Additionally, with a taller brace height, the angle of offset is shallower in the terminal stages of the power stroke, also effectively bringing the arrow "closer to center", even though the arrow is no longer on the rest by that point (see section on the "Archer's Paradox").

However, with the higher brace height, the arrow is in contact with the string for less time. Therefore the overall push or power stroke is reduced, resulting in a slower arrow and leading to the belief that a weaker spine arrow is required. The former considerably outweighs the latter, and a higher brace height allows for a stiffer arrow. Note that a slight change in brace height will not require a new set of arrows, or tuning from scratch. Through experience, you'll know how much variation your bow will allow and still be in tune.

Using the brace height to help match arrow spine to a given bow is a common and efficient practice for most archers. In reality, it may be the quickest fix for a slightly mismatched arrow.

A few tips: Because new Dacron strings tend to stretch more than other materials, the initial stretch can be hastened by "pre-stretching" the string. While there are some very expensive machines available to do this, you can accomplish the same thing with the strung bow and your legs. Place the back of the bow on the front of your thighs on the limbs near the riser, and push down on the limbs (diag 6-12). You should feel a slight elongation of the string. The string may continue to stretch afterwards simply by being shot, but only minimally.

Waxing the bowstring. Wax helps hold the strands and splice (if it's a Flemish splice string) together. Beeswax blends have long been a favorite, due to their cohesive properties, not to mention their fragrant aroma (diag 6-13).

6-12 Stretching the bowstring: Place the bow as shown on your thighs and firmly push down on the limbs. With new, non-stretched, Dacron strings, you should feel a slight give as the initial stretch (actually called a creep) sets in (right).

6-13 A well used cake of beeswax (left top) and a tube of commercial synthetic bowstring wax (left bottom).

There are also a number of synthetic bowstring waxes available which work equally well, though they may not be as aromatic. With the bow strung, rub the wax over the strands and splices, but not the serving (diag 6-14). Then take a piece of leather or heavy cloth and rub the string briskly and firmly. This will cause the wax to melt into the string and complete the process (diag 6-13b). How often to wax may be a matter of personal preference, but if the string feels slightly tacky to the touch and the strands are holding together, there's usually enough wax. I tend not to wax my bowstrings too often.

6-14 Waxing the strands of the bow string: Applying the wax to the string material, not the serving (left) and rubbing with a piece of cloth or leather to melt the wax into the string (right).

If using B-50, the thickness of the string (number of strands) needs to be proportional to the draw weight, or to the "shock" force of the bow. Shock is the force exerted on the bow by the bowstring when the forward motion of the limbs is stopped or shocked by the string. This is not the case with the newer, stronger materials.

Concerning performance, there's a physical relationship between the string, the arrow, and the bow.

1. Anything impeding the forward movement of the arrow will slow the arrow's velocity. Simple, right?

2. Any weight added on the arrow beyond that which is necessary to accept the energy imparted by the limbs would tend to slow the arrow.

3. Any weight added to the string will tend to act as weight added to the arrow.

4. Any weight added to the working part of the limbs will tend to act as weight added to the arrow.

What this means is that the strength and weight of the bowstring should be matched to the force of the bow. In the first chapter, there's a chart on the number of strands of B-50 Dacron. Similar charts are available for other string materials, and provided in Appendix B. In the case of B-50, the numbers given are more than adequate for the weights listed, but there is room for experimentation. As we said, there are 40# bows that will do quite well with a 10-strand string and 25# bows that will tolerate a 12-strand string. The lighter the string, the faster the arrow, as there's less energy required to accelerate the mass of the string and more to propel the arrow, assuming that the arrow is of sufficient weight to handle the energy imparted by the limbs. (Note: this isn't actually that simple; for example, a heavier string will tend to resist stretching on shock more than a lighter string and may factor into the resultant arrow speed, but for our purposes, those changes can be considered negligible.) Indeed, if a bow is noisy or has too much hand shock and changing the brace height isn't an option or desirable, going to a string with more strands may be a possible solution. The addition of string silencers, anything from small rubber balls to pieces of leather or fur, will serve the same purpose.

We also need to consider the effect string material has on tuning and performance. B-50 Dacron, as stable and safe as it is, may not be the best for new high-performance bows. Use of new low-weight, low-stretch string materials will increase arrow speed by virtue of those two properties. Current wisdom states that when switching from B-50 to one of the newer materials, the archer should choose arrows that are approximately 5# heavier in spine than what he was accustomed to or the rated weight of the bow. For example: if you have a 40# bow and are using a low-stretch string, you should consider using arrows spined for 45#. While that may be prudent, it's been my experience that it usually isn't necessary. Again, it has to be trial and error, and yes, your mileage may vary.

Following this discussion of energy transfer, a few words about dry-firing a bow are in order. A dry-fire, release of the bowstring without a nocked arrow either intentionally or accidentally, can be devastating to both the bow and the shooter. We can now understand why – when the shooter draws the bow, he transfers kinetic energy (energy of motion) from the movement of his drawing arm to potential energy (stored energy) in the bow's limbs. When the string is released, the potential energy stored in the limbs is then transferred to the arrow as kinetic energy. If the arrow weren't there to accept that energy on shock, the energy would be transferred back to the bow and shooter. Depending on the bow design and strength, neither the bow nor the shooter may be able to withstand the shock. Happily, most modern laminated bows are built with enough structural integrity to withstand the occasional dry-fire, but there are no guarantees, and all precautions should be taken to guard against dry fires.

Arrow tuning

We've been discussing tuning the bow to the arrow, but in some cases it is more desirable, or even necessary, to tune the arrow to the bow (diag 6-15).

Arrow tuning parameters

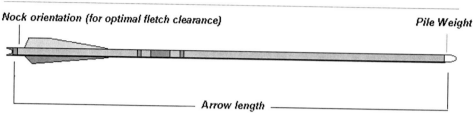

6-15 Basic arrow tuning parameters

All arrows are made up of the same components: a head or "pile" (an Old English term), shaft, fletching, and a nock. Each part can affect the archer's paradox, and so the flight of the arrow, and each part is tunable.

The head (diag 6-16) defines the purpose of the arrow. A bullet-shaped target head is designed for minimal air resistance to facilitate accurate long range shooting. Field heads are designed to limit penetration in wood or similar material and so ease extraction. Hunting heads, called broadheads, are designed with razor sharp edges to dispatch game animals quickly by hemorrhage.

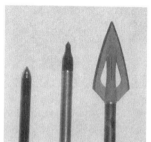

6-16 Arrowheads (top to bottom) target tip (NIBB), screw-in field point, hunting head (Bear Razorhead)

The head can affect the flight of the arrow by changing its aerodynamic characteristics (a broad head effectively adds wings to the front of an arrow). It can add to or subtract from the arrow's total weight and modify the FOC (Front of Center percentage) and spine.

The shaft is the heart of the arrow and defines its base weight and static spine. The various shaft materials and their advantages and disadvantages will be discussed in Chapter 9.

The fletching, either feathers or plastic vanes, in concert with the head provide guidance for the arrow once in flight.

The nock is designed to engage the string safely and securely during the anchor, release and power stroke.

Arrow Weight

Weight is a fairly simple concept; you can put the arrow on a scale and find out how much it weighs (diag 6-17). For a given bow, the lighter the arrow, the faster it will be accelerated during the power stroke, providing all the available energy from the limbs can be accepted by the arrow. A general rule of thumb is for the arrow to weigh approximately 9 to 11 grains per pound of the bow's draw weight. For example a 50# bow would call for an arrow between 450 and 550 grains. Target shooters tend to favor lighter arrows for additional speed. You can usually get as low as 7 or 8 grains per pound safely with modern bows. Below that, the arrow is so light you may effectively be dry firing the bow. Some hunters favor heavier arrows, as high as 12 to 14 grains per pound, due to the increased kinetic energy and momentum the arrow can attain. With aluminum arrows, if you match the spine correctly, the weight usually takes care of itself. Carbon arrows on the other hand, are remarkable for their lightness compared to other shaft materials, hence their speed advantages. With carbons it is possible to use an arrow with the proper spine, and still be severely underweight.

6-17 Arrow weight being checked on a digital grain scale (American Weight Co.)

FOC

Another aspect of weight is called FOC, or Front of Center percentage. This is a measure of where the center of gravity or balance point is in relation to the physical center of the arrow (diag 6-18).

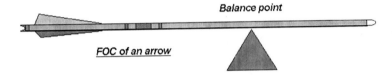

Balance point

FOC of an arrow

6-18 The FOC (Front Of Center) of an arrow

The formula is: (BPL - OAL/2)/OAL

Where:

BPL = Balance Point Length (measured from nock groove to balance point of complete shaft)
OAL = Overall Length of arrow measured from nock groove to back of head or point (BOP)

Example 1: 28" arrow with a balance point 21" from the nock groove.

(BPL - OAL/2)/OAL = FOC
(18" – 28"/2)/28" = FOC
(18" – 14")/28 = FOC
FOC = 4"/28" = 25%

Example 2: 28" arrow with a balance point 18" from the nock groove.

(BPL - OAL/2)/OAL = FOC
(16" – 28"/2)/28" = FOC
(16" – 14")/28 = FOC
FOC = 2"/28" = 7%

What does this mean? Simply, that the greater the FOC, the more stable an arrow will be in flight and the less it will be deflected by the wind. So, in theory, with a greater FOC, you should be able to shoot tighter groups. Some of you who are old enough to remember the toy balsa wood gliders from the local stationary store or hobby shop - they always had a metal weight pressed onto their noses to keep them flying straight. The same principle applies to the arrow by virtue of its FOC.

As you've probably already guessed, there is a point of diminishing returns. As you increase the FOC, you increase the overall weight of the arrow; not only does that yield a slower arrow, but the arrow tends to drop, or nose down faster, after it's expended its energy from the bow.

To see this, take an arrow with a screw-in field tip. Hold it by its balance point and drop it from as high as you can reach (standing on a chair may exaggerate the effect we're looking for). Take notice of which part of the arrow hit the floor first. Repeat the exercise, but this time remove the head. You should notice that the arrow with the head in place landed slightly more nose-down than the one without the head. The same effect happens in flight. As the nose tips over faster, the rest of the shaft needs to follow, and as its downward aspect is increased, the faster it falls (diag 6-19). The difference may be minor, but not non-existent and may be worth noting for your specific application.

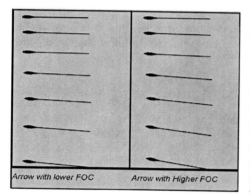

6-19 Exaggerated representation of the difference in position of an arrow shaft in free fall due to head weight or FOC.

Bow hunters like the increased FOC, as they feel the additional weight and stability increases their accuracy at the shorter distances they typically shoot. Target shooters who need to worry about extended distances, up to 90 meters, use lower FOC values to make the trajectory slightly flatter. The effect may not be significant for most casual shooters, but it is a tunable feature of which you may take advantage, should the need arise. In the examples above, Example 1 is typical of heavy-headed hunting arrow and Example 2 is consistent with most target arrows.

Arrow Spine

Arrow spine will need a little more discussion. Static spine is defined slightly differently by different organizations. The AMO (Archery Manufacturers' Organization, more recently known as the ATA – Archery Trade Association) standard is the amount of deflection, measured in inches, that a shaft demonstrates when it's supported on two points 26" apart, and a two pound weight is placed centered between the two supports (diag 6-20). Easton Archery, the largest if not the only company producing aluminum arrow shafts, uses supports spaced 28" apart and a 1.94 pound weight. Static spine is a way of reproducibly measuring or comparing the spine of one arrow to another.

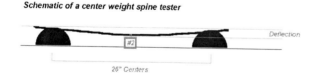

Schematic of a center weight spine tester

Deflection

#2

26" Centers

6-20 AMO arrow spine is tested by placing the arrow on two supports 26" apart, and hanging a two pound weight at its center. The distance the arrow bends (its deflection) is the spine.

The "deflection" spine in inches can be converted to the approximate draw weight spine at 28" by this simple formula:

28/deflection in inches = approximate draw weight at 28"
For example (using Easton's deflection chart):

An 1816 deflects 0.756"
28 / 0.756" = 37#

While not exact for all situations, this rule of thumb will suggest an appropriate draw weight range for a given aluminum arrow spine.

We first looked at why the spine is so important when discussing the archer's paradox and its relation to tuning; now let's look at the factors that can influence what's called dynamic spine or the actual spine deflection the shaft experiences when it's shot from a bow. That's the "spine" that we are really concerned with. When the arrow is released it is a dynamic entity and we'll need to understand each of the factors that contribute to the dynamic spine.

The first thing to consider is the shaft material and dimensions. The shafts we'll be discussing are little more than a tube, or in the case of wood arrows, a rod or dowel. (Arrow materials will be discussed in detail in Part 2.) The materials the tubes are made of give them their basic characteristics of strength, stiffness, and resiliency or modulus. In this section we are mostly concerned with stiffness or spine and its resiliency; that means the tube's diameter and wall thickness, as well as the material from which it's made. We'll use aluminum arrows as an example since they are the most standardized.

When a tube or cylinder's diameter increases, so does its stiffness, so it follows that a 2014 is stiffer than a 1914 (20/64" diameter vs. 19/64" diameter). The wall thickness of the tube also increases the stiffness, but to a lesser degree. A 1916 would be stiffer than a 1914 (0.016" wall thickness vs. 0.014" wall thickness).

Arrow comparison	Deflection	Difference
1914 to 2014	0.658" to 0.579"	0.079"
1914 to 1916	0.658" to 0.623"	0.035"

In the above example, it can be seen that the change in deflection going from a 19/64" to a 20/64" diameter shaft is more than twice that of going from a 14/1000" wall thickness to a 16/1000" wall thickness.

Easton currently makes shaft diameters from 14/64" to 27/64" and wall thicknesses from 0.011" to 0.020". Even though not every possible combination is available, you can easily match several arrow sizes to any bow from 15# - 100#+.

Next, the length of the arrow has to be factored in. Just as a six-foot pole is easier to bend than a three-foot pole of the same material, the longer the arrow, the weaker the dynamic spine (diag 6-21).

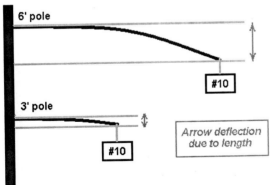

6-21 A 6' pole supported at each end will bend or flex more with a ten pound weight placed at its opposite end than will a three foot pole.

It's been suggested that a 1" change in arrow length equates to approximately 5# in draw weight spine requirements. That would mean, if you have a bow marked 35# @ 28", have a 28" draw length and use a 28" arrow, you'd check the chart below and would choose an 1816 aluminum arrow. If the arrow were cut to 29", and you still drew 28", you'd need an arrow shaft spined for 40#. No problems there as an 1816 will also work on a 40# bow. If you used a 30" arrow, that would equate to a 45#

bow, or rather require a shaft with a spine of 45#, and the 1816 might no longer work, and a 1916 might be a better choice. Naturally, if you used a 30" arrow on that 35# bow, and you actually had a 30" draw, that would mean the bow would be close to 39# or 40#, so a 1916 would be a better choice, and a 2016 would be a strong possibility.

Bow weight @ 28"	Draw length	Arrow length	Suggested arrow
35#	28"	28"	1816
35#	28"	29"	1816
35#	28"	30"	1916
35#	29"	29"	1816
35#	30"	30"	1916/2016

Many archers fine-tune their arrow's spine by modifying arrow length. They start with a full-length arrow or one that is several inches longer than their actual draw length, and then gradually shorten it by half-inch increments until the best flight is achieved. Yes, the head has to removed and reinstalled each time, and this can be quite time consuming, but may be necessary on bows without the option for center-shot adjustment due to a non-adjustable rest or strike plate.

The converse is also true. A friend of mine typically shoots arrows four to five inches longer than his draw length. When queried as to why, he answered, "Look, I got three dozen of these for free, and this is the only way I can spine them correctly for my bow." Hard to argue with that logic.

Next thing to look at is the weight of the head or pile. Think about our six-foot pole again. If we hold it horizontally by one end, its own weight will cause the far end to bend or arc downward. If we add a weight to the far end, it'll bend or flex even more (diag 6-22). Pretty intuitive, right? Well, an arrow reacts the same way during paradox. Using a heavier head weakens the dynamic spine of the arrow; a lighter head stiffens the dynamic spine. Many archers use this to fine-tune their arrows to the bow. In my experience, although small changes in pile weight might be detected during bare-shaft tuning, you'll need a significant weight change on the order of 45 to 50 grains to see a practical difference, unless you are at the very edge of the spine range for a given bow. Although less intuitive, it's been stated that adding weight to the rear of an arrow would stiffen the spine. We generally don't add weight there, except for the feathers and nock, so that usually is not too great a concern. The only way to find out how much of a difference modifying pile weight makes is to test it for yourself.

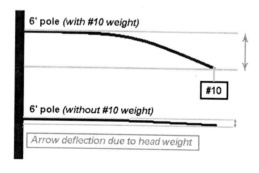

6-22 A six foot pole braced at one end will bend or flex more with a ten pound weight at the opposite end than it will from its own weight.

Use of Tapered Shafts

When dealing with wooden arrows, some archers favor tapered shafts. Tapering may increase the aerodynamics of the arrow in flight and has an effect on the dynamic spine.

There are three types of tapers. The most common is the shaftment taper where the rear 10 inches or so are slightly tapered toward the nock relative to the middle and front of the shaft (diag 6-23). This typically does little to change the static spine of the arrow, but can slightly decrease the dynamic spine. As you would expect, it also increases the FOC.

An arrow that has a larger diameter near the pile end is called "chested" or "breasted" (diag 6-24). The same theory applies; the greater weight at the front end increases the FOC and may help the aerodynamics. Also, the thicker the forward part of the shaft, the less prone it should be to breaking.

Lastly, a "barreled" arrow is thicker in the center and tapers toward both the pile and nock ends. The purpose of barreling is purely to enhance the aerodynamics (diag 6-25). Naturally, some fletchers experiment with the exact placement of the barrel to optimize performance. Interestingly, Easton top-of-the-line target arrows, the X-10 and ACE carbon/aluminum arrows, have a barreled design. In addition to improved aerodynamics, they claim to have greater durability.

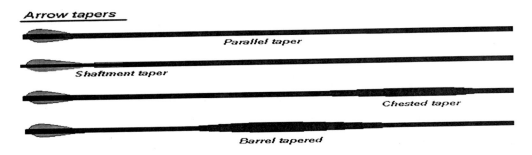

Arrow tapers

Parallel taper

Shaftment taper

Chested taper

Barrel tapered

A parallel (non-tapered) shaft compared to 6-23 A shaftment tapered shaft; 6-24 A chested shaft; 6-25 A barreled shaft

Fletching

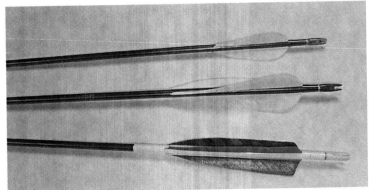

6-26 Feather fletching (from top to bottom) 3" parabolic, 5" parabolic and 5" shield cut

While fletching might not actually affect the spine of an arrow, they may appear to. The greater the surface area of the fletching, and/or the greater the offset or spin, the faster the arrow's ballistics, or rate of spin. The faster the arrow spins the faster it will stabilize and leave or diminish its paradox. So, the more stabilization, the more tolerant the bow may be to variations in arrow spine.

Fletching, feathers or vanes, while necessary to help guide the arrow, also slow it down. As we said earlier, the FOC helps to point the arrow, and in theory, given a perfect shot, that would be all you'd need to hit your target. The real world is a little different. A lot of our shots aren't perfect; probably most of them aren't, so we need a little more help. Adding fletching to an arrow, whether it be feathers, plastic vanes, or even thin wood slats, accomplishes that by doing two things. First, the larger surface area increases air resistance, and that helps to keep the tail end of the arrow behind the pointy end. Second, the fletching almost always imparts a ballistic spin. Feathers, for example, either come from the right wing or left wing of a turkey or goose. Neither right wing or left wing feathers are preferable from an accuracy standpoint, as they both have a natural right or left curvature to them, respectively. Even if attached perfectly straight without offset or helical orientation (diag 6-27), that natural curvature would cause the arrow to rotate in flight around its long axis. This rotation stabilizes the arrow, diminishes the effects of paradox sooner, and helps to keep the arrow flying in a straight line. Plastic vanes, if not applied with an offset or helical orientation, may not give a significant spin, and in that case are relying only on the increased surface and aerodynamic planing area for stability.

Arrows for shooting at aerial targets are called Flu-flu arrows (diag 6-26). They are usually heavy, stiff shafts with six untrimmed 5" or 5-1/2" feathers or full-length feathers wrapped around the shaft. Due to the affect of increased drag (stabilization) spine is not considered a factor. When shot into the air, they will fly normally for 15 to 20 yards, but the increased air resistance rapidly slows them down, and they fall to earth. They also make a very characteristic sound in flight, reminiscent of the old Robin Hood movies.

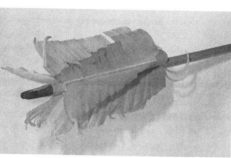

6-27 Natural curvature of a feather (5" left wing parabolic - left)

6-28 Flu-flu arrow with six uncut 5" feathers (right)

Again, we see there is a trade-off. The larger the surface area and the greater the offset or helical orientation, the faster the arrow will stabilize. Large fletching is more forgiving to shooter error and spine mismatches. However, as the arrow decelerates at a faster rate its range is markedly diminished. Hunters generally favor 5" or 5-1/2" feathers to stabilize heavy arrows with wide broadheads over short distances, while target archers use smaller fletching to decrease the arrow's trajectory over longer ranges and still maintain accuracy (diag 6-27). Archers competing in "Flight Matches" where distance is the only factor, use the smallest fletching possible, as accuracy is not critical (diag 6-29).

Flight Arrow

6-29 Example of a flight arrow as used by Harry Drake in the 1970's, an arrow of this type with a barreled shaft and small plastic fletch was shot over a mile! (left)

With excessively large fletching, a bow that is tuned very close to center-shot or an improperly tuned bow can diminish the amplitude of paradox and allow the fletching or shaft itself to strike the riser as it's being launched. Feathers and to a lesser extent plastic vanes, do yield on contact with the riser or rest, but given the timing or amplitude of paradox there may be too much contact to afford adequate clearance and an unobstructed launch. If you suspect this is the case, it can be confirmed by putting a coat of baby powder on the riser, shooting an arrow or two, and looking for tracks where the powder was brushed off by the fletching (diag 6-30). Alternatively, you can mark the edges of the fletching with lipstick or something similar, shoot an arrow, and look for pigment marks on the riser. If marks are present and your arrows are equipped with nock bushings (Easton UNI-bushings, G-nocks, etc), you may be able to rotate the nocks to improve clearance. Naturally, if you have glue-on nocks you'd have to remove and replace them. You might also want to consider smaller fletching next time! Another way of handling this situation is to shoot "cock feather in". By rotating the arrow 180 degrees, some archers find better clearance as now there is only one perpendicular feather striking the riser, instead of two at 60 degrees (diag 6-31). If the bow is tuned correctly, there should be no difference in accuracy or point of impact whether the arrow is shot with the cock feather in or out. For consistency it's best to pick one and stick with it.

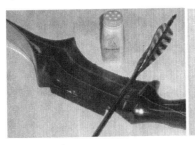 

6-30 Coating the riser and rest with powder may reveal fletching contact (left).

6-31 Shooting "cock feather in" may reduce fletching to rest or riser contact, but also may indicate an over-spined arrow (right).

Feathers vs. vanes

The use of vanes on arrows is not new. In the Middle Ages, crossbow arrows called "bolts" or "darts" used thin slats of wood for "fletching". Today, plastic vanes are quite common. They are impervious to rain water, making them a good choice for hunters who shoot in inclement conditions. They are usually less expensive than feathers and show less wear. However, when shooting tight groups, an arrow that would pass through a feather without doing any harm could puncture a vane, rendering it useless.

Plastic vanes are usually heavier than feathers of equal size and don't have the natural curvature that feathers have. They are also smoother or "slicker" than feathers. If two identical arrows were shot from the same bow, one with three 5" feathers and the other with three 5" plastic vanes, typically the feathered arrow would leave the bow slightly faster, but as the time in flight and distance increased, the vaned arrow would retain its speed longer. Put another way, the feathered arrow starts out faster, but may end up slower than a vaned arrow.

Example – Three 5" parabolic feathers weigh approximately 9 to 10 grains; three 5" parabolic vanes weigh 45 grains. Does that 35-grain difference at the rear of the arrow make a significant difference? Considering that 35 grains in total arrow weight can translate to 8 feet per second in initial speed and can slightly stiffen the arrow's dynamic spine, it's something only you can answer in your given situation.

Feathers are basically – feathers. Their size and shape can be modified to suit a specific purpose, but the basic construction remains the same. Vanes, on the other hand, are currently made from several different plastic materials with different weights, shapes and flexibility.

Arrow nocks

The diameter of the shaft will, to some degree dictate the size of the nock used. While glue-on nocks are classified by the diameter of the mouth or opening that will mate with the nock cone, or swage on the shaft, each nock size has a corresponding groove size. By using a string that's too thick or too thin, the arrow nock might not seat well on the string, being either too tight or too loose. A well-tuned system includes proper nock tension. Most shooters today use nocks that snap on to the string (diag 6-32). They are, by far, safer than the old open groove "Speed-Nocks" (diag 6-33), as they prevent the arrow from falling off the string inadvertently during the shot and producing a dry-fire. For accuracy, it's best for the snap nock to support slightly more than the arrow's weight. "Snapping" the arrow on the string can easily test the nock tension. Hold the bow horizontally with a nocked arrow pointing downward, and sharply hitting the string with your finger (diag 6-34). If the arrow falls off, the nock tension is correct. Most plastic nocks can be tuned for a perfect fit by holding them in boiling water for a few seconds and then squeezing the nock's ears or spreading them apart as needed.

Suggested glue-on nock sizes for aluminum arrows

Glue on nock size	Aluminum shaft size
7/32"	Less than 17xx
1/4"	17xx to 18xx
9/32"	19xx to 20xx
5/16"	20xx to 21xx
21/64"	21xx to 22xx
11/32"	22xx and greater

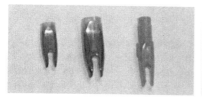

6-32 Snap on nocks: two sizes of American BJ nocks and an Easton UNI-bushing nock (left).
6-33 Speed nocks have wide grooves and do not snap onto the string (left).

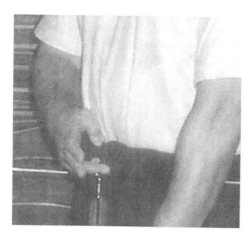

6-34 Testing for proper nock tension – gently tapping the string should cause the arrow to fall.

Gloves and Tabs

Shooting gloves

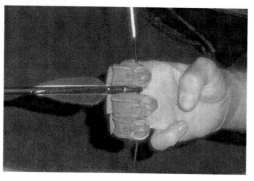

6-35 Shooting glove with long finger stalls to allow a deep grip on the string.

If you decide to use a shooting glove, then all you have to do find one that fits properly, with comfortable and adequate protection. Be sure to choose a glove whose finger stalls are long enough to extend well past the first finger joint and ensure a deep grip on the string (diag 6-35). As previously mentioned, the stalls should be snug on the fingers but not tight or constricting. Cordovan leather is a favorite due to its strength and durability; Damascus gloves are typically thinner and provide more string "feel".

Finger tabs

If you have chosen to use a tab, there's some more work we'll need to do for optimal efficiency and comfort prior to shooting. Shooting tabs are ideally designed for use with a deep hook or grip on the string. We've discussed the importance of the deep hook earlier, and now we have to adjust or trim the tab to work with that type of grip.

Diagram 6-36 shows a medium-sized tab being used with a deep hook in the string. It's quite evident that there's more material than what is actually required to protect the fingers. The extra material may become abrasive as the hand slides back along the face. A properly trimmed tab holding the string in a deep hook is shown in diagram 6-37, and diagram 6-38 shows it with the fingers extended. Once the fingers begin to relax and the release has commenced, there is no longer any need for fingertip protection. The excess material was also removed from above the index finger and below the ring finger.

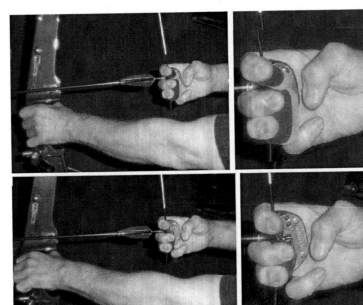

6-36 Untrimmed tab used in conjunction with a deep hook on the string reveals a considerable amount of excess material.
6-37 Properly trimmed tab protects the fingers while holding the string but has no excess material to get in the way.

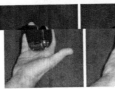

6-38 The same Win&Win 360 tabs in diagram 6-36 and 6-37 shown by themselves and on the archer's hand with fingers extended.

When trimming finger tabs, it's always safer to cut off a little at a time and test fire a few arrows. You can always remove more later on. If too much is removed, it can render a very expensive tab useless.

Finger tab and glove maintenance consists of normal leather care. They should be kept clean and checked for signs of excessive wear, cracking or other damage. Some archers regularly apply a little baby powder to the string contact areas. The powder keeps the leather slick and helps the string leave the tab or glove cleanly.

Be aware that the thickness of the tab will affect the position of the nock-end of the arrow relative to your face at anchor. This will be most evident with a side-of-the-face anchor as opposed to the under-the-chin anchor we'll discuss in the next chapter. Therefore, when going to a thicker or thinner tab or from a tab to a glove, the slight lateral displacement of the arrow nock may result in a noticeable lateral shift in the arrow's point of impact. This is not a problem, just something of which you should be aware.

Lastly, almost any change to the bow, arrows or shooting technique can and does have an effect on spine. These are usually minute and can usually be disregarded for practical purposes, but they must be considered if you are faced with a situation where the "correct" arrow doesn't seem to work correctly, or seems to have stopped working. Again, what we have discussed, are only guidelines; experimentation is always required, and yes, *Your Mileage May Vary*.

Chapter 7

Tuning with Gadgets – An Introduction to Olympic Style Shooting

7-1 Not only are Olympic style bows very precise instruments, but under certain conditions they can receive wireless broadband signals...

We've actually covered all the basic *principles* of tuning the bow and arrow. There are other gadgets that can be used to further fine-tune or rather refine the tuning of a bow based on the principles we've already learned. Most of these gadgets have been around for the last half-century. Although initially considered to be part and parcel of the "target shooters only" domain, there's no reason why they can't be applied to any bow and almost any situation – and they have been, with considerable success.

Are these devices or gadgets necessary? Not really, but are they beneficial? Without a doubt! Some archers believe that with each of these "gadgets" comes a limitation or "trade-off". Nothing could be further from the truth; each has a specific advantage in a given situation, provided the archer understands how each is used and how to exploit the potential benefits.

It would clearly be inappropriate to use an Olympic style target sight or long stabilizer on a hunting bow. Sights especially made for hunting bows and short hunting stabilizers have been around as long as recurve bows, perhaps longer, and are more appropriate for those situations. It remains with the individual archer to decide which device or gadget he wishes to try and to a larger extent, when he believes he is able to realize the benefits it offers.

This chapter assumes that you have an understanding of the principles discussed in the two preceding two chapters and your shooting form has developed to a point where you are grouping well at your typical shooting distances, for example 20 yards.

Arrow rests

The first thing that's usually added to a new bow is an arrow rest. It can be as simple as the Bear Weather Rest we discussed earlier, or one of several types of flipper rests (diag 7-2). These rests have a spring or magnetically loaded arm that moves out of the path of the arrow as it begins its flight. A novice will not notice any difference between the two types of rests, but as his shooting form improves, the flipper rest will begin to show advantages. The flipper rests have a rigid base while the arrow is at anchor, which promotes consistency and then retracts, as the arrow begins to move forward. The rubber or plastic rests behave the same way in theory, but do not provide the same rigidity nor completely get out of the way. Some flipper rests also allow for (limited) vertical adjustment of the arrow arm. This allows for very precise changes in relative nocking point height. (Modifying the placement of the arrow arm up or down has the opposite effect of moving the nocking point up or down.) There are also mechanical rests that balance the arrow between a pair of arms or a cushion plunger (see below) laterally and an arm under the arrow (diag 7-3). These are also adjustable for precise arrow placement relative to center shot and nocking point location. All of these rests do basically the same thing. In theory they provide minimal contact to support the arrow, and less contact means less resistance; that translates into a cleaner flight and easier tuning.

7-2 Bear J-2 and Weather rests and NAP Centershot and ARE flipper rests (left and middle)
7-3 Mechanical FITA style rest (Cavalier Free Flyte Elite on a Hoyt Aerotec riser - right).

Cushion Plungers

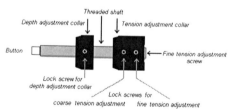

7-4, 7-4a Cartel cushion plunger and schematic

The cushion plunger serves two purposes. First, it allows very easy and precise adjustment for degree-of-center-shot and second, it allows you to "dial in" the amount of tension or resistance to the lateral pressure the arrow exerts on what was initially the rigid side plate, and is now the plunger button.

Here's the theory:
Releasing a bowstring by relaxing the fingers, while simple in concept, in practice is quite difficult to do consistently. Slight variations in the lateral pressure the archer may place on the arrow due to the uncurling of the fingers before and during the release can and will lead to variations in the dynamic spine of the arrow, and therefore how the arrow bends around the riser. The cushioning imparted by the plunger helps to negate slight variations in finger pressure. Further, by allowing you to "dial in" the amount of spring tension (or resistance) it exerts against the arrow, it gives the archer greater flexibility to customize the bow to his particular shooting needs.

A basic cushion plunger, such as the Cartel Super Plunger (diag 7-4) consists of a threaded barrel containing a spring-loaded button, a depth adjustment collar for setting the center shot position and adjustments for increasing or decreasing the spring's tension or pressure (diag 7-4a). A cushion plunger requires a threaded bushing in the riser in the area where the rest will be placed. (The standard for bow accessory bushings is 5/16" diameter x 24 threads per inch or simply 5/16"x24.)

Interestingly the concept of cushioning the lateral forces exerted by the arrow at release has been employed quite successfully on the early Hoyt Pro rests as well as the Bear Weather rest and several others (diag 7-5).

7-5 Original Hoyt Pro rest (c1969). Notice the flexible plastic piece above the arrow holder, a rudimentary but very functional cushion.

Plunger and rest tuning

The following is the classic or standard method for setting up a cushion plunger.

First the plunger and rest need to be positioned for best performance.

Flipper rests can be applied to the riser in the same manner as the simple Bear Weather rests. For serious target shooting, most archers will adjust or trim the flipper arm so that it fully supports the arrow but does not extend beyond the shaft's diameter (diag 7-5). As we have seen, any possible feather or vane interference can have a negative impact on tuning and therefore accuracy. Removing any excess length from the flipper arm is added insurance against that. Placing the arm at a slight upward angle ensures that the arrow will not fall off the rest.

The rest should be positioned so the plunger is centered on the body of the arrow shaft. That allows the plunger button to travel smoothly. Failure to do so, in addition to producing uneven travel, but may lead to premature wear on the button's surface (diag 7-6).

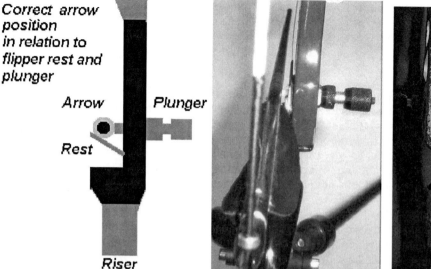

Correct arrow position in relation to flipper rest and plunger

Arrow   Plunger

Rest

Riser

7-6 Schematic of correct flipper rest and plunger placement – As shown in the diagram, the plunger tip should be centered on the arrow shaft and the flipper. The arm should be adjusted or trimmed so that it fully supports the arrow, but does not extend beyond the outer edge of the shaft. The second picture is an example of a correctly positioned plunger (left two pictures).
Concave wear on a cushion plunger that has seen several thousand arrows. In this case the arrow position in relation to the plunger button should have been slightly higher (right).

Basic plunger tuning is very similar to tuning the standard side/strike plate or rest. If an arrow appears over-spined, the button should be moved closer to the riser; if the arrow appears under-spined, the button is moved away from the riser. You also have the option to stiffen the plunger if the arrow appears too weak or soften it if the arrow appears too stiff. Since the plunger is spring loaded, and by definition designed to minimize release errors, trying to tune a bow with a built in cushion can be difficult. Therefore, it will be necessary to remove the spring or "cushion" from the cushion plunger from the equation for this part.

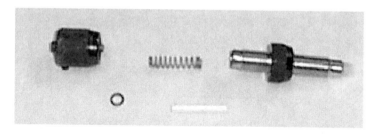

7-7 Replacing the plunger's spring with a matchstick removes the variable of the cushioning effect during tuning.

1.   Follow the instructions that came with the plunger for removing the spring. Replace the spring with a wooden matchstick or similar non-compressible rod, and reassemble. The plunger button should no longer be moveable (diag 7-7). (With some plungers, it may be possible to adjust the spring tension so tightly, that it effectively becomes stiff. If yours does, you've saved yourself a step.)

2.   Install the plunger; the button should be near the center of the arrow shaft. You may need to adjust the rest position up or down to accomplish that. Some flipper rests have an adjustable arrow arm to help align the arrow with the plunger (diag 7-5).

3.   Adjust the position so the arrow is just slightly outside (to the left of the string for a right-handed archer) the string when viewed from behind, and the string is visually centered on the limbs. To bring the arrow closer to center, turn the plunger counter-clockwise; to bring it farther from center, turn it clockwise (diag 7-7 and 7-8).

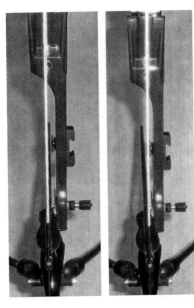

7-7 Center shot adjustment using a cushion plunger with the arrow aligned to true center shot (left).
7-8 Initial arrow placement; notice offset from center shot (right).

4. Lock the plunger in place and paper or bare-shaft tune the bow; use whichever method you prefer. Adjust the plunger position (degree-of-center-shot) as necessary to get the best arrow flight.

5. When satisfied, remove the matchstick, and replace the spring. *(It's easier to remove the plunger assembly from the bow to accomplish this.)*

6. In some cases, you may notice that even with the heaviest spring and the stiffest setting, the arrow may behave as if it were slightly weak; this is not uncommon. With lateral pressure being exerted by your fingers on a movable strike plate (button) you may be bringing the arrow a bit closer to center. If necessary, compensate by adjusting the plunger position slightly to the left.

7. Some plungers come with several springs and some with just an adjustment knob to increase or reduce the tension. Start with a medium weight spring and medium tension settings, then try using the different springs, if any, and experiment with the adjustment knob until you are satisfied with the arrow flight and your accuracy.

8. Make any final adjustments, if necessary and lock down the system with the Allen/hex-head screws.

While the above is the recommended procedure for cushion plunger tuning, for experienced archers I usually set the tension somewhere near the middle of its range and adjust the plunger to allow for arrow offset of 0 to 1 arrow diameters to the left of the bowstring. For new shooters, I set the plunger fairly stiff and use it as an adjustable strike plate. That removes one variable for a new shooter. Paper or bare-shaft tuning is then performed as usual. While not the standard procedure, I've found it perfectly adequate for my level of shooting. Which method is right for you? That is for you to decide!

What the plunger won't do:

The plunger is meant to negate minor variations in finger pressure at the moment of release. It will not save a poor release such as a pluck or collapse, or even severe variations in weight distribution from shot to shot. ***A plunger won't turn a poor shot into a good one, but it may make a good shot better and iron out slight variations between shots.***
Walk back tuning with a cushion plunger

In addition to the paper and bare shaft tuning methods described in Chapter 5, serious target archers shooting over extended distances fine-tune their bows by a procedure called walk back tuning. Developed by Vic Berger, a champion Olympic archer from the 1970's, walk back tuning requires the use of a bow sight, precision shooting skills on the part of the archer and a very calm, wind-free day. Here's the procedure:

1. Place a target face as close to the top of the target frame as possible.

2. Using fletched arrows, sight in at 20 yards and establish a group.

3. Without readjusting the sight, shoot groups of three or more arrows at the following distances: 5, 10, 15, 20, 25, 30, 35, 40, 45, and 50 yards (or as far back as your practice area will allow).

4. Note that each successive group will be lower on the target face or frame than the previous one.

5. If the groups do not align vertically, adjust the plunger position and/or spring tension as shown in the diagram 7-10.

6. If gross adjustments are required, it may be necessary to recheck the bare shaft tuning.

Walk back tuning - Berger method

7-9 Walk back tuning. These are generalized schematic patterns, yours, while similar, may not be identical. Also, expect the spacing to be farther apart at each consecutive distance.

Perfect Tuning	Plunger too far out. Move in.	Plunger too far in. Move out.	Spring too stiff. Relax tension.	Spring too soft. Increase tension.	Yards
					5
					10
					15
					20
					25
					30
					35
					40
					45
					50

Stabilizers

Most modern recurve bows come with a stabilizer bushing on the back of the bow (the part facing away from you, as you hold the bow in the shooting position) just below the grip area (diag 7-10). This is to add a stabilizer or other accessories to the bow. There are dozens, if not hundreds, of types of stabilizers on the market, ranging from simple metal bars to multi-rod models that look more like ray guns than archery equipment. Stabilizers serve two basic functions. First, they add weight to the bow, and so increase its inertia. The greater the inertia, the more stable the bow will be in your hand while aiming and on release, hence the term stabilizer. Think of it this way – if I were to strike your outstretched hand, it would move a certain amount. If I now placed a five-pound weight in your hand and hit it again, it would move less. As we want the bow to remain as motionless as possible during the shot, the added weight is a desirable feature. Second, it affects the balance of the bow and helps to minimize the effects of bow hand torque (rotational forces about the grip). Ideally, if the bow is held in an open or relaxed hand, as it should be, it should either remain vertical (diag 7-11) or the top limb should fall forward, away from the shooter (diag 7-12). Adding a forward weight accomplishes that.

7-10 A Bear one-piece hunting stabilizer (c1980) on a Martin Hunter with a Purple Heart riser. The standard thread size for the bushing is 5/16" x 24 threads per inch (left).
7-11 Bow balanced to remain in a vertical position after the shot (Hoyt 5PM Pro Medalist with twin stabilizers - middle)
7-12 Bow balanced to allow the upper limb to fall forward after the shot (Hoyt Gold Medalist with single front stabilizer - right)

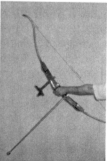

The bow remaining vertical is a very natural position. Most modern recurve bows are designed to be slightly bottom heavy – meaning the half of the bow below the pivot point (grip) will be slightly heavier than the upper half. This keeps the bow stationary and helps the arrow clear the riser as it's being shot, as any random bow hand movements that may hamper clearance are diminished.

(As an example. Let's return to use our 2"x4"x6' piece of wood. If we hold slightly above its midpoint to simulate a heavier lower half of the riser and orient it vertically, we have a single downward vector. The bow in fact will act as a pendulum. That single vector is relatively easy to counter and so, holds the wood upright. By canting the 2"x4" to 45 degrees, we've added rotational vectors to the system, and so torque to the (bow) arm. While most bows weigh less than a pine six foot 2"x4", the effect is less but not zero. As we stated earlier, a vertical bow position is also easier to reproduce consistently.)

Balancing the bow so that the top limb falls forward takes the same principle a step further, as the riser is now effectively moving in the same direction as the arrow, and it's doing so reproducibly. That forward rotation should also help reduce the archer's tendency to grab or twist the bow on release and further help to get the riser out of the arrow's path. Note that since stabilizers steady the bow and may give a cleaner launch, they may have the added advantage of giving a slightly faster arrow. Therefore, it is possible that the use of a stabilizer may require a slightly stiffer arrow, or the appropriate tuning adjustment. The effect is minor and may only show up if the arrow is at the weak end of the spectrum for the given system. It must also be stressed that for this balancing act to work correctly the bow must be held vertically and not canted or tilted. If the bow is canted, a forward weight may increase the torque about the grip and not diminish it.

Stabilizer Configurations:

The simplest stabilizer could be a weight of some sort taped to the riser below the grip area. This, while unattractive, does meet the aforementioned criteria. Before factory-installed bushings became popular in the late 1960's and early 1970's, that's exactly what was done and it worked quite well. Some companies made felt-backed base-plates that could be taped to the bow with electrical tape and were threaded to accept a small stabilizer weight (diag 7-13).

7-13 Early tape-on stabilizer (left). The same stabilizer in position on a 1974 Damon Howatt Hunter (right).

The next step is a weight, between 8 to 12 ounces and 3" to 8" long, screwed into the stabilizer bushing. That's certainly a lot neater, but serves the same purpose. These sometimes have a flexible coupling to absorb shock or vibration from the limbs. Given their relatively short size, they are usable for most target, field, or hunting situations (diag 7-14).

7-14 Short "hunting" stabilizers. These can also be used in combination with other stabilizers on a target bow.

For pure target shooting, where length isn't a major concern, a much longer stabilizer can be used. While 30" is the norm, some combinations are somewhat shorter and some considerably longer (diag 7-15). The value here is that with the longer rod or extension (called a lever arm), a lighter weight could be used to achieve the same rate of forward rotation. While it may seem counter-intuitive to use less weight, by doing so, it allows the archer to use multiple stabilizers to fine-tune the bow further without making the bow excessively heavy to hold (diag 7-16).

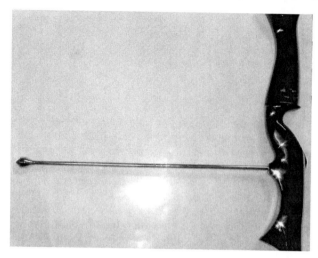

7-15 Single long target stabilizer from the late 1960's. This is a Browning Monarch target bow with a chrome plated metal rod stabilizer with interchangeable head weights.

In addition to the length, the stiffness of the stabilizer shaft also plays a role. A very stiff stabilizer shaft may not have the vibration dampening action of a more flexible one in a given situation. Stabilizers come in aluminum, carbon or combinations of the two. This gives the experienced shooter options in choosing the right weight to balance his bow and the right stiffness to help mitigate limb vibration. Some stabilizers are comprised of three separate rods held in place by spacers, which can be adjusted for vibration dampening (diag 7-17). These require additional tuning to be effective. A poorly tuned multi-rod stabilizer can actually amplify the vibration at shock.

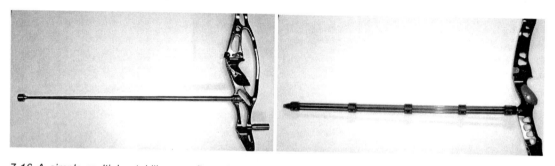

7-16 A simple multiple stabilizer configuration. The author uses a 30" tapered aluminum stabilizer with a weighted head and an 8-ounce counterbalance on his Hoyt Aerotec riser. This provides adequate physical weight and a good forward speed of rotation (left).
7-17 Beiter multi-rod stabilizer on a Hoyt Radian riser (right).

The Hoyt Archery Company introduced their Pro Medalist series in 1961, and with it came short, 3", twin stabilizers, one placed at each end of the riser; the areas were built up at each end of the riser to accept the bushings. The first ones were actually gold plated – talk about Hoyt being a class act! The theory was that since limb vibration had to pass through the riser to get to the archer's hand, adding weight to the area where the limb ended and the riser began (called the fade out, or feather area) would intercept or dampen the vibration. The theory worked. Over the years, the gold plating was replaced by chrome plating, then by bare stainless steel, and finally by hollow metal tubes. The stabilizer rods became longer and thinner to dampen vibration further. The theory evolved that a weight at the end of a flexible rod would be better able to absorb the vibration, while still giving the basic weight and balance features of the stabilizer. Later, Hoyt introduced a TFC (Torque Flight Compensator) placed between the riser and the thin stabilizer rod. These devices contained a rubber coupling that could be changed or adjusted to the amount of tension the individual archer needed or wanted to tune out the vibration or shock, and as the name implied, torque (unwanted twisting imparted by the bow and/or archer during the shot). That principle was later adopted by several other companies and is still alive and well today in one form or another on serious target bows (diag 7-16).

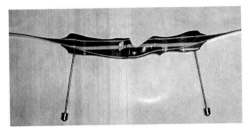

7-18 Early Hoyt chrome plated stabilizers and later hollow rod stabilizers with Torque-Flight-Compensator couplings (left). Twin stabilizer configuration on a Hoyt 5PM Pro Medalist. This configuration uses 1/4" solid rods which provide adequate flexibility for shock absorption and balance (right).

Bear Archery used a similar theory with their Omni-Coupler (diag 7-18a)

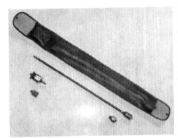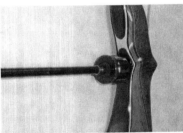

7-18a The Bear Omni stabilizer system included two interchangeable heads and rubber coupling "dampeners" to tune out vibration as well as its own carrying case (left). The Bear Omni stabilizer system on a Bear Tamerlane HC-300 target bow (right).

An interesting variation in the late 1960's by the Ben Pearson Archery Company was the use of internal mercury filled capsules, also in the fade out areas. The idea was probably taken from certain shotgun manufacturers, who used mercury in the shotgun stocks to reduce recoil. Both in the shotgun stocks and the bow's fade out areas, the mercury would literally explode within the capsule on shock and absorb excess energy before it reached the shooter. These "Mercury Cushion Capsules" were used in several of their target and hunting models, also with great success (diag 7-19). The best way to describe the experience of shooting one of these bows would be to say that the bow was dead in the hand and the archer never felt the arrow leave the bow. Some of their target bows did have provisions for a forward stabilizer as well. Unfortunately, with the publicity of mercury being a carcinogenic agent, its use was curtailed in the early 1970's.

7-19 The Ben Pearson Mercury Cushion internal stabilizers were located at the upper and lower limb fade-outs. These acted as limb vibration dampeners rather than true stabilizers, but the effect was quite remarkable.

More recently, a device appeared on the market called a Limbsaver, manufactured by SIMS-RL (SIMS Vibration Laboratories). While more of a vibration damper, they act partly as a stabilizer in the sense that they deaden shock and partly as a silencer. Limbsavers for recurve bows are paired mushroom shaped rubber buttons that adhere to the upper and lower limbs just distal to the fade-outs (diag 7-19a). At shock, vibrations travel from the string nocks down the limb and when they reach the Limbsavers, they are dampened by the additional pneumatic masses. Therefore they not only reduce the vibration felt by the shooter, but may serve to deaden any sound the bow might make.

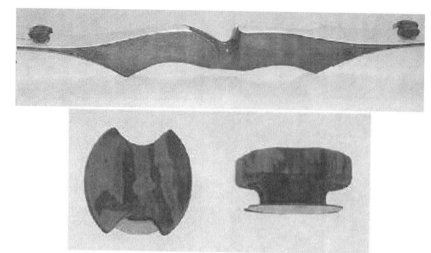

7-19a Limbsavers are mushroom shaped knobs attached to the face of the upper and lower limbs, just distal to the riser fadeouts. Here they are in place on a Ben Pearson Javelina (top).

To take this dampening effect a step further, Levin Industries markets a dampening module called the Doinker A-Bomb. Touted as being made from an Interrupted Transfer Polymer (ITP), the module is placed near the distal end of a long or short stabilizer to absorb or eliminate bow vibration and noise. These types of stabilizers are available for both target and hunting applications (diag 7-19b) and come in both single and multi-rod variants.

Doinker A-Bomb Stabilizer

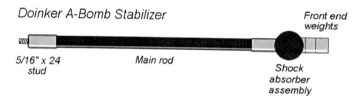

Front end weights

5/16" x 24 stud

Main rod

Shock absorber assembly

7-19b Diagram of a Doinker A-Bomb Carbon-Graphite stabilizer

Stabilizer configuration and functions

On Olympic type bows you can usually see four or more stabilizers or counterbalances. The various combinations can give the experienced shooter the exact weight, balance, or feel he or she wants during the shot. The following is a brief review of what each is designed to do. Remember that when looking at a system you need to look at the entire system, and not only the individual components (diag 7-20).

Long center stabilizer – forward weight, some additional mass, and possible dampening of limb vibration (depending on shaft flexibility).

Twin stabilizers at the fade off areas – dampening of limb vibration, some additional mass, and slight forward weight.

Rear mounted short stabilizer below the grip area – pendulum effect to keep the bow vertical, slowing the rotation caused by the long forward stabilizer, and additional weight.

Forward V-bars (attached to the center stabilizer rod, close to the main stabilizer bushing) – balance bar effect (similar to a balance bar used by a tightrope walker). They help to keep the bow vertical and either slow or accelerate the forward rotation caused by the long forward stabilizer depending on the position of the rods and end weights. While the V-bar cross member is forward of the bow, the extension rods and end weights are typically positioned back toward the shooter so the center of gravity is actually behind the grip. The exact placement of the end weights determines whether their effect diminishes or augments the forward rotation of the bow. A V-bar also adds weight to the bow, which may or may not be an advantage to a particular archer at a given point in his development.

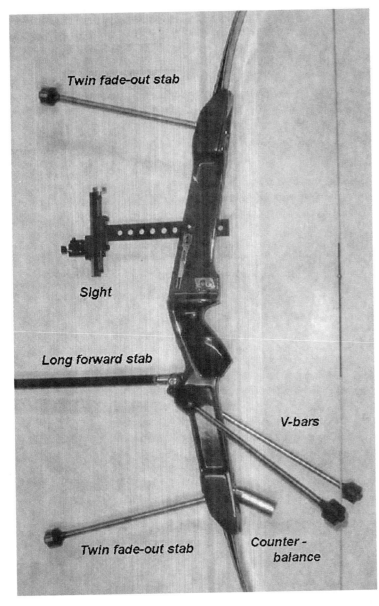

7-20 Mock up of a full-blown Olympic style target bow with numerous stabilizers, including a long center stabilizer with weighted "V" bar attachment, twin fade-out stabilizers and a rear counterbalance. With a very light weight 23" Hoyt Radian riser, this rig weighs in at a bit over six pounds. Using a heavier riser and adding a sight can easily bring the total weight over nine pounds!

Sight – The sight assembly has weight and therefore must be considered part of the balancing or stabilizing act. A bow that is perfectly balanced with a sight may not be as well balanced without it. The placement of the sight will also affect the overall balance of the bow.

Any other weight attached to the riser – used to augment or diminish any of the above effects or add additional weight. I currently use a single long forward stabilizer on my Olympic Bows and adjust the front weight to vary the speed of forward rotation after release. If necessary on some bows, I add a small rear-mounted counterbalance. These configurations demonstrate that less can be more.

Note: There are people use some or all of the above, just because it looks "cool" or because the guy who won a gold medal at the last Olympics, or the local hot shot at the range uses them. That practice usually does the owner of the local Pro Shop more good than the archer. As we can see, there's a fairly delicate balance (pun intended) required to make these things work properly. It's best to add one piece of equipment at a time when your shooting tells you it's needed, and use it long enough to evaluate its benefit honestly, as opposed to doing it because it's in fashion. Also, making several changes at one time can make it difficult to determine which change yielded which result; it's also possible that making two changes at the same time can cancel each other out.

One additional and often overlooked effect of stabilizers is their effect on the harmonics of the bow. After we release the string, the forward movement of the limbs is abruptly stopped by the bowstring. At shock, the shock waves travel from the string nocks down the limbs into the riser and the archer absorbs the waves that aren't dissipated along the way. The limb tips can clearly be seen to vibrate; harder to see, but just as evident, are riser vibrations. The riser flexes back and forth as well, usually at a high frequency. (We'll talk more about this in the next chapter on bow design.) For now, suffice it to say that anything added to the riser (or limbs) will change the harmonics of the bow, the manner in which it vibrates and flexes. In addition to all the above effects of adding stabilizers, an additional benefit may be to modify the vibrations the archer feels not only from limb shock, but also from limb and riser harmonics. Whether they modify the harmonics in a positive or negative way depends on how much weight is added and where it's placed on the bow. It's not uncommon for a given bow to be tuned correctly with regard to arrow flight, but then somehow feel out of tune with the addition of stabilizers. Occasionally, the apparent spine requirements may change, not only because of the difference in stability, but the change in harmonics.

For beginners, the myriad of stabilizers on the market and their prices can present a frightening picture. One need not spend several hundred dollars on stabilizers to find out if they actually prove beneficial or not. Home Depot or any larger hardware store has all the stabilizers you may need!

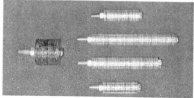

7-21 Variety of homemade stabilizers. Short stabilizers made from various lengths of 5/16x24 bolts, a few nuts and a lot of washers! Longer stabilizer was made from a 5/16" rod, threaded on both ends, and fitted with a turnbuckle for forward weight.

If you recall, we said that the standard bushing size for bow accessories is 5/16" x 24. That size threaded rod or bolts are available at most hardware stores. The shorter bolts can be loaded up with washers and held in place with a nut for hunting style stabilizers. Three-foot threaded rods can have several washers placed between two nuts at one end and the other end can be screwed into the accessory bushing. The lengths and weights are limited only by your imagination (diag 7-21).

Recipe for choosing a stabilizer or stabilizer system

There are four factors that need to be addressed in choosing a stabilizer:

1. Total weight. The bow has to be heavy enough to feel stable, but not so heavy that it can't easily be held on target for the entire course of fire.

2. Desired bow position at rest (with an open hand). You'll need to decide whether you want the bow to remain nearly vertical (popular with most bowhunters and casual shooters) or have the upper limb tip forward (the standard for most target archers) on release. If you want the bow to tip forward, then the rate of rotation becomes an issue. I like my target bows to have a considerable rate of forward rotation after release, but not so fast as to pull my arm down.

3. Lateral stability. The bow shouldn't have any side to side "flirting" if you happen to generate a little torque with your bow hand. Here you'll have to weigh the benefits of adding V-bars versus the additional weight.

4. Vibration dampening. Proper tuning can minimize most vibrations. Some bows may need a little more help and adding certain types of stabilizers in strategic locations may supply that help.

Slings

To fully utilize the balancing effect of the stabilizers, many archers use a finger sling (diag 7-22), wrist sling (diag 7-23), or bow sling (diag 7-24), to allow the bow hand to remain open during the shot. By doing that, the balance that was built into the bow is not hindered by any inadvertent action by the shooter. Most slings can be used with any bow that has a recurve style pistol grip.

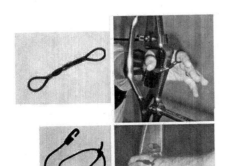
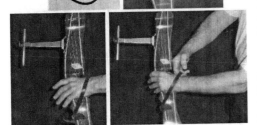
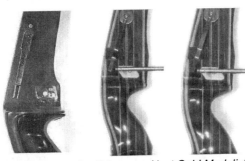

7-22 Finger sling in use on the archer's thumb and index finger with a very open hand. The finger sling is the easiest to use and requires the least adjustment. As can be seen, the end loops slip over the thumb and index finger and then are made slightly snug by adjusting the plastic collars (top).

7-23 The wrist sling is nothing more than a length of parachute cord with a loop on one end and a hook on the other. The loop goes around your wrist and the hooked end wraps around the bow and attaches to the loop. All that needs to be adjusted is the amount of slack around the bow. There should be enough to allow the bow to "jump" but not leave your hand (middle).

7-24 Older style stick-on bow sling on a Hoyt Pro Medalist. As with the wrist sling, it needs to be loose enough to allow the bow to jump, but not leave your hand (bottom).

As you begin to use a relaxed grip on the bow and realize its benefits, sooner or later you'll want to try a fully open hand position. Doing so goes a long way to keeping your bow arm relaxed during the shot and letting the bow do what it was designed to do. The downside is that with an open hand, the forward momentum of the bow on shock will carry it out of your hand and onto the floor. The sling allows the bow to "do its own thing", but catches it before it can get away from you. A sling is a fairly inexpensive investment that can really advance your shooting progress.

Clickers

A clicker is a device that tells the shooter when he is at the correct draw length for a shot (diag 7-25).There are several types of clickers currently

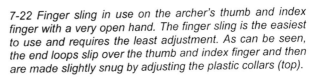

available. The most common type is a thin piece of metal (called a "blade") attached to the sight window above the arrow rest. The arrow rides under the clicker blade and will click against the riser when the arrowhead clears it (diag 7-26). Some attach to the upper or lower limb with an adhesive backing and by a cord to the bow string; they click when the cord becomes taut and bends a piece of metal within the device attached to the limb (diag 7-27).

7-25 Beiter screw-in clicker on a Hoyt Gold Medalist riser (left).
7-26 Here we see a clicker at anchor (middle), just before it "clicks" and just after (right). In most cases, as soon as the clicker strikes the riser, the arrow's released.

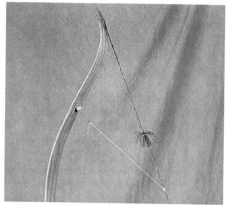

7-27 Clickety-Klicker limb clicker in position on upper limb (Photo courtesy of 3Rivers Archery) Some archers find that attaching the clicker cord closer to the loop serving or braid than shown in the picture helps to prevent tangling.

As we've been seeing, consistency is vital to good shooting. A consistent draw length, while generally a good thing to have, becomes critical as the shooting distances become longer. When shooting at 50, 70 and 90 meters, 1/4" change in draw length can easily throw your arrow above or below the target. The clicker, if used properly, solves that problem. Some archers also feel that the use of a clicker helps to ensure proper back tension (discussed in Chapter 12), as they have to deliberately "pull" through the clicker using the deep back muscles. It may also assist the archer's hold at anchor, if he begins to snap shoot or release prematurely. While these may not be its primary function, they are certainly added benefits for some archers.

There are several factors or components that determine an archer's true draw length. These components must be faithfully reproduced each time an archer draws to anchor for the shots to be consistent.

The distance to the archer's anchor point – what we commonly call the draw length is the most obvious, but not the sole factor. The degree of drawing shoulder rotation can increase or decrease the draw length (recall that the forearm of the drawing arm should be in line with the arrow at anchor), as can the rotation or alignment of the bow shoulder. Similarly, the hand position on the riser must be the same for every shot.

Lastly, the two most overlooked factors concerning draw length are the finger placement around the string and the archer's head position. While we understand that using a deep hook, with the string resting in the crease of the first joint, is the most efficient means of drawing and releasing a bowstring, the exact placement of the string can vary at anchor. This is because as the string is drawn, the forward force of the limbs begins to pull the string from the fingers. While this "string rolling" is quite natural, it's one additional reason why many archers using a clicker for the first time experience shot to shot variations in the effort required to "pull through the clicker". A very insidious shortener of draw length, especially as an archer fatigues is his head position. We were initially taught to keep the head upright, however as we fatigue it's all too common to begin to crane the neck forward to meet the string and therefore lighten the draw weight. While this may only account for a tiny fraction of an inch, less than would be noticed without the use of a clicker, once the clicker is employed, that tiny fraction of an inch can mean the difference between a relaxed pull-through and a veritable tug-of-war!

To reiterate, it is imperative that:

1. *The anchor point is well defined and reproducible.*
2. *The drawing arm is rotated the same degree every time.*
3. *The bow shoulder is aligned the same way every time.*
4. *Bow hand position must be consistent every time.*
5. *The string grip must not only begin in the exact same position for every shot, but must either stay in the same position throughout the draw or change reproducibly every time.*
6. *The head must remain vertical and not be craned forward to meet the string or back in an attempt to extend the draw.*

Installing the above-the-rest clicker:

When setting up this type of clicker, the first order of business is to make sure your arrows are cut to your draw length or more precisely, your clicker length. Or at least within the adjustment range of the clicker. (Naturally, arrow length isn't critical if you'll be using a limb-mounted cord type clicker, as discussed below.) Attach the device to the bow; they usually have an adhesive backing, or are screwed into the riser. Most Olympic risers come with a pre-drilled and tapped hole for a clicker, so if you have one of those, you're all set. If you have a non-tapped riser, unless you plan on making this a permanent addition, the adhesive-backed type is easier and safer to put on and remove.

With the "above the rest" clicker, come to your natural anchor point a few times, and have a friend take note of where the arrow front tip is. Rotate the clicker arm so it is about 1/16" to 1/8" further in (closer to you) than the tip. That means you need to pull through that extra distance for the clicker to sound. If your arrows are extending beyond the back of the bow, you'll need to cut them down, get a limb-mounted clicker, or get new arrows for use with the clicker. Optimally, the clicker bar should be as vertical as possible, but the angle is not critical as long as the clicker comes off the very tip of the arrow, and not the ogive (or tangent line) of the pile (diag 7-26). As you gain experience using the clicker you'll make minute changes to its position so it better matches your actual draw length

 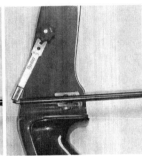

7-28 The clicker should be positioned as close to vertical as possible with the blade well below the tip of the arrowhead to ensure the blade "clicks" off the very tip of the arrowhead and not the ogive. The left picture shows correct clicker placement and the right picture shows the clicker too far forward, clicking off the ogive of the head and not the tip.

In theory, clickers are very simple to use. Slip the arrow under the clicker, draw and anchor as usual. Now, as you slightly increase the tension or "pull", as the tip of the arrow slides out from under the clicker, the clicker strikes the riser, and you release the arrow. The draw length at release has to be the same every time.

The limb clicker:

To install the limb clicker, the clicker itself adheres to the upper limb close to the tip as shown in diagram 7-27. The other end of the cord attaches to the bowstring. The length of the cord is adjusted to your draw length plus 1/16" or 1/8", as before. This is usually done by slipping the free end of the cord through the bowstring below the center serving. Drawing the bow to anchor will pull the cord to the appropriate length. Repeat the exercise a few times to confirm the correct draw length. Once you're satisfied, the free end can be secured to the bowstring. One possible advantage to the limb clicker is that you can pull through the clicker several times. One disadvantage is that overdrawing the bow may damage the clicker.

An old style hunting clicker:

Hunters knew the benefits of a clicker since the middle of the last century. The limb clicker is certainly usable on hunting bows, but some hunters objected to the audible click when stalking game. There was, however, a type of hunting clicker called a *Frydenlund Timer*, that was mounted on the sight window, above the arrow rest much like a conventional clicker. Its "clicker arm" extended beyond the back of the bow, and would "click" (actually more of a visual clue than a click) when the broadhead pushed the blade from its retainer. It was quite ingenious, very quiet, and very effective (diag 7-29) Some bowhunters simply cut their arrows so that the broadhead butts against the arrow shelf or another part of the riser. While the theory is sound, over-drawing can have nasty side effects.

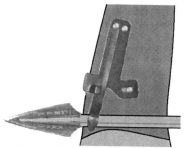

7-29 The Frydenlund Timer is a clicker designed specifically for use with hunting heads. As the broadhead is drawn back (to the left in this case) it pushes the "timer" arm away from its retainer resulting in more of a "buzz" or vibration than a click.

A common error with new clicker users is that they adjust the clicker too far beyond their normal anchor, which causes them to overdraw. Using a clicker should make you increase your draw length only slightly, if at all. It's been said that a clicker needs to be adjusted to your full draw length, not your maximum draw length. Maximum draw length means you're at your anchor point, but are overextending your draw, usually by rotating your head away from the target. This has to be avoided. Besides being bad form, it can be downright painful, as one symptom is the string clipping your nose or lip on release. Also, many first time clicker users find themselves holding longer than usual. Until you get used to the extra work, it can get very tiring, very quickly. For this reason, *I do not recommend a clicker for new shooters*. Once the archer has developed sufficient strength, he is more apt to benefit from a clicker.

The opposite is also true. Having the clicker too far forward can be problematic as you will pull through the clicker too soon and have to reset it and start over.

When coaching an archer using FITA type equipment, I typically wait until he's shooting in the 270 out of a 300 possible range on the NFAA indoor target before introducing the clicker. After it's adjusted correctly, I have the archer shoot "on click" - meaning the arrow is released as soon as the clicker sounds. After a few weeks to a month, his strength has increased to handle the additional workload and this procedure should have become almost second nature. At that point I have the archer hold for a second or more past the click. Besides having the archer take an immediate dislike to me, it stops him from developing a knee-jerk response to the clicker. That way if something either feels wrong or the sight simply isn't where it should be, he has developed the control to either correct the problem or better yet, let the arrow down and start over.

There are two exceptions to the above rule concerning new shooters. If a beginner is having difficulty maintaining a consistent draw length (I've seen some neophytes vary their draw lengths by several inches from shot to shot) then the temporary addition of a clicker may be necessary to cure the problem. The other exception is if a shooter is showing signs of snap shooting, meaning releasing the string before he is ready. Snap shooting can be one of the most detrimental problems an archer may face and needs to be curtailed as quickly as possible. A clicker is a time-proven method of curing a premature release.

Training tip: When beginning practice with an above-the-arrow clicker, start at a close distance as you did for blank bale shooting. Draw and anchor normally, but once at anchor focus on the tip of the arrow and watch it pull through the clicker. At anchor the clicker should already be very near the tip of the arrowhead and only need to come back 1/8" inch or so to clear the clicker blade. Repeating this exercise during each training session will establish a proper clicker pull-through technique. I personally find this exercise a must for all new clicker users. *(This is another variation of the "watch the arrow" exercise we began using several chapters ago!)*

A variation on this exercise for more advanced archers, is to try the exercise at 20 yards with a standard target face. Here, you draw, anchor and aim at the target normally, but once the aim has been established, shift your attention to the arrowhead and watch it pull through the clicker. In this case, besides being a clicker exercise, it will tell the shooter how steady he can hold without the sight or target as reference points. While certainly not something to try while shooting in earnest, it may prove useful for diagnosing form errors. If the arrow impacts left or right of the mark, either there is a form issue that needs to be addressed or the archer needs to modify his stance. The latter will be discussed in the chapter on form variations.

A note about alternate "clicker methods"

Some archers use triggers to know when they have reached full draw; some are better than others. For instance, one archer I spoke to waits till he feels a feather brush his nose or lip to confirm his draw. While this may indeed help with confirming the correct anchor, it does little to ensure a correct draw length. The problem lies in the fact that while the anchor may be correct, there are numerous other things that can affect the actual draw length. For example, bending the elbow of the drawing arm, hunching the shoulders or cocking the head forward can shorten the draw length and not affect the anchor point! All of the clicker devices we've discussed use the arrow as the measuring device; since the arrow's length can't change, the draw length is no longer in question.

The bow sight, its placement and configuration

We initially discussed the use of a bow sight in the section on basic shooting and fabricated a rudimentary sight to allow us to differentiate aiming errors from form errors. Olympic or FITA type shooting requires accuracy up to distances of 90 meters (approximately 98 yards) and bow sights are essential for precision shooting at those distances. The sights may be mounted on the back, side or face of the riser. Most new risers and all Olympic style risers have mounting holes on the side of the riser opposite the sight window (diag 7-30). A separate carrying case is sometimes used to protect the sight (diag 7-31). A mounting bracket is screwed into those holes and a sight extension bar (diag 7-32) is inserted into the mounting bracket usually by means of a dovetail. The extension rod allows the sighting device to be placed at various distances from the shooter's aiming eye.

7-30 Sight mounting holes on the side of a SKY Sky Hawk wood riser and an aluminum Hoyt Aerotec aluminum riser. The AMO standard for these holes is 10-24 threaded holes spaced 1.312 +/- .010" center to center. Minimum thread depth is .250" (left).
7-31 Sure-Loc Quest-X Sight in its padded carrying case. The sight can be fitted with either a pin or aperture (middle).
7-32 Killian Checkit sight extension bar assembly popular in the 1980's. Same sight showing the Spigarelli aperture (right two pictures).

The sight may be placed forward of the riser (farther away from the shooter than the riser) or behind the riser (closer to the shooter). The farther away from the shooter, the longer the "sight radius" (the distance from the shooter's eye to the sighting device). The greater the sight radius, the greater the aiming precision as smaller variations in sight movement can be detected. While that may initially sound like a good idea, since the sight will never stay perfectly still, that can be more of a detriment than a benefit to most new and intermediate level shooters. The tiny movements or "wobble" the sight makes in relation to the target can be very disconcerting. As the shooter works harder to steady the sight, the worse the wobble becomes. Bringing the sight closer to the shooter diminishes or rather "masks" some of that "wobble". Some archers go as far as mounting the sight behind the riser (closer to the aiming eye) for that reason. The apparently steadier hold of the sight on the target increases the archer's confidence and therefore his accuracy. Typically as the archer gains experience and can hold more steadily, he can extend the sight radius to increase his precision somewhat (diag 7-33)

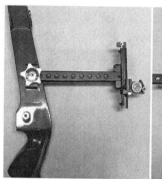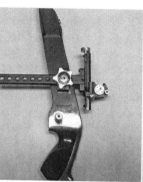

7-33 Options in placement of the bow sight as described in the above text.

Another factor in determining sight placement is its effect on the maximum distance for which the sight can be successfully calibrated. As we'll see in the chapter on aiming, as we increase our distance to the target there comes a point when the arrowhead coincides with the archer's line of sight to the target, called the point blank range. When using lighter weight bows, reaching the longer distances may become problematic, as the sight would need to be lowered to a point where it would either coincide with the arrow, or possibly be below it. Bringing the sight closer to the shooter makes the arrow's angle of elevation steeper and allows for the increased trajectory of arrows launched from the lighter bows.

The precise placement of the sight for an archer at a given level of training can be determined only by experimentation. Typically as the archer's form and hold improves, he will extend the sight farther away from the bow.

The sighting device itself may be a simple pin as we described earlier or an aperture through which the archer centers the bullseye. In either case he will have to determine how much of the target he will allow the pin to obscure or how much of the target he wishes to see through the aperture. Olympic style archers prefer the aperture, as all they need do is simply look through the opening and focus on the center of the target. While not allowed in Olympic or FITA recurve competition, scopes with magnifying lenses have been around for decades and are permitted in some shooting classes (diag 7-34).

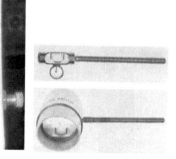

7-34 Pin sight (left) and aperture sight with level (top right) and scope with level (bottom right).

Some archers prefer the aperture to be slightly larger than the bullseye and some prefer more of the target to be visible. The size of the aperture, or rather the amount of the target visible through the aperture is of course dependent on the distance the aperture is from the archer's eye (sight placement) and distance to the target. Rather than changing apertures for different matches, some compromise is reached.

As the bow sight has weight, its placement may also affect the balance of the bow. While this may not be a concern for a novice shooter, it's something that an experienced archer will have to account for when formulating his stabilizer placement.

Diagram 7-35 reviews the sight corrections necessary to center, calibrate or "zero" the sight. However, we have been speaking in general terms and "zeroing" the sight for a single distance. In reality, archers shoot at various distances. To accommodate these changes the sight must be calibrated at each distance. These calibration marks are usually recorded on a strip of paper or tape on the sight bar (diag 7-35a). There are several computer programs on the market which allow you to enter data regarding your particular setup, however it's my feeling that trial and error is still the best method.

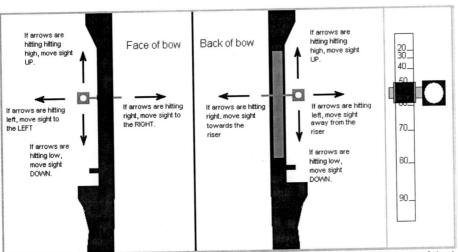

7-35 Review of sight corrections for zeroing a sight as seen from the face and back of the bow (left).
7-35a Marks for various distances on a sight bar. Notice that as the shooting distances increase the relative positions of the marks get farther and farther apart (right).

Weight and tiller adjustment

Olympic type takedown bows' limbs are adjustable for draw weight and tiller. This is accomplished by pivoting the limbs either toward or away from the shooter by means of an adjustment bolt and lockdown screw contained in each limb pocket (diag 7-36). Tilting the limbs forward, adding reflex increases the draw weight and tilting them back decreases it (or increases deflex). Most Olympic bow manufacturers claim a 10% variance in draw weight, and while some risers may allow that much, 5% is a more realistic estimate. As we'll see in chapter 8, modifying the amount of limb reflex or deflex (tilting the limbs away or toward the archer, respectively) can have a considerably greater effect on performance than increasing or decreasing of the draw weight alone should account for.

Note: While adding reflex increases performance, it is possible to add too much reflex and over-stress the limbs. The first sign of over-stressing is an inability to tune a bow correctly. Typically, if the standard size arrows for a given draw weight will not tune correctly, or changing tuning parameters, such as nocking point and degree of centershot, does not give the expected results, the limbs may be over-stressed. Most current ILF limbs start acting abnormally when the draw weight measured at an archer's draw length exceeds the rated weight of the limbs by 8# to 12#. In that case, backing off on the amount of reflex should solve the problem. In more extreme cases, over-stressing the limb may lead to premature failure. This problem is not limited to ILF limbs; one-piece bows may also exhibit the same phenomenon. This needs to be considered when attempting to tune shorter bows or dealing with archers with long draw lengths.

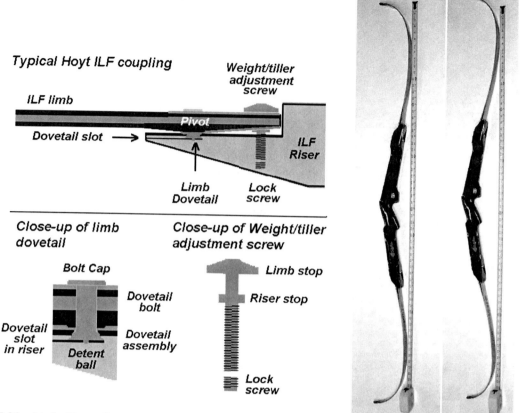

7-36a Limb tiller adjustment mechanism on an Olympic style recurve. Tightening or loosening the weight/tiller adjustment screw pivots the limb to increase or decrease the draw weight/reflex (left).
7-36b This picture clearly shows the difference between limbs in full reflex (left photo) and full deflex (right photo) on a Hoyt Gold Medalist riser.

Although we have discussed how to tune a bow to an arrow by using the brace height, strike plate, or cushion plunger, many archers are using the weight adjustment feature to match the bow perfectly to the arrow.

The limbs are adjusted to the middle of their travel and the cushion plunger is set to medium tension. The arrow's offset is then adjusted so the arrowhead is just to the left of the string, as previously described. Instead of moving the plunger in or out to compensate for the arrow's spine, the weight of the bow is adjusted up or down until the spine of the arrow is correct for the bow, as determined by paper or bare-shaft tuning.

For example:
With the bow configured as above, if the first bare-shaft test showed the bare shafts striking to the left of the fletched arrows, indicating an over-spined arrow, the archer would turn both limb adjustment bolts one half turn to the right, increasing the draw weight. The bare-shaft test is then repeated, and the bare shafts should now be closer to the fletched arrows. Further adjustments are made, until the two groups coincide. As expected, if the limb bolts are tightened too much, the bare shafts would begin grouping to the right of the fletched arrows, indicating under-spined arrows, and the draw weight would have to be reduced. If there were insufficient limb travel to accommodate the arrows, then the archer would need either to finish tuning with center-shot adjustment or switch to the correctly spined arrows.
Similar results can be accomplished by adjusting the brace height and so modifying the initial poundage and length of the power stroke.

While both scenarios are overkill for most shooters, they both match the bow to the arrow as precisely as possible. The only caveat is that unless the arrows were correctly spined in the first place, the weight adjustment requirements may be such that the limb position may render the bow either too critical or too sluggish. Likewise, changing the brace height may make the bow noisier or generate greater hand shock.

Tiller is the relative reflex/deflex of the upper limb compared to the lower and is usually measured on a strung bow from a point near the limb fade out to a point perpendicular to the string. On Olympic recurves, it's usually from the point on the limb where the limb exits the riser on the belly side of the bow (diag 7-37). Most bows are tillered to be 0/0, meaning equal tillering on the upper and lower limbs to 1/8" to 1/4" lower limb positive, meaning the lower limb's tiller distance is 1/8" to 1/4" shorter than the upper limb's tiller.

7-37 Measuring upper vs. lower relative limb tiller of a Hoyt Radian riser

Tiller is a matter of personal preference, or opinion, and 0/0 to 1/8" positive works well for most people. Hoyt Archery recommends that if a sight shooter feels the bow rising during the draw, the tiller can be increased (increasing the poundage) on the lower limb slightly, until the sight remains stationary. Conversely, if the sight seems to be sinking, the upper limb may be tightened. I recommend that tiller adjustments be left alone unless the archer is well versed in Olympic type shooting and is shooting at a fairly high level.

Understanding tiller:

We typically assume that the only force a bow imparts to an arrow is directed forward, towards the target. In reality, there are vertical forces acting on the arrow as well. These forces are due to an imbalance in the vertical axis caused by a number of factors. The most obvious reason is the fact that the arrow is always nocked at an oblique angle to the string, with the nock end slightly higher than the tip. That alone requires the lower limb to be slightly stronger than the upper limb to keep the vertical forces on the arrow in balance. In archery terms, that is giving the lower limb a slightly positive tiller. With regard to bow design, the relative strength of each limb and the distance from the pivot point of the grip to each string nock also factor into static tiller. To further complicate matters, the position of the fingers on the string and even the relative weight each finger bears at anchor and at the instant of release affect the dynamic tiller. During the tuning process, the position of the nocking point is used to balance the aforementioned forces. The effect of static tiller (bow design) is to minimize or in some cases optimize these forces the archer places on the string (dynamic tiller) to improve the quality of the shot. Most well designed and manufactured one-piece bows are built with their tillers near the center of their acceptable range; with the advent of limb pocket adjustable risers, there might be room for improvement.

It is interesting to note that Earl Hoyt demonstrated that tiller adjustments had no effect on the accuracy or grouping capability of Olympic bows. Bows tillered up to 3/8" upper limb positive shot as well as bows set to factory default of 1/4" lower limb positive. Therefore, tiller adjustment is purely a matter of personal preference.

The 10 steps for setting up an Olympic style target bow

With all the information we've covered it may surprise you how simple it is to set up a modern target bow. Here's how it's done:

1. Set the weight/tiller adjustments to either full deflex for a new shooter (to keep the bow as light as possible) or at their midpoints for a more experienced archer (to provide as much positive or negative adjustment as possible).

2. Loosen the plunger depth ring and screw it into the riser so it protrudes approximately 1/4" into the sight window (the exact amount will depend on how far past center shot the sight window has been cut).

3. Set the spring tension to medium / stiff, by turning the adjustment sleeve and the screw at the end of the plunger clockwise and locking them in place with their lock screws.

4. Place the rest on the riser and position it so the flipper arm is pointing slightly upward and will center the arrow on the plunger button as shown in diagram 7-5.

5. Adjust the plunger to give a small amount of positive arrow offset from center shot as shown in diagrams 7-7 and 7-8.

6. String the bow and affix a nocking point so that the arrow nock is approximately 1/8" – 1/4" above perpendicular.

7. Attach the sight and stabilizers (if so desired) as shown in diagram 7-33 and 7-20, respectively.

8. Stand approximately 10 yards from the target and zero the sight as shown in diagram 7-xx. Remember it's a good idea to have someone watch your alignment to the target on the first shot just in case you're off by more than a safe amount.

9. Re-zero the sight at 20 yards and start shooting!

10. When you're comfortable with the bow, begin the tuning process as described in chapter 5.

Video Taping

7-38 Video taping an archer can reveal form problems that may be difficult to see with the unaided eye. In this case a very quick "collapse" was digitally captured.

We said early on that the greatest drawback to using this or any written work, is *that the author(s) can't see what the archer is doing and neither can the archer!* Even having a very observant friend or skilled coach watching, the archer is still relying on a verbal description of what's actually taking place. The use of a video camera not only shows the archer exactly what he is doing, but allows slow motion and up close analysis from various angles of the actions and reactions taking place. The ability for the archer to see himself from various angles has also been know to settle arguments very quickly between what the archer may perceive and what actually happened. Given the price and popularity of video cameras, their use as a coaching tool should be strongly considered for shooter at an intermediate level or above. (Diag 7-38)

In the past I've had a problem with a slight collapse just before the release. Video taping myself ultimately showed the collapse had disappeared. After a brief moment of exhilaration, I decided to review the film in slow motion. To my surprise and dismay, the collapse was still there, but so small and so fast that it was invisible to the unaided eye – but the video captured it. While video taping may not be for everyone, it is a very observant and sometimes humbling critic.

The Chronograph – Friend or Foe?

A chronograph is a device for measuring the speed of an object, in this case, the speed of an arrow. It works by emitting two beams of light onto two sensors, a foot or more apart. A projectile is passed between the lights and the sensors, and the elapsed time between the interruption of the two beams is measured and translated into an appropriate unit of measure, usually feet per second (fps). Typically the device is placed directly in front of the shooter with a few feet of clearance given for safety. The readings obtained that way are for the initial velocity of the arrow (as soon as it leaves the bow).

(Most people use chronographs out of curiosity to find out how fast their bow can launch a given arrow. That's a perfectly legitimate use for the device and reflects an aspect of our human nature. It's something we just want to know and possibly claim bragging rights about – the "my bow is faster than your bow" syndrome. It also can be a reality check, as the chronograph, while not a perfect tool, really doesn't lie. It can be a confirmation that your bow is as fast you thought it was, is even faster, or unfortunately, is slower than you expected.)

7-39 Using a chronograph may not only satisfy your curiosity, but may improve your shooting!

From a technique standpoint, shooting a number of arrows through a chronograph can not only tell you the initial velocity of your bow/arrow combination; it can tell you how well you're shooting! If you are doing everything consistently, from draw length to anchor and release, then the initial velocities should be virtually identical, Certainly within a few fps. If so, then you're doing everything right. If not, there's probably something wrong with your form, or your ability to execute reproducible shots.

One occasion I found myself stringing arrows vertically, for no apparent reason; a visual inspection confirmed that the nocking point, rest and sight were not loose or moving. Naturally suspecting an equipment problem, I set up the chronograph. Initial velocities were showing a five to six fps variation between arrows. (That's where the friend or foe part comes in.) By adding a clicker, the variation was reduced to about one fps, and upon returning to the target butts, the vertical stringing had disappeared. The chronograph let me know, in no uncertain terms, that my inconsistent draw length was the weak link in the equation on that particular day.

Once your form is consistent the chronograph can help you evaluate how changes in form or equipment can affect arrow performance. For instance, what change in velocity can one expect by changing from a vertical bow position to a canted one? Most people lose some draw length when canting, the chronograph will tell you exactly how much, or if there was any at all. It can also tell what changes in equipment will do to performance. Changing arrows will change your initial velocity, as can changing the weight of the arrowhead, so can changing the bowstring or string material or adding things like string silencers. For those using Olympic bows, adjusting the draw weight or tiller will also affect the initial velocity. Even things like differences in nock tension may play a role. Without quantitative measurements, all you have is a guess. Proper use of the chronograph can help the high-tech archer choose the best possible equipment or combination for a given task.

A new device on the market is a doppler / radar chronograph that screws into the stabilizer bushing and can give an accurate velocity reading of each arrow fired. The concern with this type of device is that if it is used on a bow that is normally shot without a stabilizer or has a different stabilizer configuration compared to the archer's standard setup, then the feel or even performance of the bow may be altered.

You might be thinking, "This is a little more than I wanted to deal with; I just wanted to shoot bows and arrows." That's a valid point, and there's actually no requirement to go through the whole chronograph exercise, nor am I suggesting that a chronograph be on your next birthday's wish list. Most people don't bother, and do quite well for themselves. However, with small, portable chronographs costing less than a good set of arrows, it is an option that some may want to explore.

A final note on chronographs and bowhunters:

Remember that because of the way we set up the device, a few feet in front of the shooter, the only values we obtained were the initial velocities of the arrows. Given differences in arrow diameter, fletching material, size of feathers or vanes, offset and twist, the difference between the initial velocity and the velocity at 20 or 30 yards may not be consistent for all arrows. The initial velocity is basically a measure of an arrow's weight/mass and limb acceleration. Two arrows with the same weight/mass and spine should show the same speed. Because it doesn't take into account things like air resistance, they may have very different speeds downrange. The arrow with greater air resistance due to a larger shaft diameter and bigger fletching will have considerably less velocity at extended ranges than a small diameter shaft with small fletching. Bowhunters are concerned with the arrow's kinetic energy or momentum at impact, not when it leaves the bow. A thin arrow with very small straight vanes will retain more energy than an arrow of similar weight with a thicker diameter and large helical feathers. The only way to determine the speed at 20 or 30 yards, and so calculate the remaining kinetic energy or momentum at those distances is to have the chronograph 20 or 30 yards from the shooter and hope that his aim is good enough not to hit the machine! That's probably not a good idea, even for advanced shooters.

So, exactly how much tuning do you really need?

That's also a valid question. Clearly, someone new to archery would not benefit by some or most of the tuning measures discussed in this chapter. Quite simply, their shooting form isn't good enough to result in meaningful data, nor will they be shooting well enough to reap any real benefits. As a shooter becomes an archer, the bow will tell him what "else" needs to be done. If an archer truly believes that he has completed the shot sequence correctly and a knowledgeable observer concurs, but tighter groups or greater accuracy is required, then it's quite possible that additional tuning is in order.

Many Olympic or FITA type shooters believe that their equipment needs to be tuned to very exacting parameters to be competitive. Some believe that there may only be one specific arrow (type or spine) for a given bow. Is that really the case? The jury is still out on that one, but certainly the better an archer's form, the more precisely his equipment needs to be tuned to achieve his ultimate potential.

A word about tuning compound bows.

When compounds first appeared on the scene in the early 1970's, their owners shot them exactly as they did their previous stickbows. Those who used slights and cushion plungers on their stickbows used sights and plungers on their compounds. Those who didn't use sights or target accessories on their stickbows, also shot their new compounds without the extra equipment. What may not be obvious, is that the same laws of Physics that dictate the tuning of a stickbow carry over to the compound world.

If a compound bow is drawn and released with the fingers, as opposed to a mechanical release aid, then it follows the same rules described above for stickbows. It should be apparent that the determining factor in how a bow is tuned is more dependent on how it's shot, than the physical makeup or design of the bow.

As we saw when we discussed the archer's paradox, the initial flexing of the shaft happens because the string is moving directly forward and the arrow is off set slightly to one side. The forces on the arrow at release are what generate the spine requirements of the arrow. With the first compounds having a 35% to 50% let-off, the initial push was considerably less than a stickbow of equal peak weight. Then, the arrow experienced a second push when the cams flipped over and the peak weight (and limb acceleration) hit the arrow. Therefore, a softer-spined aluminum arrow could be used, and in that day, softer also meant a lighter arrow and, as you've guessed – a faster arrow.

The old method for compound spine determination was (peak weight + holding weight)/2. For example a 50# compound with a 35% let-off would give 35# at full draw (28") and so (50# + 35#)/2 = 37.5#. That would equate to an 1816, by our charts. At release, the arrow only experiences 35# of forward force; by the time the full peak weight of 50# hit, the arrow was effectively shorter, and so stiffer.

Several points should be noted: With a finger release, the rest on a compound needs a similar offset from center-shot as a recurve. It also needs a rest with some side pressure, be it a hard strike plate, or cushion plunger. Drop-away, fall away or under the arrow "forked" rests should not be used, as they provide minimal lateral pressure against the rotation of the string from the uncurling of the fingers at anchor and release.

A compound bow shot with a mechanical release aid can be tuned very close to center shot in lateral offset and the nockset can be located so the arrow is very close to perpendicular with the string for several reasons:

1. Since there is no lateral pressure from the release device, as is clearly present with a finger release, no lateral resistance is needed.
2. There is a single point of contact between the release device and the string and that negates the variability imparted by three separate fingers.
3. Since the string is released by the activation of a trigger, a precision intermediary between the human factor and the bow, the loosing of the string has a far greater chance of being perfect, or at least consistent, shot after shot.

In closing this section, consider the following:

Imagine the worst possible bow in design and performance ever made. Then imagine that bow strapped to a shooting machine that can hold the bow motionless while the string is drawn back to precisely the same draw length every time, and then released by a mechanical device. If the arrows being launched from that bow are identical to each other and closely matched in spine to the bow then the reality is that every arrow would land on top of the previous one in the target.

It would do that all day, at any given distance (assuming that the arrows were being shot in a no wind environment). There might be some downward shift if the string was to stretch or as temperature and humidity took a toll on the limbs, but that's about it.

The worst possible bow in the world would do the same thing, stacking arrow upon arrow in the target, as long as the shooter faithfully did his part!

As we start adding things to the bow, even something as simple as an arrow rest, we are naturally introducing points of variation or failure. Simply by going from a one-piece bow to a takedown bow, we're adding a theoretical "weak link". As we will see in the next section on bow design, a "weak link" is relative.

As discussed in the earlier tuning sections, a properly tuned system will stack arrow after arrow, even if they were not fletched. So it would stand to reason that the more moving parts, the less accurate the system would be over the long haul, simply because there are more things that could possibly fail or go out of adjustment.

A takedown limb pocket can fail or misalign, the rest can fall off the bow, a sight can be knocked out of calibration, even the feathers can fall off the arrow!

While that logic is unavoidable, we have to remember that we are human and not shooting machines. The devices we add to our equipment, arrow rests, stabilizers, even fletching, have very low failure rates. The "human" failure rate is much higher. By "our" failure rate we mean the possibility of being less than perfectly consistent on every shot, either in form or aim. These devices or gadgets minimize or dampen our inconsistencies, and in fact make us shoot more consistently over the long haul, rather than less. How's that for an "Archer's Paradox"?

Part 2

Equipment - A Detailed View

Chapter 8

Bow Design – Building a Virtual Bow

Basic Bow Design

Now that you have some shooting time under your belt, it's natural to be thinking about the mechanics of the equipment you're using and possibly your next bow. While arrows may be more important for accuracy and precision than the bow itself, without the bow, the arrows are just pointy sticks. Bow design tends to be a little more involved than arrow design. Esthetics may draw us to one style over another, but sooner or later we begin to look at bows in terms of performance. Features such as stability, speed or "cast", and forgiveness of shooter errors become at least as important as visual appeal. We want a bow that is stable in the hand, smooth to draw and forgiving of shooter errors. On top of that, we usually want the bow to be fast, or to cast an arrow well. How a bowyer combines those features is what sets his designs apart from his competitors for a specific niche of customers. At this point in our journey, we need to look at some of those features, see how they work, and understand the underlying principles.

Instead of simply defining a list of properties, or dos and don'ts, which may be mostly subjective, let's construct a ***"virtual"*** bow and examine various design scenarios and the results they yield. In the virtual world we can take advantage of things we couldn't or might not want to do in real life.

Building our virtual bow

Design 8.1 – The 2 x 4 bow (diag 8-1)

Let's start with a construction grade two-by-four inch by six foot piece of knot-free and straight grain pine. If we cut virtual string grooves on each end and put a string on it, we'd have a bow. It might be a little hard to pull, but since it's a virtual bow, that's not a problem. Let's assume that the bending will occur along the 2" thick side, and not the 4" thick side, or put another way, the face and back of the bow would be on the 4 inch sides; even in the virtual world that would make it easier to draw! Let's give it a brace height of 6". The two-by-four bow being "virtually" uniform scribes a uniform arc from nock to nock. Uniform in this case means that a straight edge placed anywhere along the back of the bow would show the same tangent (diag 8-2). We would also realize that the wood on the back of the bow would need to stretch or expand, and the wood on the belly of the bow would need to compress an equal amount. As the bow was drawn to 28" the back would need to expand even more and the belly would likewise experience greater compression, so the draw weight would increase. In this case, the wood farther away from the centerline of the bow would experience greater expansion or contraction (diag 8-3).

When we reach a draw length where either the back section can no longer expand (expansion limit or breaking point) or the belly can no longer compress (compression limit), the draw weight begins increasing at an exponential rate. At that point the bow is said to be stacking – a property that all bows will exhibit at some point. Hopefully that point will be greater than the archer's draw length. If the bow were made of a material that allowed infinite expansion and compression (remember this is a virtual bow, so we can do stuff like that) stacking may still possible. If the limbs are drawn to a point where the bending geometry is such that the bow is no longer bending, but rather the drawing force begins pulling the limbs apart longitudinally, the bow is still said to stack. To picture this, assume the draw length was so great that the limb tips were nearly parallel to each other, an extreme case, but possible. Here the bow's limbs would approximate a sideways letter "U", and as the drawing force continued, the limbs would, by necessity, be pulled apart (diag 8-4).

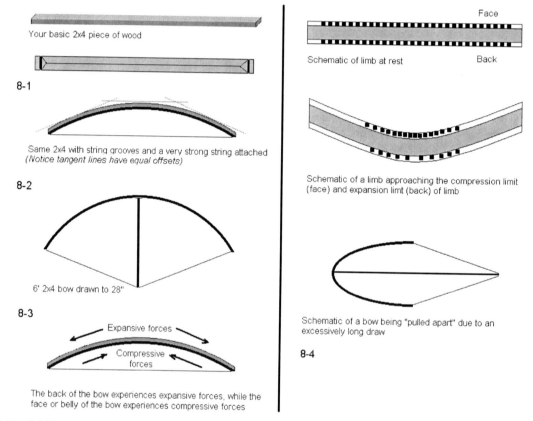

8-1 to 8-3 *Your standard 2x4 piece of wood with a few modifications (left)!*
8-4 *Exceeding the compression or expansion limits of the limb surfaces or the limbs being pulled apart rather than bent as shown here will cause stacking (right).*

Stacking either before one's full-draw length, or even at draw length is an undesirable property. It makes the bow uncomfortable to draw and shoot, and in turn hinders accuracy.

Design 8.1 Recap: The basic 2x4 bow, limb expansion/compression limits, and stacking.

Design 8.2 – The 2x4 bow, stage 1: Effects of bow length
Let's recreate the bow, but this time, instead of making it six feet long, we'll make it three feet long and give it the same brace height. The same laws of physics apply, but the bow would describe a tighter arc. At rest, there would be increased expansion and compression as compared to the original six-foot bow; the expansion and contraction would also magnify as we

drew it to the same 28" draw length. Naturally, more force would be required to draw the bow the same amount, and you'd expect that the limbs would accelerate faster when the string was released. That is exactly what happens. In this example a shorter bow should yield a faster arrow than a longer bow of similar design.

With a shorter bow, the possibility of reaching the stack point or expansion and compression limits before your full draw would also be greater. Likewise, you'd also increase the possibility of going from flexing or bending the limbs to pulling them longitudinally apart, which would also increase the feeling of stacking or actually break the bow. You would also notice that with the shorter bow, as the string was drawn back to anchor, the angle around the fingers of the drawing hand would become more acute. This is referred to as "finger pinch" and like stacking, is not a desirable property. Finger pinch is not only uncomfortable for the shooter, but can make the release more difficult, as the string will not leave the fingers cleanly (diag 8-5). Further, as discussed in the tuning section, once limbs have become over-stressed, tuning becomes impossible.

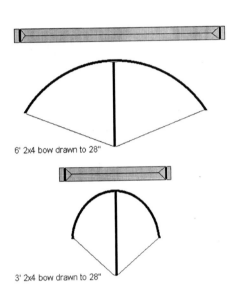

6' 2x4 bow drawn to 28"

3' 2x4 bow drawn to 28"

8-5 Differences in the arcs of a 6' bow vs. a 3' bow drawn to 28" (Note: It is not possible to draw a 36" bow to 28" – the above diagram and related text are only given as examples to demonstrate a concept. left).
8-5a This archer has a 33" draw length, combine that with most 60" bows and you'll have a problem. Notice the angle the string makes with the limb tip. In this case, the limbs were so over-stressed the bow was impossible to tune. The severe finger pinch didn't help accuracy either (right)!

For a long time, tables were drawn to suggest a specific bow length for a known draw length. This was a real concern when self bows (bows made from a single material, as our virtual two-by-four bow) were common. This was necessary to allow for a comfortable draw, maximum cast, and to prevent damage to the bow as selfbows had a tendency to fail if over-drawn. With the advent of fiberglass, wood and carbon laminated bows the concern has all but vanished. While it's true that an archer with a 32" draw would be more comfortable with a 66" or greater length bow, there are many shorter bows available that will accommodate those with a longer draw length. Whether that particular archer would be comfortable shooting a shorter bow is a matter of personal preference or possibly tolerance, but there is no physical reason why he couldn't.

Design 8.2 recap: Given two bows of the same design and material, the shorter bow will require greater force to be drawn to a specific length, but will tend to shoot an arrow faster than a longer bow. The shorter bow may be less comfortable to shoot as it will reach its stack point sooner and will have increased finger pinch.

Design 8.3 – The two-by-four bow, stage 2: Limb thickness
Even thought this is a virtual bow, a two-by-four isn't going to be the easiest thing to hold on to physically. So let's cut it in half lengthwise. Now, instead of having a two-by-four bow we have a two-by-two bow. The first thing we should notice is that the bow is now easier to draw, probably about 50% easier. As we cut the bow in half its draw weight should be roughly half of what it was before. If this were a real bow, we might notice that as the limbs are now half as wide, they may accelerate faster than when the bow was a two-by-four. There are two reasons for this; first and most importantly, the limbs have less mass – the less mass, the less inertia or internal resistance to movement and the quicker they will accelerate. A second but significantly less important reason is that since the limbs are thinner, there's less air resistance as they travel forward.

Design 8.3 Recap: A two-by-two piece of wood is easier to hold in one's hand than a two-by-four piece of wood. Thinner limbs require less force to bend than thicker ones and the less mass the limbs have, the faster they will accelerate.

Design 8.4 – The two-by-four bow, stage 3: Tapering the limbs
We now have the rudiments for a bow, albeit not an efficient one. A two by two inch by six foot piece of pine will propel an arrow, but will require considerable force (archer's strength) and will not cast an arrow very well. The parts of the bow's limbs that directly accelerate the string, and so the arrow, are the limb tips. As we have seen, the less mass, the less inertia, and the more quickly the limbs can accelerate. Instead of simply cutting the two-by-two, or bow "stave", down to one inch by one inch, let's leave it as a two-by-two section at the center of the stave and then taper the face and sides of the stave to the nock end. (Stave is an ancient term for the wooden board destined to become a bow.) The ends will be approximately 1"x 1" (diag 8-6). We'll leave the back flat (without taper) to help maintain consistent expansion as the bow is drawn.

We have again lightened the bow's draw weight, and we find that when we draw the bow the limbs no longer describe a perfect arc. The distal parts of the limbs bend into a tighter arc (have a tighter radius) than the proximal parts. We have decreased the mass where it will make the most significant benefit, at the limb tips; that should allow them to accelerate even faster (diag 8-7).

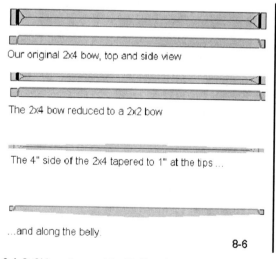

Our original 2x4 bow, top and side view

The 2x4 bow reduced to a 2x2 bow

The 4" side of the 2x4 tapered to 1" at the tips ...

...and along the belly.

8-6

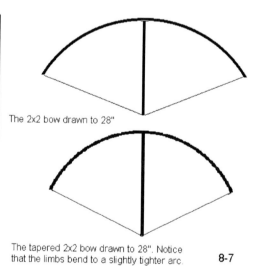

The 2x2 bow drawn to 28"

The tapered 2x2 bow drawn to 28". Notice that the limbs bend to a slightly tighter arc.

8-7

8-6 A 2x2' bow tapered to 1"x1" at the limb tips (left)
8-7 Here we see the difference in the limb arcs of the non-tapered vs. the tapered bow (right)

Note – if we were to round off all the edges, this design would actually be very similar to the original English Longbows used in the 12th through 16th centuries which are still in demand today by archers wishing to relive the past glories of archery.

Design 8.4 recap: Tapering the sides and face of the limbs results in less mass at the limb tips and allows for faster limb tip, and so, arrow acceleration.

Design 8.5 – The two-by-four bow, stage 4: Limb thickness, refined
We have narrowed the width of the limbs and have seen some improvement in performance. The next step is to reduce the limb thickness. Since the back of the limb has to expand and the belly has to compress, excessive expansion or compression can make the bow prone to failure. A way of reducing that risk of failure is to make the limb thinner. For this part of the exercise let's mark off a six inch area at the middle of the stave to be left square; do a flat taper from 2" near the center 6" block and taper the belly from that to about 3/8" at the limb tip. The bow is lighter still, and should be casting a virtual arrow a little more efficiently (diag 8-8).

To further this idea, instead of a straight taper let's make a sharp taper from the six inch center section to approximately another six inches above and below on the belly side. That means it will go from 2" to 3/8" in the six inch "fade out" or feathering area, and then remain at 3/8" to the tips. We're now starting to increase the efficiency of the bow by enhancing the "working" part of the limbs. As there is less distance between the expansion side (back) and the compression side (belly), we have lessened the draw weight (easier to shoot), made it faster (less limb mass) and have increased its durability. As the surfaces on the edges and sides are closer together, the actual expansion and compression required has been lessened (diag 8-9).

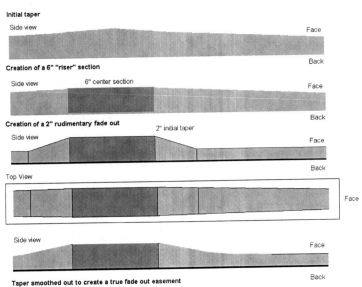

8-8 and 8-9 Further thinning of the limb tapers increases efficiency Adding fade-outs to the limb roots eases the transition from the rigid riser to the flexible limbs. (In this case both the riser and limbs are flexible, but the degrees of flexibility vary considerably.)

As we draw our "bow", one problem will become apparent. In addition to finding it lighter in draw weight and seeing that the tips are bending in a tighter arc than the rest of the limbs, we should see that there is a noticeable bend where the 6" taper area meets the 3/8" flat of the working limbs. Making the taper on the belly slightly concave and smoothing it into the working part of the limbs can alleviate this. What we have now reproduced is the evolution of the

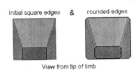

8-10 Rounding or smoothing out the sharp edges not only makes the bow look neater but will increase its durability.

English long bow design into the so-called American Flat bow. By simply rounding off all the edges, which promotes more even flexing and helps to prevent edge slivers from breaking free and attaching an appropriate string, we in theory now have a fully functional flat bow (diag 8-10).

We now have a working bow, and I know of at least one bowyer who indeed makes flat bows from commercial grade two-by-fours, in a very similar manner to our virtual bow construction. The exact dimensions of the bow, length, limb thickness and tapers are dependent on the required final draw weight of the bow and the functional theories and principles of the individual bowyer's experience. All that remains in this case is shaping the grip area to suit the shooter and applying a finish. But we're not done yet; there's a lot more that can be done in the virtual and not-so-virtual world.

Design 8.5 Recap: Less limb mass equals faster acceleration; the flatter the limb, the less expansion and compression forces the back and belly must tolerate. Rounded edges yield smoother or more even flexing and prevent limb edge slivering.

While a pine two-by-four can make a very serviceable bow, we'll see that pine may not be the best material to use for optimal performance or efficiency. For a self-bow, the properties we seek (as evidenced by the design features previously discussed) are the ability to withstand stretching and compression, low mass or weight, and also strength/durability.

Historically, English Yew (Taxus Baccata) has been a bowyer's dream wood. It's light in weight, strong and has grain patterns that, if oriented correctly, could withstand both expansion and compression. The famed English Longbows were made primarily from yew. Unfortunately, very little yew is grown in England, but so important was yew to the English war effort that a tariff was imposed on countries trading with England: with every shipment of goods imported to England, a specified number of yew staves were required to be included in the shipment.

Other bow woods of merit were Hickory, Osage Orange and Lemonwood. All made quite respectable bows, and still do, but because of actual functional properties or the prevailing sentiment, yew was considered the king of bow woods. Bamboo, while not used in England or Europe, was renowned in the Orient for bow making. Even lighter than yew, its strength and flexibility have made it an exceptional limb material. Several bowyers use it today for both longbows and recurves with outstanding results. The Howard Hill Archery company, crafting longbows in what has come to be known as the "D" or Hill style, uses several laminations of Bamboo on their high-end bows and claims an increase of six feet per second over a yew bow of equal draw weight.

Before leaving the realm of selfbows, there's one other task that needs to be considered when building a bow in the real world – tillering. Tillering is the process of modifying a limb by sanding, planing, shaving or scraping wood, usually from the belly of the limbs so that they bend evenly, or with the desired amount of unevenness. Since we are dealing with a virtual bow here, we really need not worry about tillering, but it still deserves mention. Wood, being wood, is hardly uniform, so even if great care is taken to measure the upper and lower limb dimensions precisely, the odds are when the bow is strung, the limbs may not bend uniformly. The only way to correct this is to remove wood from the part of the limb that is "strong" or isn't bending enough to match the rest of the limb or the corresponding part on the opposite limb. Depending on the actual imbalance, this can be a tedious process. Typically, bows are tillered with the lower limb slightly strong or stiff in relation to the upper limb, because there's usually more force exerted on the lower limb, due to the position of the hand on the string. There are a few different theories on tillering, each with their devotees. Happily in the virtual bow world, we don't have to worry about that too much!

Laminated bows also need to be tillered to achieve proper flexure. While the method for removing excess material may be slightly different, the principles are exactly the same. (Tillering was also briefly discussed in the chapter on Olympic style tuning. The individual limbs were tillered along their length during the manufacturing process, and given the riser adjustments, the archer can individualize the tiller to his needs or preferences.)

Another property of wood self-bows was that of "string follow". Wood, being a natural material despite its springy property, has a habit of not returning to its original position after being strung for a while and then unstrung. This property is called "following the string" or simply string follow.

While it isn't a terrible thing in itself, it did cause selfbows after a while to lose some of their draw weight and that in turn lessened cast. Old selfbows were also known to lose cast if held at anchor too long.

Beyond selfbows: Rebirth of the laminated bow

As we have seen, the real work of the limbs takes place on the back and belly surfaces of the bow and the thinner and lighter the limbs are, the faster they can accelerate. Somewhere along the historical time-line, someone had the idea to glue or laminate two or more woods together to make a better bow. The thinking was, if you could find one wood or "material" that was able to withstand the stretching required on the back of the bow and another wood or "material" that could withstand compression better on the belly, you'd have the best of both worlds.

Composite bows, as described above, actually predated the English longbows by several centuries. For example: the existence of composite war bows has been recorded in Chinese history as far back 2,000 years ago. It was not until the middle of the 20th century that they reappeared in modern form.

Design 8.6 – Use of bow laminations
From the above, is quite evident that laminated bows are nothing new. Many materials have been used to create bow laminations, including various types of woods, sinew, and various animal skins. Usually, the back of the bow was laminated, as the expansive forces caused greater concern than the compressive forces. It is far beyond the scope of this book to describe everything that has been or could be used to back or laminate a bow. Suffice it to say that laminating a bow goes a long way to increase the limbs' durability and performance. Laminations also add color and style to a bow, so there's an aesthetic benefit to be gained as well (diag 8-11).

Side view   Face

Added material "laminated" to the back of our redesigned 2x4 bow   Back
8-11

8-11 The laminated bow limb.

Design 8.6 recap: Limb laminations increase durability and performance.

Design 8.7 Fiberglass as a bow material.
In the 1950's it was found that fiberglass made a very practical bow material. It was durable, inexpensive, easy to mass-produce and unlike wood, it was unaffected by temperature and moisture. Its main drawback was that it was heavier or denser than most woods, and so solid fiberglass bows lacked the cast that the premier wooden bows of the period offered. Still, many solid fiberglass bows were and are being manufactured and are usually sold as youth or beginner bows. Most of us who began our archery careers as children of the 1960's and 70's began with a solid fiberglass bow. (I *bought* my first solid fiberglass bow and cedar arrows by selling Christmas cards at the age of eleven.) As the "Golden Age of Archery" began, the idea of laminating the back and belly of a bow with fiberglass became a reality.

Our next step is to take a sheet of lightweight wood, such as rock maple, and sandwich it between two layers of fiberglass. We have just created the beginnings of a modern fiberglass laminated bow (diag 8-12). By simply manipulating the space or distance between the two layers of fiberglass with varying widths of wood core, the draw weight of the bow could now be adjusted with a high degree of accuracy. This is possible given the higher modulus ratio of fiberglass compared to that of the wood core. The limbs are now thinner and lighter, and as we've seen from the earlier examples that has resulted in a new standard for performance.

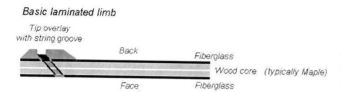

Basic laminated limb

8-12 *Adding fiberglass laminations increases the modulus (resistance to deformation under stress) of the surface areas of the bow, making the bow stronger and lighter.*

As wood contains irregularities, using two thinner layers of wood instead of one for the core allowed the bowyer to match the properties of weight and density more closely. That is exactly how modern wood core laminated bows are made. Some bowyers actually use three, four, or five layers of core material between the fiberglass to further enhance uniformity and smoothness of draw. It has been my experience that the benefits of adding layers, beyond two or three, rapidly reaches a point of diminishing returns.

Design 8.7 recap: The use of fiberglass as a bow material heralded a new age in the development of modern archery equipment. The combination of a lightweight wood core sandwiched between high modulus fiberglass sheets yielded a significant performance gain over either material alone.

Design 8.8 - Review
Let's review what we have done so far. We have a bow that is straight from end to end along its back and six feet long; it has laterally tapered limbs, starting about 3/8" at the tips to about two inches approximately nine inches from the center point (diag 8-13). The center section is six inches long and two inches round; it has a six-inch section on each side with a concave taper on the belly to approximately 3/8" at the limb tips. We'll assume that string nocks have magically appeared on each end, and that the bow now has a maple core. (Maple, as mentioned above, has been a standard for wood core laminated bows for half a century.) We'll also assume that it has layers of fiberglass (your choice of colors) glued (laminated) to its back and belly. That's the wonderful thing about making a virtual bow, the actual assembly process is painless!

8-13 *Our first completed bow.*

In addition to the increased strength and cast afforded by the lamination of fiberglass to a wood core, the lamination process also gives us the ability to change the shape of the bow, almost at will. Whatever shape the components are laminated into by the molds used to hold the bow together while the glue is curing, will be the shape in which the bow will remain indefinitely (diag 8-14). The fiberglass/wood laminations will resist string follow for decades even if the bow were to remain braced.

Heated bow press

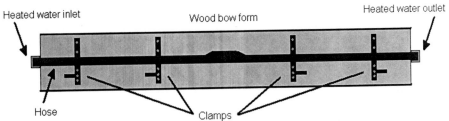

8-14 Laminating a longbow in a bow form or "bow press". This model uses a hot water hose to facilitate curing, but electric heating elements can also be used.

Building a laminated bow in a non-virtual world

Real bowyers do not have the luxury of building or selling virtual bows. To make a laminated bow, the first thing a bowyer needs is a design. With that in mind he builds a wooden form to match the outline of the face and belly of his design. The sheets of fiberglass, wood core, and riser's mating surfaces are coated with glue and sandwiched between the two halves of the "form". The form is then clamped together, and the glue is allowed to cure. Heat is sometimes applied to hasten and fortify the curing.

Once the glue has cured, the "bow" is removed, and the final curvature of the limbs is established. The riser is shaped, the limbs' edges smoothed, and string nocks cut. It's temporarily strung and if all glue joints appear solid, the bow's draw weight is checked and then it's tillered as necessary. Final shaping is done and a finish is applied.

Before we leave the topic of fiberglass as a limb backing (and facing) material, it's interesting to mention how glass color can also be a factor in overall performance. While glass color is generally considered only a cosmetic feature, experiments have shown that color does matter! We spoke of the modulus of a given material (modulus being the physical measurement of the stiffness of a material, equaling the ratio of applied load or stress to the resultant deformity), and in fiberglass the added pigment (color) affects the modulus. The greater the amount of pigment required, the poorer the modulus. It was found that gray was the worst color for fiberglass, as it required the greatest amount of pigment. White was almost as bad, and as you would expect, clear was the best, as it required no pigment to be added. Black was a close second, but the difference was minor.

If you're scratching your head now as to why target bow limbs were classically white, and current Olympic limbs have a gray color, you're not alone. The other part of the equation is white reflects light, and therefore heat, better than black or clear. Using black limbs absorbs heat, and so could change the shooting characteristics of a bow over the course of a day's outdoor shooting. The gray colors on today's carbon limbs are only painted on, and not a part of the carbon or fiberglass.

Design 8.8 recap: Review of our progress leading to our first laminated bow, and a closer look at fiberglass laminations.

Design 8.9 First shape modification – Limb reflex/deflex
For our first modification, let's tilt the limbs either out or away from the shooter ("reflexed") and then tilt them in or toward the shooter ("deflexed"). Again, thanks to the virtual world, we'll assume that we have bow forms to shape the bow any way we want and strings that will brace the bows to the same brace height, regardless of the limb position (diag 8-15).

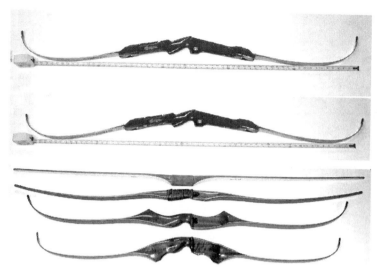

8-15a Reflex vs. deflex in limbs. A Hoyt Gold Medalist allows for tiller adjustment. The top picture shows the limbs in full reflex, increasing both draw weight and speed. The bottom picture shows the limbs in full deflex, which may add stability while diminishing performance (top two pictures).
8-15b Shows the "evolution" (bottom picture from top to bottom) from a mildly reflexed Hill style longbow (Hill Redman) to a Reflex/Deflex longbow (Jeffery Trophy) to a semi recurve (Ben Pearson Javelina) to a full working recurve (Ben Pearson Mercury Hunter).

With the reflexed limbs, the first thing we notice is that the bow is heavier to draw. That's pretty intuitive since we are bending the limbs to a greater degree and they are effectively starting farther away from the shooter. When we shoot our virtual (correctly spined) arrow, we see that it has greater cast or speed than when the limbs were not reflexed. What might be surprising, is that the increase in cast or speed is greater than what could be accounted for by the increase in draw weight alone. Hold that thought. (In our virtual world, we could prove this simply by making another bow with straight or non-reflexed limbs with the same draw weight as our reflex bow and shooting virtual arrows through a virtual chronograph.)

If we deflexed the limbs, we would expect the converse to be true, and yes, there would be a decrease in draw weight and a disproportionate decrease in cast or speed.

What we have just demonstrated is an example of how reflexed and deflexed limbs can change the degree of pre-load on the bow. The greater the pre-load, the more highly stressed the limbs are and the greater their ability to accelerate, the less pre-load, the slower the acceleration. Simply put, the pre-load is the amount of stress the limbs experience at rest and during the early stages of the draw. A bow with a higher pre-load will stress the limbs earlier and to a greater degree than one with less pre-load. Another advantage of pre-loading the limbs is that it helps stabilize the string as it returns to brace height by dampening its amplitude of vibration on shock.

The drawback that we did not demonstrate, is that if too much pre-load is designed into a bow archers will find the bow is more critical to shoot accurately or consistently, or put another way, the bow will be less forgiving to shooter error. Here too, the converse holds; the less reflex, or greater deflex, the less critical and more forgiving the bow will be to shoot. Part of the bowyer's skill in designing a bow is to be able find the best compromise between reflex/deflex and cast/forgiveness. As we discussed in the tuning section, most Olympic type bows are equipped with tiller adjustments so the archer can find the degree of reflex or deflex that works best for his or her shooting style.

Design 8.9 recap: Increasing limb reflex increases performance at the cost of forgiveness, while increasing limb deflex increases forgiveness at the cost of performance. Most bowyers try to find a compromise between the two.

Design 8.10 Second shape modification – riser reflex/deflex
What was just said about limb reflex and deflex may or may not also hold true for the riser.

Some bowyers believe that making a riser with more reflex, pointing its ends away from the shooter from the pivot point (grip), will increase performance, and making the riser more deflex will enhance forgiveness. Some bowyers believe the exact opposite. Most high performance bows today employ deflexed riser geometry and slightly reflexed limbs with moderate pre-load. While there are numerous variations, the aforementioned configuration has proven itself repeatedly since the 1960's, so that will be our next modification.

In the golden era of archery, a very popular approach was to make bows with highly deflexed risers called "V" risers and relatively reflexed limbs. That idea tried to capitalize on both principles; it actually worked quite well (diag 8-16). Target bows also evolved into a form with mildly deflexed risers and slightly reflexed limbs.

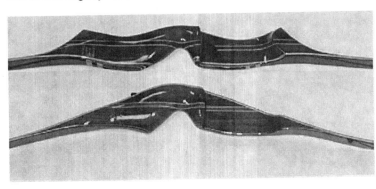

8-16 Reflex vs. deflex in the riser. Here we see two Browning recurves, The 62" Explorer II (top) shows a fairly straight or reflexed riser design and the 58" Cobra II shows a more deflexed riser.

Design 8.10 recap: A riser's reflex and/or deflex can also affect bow performance. While several theories are currently in use, a deflexed riser geometry with slightly reflexed limbs resulting in moderate pre-load seems to be the favorite.

Design 8.11 Mixing and matching
In addition to combining separate degrees of reflex and deflex in the risers and the limbs, combining reflex and deflex in various parts of the limbs alone is not only possible but also desirable. By magically manipulating the shape of our bow form, we can give one part of the limb, the part proximal to the center of the bow, a degree of reflex and the more distal part some deflex, or vice versa. The purpose here is for the bowyer to find the best combination of reflex/deflex, or R/D for short, to give the archer the best possible combination of performance and stability.

The R/D design is not theoretical, as most recurves are employing some R/D design features. Today, many bowyers are making R/D longbows with varying amount of reflex and deflex in the limbs and achieving remarkable results. The end results are so-called longbows that rival the performance and stability of the best recurves. In effect, they are recurves that have had the "curve" drawn out over the entire limb, while retaining the general straight limbed shape of a longbow when strung (diag 8-17).

8-17 R/D on this longbow is little more than the recurved part of the recurve limb extended over the length of the limb (Ancient Spirits longbow).

The idea of offsetting a limb or riser toward or away from the shooter is not new. Historical evidence, including artifacts and artwork, shows several groups of people using severe limb curvatures to enhance performance. It is unclear when the terms reflex and deflex were coined, however. It seems that with archery some things just take a little time to be rediscovered and renamed. As we've seen, to achieve these same results today, there needs to be considerable trial and error, sometimes called "Research and Development"; maybe that's where the R and D came from!

Design 8.11 recap: The combination of R/D, both in riser and limb design, can yield a bow with both outstanding performance and stability.

Design 8.12 Development of the recurve limb
Along with the idea of reflexing a limb came the idea that if the ends of the limb tips were severely reflexed away from the shooter, the effect of a reflexed limb would be enhanced. By "re" curving the distal parts of the limbs, the action of drawing the bow not only bent the limbs linearly, but also caused the limbs to uncurl. Naturally, if they uncurled during the draw, they would have to "re" curl during the power stroke. That recurling allowed the limbs to accelerate faster and cast the arrow faster. The fact that the limbs were curled in the strung resting position also allowed the overall length of the bow to be reduced while maintaining the same functional length. To say it another way, the bow was physically shorter, but behaved as if it were actually longer. As we discussed in Chapter 1 on equipment basics, the length of a bow is measured from string nock to string nock along the curvature of the back of the bow. A 70" straight limbed long bow for example is usually 71-72" in total length, owing to the length of the limb tips distal to the string grooves. A 70" recurve when measured end to end along a straight line, might only be 64" – 65", yet, both bows have the same functional length.

As with R/D longbow designs, each bowyer has his own theories based on his experiments and observations of what design, or in this case curvature, will perform the best. While the idea of recurved limbs existed before the use of modern fiberglass laminates, recurved limbs on selfbows were by and large limited to what was termed a static recurve limb tip. In that design, the distal few inches of the limbs were built up with additional wood and reflexed away from the shooter. While it did give the advantage of a reflexed limb, its static nature did not provide the uncurling and recurling of a true "working" recurve. Remarkably, some static recurves perform quite well.

Another term often heard is "semi"-recurve. A semi-recurve simply has less of a distal curvature or recurve than a full working recurve. This had the added benefit of a reflexed limb and some of the curling effect of a full working recurve, but to a much lesser extent. Semi-recurve limbs were typically used on less expensive or entry-level bows, possibly because they had wider manufacturing tolerances and could be produced more economically. Before the popularity of R/D longbows, it was considered common knowledge that pound for pound a recurve would be faster than a straight limbed long or flat bow; that thinking has been changing over recent years.

Design 8.12 recap: Recurving or curving the limb tips away from the shooter gives them the ability to uncurl during the draw and re-curl during the power stroke, increasing the speed at which the limb tips can accelerate.

Performance summary
The preceding sections discussed the basic features of limb and riser design. A bowyer with enough experience and creativity can manipulate limb length, limb thickness, degrees of taper, type of curvature and placement of the curves to create what he feels will give the shooter the best bow for his specific needs. The purpose can be elite target competition, hunting dangerous game, or casual shooting in the back yard. By modifying production techniques, he can tailor the bow to the target audience's budget.

Many archers believe that a bow's performance is based solely on limb design, and accuracy or stability on riser design. That's a very broad statement, and it doesn't really tell the whole story. While the limbs may well be the driving force behind the arrow, without a complementary or effective riser design the limbs would not be able to transfer their energy efficiently to the arrow.

Conversely, limbs that stack prematurely or draw unevenly may have a detrimental effect on the archer's accuracy. A well-designed and well-made bow really is a package deal. In the next section we'll try to show the role riser design can play in both shooter accuracy and performance.

Efficiency

Before we leave the topic of performance, we need to discuss bow efficiency. What we mean by efficiency is the amount of work we put into a system, compared to the amount we get out. No system is 100% efficient, but the closer it is to 100%, the better. If we look at a bow's efficiency, we are comparing the amount of force we put in, the draw weight at our draw length, with the force of the arrow has either leaving the bow or when it hits the target.

If we use a 50#@28" bow as an example, it takes 50# to draw the string back to 28" and keep the system in equilibrium. When the string is released, that 50# should be used to accelerate the limbs forward or back to their braced or resting position. Unfortunately, there are several things going on that reduce the force that the arrow will ultimately have before it reaches its target.

- As the limb is being bent, materials are being compressed and stretched. That compression and stretching uses energy that would otherwise end up in the arrow.

- As the limbs move forward, friction within the limb materials on a molecular level also wastes energy.

- The limbs have to move their own weight, as well as the weight of the string and anything on the string, such as string silencers, serving material, and even nocking points.

- The riser, depending on its rigidity, may also dissipate energy.

- The farther a bow is from center-shot, the more energy is required to bend the arrow during paradox, which otherwise could have been used to propel the arrow forward.

There are other factors involved, but it's clear that there are energy losses. An efficiency rating of 80% to 90% is considered extremely high and 70% to 80%, very good. Most bows fall into an efficiency range of 55% - 70%. We'll discuss how to calculate or rather approximate bow efficiency later.

Design 8.13 – Refining the handle or "getting a grip"

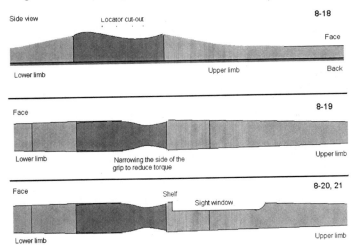

8-18 Creating a locator grip on the 2x2 bow helps the archer maintain a more consistent grip.

8-19 Creating a smaller grip near the upper section called the throat can help reduce hand torque.

8-20 and 8-21 Creating a sight window allows the arrow to be closer to center shot and provides a better view of the target and a shelf provides consistent arrow placement.

Our virtual bow still has a 2" x 2" rounded, 6" long midsection for a handle or grip. While it's utilitarian and functional, it is not very comfortable, nor conducive to accuracy or consistency. One thing we can do to help in the accuracy department is to create a locator grip. That simply means removing some of the wood from the belly side, giving it a more concave shape deepest near the top of the grip (diag 8-18). That will help our hands return to the same place every time we take hold of the bow. Next, we might remove some wood from the sides of the handle section. The thinner handle may fit our hands better and also help reduce torque (diag 8-19). We might also remove a wedge of wood from the left side (when viewed from the back) to create a sight window and shelf (diag 8-20).

8-21a The Ancient Spirits longbow has a locator grip, actually quite similar to today's compound bows!

Creating a sight window will do three things:

- Get the arrow closer to center shot, which should help in tuning
- Give us a constant position for the arrow on the bow, which helps our consistency
- Give us a better view past the riser, if we hold the bow vertically

The length of the sight window will, of course, depend on the length of the newly defined riser section. Let's say, we've designed a sight window cutout similar to what's in current use on most recurve bows. That will give us a vertical flat area parallel to the opposite side of the riser, and an arrow shelf perpendicular to the long axis of the bow (diag 8-21). As we've learned in the basic setup and bow tuning sections, while it's possible simply to shoot off the shelf, a far better option would be to use some kind of arrow rest. It's also advantageous to be able to adjust the degree of center shot to tune-in the correct dynamic arrow spine, so let's install a bushing to allow the use of an adjustable arrow plate. This can be as simple as a threaded bushing and screw with a lock nut to move the arrow away from the riser the desired amount (diag 8-22a) or a cushion plunger to allow further tuning options (diag 22b).

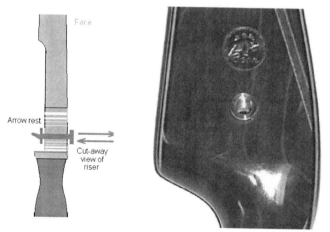

8-22a Placement of an adjustable arrow rest on the newly formed sight window (left).

8-22b Insertion of a bushing for a rest or cushion plunger on a Bear Tamerlane (right).

The next logical step would be to reshape the riser section into more of a pistol grip that fits into the hand more naturally. Since this is virtual bow we can even make it form fitting to the shooter's hand (diag 8-23). Remember that the grip is the interface between the archer and the bow; the better and more comfortable the grip, the better the shot.

Side view

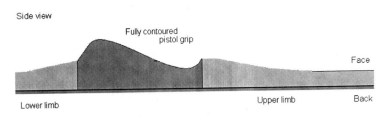

Fully contoured pistol grip

Face

Lower limb   Upper limb   Back

8-23 *Further refining the grip to a pistol grip configuration.*

If you recall our discussion on shooting technique, grabbing the bow on release and twisting or torqueing the handle usually has a negative effect on our shooting accuracy. The typical symptom is an unexplained left group for a right-handed shooter. This was considered so critical that in the 1970's many bow manufacturers designed their target bows and some of their hunting bows with very small "torque-free" grip areas. In addition to metal-risered bows of that era which sported exceptionally small grips, the Wing Archery Slim line series was based on that principle and the Bear Super Kodiak hunting bows sported very small "throat" areas for several years (diag 8-24 and 8-25).

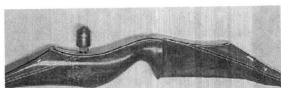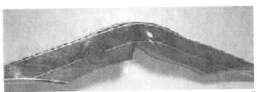

8-24 and 8-25 Bear Super Kodiak (left) and Wing Slim Line bows (right) took advantage of the very small torque-free grip design.

It must be mentioned that there are a number of archers who actually prefer the blocky, squared off grip that's still standard fare on many longbows. They believe that type of grip fits in their hands well and there is no need to change to anything else. It's unclear where that notion came from, but it can possibly be traced back to a quote from Howard Hill who stated in his memoirs that he preferred a straight-risered longbow. Most people find the exact opposite to be true. A pistol type grip provides both shot comfort and shot consistency, and therefore, accuracy.

Design 8.13 Recap: The addition of a locator or pistol type grip and arrow shelf can enhance both shooting comfort and accuracy. Adding the ability to adjust the degree of center shot makes bow tuning easier.

Design 8.14 Riser length vs. limb length
Now we have a bow with straight, R/D, recurved limbs, or some combination of the three, a length of 70" or less and a riser with some type of contoured grip and arrow shelf. Not too bad actually, but there's still work to be done.

If we keep the bow full length, the riser section including the fade out areas still measures about 18" and each limb about 27". Through the continuing magic of virtual reality, let's change the dimensions so the riser is now 36" from fade out to fade out and the limbs become approximately 14" each. This is an extreme case, but it's a virtual bow so we can do whatever we want and fix it later if we have to! What we now see is that the very short limbs need to bend into a tighter arc to reach the same draw length than they had to before we shortened them. This results in a draw weight increase and the arrow's cast should also increase. We'll also reach the stack point of the limbs earlier in the draw, but the string angle around our fingers hasn't changed to any appreciable degree.

If we were to keep the overall bow length the same but modify the riser, and so the limb length, we'd reach a point where there would still be a performance gain over the initial design. We would also maintain a smooth draw to archer's anchor if we chose our lengths correctly.

For our purposes, let's arbitrarily say that through virtual trial and error, we've determined that our optimal configuration is a 24" riser and a pair of 21" limbs. Some quick math shows that we now have a 66" bow that draws smoothly to our draw length and has optimal performance.

At this time it is probably a good idea to step out of the virtual world for a few moments and discuss non-virtual reality. In the real world, if we have two bows, the bow that shoots a faster arrow at a 28" draw length will shoot faster than the other bow even at a 25" draw length, a 32" draw length or any draw length in between. There really isn't a magic draw length where a given set of limbs will "come alive". An archer with a longer draw length will always get more performance out of a given bow than would an archer with a shorter draw length. It's been shown that an extra inch in draw length will result in an extra 8-10 fps, providing the same weight arrow is used. *Put another way, adding an inch to one's draw length may increase the draw weight by 2 to 3 pounds, but will increase the performance of the bow as if its draw weight had actually been increased by 10 pounds.*

Also, in theory, and the key word is THEORY, you should get the same results, meaning a faster arrow, if you were able to shrink a given bow, say from our 70" virtual bow to a 60" virtual bow and maintain the exact same design and weight. Unfortunately, when you change the length, you usually do impart some design changes. If you recall, that's what we demonstrated in Design 8.1.

In the 60's and 70's, the Browning Firearms Company made some excellent hunting bows. Most models came in a "1" series and a "2" series, For example, an Explorer 1 was 56" and an Explorer 2 was 62", the Cobra 1 was 56" and the Cobra 2 was 60". The shorter bows showed a modest speed increase, but they were a little quirkier to shoot accurately, especially over extended shooting sessions.

Design 8.14 recap: Modifying the relative length of the riser and limbs can change the shooting characteristics of a given bow for a given shooter.

Design 8.15 Subjective (and not so subjective) features
We've discussed a lot of objective data regarding bow design, in a "tip of the iceberg" sort of way. Before we look at some more concrete examples on how this stuff works outside the virtual world, we really need to look at some subjective features that can play as important a role in defining a perfect bow for a particular archer as the objective ones.

We should now have a 66" bow with some R/D, or recurve in the limbs, a pistol style grip and a riser to limb ratio of approximately 1:1. The bow is probably a virtual shooter. Like the man said, "It's good; we'll make it better".

The riser is still basically a narrow cylinder that is shaped to fit the user's hand and has an arrow shelf cut into it. What if we widened it from back to belly? Instead of 2" deep we made it 4" deep? By the laws of physics we just increased the bow's mass and so its weight. If you were planning to carry the bow for days on end, that might not be a good thing, but if you wanted the bow to be as stable as possible for shorter shooting sessions, then it might be just the thing to do. (Adding a few inches of wood to a riser certainly wouldn't make it too heavy to carry for extended periods, so we'll take the above as a figurative example.) We used an analogy earlier when discussing stabilizers: If you held your arm out, and I hit it, it would move in proportion to the force that was used. If you were holding a five-pound weight in your hand and I hit it again, it would move less, due to the increased inertia. By adding wood to the riser, we effectively put a (figurative) five-pound weight in your hand; any movement imparted by shooter error would also be dampened by virtue of the added weight.

Not only does adding weight to the riser help by increasing inertial resistance, but the placement of the extra weight can also have beneficial (or detrimental) effects on the feel of the shot. If we add weight uniformly from fade out to fade out, all we've done is increase the inertia of the system. While that's beneficial, it's not optimal. If we add more weight below the grip area than above, we've created a pendulum effect. That effect helps to keep the bow upright during and after the shot, acting like the stabilizers we discussed in Chapter 7. Most archers find that adding that type of stabilizing weight makes the bow point better and hold steadier on target.

Another area where extra weight can be beneficial is just central to the fade-out areas. If you recall, at shock, the bowstring abruptly stops the limb's forward movement, hence the term "shock". The shock waves then travel down the limbs and meet somewhere near the center point of the bow/riser, usually in the grip area. The shooter feels this as hand shock, a generally uncomfortable feeling that can, in severe cases, be transmitted up the bow arm to the shoulder. *One archer described a bow with a particularly noticeable hand shock as "shaking his fillings loose"!*

Reasons for a particular bow having excessive hand shock include poor overall design or tillering, low physical mass/weight, insufficient arrow weight, and improper tuning. Poor shooting technique can also be a contributing factor. Adding mass to the riser helps, but adding mass to both fade-out areas can act as a shock absorber, or more accurately, a shock dampener. As the shock wave travels down the limbs, some of its energy is dissipated by the mass of the limb itself. If the shock wave reaches an area of increased mass along its path, more energy can be dissipated.

This concept was fairly well known in the 1960's and 70's. A great many high-end target bows and quite a few hunting bows had extra wood positioned at the fade-outs, some both on the back and the belly. Some of the larger ones were lovingly called "Bat-wings", and as strange as they may have looked, they performed exactly as advertised (diag 8-26).

8-26 "Bat-Wing" risers. Pictured here is an early Bear Tamerlane (c1966).

Another reason for adding wood to the riser section was that it simply made the bow look better. During the golden age of archery, deeply grained Rosewoods, Curly Maples, Bubingas, Osage and dozens of other exotic woods were used for risers and riser accents. The extra wood gave the bowyer of that era more room to be creative. The heavy-risered bows appeared to be sculpted as fine furniture and the better bowyers were adept at making the seemingly decorative shapes quite functional as well as attractive. By choosing woods carefully, light and heavy woods could be combined to give the bow any balance the bowyer wanted. Strips of wood, fiberglass and/or plastic were and still are being used in wood risers, not only for visual appeal, but if placed correctly, to enhance the strength of the riser.

One company used a total of five wood laminations of alternating colors in the riser. The appearance was spectacular, however the laminations did not pass through the pivot or throat of the grip. I have had one such bow break in two at the pivot point while being strung!

Design 8.15 recap: Adding weight to the riser will help stabilize the bow during and after the shot. The proper placement of additional weight can further balance the bow, act as a shock dampener, and greatly enhance the beauty of the bow.

You may be asking – why are we discussing bow aesthetics here? The answer can be found in the first chapter. If a bow, and arrows for that matter, do not appeal to the archer on some visceral level, the desire to use them will be severely diminished. If the desire is even slightly lessened, the proficiency will ultimately be lessened as well. It may not make logical sense but that's the way it works for most of us.

Design 8.16 Miscellaneous things that go bump in the night
Working from the preceding sections and the chapters on tuning, we see that anything that increases the pre-load on the limbs will increase draw weight and usually increase performance to a greater degree than the extra pounds alone would warrant. In addition to adding reflex to the limbs, placing the limbs farther behind the grip (closer to the shooter) may increase pre-load. As mentioned earlier, sometimes increasing pre-load by whatever means can make a bow more sensitive to shooter error.

Things that can affect the rate of limb tip movement directly affect arrow speed. Classically, that's why the limbs are tapered toward the tips, to make them lighter and livelier. The disadvantage with that theory lies in the "livelier" part. Yes, they will move (accelerate) faster but the light weight may also increase the limb vibration. Vibration is not a bad thing in and of itself, and it's a necessary property of the limb harmonics. Simply stated, if the limbs didn't vibrate, they would break. However, excessive vibration can be bothersome and possibly harmful to the shooter. A shooter experiencing excessive vibration for prolonged periods of time may develop joint injury or tendonitis of the elbow. The bowyer needs to find a compromise here as well, or make it known to the perspective buyer, that to achieve a certain level of performance the buyer needs to accept that vibration as part of the package.

A more serious concern about bow tips is strength. Anyway you look at it, it's the string nocks that are the first recipients of the shock when the string stops the limb's forward motion. We'll discuss various string properties in a later chapter; suffice it to say some string materials shock the limbs more than others do but they all exert considerable force. Most bows have tip overlays of various materials, including wood, fiberglass, plastics or phenolic resin, to name a few. These are not only decorative but also serve to reinforce the nock and tip area.

Additionally, some bowyers or manufacturers extend these overlays in the working part of the recurve to stiffen the distal few inches. While this may seem counterintuitive at first glance, recall that each bowyer has his own ideas on how and when, or even if, the ends of the recurves should uncurl. Adding overlays is an expedient way of slowing or stiffening the limb action, whether to increase performance, stability or longevity.

Design 8.16 recap: Moving the limbs closer toward the shooter can increase pre-load. Limb tips can be strengthened by the use of tip overlays, which can also be used to fine-tune limb tip and recurve performance.

Looks like we've developed a pretty decent-shooting wooden-risered bow. We've even used synthetic material (fiberglass) in the limbs for strength and speed. While it may not seem traditional to some, the use of other synthetic materials has found its way into the archery market. We'll see this quite clearly in the next chapters on arrows and strings. Before we go on to carbon limbs and metal risers, here is a real world example of most of the properties we discussed combined into two representative bows.

This is a HIT Black Diamond target bow circa 1965. It's 66" and 35# a 28" draw (diag 8-27).

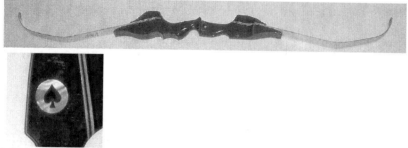

8-27 Hit Black Diamond Target bow, circa mid 1960's and mother-of-pearl inlay

The riser is a dense close-grain hardwood giving the bow considerable mass.
1. The riser at first glance seems symmetrical above and below the grip, but is actually weighted well below the grip area. There is more wood in the lower half of the riser, than the upper, yielding the aforementioned pendulum effect.
2. The riser is mildly deflexed.
3. Extra weight was placed over the fade-outs to absorb shock.
4. The riser to limb length ratio is approximately 1:1.
5. The grip is a medium pistol type grip with a small torque-free throat.
6. The limb fade-outs are tapered by the addition of a wedge of riser-colored wood between the maple limb cores.
7. The riser is cut out to follow the curvature of the limbs at full draw, but acts as a stop point to force the limbs to stress at the appropriate time.
8. The limbs begin with a fair amount of deflex from the fade-outs and then have a sharp or "forced" reflex starting approximately eleven inches from the tip.
9. The limb tips are small past the string nocks to reduce excess weight.
10. For aesthetics, the bow even has a mother of pearl inlay with a black ace of spades on the riser.

The bow, as expected, shoots quite well. HIT Archery was known for designing and manufacturing innovative and elaborate bows, incorporating many of the design features we've been discussing. Unfortunately, as was the case with many small bowyers of that era, the end of the golden age of archery forced them to close up shop.

Another bow from that era, that happily did survive and has become the template for most current Olympic style target bows, was the Hoyt Pro Medalist. Hoyt was able to perfect and incorporate many of the design features we've discussed, while keeping the lines of the bow remarkably simple and classic.

This is a rosewood 5PM series bow, circa 1970.
It's 69" long and 34# @ 28" (diag 8-28).

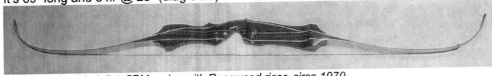

8-28 Hoyt Pro Medalist, 5PM series with Rosewood riser, circa 1970

1. Riser made of dense rosewood with multiple laminations for beauty and strength.
2. Riser weight is symmetrical above and below the pivot point, and designed to be used with twin stabilizers, just central to the fade-outs.
3. Extra weight placed central to fade-out areas, both on the back and face of the bow.
4. Riser to limb length ratio is approximately 5:3 (end of fade-out to end of fade-out). The shorter limbs added speed.
5. Riser geometry is mildly deflexed, adding remarkable stability.
6. Grip is contoured to a full pistol grip shape with thumb rest.
7. Limbs are mildly reflexed to maximize performance.
8. Limbs are bilaterally tapered, both in width and thickness.
9. Thin, tapered and reinforced limb tips.

Design 8.17 Carbon limbs have several advantages over wood core limbs
Since carbon fiber is a lighter material than wood it will accelerate faster during the power stroke, and being lighter, it will impart less shock when stopped by the string. Being synthetic, it has no irregularities or inconsistencies compared to wood. Equally as important, it is "virtually" unaffected by temperature, moisture, sunlight, and termites. It can be manipulated to very exacting tolerances and so, draw force curves can be regulated to very high degrees of precision. There

are really only two downsides – the most striking is cost. Depending on the construction methods, carbon and carbon composite limbs can cost anywhere from 50% to 200% more than basic wood core limbs. Second, is that they're not wood. Some people cling to the notion that archery, by definition, implies wood in both the bow and the arrows. That might be a hard sell, if the discussion were to include some top competitive archers. Even top longbow competitors are using carbon limbs in their new R/D longbows.

As with limb and riser design, each manufacturer has his own method for constructing carbon and carbon composite limbs. An often-asked question is "Who makes the best limbs?" or "What are the best limbs being made?" Those questions almost need the qualifier, "this week". It seems that every season there's a new favorite on the market. Manufacturers are either touting the fastest speed per pound or the smoothest draw, and usually adding "through the clicker" to the smoothness of draw claim for the Olympic or FITA shooters. The fact of the matter is that for 99% of the archers buying those limbs, the difference between one manufacturer's limbs and another's or one high-end limb model and another model from the same manufacturer will be indiscernible. Or, to put it very simply – they are all good!

Author's note: There has been a recent promotion by many Olympic/FITA limb manufacturers that smoothness of draw (especially pulling through the clicker) is of greater importance for accurate and consistent shooting than arrow speed per pound of draw weight. At first glance, this seems quite reasonable, but let's examine the theory a little more closely.

Olympic or FITA shooters typically shoot many arrows at ranges up to 70 and 90 meters, respectively; that by itself requires considerable strength, stamina, and consistency. A clicker is necessary to ensure a consistent draw length. At those distances, changes in draw length of 1/4" can easily send the arrow flying above or below the target; smoothness, or the absence of stacking, through the clicker region of the draw is indeed a desirable property. If we assume that a particular archer believes he or she needs a specific initial arrow speed to reach the longer distances comfortably, a draw weight and arrow combination will be chosen to achieve that speed. Makes sense so far. Now, a given set of limbs, "set A", is touted as being smoother through the clicker than another, "set B", but yields a slower arrow flight. So, if we say that an archer believes he needs 200 feet per second to reach the 90 meter target comfortably, he knows the A limbs would require a draw weight of 50#. The B limbs aren't as "smooth through the clicker", but are faster, and the same 200 feet per second requires a draw weight of only 45#. It's my strong belief that set A would have to be an awful lot smoother than set B to make up for the additional #5 the archer will need to hold at anchor for the 144 arrows in a full FITA course of fire. While it's possible that a smoother set of limbs could actually feel lighter on the initial draw, after several shots the additional weight begins to take a toll on the archer.

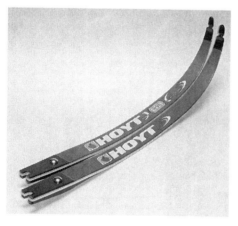

That may be an over-simplification, as different limbs (and risers for that matter) do have different feels to them or, more correctly, different draw force curves. There certainly are smoother drawing limbs and there are faster shooting limbs available, and those features are not mutually exclusive. As we've seen so far, it is still up to the archer to determine for himself what will be the most effective combination in his hands (diag 8-30).

8-29 Hoyt G3 Carbon Foam limbs

A draw force/curve is a graph of the measured draw weight of a bow plotted against various draw lengths. Draw/force curves clearly show the nature of how a given bow increases in weight, as well as the stacking point if the curve is extended far enough (diag 8-30).

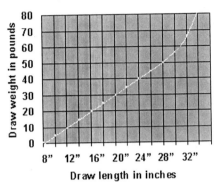

Draw length	Stickbow #
8"	0
10"	5
12"	10
14"	15
16"	20
18"	25
20"	30
22"	35
24"	40
26"	45
28"	50
30"	56
32"	64

8-30 Typical draw force curve data (left) and graph (right).

Design 8.17 recap: Carbon limbs can produce greater arrow speeds per given draw weight than wood core limbs; they are unaffected by temperature and moisture. Being synthetic, they can be manufactured to high tolerances.

Design 8.18 Metal risers

We've seen how riser material, as well as design, can affect the overall performance and stability of a bow. Our previous considerations were limited to wooden risers, but a trip to most archery ranges will show that wood, except in some die-hard traditional circles, isn't the only, or even the preferred choice for risers. In the 1960's, several manufacturers began introducing metal risers. By necessity, these were for takedown (T/D) bows where the limbs either fit into pockets on each end of the risers or were bolted onto the riser using tracks, pins, or both, for alignment. The metal risers didn't need the finishing work that wood did; usually machine polishing and painting was all that was required. That made the manufacturers happy. As long as proper manufacturing principles were adhered to, each riser was identical to every other riser in that production line, as the natural variation seen in wood didn't enter the picture. (To the customer, that could be a plus or a minus depending on his or her preferences.) It seemed that a lot of the new-fangled metal-risered bows were actually out-performing their wooden counterparts. One of the performance theories was that the more rigid the riser, the faster the limbs could accelerate the arrow. The reason was that a rigid riser wouldn't absorb or dissipate as much energy from the limbs as a softer or more flexible riser would. As we've seen in the case with carbon limbs, removing the wood from the picture also made the riser resistant to changes due to temperature and moisture.

Most metal risers were initially made from magnesium and some from aluminum. Early on, magnesium was favored because it was relatively light, inexpensive and rigid. Except for the fact that magnesium dust is highly flammable, it's also easy to work with. Most magnesium risers were simply cast, polished and painted. One of the earliest successful three section production takedown bows, the Bear Victor T/D, used magnesium quite successfully, offering three riser sizes, and three limb lengths. Combining various risers and limbs, bows from 56" to 70", and 20# to over 70# could be created. They also used an ingenious pocket and latch system that required no tools for assembly and disassembly (diag 8-31). Bear Archery also offered a wooden version of the risers, but at a considerably higher cost. Soon after, most other companies offered their own versions of T/D bows, most often with a metal riser. (In addition to the rigidity of the metal riser, the convenience of being able to disassemble a bow for storage and travel made the T/Ds grow quickly in popularity.)

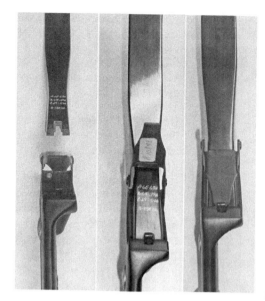

8-31 Bear "tool-free" Take-down limb coupling. The latch was simply to hold the limb in place before the bow was strung. Once strung, the force of the string against the limbs locked the limbs into their sockets. These bows came with a lifetime warranty!

While magnesium is a relatively lightweight metal, it couldn't be called "light" when compared to aluminum, and some massive magnesium risers became quite heavy. The extra weight was usually an advantage on the target range, but carrying one in the field was another story. Aluminum was the next logical choice; being much lighter also made it less rigid, and so additional engineering was required to regain some rigidity. The stiffness was necessary – not only for performance but to stress-relieve the riser adequately so it would remain straight under pressure. Early aluminum risers did, in fact, have a tendency to be out of true, and a knowledgeable archer needed to be careful of this when purchasing one. Aluminum risers were generally not cast as were their magnesium counterparts, but were "carved" on duplicating (CDC) machines, and anodized instead of painted.

Today, nearly all top-flight Olympic/FITA bows have aluminum risers. The light-weight aluminum alloy allows the archer to add additional weight where he wants it to customize the balance. A very lightweight riser may weigh two pounds by itself but can reach eight or more pounds after the stabilizers, sights and other paraphernalia are added. The problem of rigidity or greater flexibility has been addressed in several ways; one very novel approach was the saber grip or flying buttress used in Hoyt-USA's Tec series (diag 8-32). Here, the back strap adds rigidity without adding too much additional weight. It also gave the riser a very futuristic appearance, which some archers found intriguing.

8-32 First of Hoyt-USA's TEC line of recurve risers, the AXIS was a proven winner.

We briefly mentioned bow harmonics in the last chapter on Olympic style tuning. At shock, the shock waves travel down the limbs into the riser and should meet near the center of the bow. That happens on any bow, regardless of the materials. While wood has a natural dampening quality to it, metals will transmit vibrations quite well and will generate more noticeable harmonics. There is usually less hand shock on a metal-risered bow, but it's not uncommon for the archer to feel more vibration after a shot. The vibration may actually last several seconds, especially if a soft string like Dacron is used. The better a bow is designed, the less vibration the shooter will experience. The ability to adjust tiller and weight and add stabilizers to various points on the riser can also serve to dampen a bow's vibration.

Lastly, we mentioned that the early wooden Hoyt Pro Medalists were the templates of modern magnesium and aluminum Olympic style target bows. To see that, all you would have to do is lay a wooden Pro Medalist and the newer magnesium or aluminum bows side by side and the similarity is unmistakable (diag 8-33).

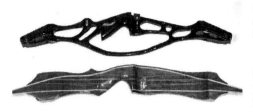

8-33 Comparing the Hoyt-USA Aerotec circa 2002 (top) and a Hoyt 5PM circa 1970 (bottom) we see striking similarities in geometry.

Metal risers can be painted or anodized any color or pattern you like. I guess you could do the same with wood, but that just doesn't seem right somehow.

Design 8.18 recap: The use of metal risers adds rigidity to the system, which can increase performance, but can also magnify the transmission of harmonic vibrations after the shot. They are not affected by temperature and moisture, but generally require the use of T/D mechanisms. They can be painted or anodized to any desired color.

Design 8.19 A few additional notes on takedown bows
Probably one of the biggest problems in the archery game is traveling with your equipment. Most people movers can deal with oddly shaped baggage, but still you might find it easier transporting a 36" or 40" box than a 70" one; and even easier if you could pack your bow right in your luggage. The idea of a takedown bow did not originate in the 1970's. Takedown longbows have been around for hundreds of years in one form or another. The original mechanism was simply a sleeved riser so that the bow could be pulled apart in two pieces when unstrung and that design is still in use today on certain T/D longbows. A metal sleeve is inserted into the lower half of the riser, and the upper half, also sleeved, slides into the lower fitting. This naturally made transport easier but lost the advantage of being able to change limbs to vary the length and draw weight. One of the selling features of the early three piece T/D bows was that an archer could easily shoot targets all day with a light set of limbs and then hunt the next day with the same bow by merely changing the limbs, and of course, the arrows.

Ben Pearson Archery initially used an idea similar to the sleeved T/Ds but with an aluminum knuckle "joint" held together by a through bolt. That design was used on both their target and hunting model bows (diag 8-34). It had the same limitation as the longbow sleeve, that while it permitted easy assembly and disassembly, you didn't have the option of changing limbs. The knuckle joints were held in place by a plate that was glued into the two halves of the wooden riser. There have been reports of these plates separating from the wood over time, and some have suggested the owner of such a bow run a bolt or two through the upper and lower riser halves, perpendicular to the plates, to hold them in place. While not aesthetically pleasing, that might not be a bad idea, for safety's sake. I have two such bows from the 1970's and neither has shown any sign of separation. However, given the softness of aluminum, those bows are rarely disassembled.

Several other manufacturers have had proprietary limb coupling schemes. As with the aforementioned Bear Archery T/D system, Herter's Archery also had a "slip-in" limb system, but most others used a bolt and pin or track system. These usually required an Allen or hex-head wrench, and while not as quick to assemble or disassemble as the slip-in or latch systems, they were entirely adequate and user friendly (diag 8-35).

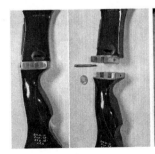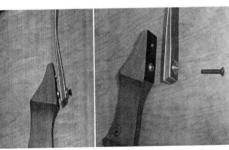

8-34 Ben Pearson takedown bow (Silencer model, circa 1972) used aluminum "knuckles" and a through-bolt for a very secure coupling (left). 8-35 Bolt on limb system (Ragim / PSE Impala - right).

Today, almost every archery manufacturer or bowyer offers takedown models in their catalogs, with both wood and metal risers. Anyone choosing a takedown bow over a one-piece bow need not be concerned about the limb joint being a weak link in the system. For the most part, takedown bows are no more prone to failure than their one-piece counterparts, and that's a very, very low percentage.

One problem that plagued target archers for some time was that each of the major producers of archery equipment had their own proprietary limb coupling system. Some companies even changed their systems every few years. In the early 1990's, Hoyt-USA designed the ILF or International Limb Fitting (diag 8-36). Several other companies quickly adopted the ILF, and it has become a de facto standard. Here the end of the limb had a standardized notch that mated with

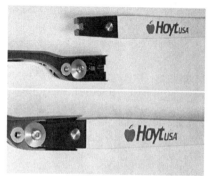

an adjustable bolt at the deep end of the limb pocket. It also had a detent-enabled dovetail to fit into a slot on the riser for alignment and to keep the limbs in place until the bow was strung. Any company adhering to the ILF standard could interchange limbs or risers with another company's products. Additionally, the ILFs were usually adjustable for limb position so draw weight and tiller could be adjusted to suit the individual archer (see Chapter 7 on Tuning with Gadgets – Olympic Style).

8-36 Typical ILF limb coupling (Hoyt-USA Radian riser and maple core limbs, circa 1994).

It has been postulated that since Olympic/FITA limbs typically go up to only 50#, the ILF coupling, or possibly the risers, couldn't handle the stress from heavier limbs, but this is not the case. There simply hasn't been a need or demand for heavier limbs in that type of competition. A pair of 50# limbs in full reflex position should yield approximately 54# to 55#, depending on the riser. Add to that the possibility of the archer having a draw length over 28", and the actual draw weight can be considerably more. To the best of my knowledge, there have been no reported failures of ILFs to date due to excessive draw weight.

Some independent manufacturers are adapting shorter risers, either older compound bow risers or newly minted ones to accept the ILF limbs. Since the risers are shorter, the draw weight can be as much as 6# to 8# more than the weight marked on the limbs. Again, add to this the ability to increase the limb reflex and the possibility of an archer with a longer draw, and draw weights in the 60#+ range can be realized.

Design 8.19 recap: Several mechanisms have been utilized in creating T/D bows. Two piece T/D bows make storage and transport easier but lack the limb interchangeability and the associated benefits. The ILF brought a standard coupling mechanism to Olympic/FITA type target bows.

Design 8.20 Compound bows
While compound bows are typically not considered "stickbows", we often forget that they are not as different as initial appearances would have some people believe.

A brief explanation of how a compound bow works:
Since we've already built a virtual bow, we can continue the process and turn it into a compound bow. The traditional (stickbow) purists might not like it but since it's a virtual bow, we can turn it back any time we want, and stay out of trouble.

If we attach brackets to the upper and lower limbs somewhere near the tips, place pulleys in those brackets (diag 8-39), then loop a string around the pulleys, and fasten the ends to the pulleys' axles or thereabout, we'd have a compound bow. It would be a pretty inefficient one, since with that configuration, as we drew the string back, all we would have accomplished is to lessen the draw weight. (Since the string is now nearly twice as long and passing through a pair of pulleys with concentric axles, the amount the limbs will bend per unit of draw length is roughly halved.) If you recall your high school Physics, this should sound familiar to you. If not, you'll either have to take my word for it, or crack open the old Physics books, if you can find them!

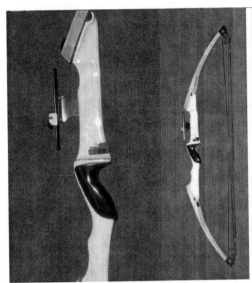 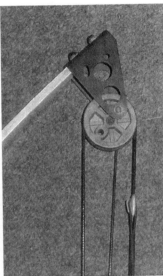

8-37 Attaching brackets and pulleys to recurve limbs to create an early "compound" bow. This is a Canterbury model from Robinhood Archery. By looking at the first picture, you'd think it was just a T/D recurve, right. The odds are, it more than likely was a recurve before the pulleys were attached! Notice the Flipper II rest and cushion plunger (left)!
8-38 Close up of limb pulley attachment from the Canterbury (right).

So the first thing we may need to do is give the bow a little more draw weight. Referring back to Design 8.1, if we shorten the bow (limbs) we'll increase the draw weight. So let's "shorten the limbs" by moving the brackets closer to the center of the bow. Also, if you recall, any excess weight on the limbs will ultimately act as weight on the arrow. What that means is that we don't need or want the parts of the limb distal to the brackets, so let's cut them off. You're probably noticing that our well-designed stickbow is now starting to look a lot more like an early compound bow. All we've done so far is add pulleys, a longer string, and shorten the limbs. We haven't gained a lot, so far.

Now, let's put the "compound" in a compound bow. We'll use the same configuration as above, but this time the pulleys' axles won't be concentric, but eccentric. That means the axle isn't in the middle of the pulley, but off-center to some degree. We have just turned the pulley into a cam, which by definition is an eccentric pulley, so we're still within the realm of basic Physics.

If after some trial and error we orient the cams correctly, an interesting thing begins to happen. As we observe our virtual limbs as we begin the draw, the limbs begin to bend as they always have, just a little faster than they did before. As we continue to draw the string and the cams eccentrically rotate when we pass the crest or peak of the cam, the limbs actually begin to "unbend"; to the person pulling the string, the weight is getting lighter. As we continue to pull the string back, the draw weight again begins to increase. While this is a well-known occurrence to anyone who has shot a compound bow, to help those who haven't, here are some virtual numbers (diag 8-39). Part of the trial and error is to position the eccentrics or "time" them so they are synchronized with each other and the weight is at its lowest point at the person's full draw.

Drawforce curve for typical recurve and compound bows
(compound with 50% let off)

Draw length	Stickbow #	Compound #
8" (at brace height)	0	0
10"	5	10
12"	10	20
14"	15	30
16"	20	40
18"	25	48
20"	30	50
22"	35	35
24"	40	28
26"	45	26
28"	50	25
30"	56	35*
32"	64	50*

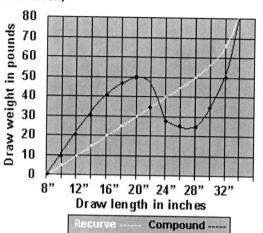

8-39 Theoretical draw/force curves for a 50# stickbow and 50# compound bow (with a 50% let-off).

*Most compound bows, even basic ones, as in this hypothetical demonstration, have "stops" built in that prevent the string from being drawn beyond a certain point, usually corresponding to the shooter's draw length. For this example, we've "pulled out the stops", so to speak.

Notice that as the shooter goes beyond the low point, on this type of compound bow the weight begins to increase again; that's because as the cams continue to rotate, the limbs are once again bending, but to a greater extent.

That explains why a compound breaks down after it's reached its peak weight, and that's certainly a benefit for the shooter, since he can now hold less weight at full draw. The other half of the story is what happens when the string is released. Since the limbs have slightly uncurled at full draw, as they move forward after the release, they have to re-curl when they pass the hump in the force curve, as the cams roll over again, but in the opposite direction. The limbs are giving their full thrust at mid draw and not full draw as in a stickbow. That allows for greater arrow acceleration and to some extent a reduction in the required archer's paradox (which allows for a slightly weaker spined arrow).

Notice that the last two weights shown for the compound seem to be heavier than expected. Even though the cams have allowed the limbs to uncurl, the limbs are still being flexed; given the shorter size, are reaching their stack point.

Our virtual bow has actually become an example of the early compounds as designed by companies such as Jennings and Allen in the early 1970's. The average let-off on the early bows was about 35% to 50%, meaning that a compound with a peak weight of 50# would only relax at full draw to approximately 32.5# or 25#, respectively. That plus the added acceleration, "compounded" by the fact that a lighter and weaker spined and therefore faster arrow could be used, drew in a lot of people. This was especially appealing to new archers and some old hands that wanted or needed to do less physical work while shooting and still have a bow with "oomph".

I remember the first time I heard the term "compound" bow. I was at my old archery range, during the early 70's. I was talking to the president of our club, an older member joined the conversation. He asked whether he would be allowed to shoot a compound bow at the range, as he didn't have the strength or stamina to shoot a recurve any more. I didn't know what he was talking about; fortunately the president of the club did. His reply was that he could certainly use it at the range, but since the NFAA didn't allow it, and we were an NFAA affiliated club, he couldn't use it in any competitions. That seemed satisfy everyone. Within the next two years we had to modify every bow rack at the range to accommodate compound bows.

The very simplistic example we just used was not completely fabricated. Several archery companies sold "Compound Conversion Kits" which contained two eccentric pulleys mounted in brackets to be screwed into the upper and lower limbs of recurve bows, and a new string to accommodate the pulleys. Instructions were given as to where on the limb the brackets should be attached, and how to "time" the cams. While I'd like to believe no one actually performed that operation on any of the high end or classic target and hunting bows of that era, I have seen more than a few bows so modified. It must be remembered that the early compound bows were nothing more than stickbows with lower holding weights and a speed advantage, both of which were relatively minor. The new compound bows were shot exactly the same way their predecessors were; they were drawn with fingers, used the same rests, stabilizers, sights, and yes, even the same release aids that were used on the stickbows.

As the compound technology developed, the newer bows became more and more complex. There were four and six wheel compounds, and for a while, no serious self-respecting shooter would be seen with a two-wheeler. Add to that the myriad of stabilizers already in use by the top tournament archers of the time, and it appeared that that bows could not only shoot by themselves, but as with their target recurve counterparts, they could receive VHF and UHF broadcasts (diag 8-40). If seen today and described in today's terms, they would probably be called broadband capable.

8-40 Fully accessorized target compound bow, with front stabilizer, V-bars, sight and peep.

In the three decades that ensued, technology advanced rapidly and the two wheel compound bow, or rather two-cam compound (they didn't resemble wheels anymore) became more efficient. The need for extra moving parts disappeared. The compound had become shorter and shorter to a point where it was impractical to draw the string back with the fingers and so mechanical releases became increasingly popular, even necessary. The let-off also increased to a point that a 65% let-off is nominal, 80% common and there's at least one company that's currently boasting a 99% let-off. As efficiency increased so did arrow speeds, with several models claiming initial velocities well in excess of 300 feet per second. (The best stickbows tuned specifically for speed shoot in the neighborhood of 235 feet per second, with light target arrows.)

The details of each type of compound bow on the market today, and the workings of their cam systems are beyond the scope of this book, which is called <u>Shooting the Stickbow</u>, after all. All the major compound bow manufacturers have ample literature demonstrating the latest advances in the technology of archery.

Design 8.20 recap: The compound bow derives its advantages of lower holding weight and faster arrow speed by virtue of the cams or pulleys at the ends of each limb, which allow the limbs to relax during the draw, and regain their energy as the arrow is released.

Final summation and closing thoughts

Well, that's the theory of building a bow. Hopefully, you now have an idea of how design features can change the performance characteristics of a bow. The basic principles haven't changed that much since the first stick was bent and braced with a string. Archery is still just two sticks and a string, and the desire of the man bending the longer stick to hit a mark off in the distance with the shorter stick. Bowyers have always wanted to make bows shoot faster and cast an arrow farther. They have also tried to make the design of the bow better fit the task at hand. You probably didn't think we'd end up with a compound bow, did you? It would be difficult not to, as increasing the mechanical advantage of a device is what progress is all about. What must be remembered is that while changes in technology may decrease the workload on the practitioner, the end result is still the same. In the final analysis, it's not the tool, but the man who uses it that matters.

For us, we have chosen to use a stickbow, for lack of a better term, one with no mechanical differences from those used for thousands of years, but the differences are still there. Technologies and materials in use 1,000 years ago are not common today, except possibly in historical reenactments or by those interested in "primitive" archery. Newer and better materials will no doubt supplant the materials that we are using today. Arrows will fly faster and truer but the soul of the archer will remain unchanged, he or she will still believe and say with pride and conviction –

I am an Archer.

I am not a traditional archer, bowhunter, compound shooter, or target archer.

I draw a bow with the first three fingers of my hand. The bow's limbs bend in direct proportion to my strength and to the length of my draw. My fingers are callused and my back is strong from years of shooting.

I focus completely on the one target I wish to hit. I use no device to direct my arrow toward its mark, save my eyes and my will.

As long as I have the strength to bend a bow, the eyesight to direct my arrow, and the mental faculty to understand what that means,

I am an Archer.

Those simple statements are applied to how I try to live my life. I do and I am many things, as we all do and are, but the loosing of a well-aimed arrow defines how I try to do all those things.

For those of you who understand these simple words, there is no doubt, as to what we do, or who we are.

Chapter 9

Arrows

I t's been said, "Any bow can be made to shoot well, but good arrows are worth their weight in gold". Almost any bow will launch an arrow the same way every time, if it's drawn to the same point and released in the same manner. The arrows are a different story; they must all be identical in weight, spine (stiffness) and configuration. They must also be matched to the bow, within given parameters and tolerances. From our discussions on tuning, and the following discussion on arrow materials, it will be seen that those requirements are more easily achieved with some materials than with others. Let's start by reviewing the parts and properties of an arrow from Chapter 1 (diag 9-1).

Typical arrow nomenclature

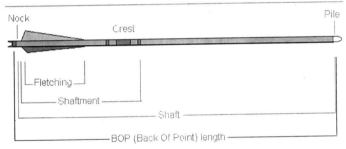

9-1 Generic arrow components: remember this from Chapter 1?

Arrow nomenclature:

Arrow – the long, thin stick with a point on one end and fletching on the other end.

Shaft – the rod or tube the arrow is made from.

BOP (Back Of Point) length – The length of the arrow measured from the throat of the nock to the back of the arrowhead.

Shaftment – the rear 8" to 12" of the arrow shaft.

Head, tip, point or pile – the pointy business end of the arrow, the part of the arrow that defines its purpose.

Nock – the grooved, usually plastic piece that is attached to the rear of the arrow and engages the string.

Fletching – the feathers, typically from a turkey or goose, attached to the shaftment, which steer the arrow. Various types of plastic fletching called vanes are also used.

Cresting – optional colored bands painted on the forward end of the shaftment for decorative or identification purposes.

Arrow Properties

Length – Measurement from the deepest cut in the nock groove to the back of the point (arrowhead). Also known as the BOP (Back Of Point) length. Measured in inches.

Weight – Weight of the complete arrow measured in grains.

Spine (static) – Amount of deflection caused by placing a two pound weight at the center of a shaft supported on 26" centers (diag 9-2). The deflection causes the pointer to pivot and the spine is read from the curved scale.

Spine (dynamic) – Amount of deflection an arrow experiences when being shot from a non-center shot bow (diag 9-3).

9-2 An excellent commercial spine tester from Hobbyist (Photo courtesy of 3Rivers Archery)

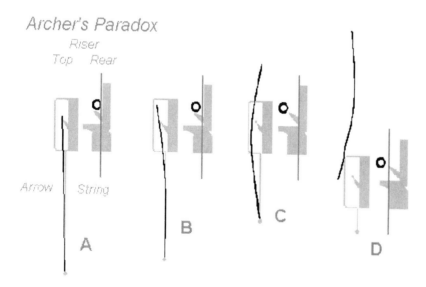

Archer's Paradox

Riser
Top   Rear

Arrow   String

A   B   C   D

9-3 Effects of the archer's paradox – dynamic arrow spine

With that in mind, let's look at each component, starting with the shaft itself.

Arrow shaft materials

Wood (diag 9-4)

9-4 Wood arrows

Wood was probably the first material used to make arrow shafts. Remarkably, it has many qualities that still make it an excellent choice for shafts. Unfortunately it also has a number of disadvantages that make it less than desirable given today's other options. It should be noted that in the 1960's, 70's and 80's, considered by some to be the Golden Era of Archery, as it was the most rapidly growing sport in the US, very few, if any, serious archers used wood arrows. At that time archery was all about accuracy, not a trivial concept, and wood didn't fit well into that picture.

The resurgence of wooden arrows within the last 15 to 20 years has been in large part due to the increased interest of some people to practice a more traditional form of archery. Perhaps historical or primitive would be better words to describe that style, without all the technological advances currently available, and to many that includes, almost by definition, the use of wooden arrows. Today, wooden arrows, depending on the type of wood and degree of preparation, can cost anywhere from a few dollars for raw shafts to over $100 per dozen for completed arrows.

For any given species of wood, the spine of wood arrow is determined first by the natural stiffness of the wood and second by the diameter of the dowel that the arrow will be made from. Wooden arrows are either machine (factory) spined or hand spined, and there are significant differences in spine tolerances between factory spined and hand spined arrows.

"Factory spined" arrows are simply classified by their diameter with random shafts being spot-checked for accuracy. Some companies test the spine electronically, but there's still room for improvement.

"Hand spined" means that each arrow is spine tested by a human hand using a spine gauge or electronic tester. A much higher level of consistency is realized, but at an increased cost.

Many experienced archers who choose to shoot wood arrows buy their dowels in lots of a hundred or more, and then hand check each to find the dozen with the most consistent weight and spine. Hopefully, there'll be more than a dozen in a given lot. Those shafts become the archer's primary or "best" arrows. Subsequent arrows are classified accordingly and any that don't make the cut are either culled out as practice arrows or simply used for firewood.

There are three main reasons for people choosing wood arrows today. The major reason is their historical or traditional significance. Until the early part of the last century, that's all that was available, and wood does have a proven track record of several thousand years' duration. They can be finished to show off their grain and be turned into virtual works of art. Indeed, arrow making or "fletching" can become a hobby unto itself, and has for many archers. The second reason some people (primarily "traditional" bowhunters) prefer wood is that it is natively heavier than most other materials, and so can help quiet a noisy hunting bow or reduce hand-shock. While it's been shown that for any given bow a heavier arrow will not necessarily penetrate further into game (and so be more lethal) than a lighter arrow, many bowhunters hold on to the theory that it does, therefore wooden arrows remain a viable industry in today's archery market. Lastly, several archery organizations allow the use of only wood arrows in their traditional or longbow competitive classes. An archer choosing to compete in those classes has no choice but to use wood. A lesser known or understood factor is that the natural elasticity of wood actually makes it recover faster from paradox than aluminum, but not quite as fast as carbon, so there may be some valid rationale to choosing wood as an arrow material.

With all these factors in wood's favor, it's remarkable that it's not the first choice for all archers. Unfortunately, it does however have some serious disadvantages. Being a naturally occurring substance, it has inherent inconsistencies and weaknesses and so it requires considerable cost and effort, both in assembly and maintenance. For example, during assembly, care needs to be taken with respect to wood grain. As wood grain is not uniform, it needs to be oriented so that the effects of the archer's paradox neither over-compress nor over-stress the denser or weaker sections. Failure to do so can and has resulted in shaft failure and injury to the archer. Wood, being wood, also has a tendency to be less than uniform in overall density, and therefore, weight and spine. Furthermore, wood has a natural tendency to warp. Once straight, the arrows need to be checked constantly for straightness as well as damage. Proper sealing of the wood and certain types of impregnation, as well as lamination, can go a long way to diminish the warping, but not completely eliminate it. Even when the straightest and most uniform 12 shafts are chosen from a lot of a hundred, they will not be as straight as the lowest grade aluminum or carbon arrows. Many archers who shoot wood arrows have, out of necessity, become quite adept at hand straightening their shafts. Regarding damage, in addition to checking for straightness, wooden arrows must be checked for damage. Dents, nicks, cracks, splits or any questionable appearance needs to be considered suspect, and more than likely, the arrow destroyed and discarded. Also, while the added weight of the wood shafts may appeal to some archers, the performance loss can be significant and is unacceptable to others.

Types of wood arrows

Port Oxford Cedar (*Chamaecyparis Lawsoniana*, also called Port Orford cedar) – For those of us who began our archery careers in our youth, decades ago, our first arrows were probably made of cedar. They were relatively inexpensive, certainly adequate for backyard or very casual shooting, and they had that wonderful cedar aroma. If the lure of the bow wasn't enough to get you hooked on archery, that smell was. Most of us still remember opening a new box of cedar arrows, and having to stop for a moment as that aroma took us by surprise and brought a smile to our faces. Unfortunately, we broke as many arrows as we lost, and Olympic level accuracy wasn't that important then, even if we thought it was.

Cedar is known for its light weight and straightness, but not its durability. A variation is Alaskan Yellow Cedar, which actually isn't yellow in color, but white and is a little more durable the Port Oxford Cedar.

Sitka Spruce (*Picea Sitchensis*) – More expensive than cedar, but more durable.

Birch (several species of the *Betula* family) – Also another durable wood; some species are fairly soft and easy to work with.

Ash – Also more durable and heavier than cedar, but harder to straighten.

Chundoo or Lodgepole Pine – (*Pinus Contorta*) As the name implies, Lodgepole Pine was used by Native Americans to build lodges or teepees. It's a fairly hard wood, and given its strength, has also been used in making railroad ties.

Forgewood – Forgewood was a compressed hardwood arrow shaft that was manufactured by Sweetland Archery in the 1960's. The compression process added to the strength and weight of the arrow and made it more resistant to warping. Their strength was usually demonstrated by hammering Forgewood dowels through a piece of plywood. Sweetland Archery is no longer in business, but similar materials may be available through a few other manufacturers.

Footed arrow shafts – As far back as the Middle Ages, wood's durability, or lack thereof, became apparent and proved problematic. A common point of failure was the part of the shaft just behind the arrowhead. To help alleviate this, some fletchers (arrow makers) began footing, or splicing harder, more durable, woods to what would become the front of the arrow. That practice is still in use today, with woods such as Purple Heart and Osage spliced to the leading part of the arrow shaft. In addition to strengthening the weakest part of the shaft, it also added weight to the front of the arrow and provided a very distinctive finished arrow. Only a small portion of the shaft can be footed, else the spine of the arrow would be affected more than it would by simply adding weight to the pile end (diag 9-5).

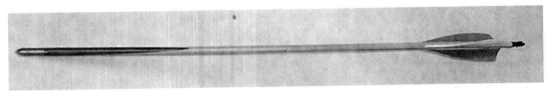

9-5 A walnut footed cedar arrow

Laminated wood shafts – The next step to increase strength, durability and weight would be to use layers of different woods laminated together. This has been done with several woods, and has yielded excellent results. The most notable laminated arrows are hex shafts, described below.

Hex shafts – are not hexagonal in shape, but are round shafts made of six wedged/triangular shaped pieces of wood, typically Lodgepole Pine, that are glued or laminated together and then rounded to form a dowel (diag 9-6). Using multiple pieces of wood reduces the inconsistencies normally found in a single dowel and increases the overall strength. In most regards, they can be treated as regular wood arrows.

Hex Shaft

9-6 Hex shafts are made from six pieces of wood glued together in a pie configuration

Fake wood arrows – Not really sure where these entities should go. Aluminum and carbon arrows are available with anodized or photo film finishes to simulate wood (diag 9-7). That would provide the ultimate arrow for those who desire the look of wood, but need the advantages of the newer, stronger, and lighter materials.

9-7 Easton Legacy, Beman ICS Classic and Vapor arrows
Wood arrow maintenance

Wood arrows are high maintenance items, for both accuracy and safety. Wood arrows need to be checked frequently for straightness, and then either straightened by hand (diag 9-8), by applying gentle pressure in the opposite direction of the bend, or by use of a straightening hook (diag 9-9). The straightening hook is a small diameter hook with a handle on the opposite end to apply more precise pressure to the center of the bend, also called the "wow" (diag 9-10). Using a hook may leave a slight dent or compression at the contact point but will not harm the shaft or shorten its life span. As previously stated and this bears repeating – wood arrows also need to be regularly inspected for damage; any signs of splitting, dents, or any other damage should be taken seriously, and the arrow destroyed to prevent further use.

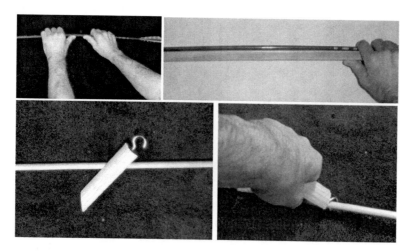

9-8 Hand straightening a wooden arrow. While simple in theory, this process can take time and patience (top left).
9-9 Wooden arrow "hooks" can be purchased or made by simply screwing a Cap Hook into a scrap piece of dowel (bottom left). Using a "hook" to straighten a wooden arrow is fairly intuitive (bottom right).
9-10 High point or "WOW" of a warped wood arrow as seen against a wooden straight edge. (top left).

Wood arrow components

In addition to the shaft material, the components are quite simple: a sealing agent for the wood, staining and/or paint as desired, feathers, heads and nocks. The wood dowels are usually tapered at each end to receive the heads and nocks with a tapering tool. The standard head taper is 5 degrees and the nock taper is 11 degrees (diag 9-11). The simplest tools are similar to hand-held pencil sharpeners (diag 9-12). More elaborate tools hold the arrow at the requisite angle and an electric sanding disk or scraper creates the taper (diag 9-13). The nocks on wooden arrows need to be aligned so that the cock feather is roughly parallel to the grain of the shaft with the densest part of the grain against the riser's strike plate.

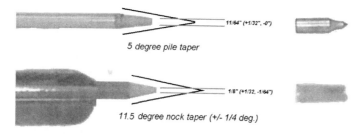

AMO Standard wood arrow pile and nock tapers

11/64" (+1/32", -0")

5 degree pile taper

1/8" (+1/32, -1/64")

11.5 degree nock taper (+/- 1/4 deg.)

9-11 Standard wood arrow pile and nock taper dimensions

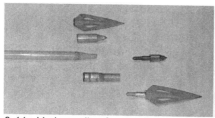

9-11a Various piles for wood arrows. Bear Razorhead and field point with 5 degree tapers to attach directly to the shaft. Below is an early wood arrow adapter that glues onto the shaft and allows the use of screw-in heads (left).
9-12 Pencil sharpener style tapering tool (Photo courtesy of 3Rivers Archery). This cutter provides both 5 and 11 degree tapers (middle).
9-13 "Woodchuck" sanding/bench type tapering jig (Photo courtesy of 3Rivers Archery). The wood shaft sits in one of two channels to yield a 5 or 11 degree taper (right).

Once the arrow has been cut to length and tapered on both ends, it needs to be sealed, painted and the nocks and piles glued on. The fletching procedure is the same as with other shaft materials; just be certain that the fletching cement is compatible with the finish. See the next chapter on arrow building for details.

Wood arrow shafts are typically of parallel design, meaning they have the same diameter throughout their length. With wood, and as we'll see, with carbon composite shafts it is possible to taper the shafts for better aerodynamics and finer tuning. The various taper designs were discussed in Chapter 6 on arrow tuning.

Fiberglass arrows

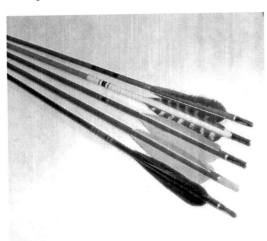

9-14 Fiberglass arrows. (Top to bottom Microflight (refletched), Bear Microflight (factory), Bear Kodiak Supreme, Bear Kodiak, and Robinhood Fiberglass (Robinhood Archery).

Fiberglass arrows appeared on the archery scene in the 1950's, originally made from sheets of resin impregnated fiberglass, and rolled into a tube on a steel mandrel. Gordon Plastics, in the 1960's, improved on that idea by using a parallel fiber method, employing two sheets of longitudinal fibers surrounded by four sheets of horizontal fibers. This added considerable strength and consistency to the shaft and the fiberglass arrow thereafter became a success. The Microflight brand was another excellent fiberglass arrow and was possibly better known or remembered than Gordon. There were several other manufacturers as well, each with a slightly different approach to arrow construction.

Most of the major archery manufacturers either marketed their own brands or sold Gordon or Microflight shafts that they assembled into arrows and labeled as their own. They were heavy and durable arrows available in spines that could accommodate bows from about 15# to well over 80#. They were probably the most durable arrows of the time, and they never lost their straightness; it was said that a fiberglass arrow was either straight or broken. That, plus the fact that they were less expensive than aluminum made them an excellent choice for schools and archery clubs. Their weight compared to aluminum also made them an attractive choice to bowhunters who favored a heavier arrow. They are no longer being produced in significant quantities, if at all, and are rarely used today. The older ones are occasionally seen at auctions, such as eBay, or flea markets, sometimes at very attractive prices. If fiberglass arrows appear to be in good condition, there should be little concern about using them. I have several dozen that have held up quite well through the years and show no signs of wear.

Fiberglass arrow maintenance

As fiberglass arrows were very durable, little maintenance was required. The typical point of failure was the area just behind the pile, usually after impact with a hard object. Fiberglass arrow manufacturers sold metal sleeves that could be placed behind the pile insert to strengthen that part of the shaft. Any splits or cracks rendered the arrow unusable. As we'll see with carbon arrows, fiberglass splinters can be quite sharp, therefore damaged arrows should be disposed of carefully.

Fiberglass arrow components

Components include the shaft itself, the pile, nock inserts with appropriate tips and nocks, feathers, and if so desired, paint (diag 9-15). The hollow fiberglass tubes used aluminum inserts for the nocks and heads with standard tapers, 5 degrees for the piles and 11 for the nocks. They were usually epoxied into the shafts, and the nocks were attached with regular Fletch-tite cement and the piles with hot stick (Ferrile-tite). (As fiberglass was not heat tolerant, care needed to be exercised when attaching the pile to the insert.) The spine of fiberglass arrows was determined by the diameter of the shaft.

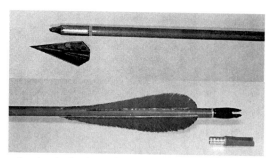

9-15 Fiberglass arrow components: (Microflight) Shaft, field and Bodkin heads, nocks, inserts and feathers.

A specialized type of fiberglass arrow, either solid or very thick walled, was used for "bowfishing" (shooting fish near the water's surface with an arrow). These were very heavy arrows with barbed points and typically plastic or rubber fletching, if any at all. A small hole was drilled behind the fletching for a fishing line to be attached. As bow fishing was practiced at very close range, the distance measured in feet, not yards, there were no spine requirements. Truly a one size fits all arrow (diag 9-15a).

9-15a A Sting-A-Ree solid fiberglass fishing arrow with plastic fletch and a retractable barbed point (circa 1977).

Graphite (diag 9-16)

9-16 Graphflex shafts from Stemmler Archery.

Graphite arrows were similar to fiberglass, but lighter and stiffer. One of the largest producers of graphite composite arrows was the Stemmler Archery Company who manufactured Graphite arrows under the name Graphlex Shafts. These were very stiffly spined arrows suitable for both stickbows and compounds, especially at the higher draw weights. There is extensive information on Graphlex Shafts in Appendix B. As with fiberglass, they are no longer being produced in any significant amounts. If found, they can be treated as fiberglass or carbon shafts with regard to construction and maintenance. Also, as with fiberglass, the spine was determined by the diameter of the shaft.

Aluminum arrows

Easton has been producing aluminum products since 1922 and has been the leading manufacturer of aluminum arrows since 1946, when they introduced the first production aluminum arrow, the 24srt-x. Unlike wood, fiberglass or even carbon arrows, which have always had numerous manufacturers or distributors, Easton has always dominated the aluminum arrow market.

Aluminum arrows have the advantages of strength, durability, and extreme consistency in weight, spine, and straightness compared to all other arrow materials, except for the most expensive carbon and carbon/aluminum composite arrows. The sizes of aluminum arrows available range in diameter from 12/64" to 27/64", and wall thickness from 11/1000" to 20/1000". The right arrow can be found for bows of any draw weight and archers of any draw length. The softest-spined arrow currently available is a 1214, deflecting 2.051", and the lightest is a 1413 weighing 5.88 grains/inch. The stiffest spine currently available is a gigantic 2712 with a deflection of 0.260", and the heaviest is a 2419 with a weight of 14.56 grains/inch. For some folks who actually believe that's not enough, it is of course possible to fit one shaft inside another, and thus both stiffen the spine and increase the weight. As bizarre as that might sound, it's actually being done by some people with very heavy bows.

Aluminum arrows do have some disadvantages, however. Aluminum, being a metal, does not have the resiliency, or more aptly, the speed of recovery from flexing, of carbon, fiberglass or even wood. It actually takes aluminum arrows longer to leave the archer's paradox (stop flexing after paradox) than arrows made from most other materials. Technically, this means that more energy is expended during paradox than with other arrows, theoretically making them less efficient. While a quantifiable difference, it hasn't made aluminum a poor choice for most archers, given its other positive qualities. Also, until the appearance of lightweight carbon arrows, aluminum arrows were the lightest shafts available, which translated into the fastest arrows available. We'll see in the next section that carbon arrows can usually be considerably lighter, and so have almost cornered the market on arrow speed.

Easton has always provided arrow spine charts to help archers choose the best arrows for their needs. If you examine the current recommendations, they may seem considerably over-spined compared to the charts presented earlier in this book. The information I've included here has been derived from the Easton charts of a few decades past. No, arrows haven't gotten weaker over the years, nor have bows changed significantly in their design or performance. The recommendations that Easton now gives are for what may be considered a worst case scenario bow; a very fast Olympic or similar type bow that is tuned very close to center shot. As we saw in the tuning sections, the faster a bow is and the closer it is to center shot, the stiffer the arrow needs to be. In that regard, the Easton charts may be accurate; however, most recurves and longbows do not fall into that category. That's not a good or bad thing, just a statement of fact. While stiffer and heavier arrows can be tuned to fly correctly, it's my feeling that for most applications, properly spined and therefore lighter arrows will yield better performance from most bows. Even my fast-shooting, near center shot Olympic bows are tuned to accept softer-spined aluminum arrows than the current Easton charts would suggest.

This does not mean the Easton charts and software (available from their web site, listed in Appendix C) can't be a useful tool; quite the contrary, they can be very useful, once you understand a variation on how to use them.

Here's the reference from Appendix B

weight at your draw length	Arrow length 25"	Arrow length 26"	Arrow length 27"	Arrow length 28"	Arrow length 29"	Arrow length 30"	Arrow length 31"
30#	1616	1616	1616	1616	1716	1816	1816
35#	1616	1616	1716	1716	1816	1816	1916
40#	1616	1716	1716	1816	1816	1916	1916
45#	1716	1716	1816	1916	1916	2016	2016
50#	1716	1816	1916	1916	2016	2016	2018/2114
55#	1816	1916	1916	2016	2016/2114	2018/2114	2018/2114
60#	1916	1916	2016	2016/2114	2018/2114	2018/2114	2020/2117
65#	1916	2016	2018/2114	2018/2114	2020/2117	2020/2117	2117
70#	2016	2018/2114	2018/2114	2020/2117	2020/2117	2117	2216
75#	2018	2018/2114	2020/2117	2020/2117	2117	2216	2219
80#	2018/2114	2020/2117	2020/2117	2117	2216	2219	2219

Arrows selected based on the above chart will work quite well for most people, but *well* and *optimal* may not always be the same thing. The following is a section of a table I compiled from the current Easton data for a 29" arrow (the full chart is also given in Appendix B).

Arrow Size	Spine (inches)	Raw Weight (grains)
1716	0.880	261
1813	0.874	228
1814	0.799	249
1816	0.756	269
1912	0.776	220
1913	0.733	242
1914	0.658	269
1916	0.623	291
2012	0.680	232
2013	0.610	261
2014	0.579	277
2016	0.531	306
2018	0.464	356
2020	0.426	391
2112	0.590	244
2113	0.610	261
2114	0.510	286

This shows arrow sizes from 17/64" to 21/64", their SPINE (deflection in inches) is determined by supporting the arrow on two posts 28" apart and hanging a 2# weight near the center of the shaft. Raw WEIGHT means the weight of the shaft without heads, nock, feathers or paint, measured in grains. It may look daunting, but it's really very simple, once you get used to it.

Here's an example:

Let's say you have a bow that's marked 36# @ 28" and you have a draw length of 29" and will be using a 29" arrow. By the formula from the tuning section, you figure the bow should have a draw weight of approximately 38# at your 29" draw. Going by the original chart, you see the closest entry for a 29" arrow on a 38# bow is a 40# bow, and that calls for an 1816.

weight at your draw length	25"	26"	27"	28"	29"	30"	31"
40#	1616	1716	1716	1816	**1816**	1916	1916

By test firing, and either paper or bare-shaft tuning, you see that the 1816s are a little weak (under-spined). You could either tune that out by bringing the arrow plate further away from the bow, reducing the degree of center shot, or reducing the weight of the pile. That would be fine, and certainly is the least expensive option, but by understanding the table below we see we have more options at our disposal.

Arrow Size	Spine inches	Weight grains
1716	0.880	261
1813	0.874	228
1814	0.799	249
1816	**0.756**	**269**
1912	0.776	220
1913	0.733	242
1914	0.658	269
1916	0.623	291
2012	0.680	232
2013	0.610	261
2014	0.579	277

The 1816's have a deflection of 0.756" and weigh 269 grains (raw). We'll assume that we'll be using the same feathers, nocks and piles on whatever arrow we choose, so they effectively cancel out of the equation, and therefore we can deal with just the raw shaft weight for this exercise. What you can also see is that a 1913 is slightly stiffer in spine, and slightly lighter in weight. The 1914 is stiffer yet, and weighs the same as the 1816, and the 1916 is even stiffer but also weighs more. Also by the chart, we see that the 2012 might also be an option, stiffer and a lot lighter.

A few things should become apparent:
- Both OD (outside diameter) and wall thickness are factors in determining weight and spine.
- The OD has a greater effect on spine than does wall thickness.
- The wall thickness has a greater effect on weight than does the OD.

So, which arrow should you choose when it comes time to replace your current 1816's, if you do indeed decide a change is needed? For most applications, we're not looking to go up in weight, as that would result in a slower arrow and a greater trajectory. Unless there's a compelling need for additional weight, it's generally not a desirable option. Initially, from a performance point of view, the 2012 looks good – increased spine and reduced weight. And for some applications, such as indoor target shooting where the archer is shooting at multiple target spots, that would be a great choice. The lighter weight would provide a faster arrow, the larger OD may help to place the arrow into the higher scoring area, and since we stated that the archer would use a multiple spot target, there's little chance of arrows striking and damaging each other. But let's look deeper. If you're shooting outdoors at extended ranges, the larger OD may not be an advantage. The thicker arrow will have greater the wind resistance, and while it would be launched at a higher speed, the larger OD may not only work against a flatter trajectory downrange, it would be affected more by crosswinds. Also a 12/1000" shaft wall is very thin, and therefore less durable than a thicker one. The 2013's have a slightly thicker wall, but are considerably stiffer; and the 2014's wall is thicker still, but probably too stiff for the bow in question, and you still have that air resistance problem to contend with. Looking at the 19/64" sized shafts, you have 1913's and 1914's (the 1912's have a weaker spine than the 1816's, and so are not an option). The 1913's are slightly stiffer, but not really enough to make a difference, and you still have a relatively thin wall to contend with. That pretty much leaves the 1914's; they have a stiffer spine than the 1816's and no weight deficit.

This is a lot of information to digest, until you gain experience using the arrow's variables and have a little more shooting experience under your belt. That experience will come, and with the tuning techniques we've already discussed, it becomes almost second nature.

Most vintage and current bows will shoot a variety of arrows with proper tuning. Ultimately it is up to the individual archer to decide on which arrow (spine, weight and length) works best for him in a given situation. As we said – there are always options!

A brief historical perspective on Easton arrows:

By the 1960's, Easton had three classes of aluminum arrows available to target archers and bowhunters.

The 24srt-x (diag 9-17), Easton's original aluminum arrow, had become their economy grade arrow for both hunting and target. The arrows were bare aluminum, and had a tensile strength of 88,000 to 90,000 psi (pounds per square inch). Quite good as entry level arrows, but due to the lack of anodization, they were known to tarnish, not badly, but enough that the oxidation did rub off on the archers hands after a day of shooting and pulling arrows. They are no longer being produced.

9-17 Easton 24-srt-x shafts assembled by Indian Archery, c1968; notice the "sprayed" crest.

The XX75 (diag 9-18) was the next step up. Debuted in 1958, these were also available in target and hunting weights and spines, but were anodized in silver and in what Easton called an Autumn Orange color, and had a tensile strength of 96,000 to 100,000 psi. They are still being produced in several color schemes, but not in the original colors, and are primarily considered hunting arrows.

9-18 Easton early xx75 shafts in Autumn Orange.

The X7 (diag 9-19), released in 1966, was the top of the line target arrow of that era. Anodized to a matte gray finish, sporting a tensile strength of 105,000 to 110,000 psi, and trueness (straightness) of .001" to .002", they were considered the ultimate in accuracy and consistency, and won about every national and international competition at that time. The Bear Archery Co. marketed their high-end Magnum series of aluminum hunting arrows, which were rumored to be thick walled Easton X7s.

9-19 Original Easton X7 shafts sported a matte (brushed) aluminum finish.

In subsequent years, Easton added additional classes of arrows, including the Swift, aimed at the youth and beginner target market, and the original GameGetter "hunter" shafts (diag 9-20). An interesting note about the original GameGetter shafts was that they had a dark green anodization that never quite stayed on the shaft very well. It was common to see dark green Gamegetters with bright silver foreshafts where the anodization had worn off. It's been speculated that the early Gamegetters were simply anodized 24srt-x's.

9-20 Original Green GameGetter arrows, notice how the green anodization has been worn away from the pile end of the shaft.

Current Easton aluminum offerings:

Scout – An aluminum arrow designed for young archers. Low PSI rating, 1618 shaft size using over-nocks and one-piece piles. Silver color.

Genesis – Youth / Intermediate grade arrow, higher PSI rating than the Scout arrow and thick walled 1820 shaft makes this a very tough arrow. The shaft specifications spine to about 50#. Blue anodized finish, conventional nocks.

Jazz – Same alloy and PSI specifications as the Genesis arrows, but available in sizes from 1214 through 2013. Excellent entry grade target arrows for younger archers. Purple anodized pattern finish, conventional nocks.

Stalker – Economy grade general-purpose arrow. Low PSI rating makes these arrows more fragile than the XX75 grade, but they will hold up quite well with normal care. Available in gold and black anodized finish. Conventional nocks.

XX75 – Truly Easton's general-purpose arrow. High PSI and spine/weight tolerances make this a very good shaft for target, field and hunting. Available in a "Platinum Plus" silver anodized finish for target archers as well as numerous camouflage and wood grained anodized patterns for hunting. They are available with both conventional nocks and UNI-bushings (see section on aluminum shaft components).

XX78 – Higher PSI and trueness ratings than XX75 shafts. The difference in PSI and trueness between XX75 and XX78 is minimal in most situations These shafts are camouflage anodized for hunting and come with UNI-bushing nocks.

X7 – Easton's top of the line target arrows, boasting the highest PSI and spine/weight tolerances. X7 shafts have a maximum wall thickness of 14/1000" and are typically fitted with "G" nocks or UNI-bushings. Earlier versions of X7 were available in 16/1000" wall thickness and conventional nocks. Hard anodized black (Eclipse) and blue (Cobalt).

Aluminum shaft alloy comparisons

Shaft	Alloy	PSI	Trueness	Weight tolerance	Comments
Scout	5086	58,000	N/A	N/A	Youth arrows 1618 shaft size
Genesis	7075	85,000	.006"	+/- 2	Youth / Intermediate arrows 1820 shaft size
Jazz	7075	85,000	.006"	+/- 2	Youth / Intermediate arrows
Stalker	5086	58,000	N/A	N/A	Economy aluminum arrows
XX75	7075-T9	95,000	+/- .002"	+/- 1%	Legacy PSI 95,000 Gamegetter trueness +/- .003
XX78 Superslam	7078-T9	100,000	+/- .0015"	+/-1%	Slightly higher PSI and trueness tolerances
X7 (Eclipse/Cobalt)	7078-T9	105,000	+/- .001"	+/-¾ %	Target arrows with a maximum wall thickness of 14/1000"*

In today's market, Easton has numerous offerings in the aluminum, carbon and composite arenas. A detailed list is provided in Appendix B.

Aluminum arrow maintenance

Aluminum has the advantage of needing the least amount of maintenance of all the arrow materials. That doesn't mean "no" maintenance, however.

If an aluminum arrow collides with something other than the intended target, usually something hard, the resultant damage is readily apparent. The usual damage is bending, although arrows are designed to flex a certain amount during paradox; if that amount of flex is exceeded, or it occurs too rapidly, then the shaft doesn't return to true after the collision. If this happens to a wood, fiberglass or carbon arrow, the result is usually a broken shaft; with aluminum, it's a bent arrow, which may be repairable. There are several devices on the market to straighten aluminum arrows. The most common and most precise tool combines twin moveable rollers to support the arrow, a dial indicator, usually graduated in 1/1000's of an inch, and a lever to remove the bend in the arrow by applying pressure against the high point of the bend (diag 9-21). Instructions usually come with the device, but basically the arrow is rolled on the supports, and the dial indicator locates the center of the bend or bends by noting the point of greatest deflection (high point); force is then applied in the opposite direction to straighten the arrow. The archer decides what level of straightness is necessary, and then begins to re-straighten the shaft, repeating the process as necessary. With these straighteners, and a little patience, it's very possible to return an arrow to .002", or better.

9-21 Dial type arrow straightener

When straightening arrows there are two types of bends that may be encountered. A slow or long bend that may extend for half the length of the shaft or more, and much shorter and sharper bends, where part of the arrow seems to have formed a flattened "V". Both types are repairable, but the slow bend may extend beyond the length of the arrow straightener and may take considerable time to work out. "S" shaped bends are handled as two slow bends. The sharper bends tend to be easier, unless they're very close to the pile or nock and there isn't a sufficient length of shaft on either side of the arrow to be supported by the jig. Any arrows with a crimp or dent should not be considered repairable. Also, be aware that thin walled shafts may not tolerate the straightening process well, and may be dented by the supports or straightening lever when pressure is applied. For that reason, I recommend and personally use only shafts with a minimum wall thickness of 14/1000 of an inch.

The other common type of damage due to collision with a hard object is the head and insert being pushed into the shaft (diag 9-22). This usually, but not always, comes with a bend or two in the arrow. The only real fix for this is to remove the head (and insert), and cut off the damaged section of the shaft and replace the head. Usually 1/2" is sufficient, and then remove the bends as described above. Unfortunately, this means that you now have one arrow shorter than the remaining arrows. If your arrows were initially cut slightly long, there's probably no reason why it can't be used as a practice arrow for close shots. I would hesitate to use it for serious shooting or at longer distances; the purpose of the exercise is consistency, and a shorter arrow would, by definition, have not only less weight and a stiffer dynamic spine. If the arrow flies well, you could certainly cut the remaining arrows to that length, but that would be a personal call. Usually if there is direct impact to the head, it's very common for the nock or nock insert to fly off the other end. This is due to the shock wave traveling down the arrow and breaking the nock or insert's glue line. This is usually easy to repair, as described in the next sections.

As your skill improves and your groups become smaller and tighter, it's very common for arrows to side-slap each other in the target. This can result in long silver streaks lengthwise down the arrow shaft, most noticeable on dark colored/anodized arrows (diag 9-23). Unless there's an actual crease in the wall, which is rare, these streaks are not dangerous and are a testament to your shooting ability. Creases, nicks, or dents in the arrow shaft, on the other hand, should not be taken lightly (diag 9-24). While people do shoot with such arrows for years, given the forces the arrow experiences during paradox and depending on the location of the damage, shaft failure is entirely possible. Any arrows with creases, nicks or dents should be destroyed to prevent further use and the possibility of injury.

Many archers find it enjoyable to take a damaged arrow, cut off the shaftment (the last 8 to 12 inches) and glue a pen or pen refill into the shaft (9-25). Unfortunately, the number of arrow pens an archer amasses is typically inversely proportional to his skill, so it may not be a good idea to have too many of them in lying around in plain sight!

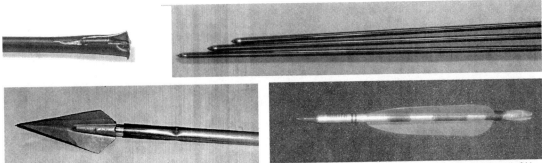

9-22 Arrowhead and insert forced into an aluminum shaft caused by hitting an unreceptive target (top left)!
9-23 Silver streaking on dark anodized aluminum shafts (Easton X7 Eclipse shafts) is a testament to your shooting ability (top right).
9-24 Dents or creases in aluminum arrows should always be considered serious and the arrow destroyed to prevent accidental use (bottom left).
9-25 Arrow pen – careful, don't collect too many of these (bottom right)!

The most common occurrence a skilled archer will face is shooting the nocks off the ends of arrows (diag 9-26). This is quite common amongst experienced archers who shoot small, tight groups and the situation is readily rectifiable. In the case of glue-on nocks, Easton recommends that the damaged nock be heated until it softens and then pulled off with a pair of pliers. Any remaining residue should then be removed by soaking in lacquer thinner. They also advise against cutting nock remnants off with a knife blade or razor, due to the possibility of damage to the aluminum swag cone, resulting in misalignment of the replacement nock. That may be good advice, but in the nearly four decades I've been shooting, I've never had that problem if care was taken while cutting off the remains of the nock (diag 9-27). With the internal or push-in nocks, such as G-nocks or UNI-bushing nocks, the damaged nock is just pulled out of the insert and a new one pressed in and aligned with the cock feather (diag 9-28).

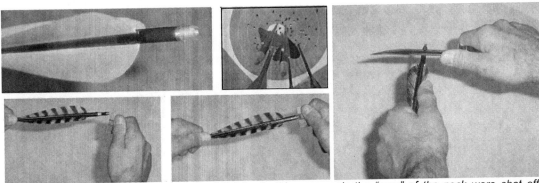

9-26 Nock damage due to grouping "too" tightly. In this case, only the "ears" of the nock were shot off, typically the entire nock is shot off. In the second picture, the author somehow shot two nocks off with one arrow I'll let the reader figure out how that happened (top left)!
9-27 Removal of a glue-on nock using a sharp knife. Be careful not to cut into the swaged nock cone (right).
9-28 Replacing a "G" or UNI-bushing nock. Push the shank of the nock into the bushing and then force it in the rest of the way with the tool provided with the nocks. Once fully seated, use the tool to orient the nock groove as needed (bottom left).

Another rare and usually fatal occurrence (for the arrow) is a "Robinhood". As in the legend, the archer shoots one arrow into the center of the bullseye and splits it lengthwise with a second arrow. In the case of aluminum arrows the splitting is more of a fluting, with one arrow ending up "telescoped" inside the tail end of the other. The second arrow is usually salvageable, but most folks keep the two together as a souvenir, at least, their first one or two. After you get a few, the novelty wears off as the price of arrow replacement mounts (diag 9-29).

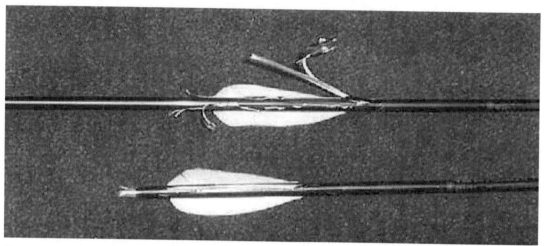

9-29 Ouch!!! The top arrow is called a "Robinhood" for obvious reasons and the bottom arrow came close!

Aluminum arrow components

There are several options with aluminum arrows that allow you to mix and match certain components. We'll take them one step at a time for clarity.

With the most basic aluminum arrows, you have the shaft itself, with the tail end swaged to an 11 degree taper to accept standard glue-on nocks. The other end is open and will accept the pile or insert (diag 9-30).

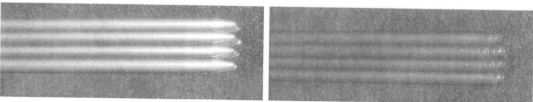

9-30 Swaged nock end and open pile end on aluminum arrows

Originally, target archers used one-piece conical piles with a shank of a specific weight that was simply glued into the shaft. Bowhunters used inserts or "broadhead adapters" that glued into the shaft and had a 5 degree taper to accept the pile, either a field tip or broadhead (diag 9-31).

These days, the conical target tip has been all but replaced by bullet (parabolic) shaped points or NIBB points. NIBBs *(New Improved Balance Bullet)* are target points made specifically for each shaft size to yield a 7% or 9% FOC (diag 9-32). Other one-piece piles are available that have extra long shanks that are scored and can be broken off in sections to give the archer the desired weight and FOC. All of the above piles are glued in place with Ferrule-tite.

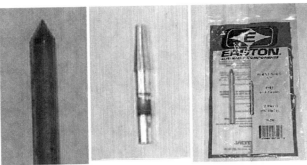

9-31 Glue-in conical target tip and 5 degree tapered broadhead/field point adapter (left). 9-32 Standard bullet target points and NIBBs look identical when glued into a shaft. The only difference is that the target tips are provided in one or two weights (heavy and light or standard) and NIBBs are specifically weighted to provide a specific FOC for a particular shaft (right).

The more common option is to use a threaded insert instead of a one-piece pile. Once the insert is glued into the shaft, any pile with a threaded shank can be utilized (diag 9-33). Interestingly, screw-in adapters were first developed with bowhunters in mind. They could practice with field or target tips, and quickly switch to broadheads of the same weight when hunting season opened. Some bowhunters weren't too fond of them, however. A problem with broadheads, not seen with target or field points, is that the blades needed to be aligned a certain way, usually vertically, for optimal flight. Seems that with the screw-in heads, the bowhunter was never quite sure that they would get the right alignment, so they preferred to just glue them on in the right position and be done with it!

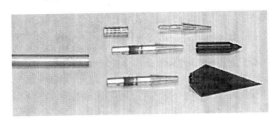

9-33 Aluminum inserts and various glue on heads/inserts. (Top clockwise: screw-in insert, 5 degree screw-in broadhead adapter, old style 5 degree glue-on field point and Bodkin glue-on broadhead, glue-in 5 degree adapter.)

Also popular in the 1960's and 70's were swaged tip arrows. Some archers began to realize the accuracy benefits of the lower FOCs for long range shooting. Several companies began swaging the pile ends of aluminum shafts to a standard 5-degree taper, allowing the head to be glued directly to the shaft (diag 9-34). The obvious disadvantage was that the arrow had to be made to the exact length the archer specified, as the shaft couldn't be shortened if necessary. While still available, they have fallen out of favor with most archers due to the large number of currently available head weights.

Schematic of swaged shaft

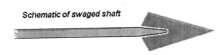

9-34 Swaged pile end shaft and broadhead

The 11 degree swaged nock end of the arrow had been the Easton standard for decades, until it was discovered that perfect shaft/nock alignment was difficult, if not impossible, with glue-on nocks. The next advancement was the use of nock bushings. G-Nocks, UNI- or Super UNI-bushing nocks are now standard on most mid and high-end arrows. Here a nock insert or bushing is glued into an open ended arrow shaft, and the nock's shank is pushed into the insert and aligned as needed (diag 9-35). In addition to increasing the concentricity of the nock to the shaft and the ease of replacement, it made possible minor changes in nock to feather orientation.

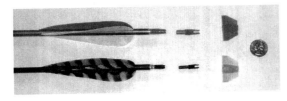

9-35 "G" nocks and UNI-bushing Super nocks. Both nocks are pressed into bushings by means of a tool supplied by Easton and a fair amount of effort on the part of the archer. A US quarter is shown to the right for size comparison.

Carbon Shafts

9-36 Beman ICS carbon arrow

Carbon, or more correctly, carbon fiber arrows have been in use as arrow shaft material since the 1980's. They provide several advantages over aluminum and some disadvantages.

Carbon shafts are inherently stiffer and have greater resiliency than aluminum. They can be made lighter and thinner than most aluminum arrows and may show significant increases in speed and reduced wind resistance. Less obvious is that because of the increased stiffness and resiliency they recover from paradox quicker than aluminum and therefore retain more energy. They can also be quite durable under normal use and like fiberglass, they are either straight or broken.

On the downside, carbon arrows are a newer technology, relative to aluminum. Some of the lower priced carbons do not have the consistency in spine or weight that aluminum arrows have, occasionally even within the same batch or dozen. While rare, it does happen, and if you use carbon arrows and one arrow refuses to group with the rest, the possibility that it may be out of spec, weight or spine-wise, must be considered. The high-end carbon and carbon aluminum composites do not have that shortcoming. While carbon arrows are touted for their durability, they do not stand up very well to side-slaps and direct impact. It's also possible that a carbon arrow can become damaged or cracked, and the crack go undetected by the shooter until the shaft actually fails. "Failing" usually occurs on release, and may result in injury to the shooter. These instances are also rare, but a carbon arrow shooter needs to inspect his arrows a little more carefully and frequently than someone shooting aluminum. In addition to visually inspecting the arrow, particularly near the pile and nock ends, there are two additional techniques for checking the integrity of carbon arrows. The first is to tap one arrow against another. The tapping sound should be singular and clean; any other type of sound should be readily apparent, considered suspect, and lead to further inspection. The second is to grab the arrow at each end and twist the shaft along its axis, while carefully listening for any creaking sounds. If either test suggests shaft damage, the arrow needs to be discarded. Carbon splinters are quite sharp and difficult to remove once embedded in the skin, so please use care with carbon arrows.

There are three types of carbon arrows currently available.

Pultruded shafts are made from unidirectional fibers and so don't offer as much strength as the other types. Pultruded carbon arrows are typically quite thin and cannot use internal inserts for heads and nocks. They require external "outserts" which, as the name implies, go outside the shaft wall, or rather, the shaft goes inside a cylindrical cavity in the outserts. Pultruded shafts haven't undergone any serious development in recent years and are considered to be economy or entry-grade arrows (diag 9-37).

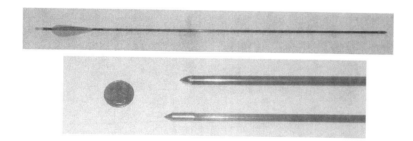

9-37 Pultruded carbon arrows are very thin and marketed towards new and young shooters (top). In the second picture we see an aluminum 1816 (top arrow) next to a 35/50# pultruded carbon arrow. The US quarter to the left is for size reference.

Carbon shafts made from fibers in alternating layers are called **internal component shafts (ICS).** They are considerably stronger than pultruded shafts and as the name implies, they can utilize internal head and nock inserts (diag 9-38). These are the most common carbon arrows in use today.

9-38 Internal Component Shafts (ICS) arrow (Beman ICS)

Spine conventions: Arrow numbers typically denote actual deflections. (A 500 series arrow placed on supports 28" apart will deflect 0.500" when a 2# force is applied to the midpoint of the shaft.)

Carbon composite arrows or **hybrids** are composed of carbon and aluminum. They are made to very tight tolerances, heavier than carbon alone and can be very thin in diameter (diag 9-39).

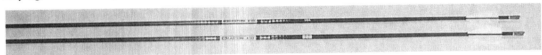

9-39 Easton X-10 carbon aluminum shaft

Most elite Olympic / FITA shooters are using composite arrows for outdoor competitions these days with great success. Their greatest downside is their price. A dozen top-end arrows can easily cost over $350. With proper components, the total can reach nearly $600, at the time of this printing. In addition to Easton, several manufacturers are offering carbon composite arrow of general use and hunting purposes.

Easton composite arrows

Easton currently offers five aluminum/carbon composite arrows, three for target archers, one for both target and hunting and one designed specifically for hunting use.

Axis Full Metal Jacket – Hunting arrows with a carbon core and aluminum outer casing. Axis FMJ's are thin shafted arrows using "X" nocks and HIT (Easton's Hidden Insert Technology) inserts.

Spine conventions: Arrow numbers denote actual deflections. *(A 500 series arrow placed on supports 28" apart will deflect 0.500" when a 2# force is applied to the midpoint of the shaft.)*

ACC (Aluminum/Carbon/Composite) – They are available in spines suitable for both target and hunting bows. ACCs use a thin, parallel shaft design and can be configured with HIT components for hunting applications and standard target components for target use. Spine conventions: Probably Easton's most confusing nomenclature! ACC arrows use two sets of numbers, separated by a hyphen for example 2-00, 3-49. The first number (2 or 3) indicates the relative thickness of the carbon (actually graphite) that is bonded to the aluminum core. The second two-digit number signifies thousandths of an inch over 0.200" of the aluminum core tube diameter. For example: a **3-49** ACC has a carbon layer relative thickness of **3** and an aluminum core diameter of 0.249". To make matters worse, Easton uses the letters "L" and "X" after the first number. "L" (as in 3L-04) signifies a shaft with a lighter spine than a 3-04 without the "L". The "X" (3**X**-04) indicates the lightest spine for a given core.

AC Navigators – Easton's entry level composite target shaft, also using a thin parallel shaft design and ACE or Navigator pile components. Navigators can be fitted with either "G" nock bushings or "pin" nocks.

Spine conventions: Arrow numbers denote actual deflections. *(A 500 series arrow placed on supports 28" apart will deflect 0.500" when a 2# force is applied to the midpoint of the shaft.)*

ACE (Aluminum/Carbon/Extreme) – These shafts are barreled for enhanced aerodynamics and utilize "G" or "pin" nocks and specific ACE one piece or screw-in piles. ACEs have tighter weight and spine tolerances than the ACC or AC Navigators.

Spine conventions: Arrow numbers denote actual deflections. *(A 500 series arrow placed on supports 28" apart will deflect 0.500" when a 2# force is applied to the midpoint of the shaft.)*

X-10 — Easton's top of the line Aluminum/Carbon target arrows feature barreled shafts and can use only "pin" nocks and specific X-10 piles. (see diagram 9-39) A new addition to the Easton line is the X-10 Pro Tour arrow. They are the essentially the same as the standard X-10, except for a modified taper which remains thicker through the shaftment. The Pro Tours are designed for compound bows which may benefit from the stiffer spine in the rear of the arrow.

Spine conventions: Arrow numbers denote actual deflections. *(A 500 series arrow placed on supports 28" apart will deflect 0.500" when a 2# force is applied to the midpoint of the shaft.)*

Cartel Archery (a Korean based archery manufacturer dealing primarily with target equipment and accessories) recently entered the composite arrow market with a new arrow called the "Triples". They are a parallel shaft design and have shown excellent tolerances in weight and spine.
Spine conventions: Arrow numbers denote actual deflections. *(A 500 series arrow placed on supports 28" apart will deflect 0.500" when a 2# force is applied to the midpoint of the shaft.)*

Carbon arrows are usually classified by spine deflection; for example, a carbon arrow marked 400 would have a deflection of .400 inches, or thereabouts. Each manufacturer publishes their specifications on the actual deflection of each arrow. Some manufacturers simply state the appropriate draw weights; for example, a 35/55 or 3555 carbon arrow would be suitable for bows between 35# and 55#. Other manufacturers simply use the shaft OD and others have their own naming conventions. Since carbon arrows do offer greater resiliency to flexing during paradox, and a quicker recovery, a particular arrow spine will tolerate a wider range of draw weights. While that may sound like an advantage to new shooters, because of the one size (or a few sizes) fits all theory, some archers may find that carbon arrows may be a little trickier to tune than aluminum arrows.

Typical spine ranges for carbon arrows:

500 series arrows will work with bows from 45# to 55#
400 series arrows will work with bows from 55# to 65#
300 series arrows will work with bows from 65# to 75#

There are many carbon arrow manufacturers and their offerings change from year to year; it would be impossible to mention each. Some of the more popular carbon arrows are listed in Appendix B.

It is imperative that you consult with each manufacturer or a knowledgeable dealer when ordering carbon arrows, as the same number designation from one manufacturer may not have exactly the same specifications as another manufacturer.

Carbon arrow maintenance

Carbon arrows are very durable except in the instances described above. The Internal Component Shafts may be more prone to "Robinhooding" due to their one-piece internal nocks. I'll let the reader decide whether that's a plus or minus.

Carbon arrow components

Pultruded shafts use only outsert piles and nocks (diag 9-40).

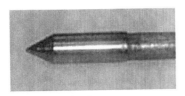

9-40 *Pultruded carbon shaft components with nock and pile "Excerts" slipped over the shaft ends*

Internal Component Shafts typically use one-piece nocks, but can be fitted with nock inserts to allow "UNI-bushing" type nocks and use screw-in pile inserts (diag 9-41).

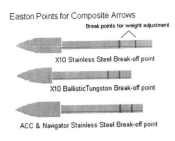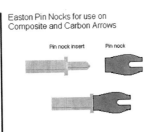

9-41 *ICS shaft with insert*

Composite Aluminum/Carbon shafts are fitted with specialized nock bushings with push-in nocks or pin nocks and usually glue-in piles which are weight-adjustable by varying the length of the shank (diag 9-42) Diagram 9-42a shows pin nock assemblies on Easton ACE arrows.

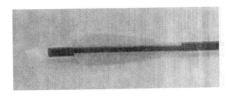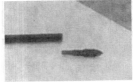

9-42 *Aluminum/Carbon composite arrow components (Easton Archery).*
9-42a *Easton Pin nocks on ACE arrows.*

Spine charts and specific composite arrow nock and pile options for some current and vintage arrows are given in Appendix B.

Arrowheads

The arrowhead defines the purpose of the arrow. As simple a statement as that may appear, it defines the very purpose of archery.

Target tip – used for target shooting, aerodynamic and weighted for maximum accuracy over longer ranges. Initially, target tips were conical in shape, as that design allowed the greatest degree of precision in manufacturing with regard to weight and shape. Later, they became more parabolic in shape to decrease aerodynamic drag (diag 9-43).

Field point – similar to a target tip, but with a shoulder past the actual point to hinder penetration if shot into wood, either deliberately or inadvertently (diag 9-44).

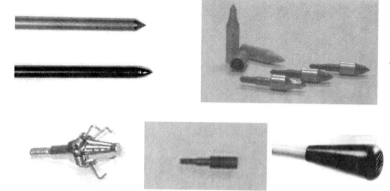

9-43 Early conical steel point and standard bullet shaped NIBB point (left)
9-44 Field points: glue-on and screw-on types (right)

9-45 Judo point (left)
9-46 Blunt heads for small game, metal screw-in (middle) and rubber push-on (right) types

Judo point – Specialized tip for use in roving or "stump shooting". The descriptive term stump shooting, or more colloquially "stumpin'", simply means walking around a wooded area, picking out an appropriate tree stump and shooting at it, or a part of it. While field tips may hinder penetration if the stump is actually hit, more often than not, arrows miss their marks and hit the ground, usually burying themselves under leaves or soil. The Judo point, with four wire arms snags the ground or something on it, and flips the arrow over, hence the martial arts reference. It has a small blunt metal center, which makes it equally efficient for small game (diag 9-45).

Blunt head – Made of either rubber or metal, these heads are used to dispatch small game. Blunt heads kill by shock and are not meant to penetrate the animal (diag 9-46).

Broadheads or Hunting heads – These arrowheads are designed to dispatch large game animals. They are equipped with 2 to 4 or more sharpened blades that kill by hemorrhage. There have been various designs on the market over the years and each has its devotees (diag 9-47).

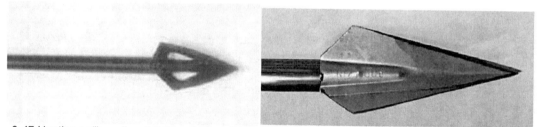

9-47 Hunting or "broadheads": Classic Bear Razorhead and Bodkin tri-blade, popular in the 1970's.

Nocks

The nock is the one part of the arrow that engages the string. It must do so securely and with uniform tension from arrow to arrow while maintaining concentricity with the shaft.

Except in some primitive style archery circles, long gone are the days of self-nocks made by cutting a groove in the tail of a wooden arrow and binding the shaft with string or twine (diag 9-48). Throughout the latter half to two-thirds of the last century, the most common arrow nock was the so-called "Speed-nock" (diag 9-49). It was a plastic nock with the standard 11-degree taper to fit the arrow, and a chamfered throat to allow easy engagement of the string (diag). Not only did it quickly slip onto the string, since it didn't clip on in any way, it guaranteed consistent tension on disengagement. Many speed nocks also had a ridge or "index" that gave the archer a tactile indication of the arrow's orientation to the riser. (The index was aligned with the cock feather, so all the archer needed to do was position the index ridge under his thumb.)

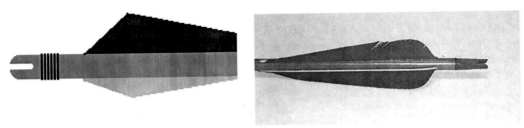

9-48 Self nock on a wood arrow (left)
9-49 Speed nocks with wide open throats for quick string engagement (right)

As the speed nocks did not snap or clip onto the string, there was always a risk, especially with new shooters, that the nock would come off the string prematurely. When that happened, the resultant dry fire not only shocked the shooter, but also could have potentially damaged the bow. By the 1960's there were several brands of nocks on the market that clipped onto the bowstring (diag 9-50). These greatly reduced the possibility of a nock slipping off the string, and some were even indexed as speed nocks were.

9-50 Snap-on nocks secure the arrow to the string and need to be checked and tuned for the correct amount of tension.

With the acceptance of glue on "snap-nocks" (also called "conventional" nocks) the next thing the serious competitor needed to worry about was whether the nocks were too tight, too loose or had inconsistent tension on the string. This could be achieved by either finding the right sized nocks (the preferred method), modifying the thickness of the string or serving, or modifying the nock's opening. The last option was easily accomplished by holding the nock in boiling water for a few seconds and then spreading or pinching the ears to the correct size for a given string. As we stated in the tuning section, it's not advisable to sand or file down the inside of nock groove, as removing material may weaken the nock. A nock with correct tension should hold slightly more than the weight of the arrow.

Maintaining nock concentricity with the shaft became increasingly critical, as higher levels of precision were required at longer distances. The glue-on nocks, while generally quite adequate for most archers, became problematic for elite archers shooting at longer ranges. Easton then developed the nock bushing. Not entirely a new idea, the bushing was a nock insert as had been used on fiberglass and graphite arrows; instead of an 11-degree tapered cone to accept a glue-on nock, these bushings had a precision ground hole to accept the shank of a push-in nock. There are several varieties based on shaft size and type of shaft material. Despite their slightly higher cost, they are becoming increasingly popular An added benefit, a damaged nock could be instantly replaced without the need for glue and since the nock bushing added a certain amount of strength to the rear of the arrow, it made splitting an arrow more difficult.

UNI-bushings and beyond

To use the push-in type nocks UNI (Universal Nock Insert) bushings of the appropriate size are factory installed with a hot melt type of glue. The nocks, either "G", "H" or "X" nocks for smaller diameter arrows or "Super" nocks for larger diameter shafts, are pressed into the bushing. A special tool or "key" is provided with these nocks to aid insertion and to help align the nock as the archer requires (see diag 9-28). Some carbon shafts are designed to accept the "Super" nocks or nock of similar design directly into the shaft without the need for a bushing. While convenient, the possibility of *"robinhooding"* an arrow is greatly increased

The extremely thin arrows used by Olympic style target archers made use of the UNI bushing impossible. For arrows such as the X-10, ACEs, Navigators and ACCs "nock pins" were developed. A nock *pin* is a solid metal shaft that fits inside a thin arrow and has a male end onto which the pin *nock* is pushed. Some of the larger diameter target shafts give the archer the choice of UNI bushings or pin nocks (see diag 9-42)

Fletching

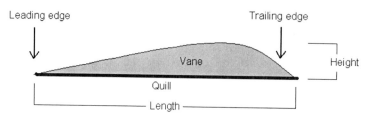

Feather nomenclature

9-51 Basic feather nomenclature, parabolic cut, and yes, the main section is called a "vane"!

The fletching, comprised of either turkey or goose feathers or plastic vanes, is responsible for giving the arrow most of its flight characteristics. It stabilizes the arrow, hastens its departure from paradox and continues to steer the arrow while in flight.

We discussed in detail the purpose and effects of fletching in the tuning section. Before we embark on building our own arrows, or rather, *fletching* them, a brief word is necessary about the available shapes of the feathers or vanes.

The most popular feather or vane shape is called "parabolic", as it describes the shape of a lop-sided parabola, a mathematical plot given by the general formula $x=y^2$ (9-52). Besides aesthetic appeal, parabolic cut feathers tend to yield a smoother air-flow and therefore less turbulence behind the trailing edge than other types of feather shapes. A more traditional, and so possibly older, design is the shield cut, which looks like a narrowed medieval knight's shield, halved lengthwise (diag 9-53). Shield cut feathers will give the characteristic "whooshing" noise, which may be exacerbated or diminished by the angle of the trailing edge and the degree of offset or helical orientation. *(The whistling or "whooshing" noise that was typically heard when arrows were loosed in old movies, was due to amplifying the sound of arrow with exceptionally large fletching.)* Both shapes will equally stabilize an arrow, and the choice is one of personal taste. Also, both are typically available in sizes from 1.5" to 5.5".

Standard Parabola $x=y^2$

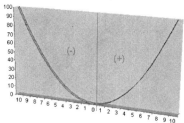

9-52 Mathematical graph of a parabola $x=y^2$
9-53 Parabolic cut feathers in 3" and 5" lengths (left) and shield cut feathers in 5" length (right)

Another feature of feather shape to be considered is height – the distance from the quill to the tallest point on the leading edge. As previously discussed the greater the surface area of the fletching, the quicker the arrow will stabilize in flight. While 5" feathers (and vanes) are approximately 5/8" in height, high-back feathers are available with heights of 3/4" or more. They are designed to stabilize large broadheads, but typically see more service in masking the shooter's form or equipment tuning problems. They may also lead to interference with the arrow rest or riser and therefore result in erratic fight characteristics. For those reasons, they are unnecessary and should be avoided. A well-tuned bow and arrow combination eliminates the need for excessively large fletching even when using the largest broadheads.

Also used today by some traditional archers are "banana cut" or so called "Magnum" feathers. They are usually 5.5" long high back feathers with equal slopes on the leading and trailing edges. Their purpose is to provide a large surface area to stabilize the arrow quickly, while giving a surface for a smoother airflow and thus eliminating the whooshing sound. As with high-back parabolic feathers, they may give clearance problems and should be used with caution, if at all. I have had no trouble stabilizing the largest broadheads with 5" parabolic feathers (diag 9-54).

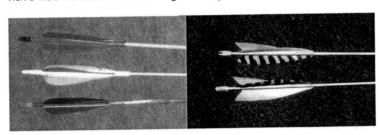

9-54 High back feathers (top two left) compared to standard height feathers bottom left) and high back feathers in a "traditional shield" cut.

There have been other shapes used over the years, such as balloon, triangular or straight cut feathers, but few are in common use today (diag 5-55).

Comparison of feather shapes

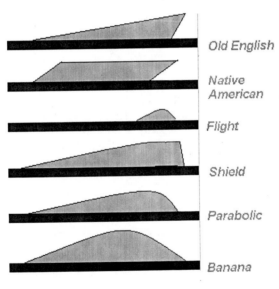

Old English

Native American

Flight

Shield

Parabolic

Banana

9-55 Comparison of feather shapes (left).

Most people these days buy pre-cut feathers in the shape, size and color they need. Some folks who'd rather do it themselves can buy full length, uncut feathers and cut them to size. These may be pre-dyed or raw, if the fletcher decides he'd rather dye them himself.

There are two methods of cutting feathers. The first and easiest is with a feather "chopper" (diag 9-56). The chopper has a sharpened blade curved to the required shape and size and held between two blocks of wood. The feather is placed under the blade, the top block of wood is hit with a hammer, cutting the feather to shape. The other method is a feather burner. The burner is a length of high resistance wire, typically nichrome, bent to the required shape and attached to an electrical transformer (diag 9-57). When an electric current is applied, the wire gets hot and the fletched arrow, usually with its nock supported in a bushing, is rotated so the uncut feathers come in contact with the hot wire and are burnt to size. The charred edges are then sanded down. While a very efficient method of trimming feathers, the smell of burning feathers is potent enough to warrant the procedure being taken outdoors, or at least away from family members who might not share the fletcher's enthusiasm.

Flu-flu arrows may use 4 or 6, 5" to 6" uncut feathers or a single long feather wrapped several times around the shaft. They are used for aerial targets, either paper discs or flying game birds.

After approximately 15 to 20 yards of relatively normal flight, they rapidly decelerate and fall to earth due to their large surface area. They also make a very loud characteristic sound in flight. Because of the rapid stabilization, spine is not a concern and the flu-flu shafts are typically over-spined, almost to a one-size-fits-all scenario (diag 9-58).

9-56 "Little Chopper" feather chopper and 9-57 Young feather burner (Photos courtesy of 3Rivers Archery) 9-58 Six feathered Flu-flu arrow

Typical feather specifications:

Feather type	Height Cut	Shape	Number of feathers
Standard 3" feather	7/16"	Parabolic or shield	3
Standard 5" feather	5/8"	Parabolic or shield	3 or 4
High-back 5" or 5.5"	3/4"	Parabolic or shield	3 or 4
Flu-flu 5" to 6"	1-3/4"	Uncut	4 or 6

Barred, plain or spliced?

Barred feathers have uneven stripes running in the direction of the side branches or "barbs". They come from the undersides of birds and are believed to be stronger than the plain or unbarred feathers. They are becoming increasingly expensive and difficult to get. Some companies are selling faux-barred feathers, which have the stripes or "bars" dyed in. Still more expensive than plain or single colored feathers, they do add a touch of traditional charm to arrows. Plain, or unbarred feathers begin typically white or off white, and the feather "re-manufacturers'" bleach and/or dye them to specific colors. Some, in addition to the previously noted faux-barred feathers, also offer camouflage, or streaked feathers, to add visual variety. Some companies and individuals splice two or more different color feathers together, cutting them at equal distances from one end, and joining them together for a two-tone or multicolor effect. (diag 9-61)

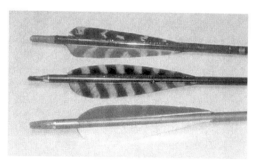

9-61 Barred (top left), faux barred (center left) and plain (bottom left) fletched arrows.

Fletching, dipping and cresting arrows will be covered in chapter 10.

Miscellaneous notes on arrows

Note on target arrow dimensions and requirements: In 2004, FITA rules set a maximum shaft diameter of 9.3mm or roughly 23/63"; the IBO, NFAA and other organizations have yet to adopt that change.

To make matters worse, the OD, the first two digits of an aluminum arrow's designation, is only a nominal figure. If you were to measure the OD of various shafts with the same OD numbers but different wall thickness numbers with a dial caliper, you'd find slight variations. This may seem trivial, but for FITA competition, the 9.3mm maximum arrow diameter allows the 2312, 2314 and 2315, but not the 2317.

Arrow speeds and standards: The only accurate way to measure arrow speed is with a chronograph. There are two organizations that have standards for arrow speeds.

AMO (Archery Manufacturers Organization) standard:
- Maximum draw weight of 60#
- Arrow weight of 540 grains (9 grains per pound of draw weight)
- A draw length of 30 inches
- The chronograph set to detect the initial speed of the arrow as it leaves the bow

IBO (International Bowhunters Organization) standard:
- Maximum draw weight of 70#
- Arrow weight of 350 grains (5 grains per pound of draw weight)
- A draw length of 30 inches
- The chronograph set to detect the initial speed of the arrow as it leaves the bow

It should be fairly clear that the above standards are for comparisons only. Not all archers have 30 inch draw lengths, use 60# or 70# bows or use exactly 9gr/lb or 5gr/lb arrows. The 5gr/lb arrow specifications are intended for compound bows and under no circumstances should stickbow shooters go that low in weight. Minimum tolerances for currently manufactured high performance bows are around 7 gr/lb and older bows should stay within the 8-9gr/lb range or greater.

Chapter 10

Fletching, the Art of Building an Arrow

B y this point, it's probably a good time to get to some practical applications of all this stuff we're talking about. Time to make some arrows!

We'll use aluminum arrows as an example, as they are still the most popular with new shooters, and the easiest to work with. From a practical standpoint, most archers' first fletching job isn't making a brand new set of arrows, but re-fletching arrows with worn feathers, so we'll start there.

You'll need (diag 10-1):

- a dozen or so arrows with tattered feathers (a fairly readily available commodity, if you've been shooting for awhile)
- 36 new pre-cut feathers, usually 24 of one color and 12 of another (a few extra usually won't hurt, just in case!)
- a fletching jig; I'll use a Jo-Jan Multi-fletcher for this example
- fletching glue (Fletch-tite) or fletching tape (Fletch-tape)
- a knife or feather stripping tool
- a container of Comet or a similar abrasive cleanser and some rags or paper towels

10-1 Components and materials required to fletch arrows

Removing the old feathers

Several methods have been suggested over the years, but the safest is simply to cut or shave the worn feathers off with a sharp knife. There are also commercially available feather/vane removal tools, or strippers, that have a curved blade to follow the contour of the arrow shaft more closely (diag 10-2). Another alternative is a #12 blade disposable scalpel, or a hobby knife with a #28 X-Acto blade. The #12 scalpel blade, and the #28 X-Acto blade have a concave cutting surface, and work as well as the feather stripping tools. They can be bought at most surgical supply stores and hobby shops, respectively (diag 10-3).

10-2 "The Stripper" commercial feather stripping tool (Photo courtesy of 3Rivers Archery, left)
10-3 #12 scalpel blade affixed to a #3 scalpel handle (right)

Simply cut the feather off the shaft by putting the blade under the quill and slicing away from you (diag 10-4). Continue the cutting action and you will feel remaining slivers of the quill and glue being removed (diag 10-5). Once there's no more resistance to the blade's movement, that means that the feather and glue residues are gone. Repeat for the remaining feathers and then go on to the next arrow.

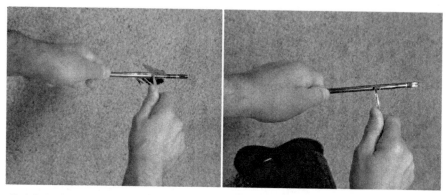

10-4 Stripping feathers with a #12 scalpel blade (left)
10-5 Removing any remaining glue residue. Once the blade slides smoothly over the shaft, the residue is gone (right).

Most arrows today aren't painted, but if the arrows you're working on have a painted shaftment, the paint will have to be removed. Some advocate letting the shaftment soak in acetone for a few hours, while others use paint remover; still others just scrape it off with a knife blade. All are viable methods and which to use is really your choice. If you do use the paint remover method, the gel type is easier to work with as it adheres well to the shaft. It's a good idea to wrap the nock with masking tape, as the paint remover may soften the nock. Naturally, follow the instructions on the container and work with adequate ventilation. If the arrow has a crest you want to preserve, mask the crest as well as the nock, and simply remove the paint from the area that will hold the feathers.

Note: some chemicals in paint removers may attack the resin in fiberglass or carbon shafts, and weaken them. If you choose to use a paint remover, use one that is safe for plastic/resin surfaces and leave it in contact with the shaft only as long as necessary to allow the paint to be removed. Then thoroughly wash the shaft to remove all traces of it. While I have never found this to be an issue, given the number of solvents and shaft materials, caution must be advised. Letting a damaged shaft soak in the solvent overnight and checking for signs of weakening or discoloration would be a prudent approach.

When the feathers and glue residue and paint (if any) are gone, take the arrows over to the kitchen sink, and scrub them down with an abrasive cleanser, such as Comet or Ajax. This helps to remove any remaining glue from the shaft, as well as any oil from your hands on the shaftment. It also roughens up the surface, which helps the new glue adhere better. This also has to be done with new shafts, as most will have an oil film from the manufacturing process or at the very least oil from the hands of the people handling them. Rinse with clear water and paper towel dry. From this point on, nothing should touch the shaftment until the feathers have been applied (diag 10-6).

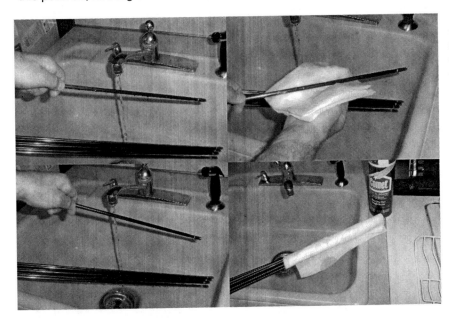

10-6 A stream of water running over the scrapped shaft shows water droplets, indicating dirt or oil residue that will hinder adhesion (top left). Scrubbing the shaftment with a scouring cleanser on a paper towel (top right). Water flowing off the shaft without droplet formation means the shaft is clean (bottom left). Wrapping a paper towel around the clean shafts ensures they'll remain clean until fletched (bottom right).

Setting up the fletching jig

Set up the fletching jig as shown in the instructions that came with it. There are several types on the market, and each will be a little different. We'll use a Jo-Jan Multi-fletcher for this example. If you are using fletching glue, this jig has the advantage of being able to fletch six arrows at once. If you decide to use the fletching tape that benefit is somewhat diminished, as the tape has little if any drying time. The Jo-Jan Multi-fletcher is available with straight fletch and right or left helical clamps (diag 10-7). The left helical clamps will be used for this example.

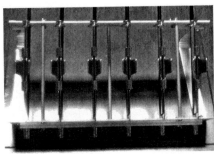 

10-7a Jo-Jan jig with straight clamps (left) and left wing helical clamps (right).

1. Indexing the cock feather: The Multi-fletcher uses the arrow nock as an index. Position the six nock-receivers so that the index plate (the metal plate the arrow's nock engages) is horizontal (diag 10-8). That way, the first feather will always be the cock feather. Since we're assuming this is your first time using this fletching jig, you'll need to calibrate it for feather position from the nock and for offset.

10-8 Set all nock receiver index blades to horizontal. The receivers sit in a piece of aluminum that can be positioned left or right to adjust the offset of the feather's trailing edge. A similar plate on the other side of the jig cradles the arrow and allows for leading edge adjustment.

2. Establishing feather position from the nock: Take a fletched arrow and place it in the jig. Slip the clamp over the feather; it doesn't have to be perfect. See where the trailing (rear) end of the feather is on the edge of the clamp. Mark that spot with a pen or felt tip marker (diag 10-8). Repeat the process for the other five clamps. When done, measure each mark and confirm that all six marks are the same distance from the rear end of the clamps. If not, recheck and correct the inconsistencies. Generally, the trailing edge of the feather should be about 1-1/4" to 1-1/2" from the nock groove. It doesn't matter if it's not exactly 1-1/4" or 1-1/2", but all clamps should be identical. If it's less than 1-1/4", there's a chance that your fingers will contact the feathers while drawing and anchoring. On aluminum jigs like the Multi-fletcher, once the position has been established, cutting or filing a small notch in the clamp edge permanently marks the position (diag 10-9).

Note that the some of the newer straight Jo-Jan jigs have clamps that are notched on the trailing end for consistent feather placement. If yours has these notches, marking the clamps as described above is unnecessary (diag 10-9a).

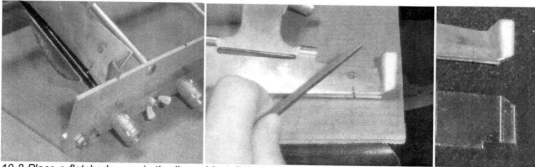

10-8 Place a fletched arrow in the jig and install the clamp over the feather. Mark the position of the trailing edge of the feather on the clamp. Notice also that the clamp and jig base are numbered so the same clamp is always used in the same slot (left).
10-9 Here, a small file is used to make the trailing edge position mark permanent (right).
10-9a Comparison of flat edge and notched clamps. The trailing edge of the feather is set flush against the perpendicular cut on the notch.

3. It is also beneficial to number the clamps and jig positions. That way, the #1 clamp is always in the #1 slot on the jig. While each clamp should be identical, slight variations are always possible; knowing that the same clamp is always in the same slot is somewhat reassuring.

4. Positioning the offset of the feather: Offset is the lateral displacement between the leading and trailing end of the feather. Most jigs allow for offset variation. The Multi-fletcher has two rails that support the arrow and they can be adjusted for front (leading edge) and rear (trailing edge) offset. Simply loosen the wing nuts and slide the front and rear rails until the desired offset is achieved. Place a bare shaft in the jig, and a feather in the clamp with its trailing edge at the mark, as described in step 1. Place the clamp in the jig.

If you have straight clamps (no helical curvature) move the front and back rails so that the quill is in line with and centered on the shaft. That's your neutral position for that arrow, and theoretically any arrow on that jig. You can adjust the front and rear rails to give the desired amount of offset. Diagram 10-10 shows the options or fletch orientation (diag 10). Just be careful that you retain enough contact between the quill and the shaft for adequate glue adhesion.

If you have right or left helical clamps (and therefore are using right or left wing feathers) you follow the same procedure; align the rails so that there's maximum contact between the quill and the shaft (diag 11-11). Again, you have some room to adjust the amount of offset, but less than with the straight clamps. Fletch-tite cement is quite strong, but the more contact between the quill and the shaft, the better the adhesion. Properly fletched arrows should never lose their feathers and they should actually be slightly difficult to remove when it comes time to refletch.

Tighten down the rails with the thumbscrews or wing nuts, and you're ready to start fletching. When you need to fletch different diameter shafts, you'll need to repeat step 2 if you're using helical clamps.

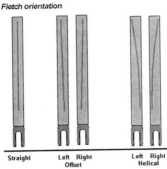

Fletch orientation

Straight   Left   Right   Left   Right
           Offset   Helical

11-10 Options for fletch orientation (left)

10-11 Proper contact between the quill and the shaft guarantees a solid bond. There are no gaps or spaces in this glue line (right).

Fletching the arrows

To fletch the arrows, place an arrow in each of the jig's receivers and a feather, leading edge forward in each clamp, with the trailing edge at the mark you previously made. Some fletchers like to leave 1/16" of feather showing between the quill and the clamp edge so the clamp forces the feather against the shaft. Next, run a thin bead of Fletch-tite along the flat of the quill, then slip clamp #1 into the slot #1 on the jig and visually inspect its position to make sure the quill is fully seated against the arrow shaft (diag 10-12). If not, adjust it as necessary. If it is, move on to the next arrow. Fletch-tite has a relatively quick drying time. After you've completed the first feather on the six arrows, wait about 15 to 20 minutes. Then remove clamp #1, and examine the arrow to confirm a solid bond. Rotate the nock receiver clockwise to the next detent and repeat the process for the second arrow, and so on (diag 10-13).

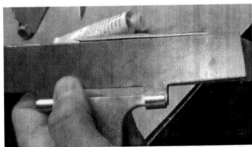

10-12 A nice, even bead of glue on the quill (left) The clamp in position as in diagram 10-11, but this time with glue bonding the feather to the shaft (right).

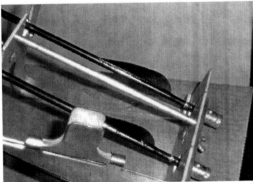

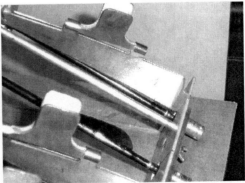

10-13 The first (cock) feathers in place on their shafts (left) Rotate the nock receiver to affix the first hen feather (right).

Since the first feather was the cock feather, the second and third feathers will be hen feathers of a different color. Repeat the process for the remaining arrows and for the third feather. You should now have a half dozen arrows fletched. The next six should be easier as all the calibrations have been made already. Within an elapsed time of about two hours, you'll have a dozen newly fletched arrows (diag 10-14). Despite Fletch-tite's quick set up time, it's a good idea to let the glue cure for 24 hours, or at least overnight.

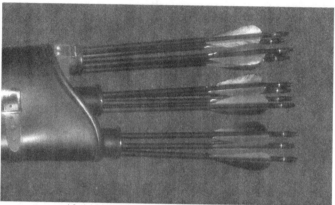

10-14 Your first dozen re-fletched arrows

An alternative method is to use fletching tape. Fletching tape is very thin and narrow double-sided or "double-stick" tape with very strong bonding properties. To use it you simply place a feather in the clamp, affix the tape to the quill, slide the clamp into the jig and onto the shaft, and trim off the excess tape (diag 10-15). The initial bonding is immediate, and so you can go immediately to the next feather. The bond should be allowed a few hours to set, to ensure maximum adhesion. Many archers have switched from glue to tape with excellent results.

10-15 Fletch-tape is a viable option to Fletch-tite glue for those who need a quick bond with little or no mess.

Whether glue or tape is used, a small drop of glue should be placed at each end of the feather. This ensures that there isn't an edge sticking up to cause either an untimely dissociation of the feather from the shaft, or a sharp edge to stick an unsuspecting archer (diag 10-16a). When feathers are dyed, the dye typically doesn't fully color the quill. A white quill is not aesthetically pleasing between a dark colored feather and dark shaft. A simple trick to camouflage the quill is to touch it up with a felt tip pen of an appropriate color. The pen color may match either the feather color or the shaft color. Depending on the colors being used, the touchup may need to be done either before or after the feather is glued to the shaft. Usually one or two passes over the quill is sufficient and adds a very professional finish to your arrows (diag 10-16b).

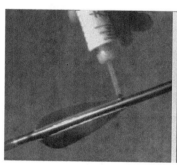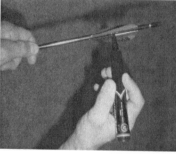

10-16a A small drop of glue on the leading and trailing edges of the quill ensures a solid bond (left).
10-16b Camouflaging the quill with a felt tipped marker (right).

We've used the Jo-Jan Multi-fletcher here, but there are numerous fletching jigs on the market today. The Multi-fletcher originally marketed by

J G Gebhardt has been around since the middle of the last century and has the advantage off allowing six arrows to be fletched identically at the same time. The Bitzenburger jig (diag 10-17) has long been considered the gold standard and allows very precise adjustment in offset. With these jigs, along with several newer entries, the archer/fletcher would be hard pressed not to achieve professional results.

10-17 Bitzenburger has been the gold standard for fletching jigs for decades. Magnets hold the feather clamp in place to allow for optimal alignment.

If you are fletching new or raw shafts, you'll also need to cut them to the proper length and attach the nocks and points. Again, we'll use aluminum arrows for our example.

If your shafts have swaged nock tapers, a small amount of Fletch-tite in the nock's cavity is sufficient. Once the glue is applied, push the nock on to the swage and rotate it slightly to get an even coating of glue (diag 10 18). Most fletchers align the nock with the logo on the shaft. While not serving any practical purpose, it does give a professional look to the finished arrow. If aluminum nock inserts are used, they are installed the same way as the piles, in the next section. The matching nock is then simply pressed into the insert and aligned to a logo or mark on the shaft.

Cutting the shaft really requires an arrow or tubing cut-off saw. Several non-commercial models are available for about $30.00 (diag 10-19). While it is possible to use a hacksaw or tubing cutter on aluminum arrows, the results are never as clean as when using the proper tools. *(Carbon arrows should never be cut with a hacksaw!)* If you don't have access to one, it might be better either to order your shafts cut to length or have them cut by the local Pro-Shop. After they are cut, the inner edge needs to be chamfered to remove any burrs and allow easy entry of the pile or pile insert (diag 10-20). These chamfer/deburring tools are also used by gun enthusiasts who reload their own ammo and so are available at most gun shops for a few dollars. Only a light chamfering is necessary for our purposes.

10-18 Applying glue to the mouth of a glue-on nock and affixing it to the shaft (left).
10-19 An inexpensive arrow cut-off saw mounted on a graduated board is all that is needed to cut arrow shafts uniformly (right).

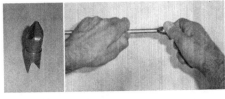

10-20 A de-burring tool neatly cleans the mouth of the shaft to allow easy entry of the head or insert.

Piles or inserts are generally glued into aluminum shafts with a hot stick (Ferrule-tite, or similar) glue. This is not the same type of glue available in craft stores for use with hot glue guns. Both the insert and the inside of the shaft should be free of debris or oil before assembly. The inserts can be wiped with isopropyl alcohol, and the shaft's inner surface can be cleaned with a cotton swab dipped in alcohol. For aluminum arrows – the shank of the pile or insert should be held in a pair of pliers and heated over a propane torch, or kitchen burner, as should the end of the shaft. Care should be taken not to overheat the insert or shaft so as not to damage either. The hot insert is then rubbed against the end of the Hot Glue stick, melting the glue. It is then pushed into the warm open end of the shaft (diag 10-21 to 10-23). As soon as the assembly is cool to the touch, it's ready to be used. If inserts were used, then the appropriate heads can be screwed in. If there is any excess glue on the outside of the shaft, it can be removed when cool with your fingernail or a knife. Another advantage to the hot glues is that if the head or insert ever needs to be removed or repositioned, reapplying heat softens the glue and allows the change or adjustment.

10-21 With the insert held in a pair of needle-nose pliers, apply heat directly to the pile or insert and the end of the shaft, in this case with a torch (left).
10-22 Touch the shank of the insert to the hot-glue stick (middle).
10-23 Push the insert into the shaft opening (right).

While the same general principles apply to other shaft materials, there are some differences that we need to be aware of.

Wood shafts

First and foremost, a bare wood shaft makes a very poor arrow. It will absorb moisture, warp quickly and will damage very easily. Wood arrows must therefore be sealed with some type of finish before being fletched. Fletchers use urethane, spar varnish, simple stains, or even paint, before assembly. See the cresting section below, on painting or "dipping" arrows.

Wood arrows need to be aligned so that the nock groove is perpendicular with the grain lines, and the densest part of the grain is oriented so that when the arrow is nocked, it is against the strike plate on the riser. This is necessary for both self-nocks and glue on nocks for the following reasons:

1. Greater resistance to splitting on release
2. May provide the stiffest and most uniform spine
3. If the arrow should break during acceleration the jagged ends of the break are oriented up and down instead of towards the archer's arm and might add a slight measure of protection in the event of failure.

Nocks can be cemented on with Fletch-tite and piles can be attached with Hot Stick glue as with aluminum, but only the pile should be heated, as it's generally a bad idea to try to heat a wood shaft over a flame. While Hot Stick glue (Ferrule-tite) is an archery standard, some wood arrow fletchers prefer to use a two part epoxy, claiming it has a stronger bond. Typically the epoxy needs to cure for 24 hours to achieve adequate adhesion.

Carbon shafts

Carbon arrows may or may not need to be cleaned prior to fletching. Each manufacturer has its own recommendations, and they should be followed for optimal adhesion. Also, Hot Stick glue is generally not used for carbon arrows, as the carbon has poor heat tolerance. Two-part epoxy is the glue of choice and should be used as stated in the package directions. As above, epoxy should be given 24 hours to cure before use. Another option is a cyano-acrylate *(CA)*, such as

Crazy-Glue, which has the advantage of being removable by placing the end of the shaft in boiling water. The cyano-acrylates break down at approximately 180 degrees.

Fiberglass and older Graphite shafts

The older fiberglass shafts can be treated like carbon shafts. I have used gel type paint removers successfully, but would be careful about soaking the arrows in solvents, such as acetone, for any length of time. They do require nock and pile inserts and as with carbon, epoxy should be used. Hot Stick can also be used, but only the inserts and not the fiberglass shaft should be heated.

Carbon, graphite and fiberglass shafts may need their ends chamfered before inserting the pile or nock inserts. An emery cloth (a type of sandpaper) is used in place of the chamfering/deburring tools described in the section on aluminum arrow preparation.

Cresting Arrows

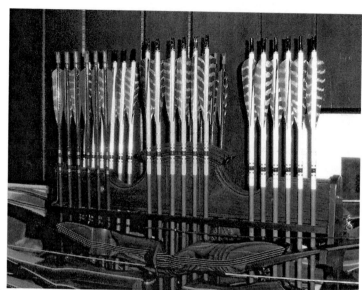

10-25 Elaborately dipped and crested arrows: homemade wood arrows (left) and Bear/Microflight fiberglass arrows, circa 1968 (right)

Decorating arrows by painting the shaftment and cresting (painting colored bands on the shaftment) still remains popular with the traditional archery crowd.

Pros

- May make the arrow look better, to some people's tastes.
- Can be used as a way of distinguishing one archer's arrows from another's in the target.
- It can become a hobby unto itself, in addition to shooting.
- May instill a sense of pride in one's workmanship.
- Wooden arrows require sealing for durability.

Cons

- May make the arrow look less attractive, to some people's tastes.
- Time consuming to paint and crest.
- Time consuming to remove the paint when it's time to refletch.
- Adds an additional expense.
- Doesn't really help your shooting, except possibly psychologically.
- May add weight variables to the finished arrows.

Except for wood arrows that require sealing, each archer must decide whether painting the arrow shaft is a practice he wishes to undertake.

Typically, cap dips or painting the shaftment is done with a plastic dipping tube filled with the color paint of the archer's choice. Dipping tubes come in various sizes, to accommodate painting requirements from a few inches to the entire shaft (diag 10-26). White paint is a favorite as it aids visibility, especially if matched to brightly colored feathers. Varnishes or stains are used for wooden arrows, and may be rubbed or wiped on instead of dipped. The only requirement is that the paints or finishes are compatible with the fletching adhesive you're going to use. Some people have used household type spray paints to paint the shaft or shaftment. While I have no personal experience with this practice, there are enough reports that it is being used successfully that for those so inclined, it may be worth the time to experiment.

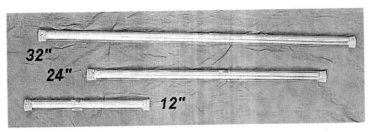

10-26 "Big and Little Dipper" arrow dipping tubes are available in various lengths (Photo courtesy of 3Rivers Archery).

The Bohning Company has been producing an excellent line of adhesives, paints, brushes, and related dipping and cresting equipment for decades. Their products are compatible with one another and therefore remove the guesswork from the equation. They also offer complete fletching and cresting kits that include all equipment and materials to fletch and finish arrows (diag 10-27 and 10-28). Bohning also makes Fletch-tite adhesives and Fletching Tape discussed in the previous section.

10-27 and 10-28 Bohning arrow Fletching and Cresting Kits. (Photo courtesy of Bohning Inc.)

The following is a brief description of how to dip and crest an arrow.

1. Obtain a dipping tube, at least a few inches longer than the length of the cap dip you wish to apply.
2. Mark the end point of the cap dip on each arrow, usually about 10" from the nock end.
3. Mask the nock or swage with masking tape, as we don't want to paint that.
4. Fill the tube with paint about 1" beyond the length of the dip.
5. Dip the arrow in the tube to the mark you made on the arrow, or dip the entire shaft.
6. Slowly withdraw the arrow from the tube, allowing the excess paint to drip off.
7. Set the arrow aside, preferably in a vertical position, to allow the paint to continue to drip off and level itself.
8. Once dry remove the masking tape from the nock or swage.

If preparing wooden arrows, then the entire shaft is dipped, including the nock taper.

Cresting

Not too long ago, it was common for fletchers to crest by hand, slowly rotating the arrow on a pair of wooden "V" blocks, touching a fine paintbrush against the arrow shaft to apply a band of color and I'm sure it's still done that way in some circles. It's more common, and easier, for most folks to use some kind of cresting lathe to spin the arrow and apply the paint. A cresting lathe is nothing more than a low speed electric motor with a chuck to hold the nock end of the arrow and "V" notches to support the shaft while the paint is applied. Cresting lathes are available commercially (diag 10-29) or can be made with an old motor, some rubber or plastic tubing, and a few pieces of wood.

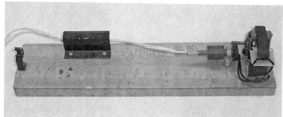

10-29 Cresting lathe from Bingham Archery Products (c1974)

Making a simple cresting lathe (diag 10-34)

1.   Attach the motor to one end of a piece of wood at least 24" long and wide enough to support the motor. The axle of the motor needs to be in line with the long axis of the wood.

2.   Place a piece of rubber tubing tightly over the axle and let it extend out about an additional inch or so. The tubing should have a slightly smaller diameter than the smallest arrow nock or shaft you plan on using.

3.   Take two smaller pieces of wood and cut "V" notches in them and attach them to the base as shown in the diagram, as arrow supports. You can line the "V" notches with felt, leather or plastic to protect the arrow as it spins. Place one just past the end of the tubing and another about 12" to 14" farther away from the first. While the rubber tubing will cover a slight misalignment, care must be taken to have the "V" notch line up closely with the motor's axle. When aligned, secure them with carpenter's wood glue. (Fine adjustments can be made by widening or deepening the "V" notches.)

4.   A third piece of wood should be attached to the board approximately 6" to 8" from the "V" block closest to the motor, slightly behind the position of the arrow. This acts as a stage to fasten a card with your crest design, so you'll have a reproducible pattern to follow.

5.   More detailed instructions are available on the Internet if you want to make a more sophisticated lathe, but this one should suffice. There are also several styles available commercially in various price ranges.

Cresting lathe

10-30 Schematic for building a simple cresting lathe

1. Components

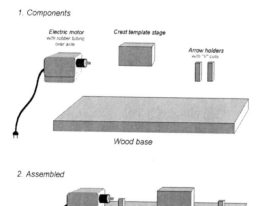

Electric motor
with rubber tubing
over axle

Crest template stage

Arrow holders
with "V" cuts

Wood base

2. Assembled

3. With arrow shaft in place

Cresting an arrow

Testing the cresting lathe – Press the nock of an arrow (or swage, if nocks have not been applied yet) into the rubber tubing and lay the arrow in the "V" grooves. Start the motor and the arrow will begin to spin. Hopefully, the motor and the "V" notches have lined up adequately, and any small deviation will be masked by the flexibility of the rubber tubing (diag 10-31). If so, you are ready to start cresting, if not, you may need to adjust the height of one or both of the notched blocks. It helps to place a finger on top of the spinning shaft over the "V" block closest to the motor or near the cresting area to stabilize the shaft.

Testing the lathe

10-31 Testing the cresting lathe for true arrow spin by applying slight pressure on the shaft near the shaft of the motor.

If all is well, the next thing to do is decide on a crest pattern. The choice is yours. You can copy a preexisting one you're fond of, or get as creative as you like. The crests are usually several inches forward of the fletching, but can also be under the feathers (providing the feathers haven't been applied yet). Decide what you'd like and draw it on an index card or small piece of paper. The drawing needs to be the actual size of the real crest. Attach it to the staging block, so the design is where you'd like it to appear on the arrow (diag 10-32). Assemble the requisite colors of paint and paintbrush sizes, start the motor and start cresting!

10-32 Place your crest template on the cresting "stage". In this case, a piece of paper with the major bands marked with a felt tipped pen.

A lot will be trial and error (which you should be used to by now), but here are a few basic painting tips:

1. Paint larger areas first, and use a wide brush, usually a 1/2" flat brush works well.
2. Paint lighter colors before darker ones. Some light paints do not cover well.
3. Let the first paint color dry before applying a second color.
4. For pinstripes, you can use either very small artist's brushes (0000 is fairly small) or small, angled chisel tipped brushes.
5. As stated before, make sure that the paint you use for the cresting is compatible with the dipping paint and the fletching glue if you plan to crest under the feathers.
6. If you do plan on having a crest under the feathers, it should be done before the arrow is fletched!
7. After the crest has dried, you may want to apply a coat of clear paint to protect your work. (diags 10-33a-d)

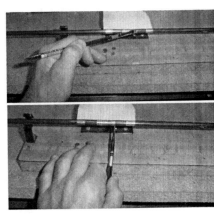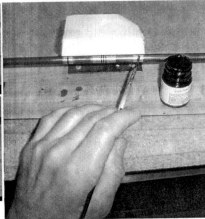

10-33a-c Steps in cresting an arrow. Paint the larger or base bands first with a wide brush (top left). A smaller brush or the brush's edge can be used to define the edges (bottom left). A fine brush is used for detailing "pin stripes".

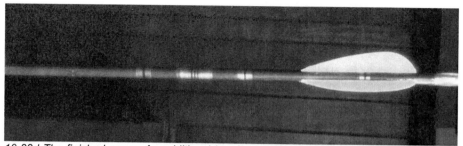

10-33d The finished arrow. An additional band was placed under the midpoint of the fletching; yes, it was painted before the arrow was fletched!

Some arrow makers have crested arrows using enamel or acrylic paint markers for the wider bands and "Sharpie" felt tipped pens for the pin stripes. Experiment and see what works for you; feel free to be creative!

Arrow wraps – the lazy man's answer to dipping and cresting

A few years back, someone came up with the idea of making a pre-colored, pre-crested plastic wrap to allow the archer/fletcher to "dip and crest" his arrow without the need for a lathe or paint. The plastic film, basically a thin contact paper, similar to that used as kitchen cabinet shelf liners, is rolled onto a cleaned shaft. *(You can also use contact paper from a craft store if you find one in a color or pattern you like!)* The fletching is applied to the wrap with either Fletch-tite or fletching tape, and the results are remarkably professional looking. Wraps can be used on aluminum, carbon, wood and fiberglass (diag 10-34).

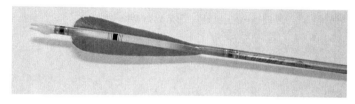

10-34 Arrow wrap applied to the shaftment of an Easton Legacy arrow

To remove the wrap, and the feathers, several methods have been recommended. The simplest is to place the entire shaft in boiling water or hold it over a streamer, and when the adhesive softens, simply peel the wrap and feathers off. Care must be taken, however; if you recall, boiling water can soften the nocks, so they should either be placed in the water without any pressure, or be inspected afterwards for any deformities. Others use acetone, which can also soften some nocks, and others insist on scraping them off with a knife blade.

The information on the preceding pages has been a generalized overview of arrow making. Most arrow manufacturer's websites have detailed instructions for each type of shaft that they produce. Easton Archery (www.eastonarchery.com) has an excellent download on arrow building.

Chapter 11

Bowstrings

The string, as simple as it seems, is the one thing that turns two sticks into a weapons system. In this chapter we'll discuss both bowstring materials and methods of construction. We'll see that the material used has a much greater effect on the shot characteristics and performance of a given string than the construction methods, though the latter also plays a role.

Bowstring materials

There are dozens of bowstring materials on the market today. Companies are continually trying to improve on the performance, durability and, yes, even the appearance of the bowstring. The qualities that go into a good bowstring however, haven't changed considerably since a string braced the first stick and turned it into a bow. Those qualities are strength, durability and the right amount of stretch or "give" on shock to protect the bow. Shock, if you recall, is the term we used to describe the action of the limb's forward movement being abruptly stopped by the string. The more a string will stretch or give on shock, the greater its cushioning or protective effect on the limbs. On the downside, that cushioning may rob the arrow of some speed as energy is utilized to stretch the string that could have been used to propel the arrow. That cushioning may also increase the limb vibration. The former is clearly undesirable from a performance perspective, and the latter may be uncomfortable for the shooter, if the vibrations are transmitted through the riser to the shooter's hand.

Qualities of a bowstring

Strength – Strength is the ability of the string to withstand the effects of shock, while retaining a reasonable diameter and weight. If the string is too weak, it will break on shock, and if made thicker to withstand that force, its added weight will reduce arrow speed and its diameter may be too large to accept an appropriate arrow nock. The new low stretch synthetic fibers are not only stronger than their previous counterparts, but lighter and more stretch-resistant as well.

Durability – Durability is the string's ability to last over an extended period of time. Most synthetic fibers have more than adequate durability; I personally have B-50 Dacron strings made in the 1970's, and would use them today without a second thought. In the 30 years I have been making bowstrings, I've had only three string failures. One string came a little too close to a very sharp hunting head, one was cut by a sharp edge on a limb nock, and crimping a nockset too tightly damaged the third string.

In the late 1970's, Kevlar (aramid fibers), the stuff from which football helmets and other protective gear are made, appeared on the market as a bowstring material. It was very strong and stretch-resistant due to its parallel fiber construction, and very lightweight; it was basically a "fast" string. Unfortunately, it lacked durability and usually failed after 1,000 or so shots. For competitive shooters, 1,000 shots meant replacing a string every week. Subsequent versions mixed Kevlar with other materials, and while that did increase its durability, it fell largely out of favor soon after. I would seriously avoid using Kevlar-based strings today.

Stretch – All materials stretch. A stainless steel bar if pulled with enough force and measured with sufficient accuracy will show signs of stretching. A certain amount of bowstring stretching is necessary to prevent damage to the bow on shock. The less a bowstring stretches on shock, the less energy is lost to the string, and therefore more energy is available to be transferred from the limbs to the arrow. That results in greater arrow speed. However, bow limbs and risers have only a finite amount of strength. If the amount of force the bow experiences at shock is more than it can structurally handle, something will break – unfortunately, usually the bow.

Technical note: Stretch vs. creep. Stretch, as when we "elongate" and release a rubber band, is recoverable, meaning the rubber band returns to its original size. Creep, on the other hand, is what occurs when something is elongated to a point where it cannot recover or return to its original size. Bowstrings exhibit both stretch and creep. While "stretch" in archery jargon is used to describe both occurrences, technically, stretch is what happens at shock and creep is what happens as a new bowstring elongates before its brace height stabilizes. For simplicity, we'll consider both cases as "stretching".

For that reason, some stretch is not only beneficial, but necessary. Selfbows and older laminated bows from the 1960's, 70's, and 80's with maple/fiberglass construction, and wood or fiberglass tip reinforcements, were designed to withstand the shock exerted by Dacron, but not the shock exerted by the new low-stretch materials. Newer, lighter materials with less stretch have been known to sheer off bow limb tips from bows of that era. Some current production bows, not specified as Fast Flight compatible by their manufacturers, have met similar fates due to their owners trying to squeeze out a few additional feet-per-second of arrow speed. Some metal-risered takedown bows with thin "torque-free" grips manufactured before the introduction of Fast Flight or Spectra strings were known to fail at the pivot point of the grip. The manufacturer subsequently recalled the risers and a design revision with thicker grips resulted. It's a well-accepted fact that B-50 Dacron is the only currently produced bowstring material that is safe for any bow in sound condition.

Bowstring Trivia – B-50 Dacron, pound for pound, has a higher tensile strength than the steel bar mentioned in the preceding paragraph. Further, B-50 is one of the weakest of all the string materials we'll be discussing (only S4 Thin is weaker according to Brownell's documentation)!

The speed advantage of the newer bowstrings over B-50 is typically on the order of 5 to 10 feet-per-second. That performance increase is due both to the new materials' decreased stretch on shock and to a greater extent, the materials' lighter weight. As we've discussed earlier, any additional weight on the limb or string (or in this case "of the string") will act as additional weight on the arrow, slowing it down. Some archers do find that the newer string materials feel more solid than B-50, which has been said to have a "soft" or "spongy" feel by some. I haven't noticed this to be the case, however given its tendency to stretch, over a long course of shooting there may be a small but troublesome change in brace height, especially with a newly minted string.

It is imperative before using a new low-stretch lightweight string on any bow, that you confirm with the bowyer or manufacturer that the bow was designed to handle the forces those strings will impart to the bow.

Bowstring construction methods

There are two methods of bowstring construction in use today, the Endless Loop and the Flemish Splice.

Endless Loop (diag 11-1)
The Endless Loop string is, exactly as the name implies, a single strand of string material looped around several posts and then bound together by serving material at each end to form the loops. It is somewhat less prone to stretching than a Flemish Splice string and therefore slightly more consistent and possibly faster. Although slightly faster, they may also be slightly harsher on bows (at shock). Making Endless Loop strings requires a large dedicated jig.

11-1 Endless Loop bowstring

Flemish Splice (diag 11-2)
The Flemish Splice string is a much older design than the Endless Loop and is more aptly called a hand-laid string. It has recently regained popularity with the emergence of "traditional" archery, as it can be assembled fairly quickly, with or without a jig, once the procedure for making one is understood. It also has a more rustic appearance compared to the neatly finished Endless Loop strings. Because the loops are held together by braiding, string twists are required to keep the strands together. By the nature of the braids, the Flemish Splice strings tend to stretch more, are softer on the bow than Endless Loop strings, and therefore may be slightly slower. However, as we've stated, the determining factor is still the string material, and not the method of string construction. Also, some Flemish Splice strings are made with only one loop. That loop slides up the upper limb and engages the nocks when strung. The other braided end is simply tied to the lower nock. While not in common use anymore, it's still an expedient way of determining the best string length and brace height for a new bow. For a bow needing to be retuned, the knot can be untied and repositioned to adjust the string length.

11-2 Flemish Splice bowstring

Both string types are more than adequate for any bow. Flemish strings are generally favored by more "traditional" types because of their rustic appearance and Endless Loop strings are favored by target and competitive types due to their greater efficiency and consistency.

A common belief is that the Flemish Splice is more durable than the Endless Loop string. By nature of its construction it has twice the number of strands in each loop. While technically correct, string loop failure is not a serious concern with either string type, provided the strings are properly made and the bow is sound.

There is also a term "reverse splice" is sometimes used in string making. It more aptly applies to rope making and should not be confused with the Flemish Splice, which by the way, is neither of Flemish origin nor a true splice!

Care and feeding of bowstrings

Synthetic strings, unlike their predecessors, for example, linen and hemp, do not need to be guarded from moisture and most elements. Some basic precautions are required, however. Naturally, keep any and all sharp objects away from them, especially when the bow is strung (diag 11-3). See the note above! If a string is damaged, the damage may not show until the bow is strung, or at shock. If you suspect any contact with sharp or cutting objects, inspect the string very carefully, and if there is any doubt, destroy the string by cutting it in half and discarding it; that way, neither you nor anyone else can use it inadvertently.

11-3 A bowstring and a sharp broadhead
should NEVER be this close!

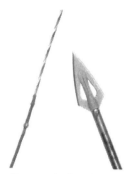

Most bowstrings have twists in two functions; the first is to the brace height. The second is "ballooning". When strings are each strand equal tension. While not always perfect. Slight combined with air resistance on cause separation of the strands adding twists to the string, that eliminated. A lesser-known string is that the more twists, the them (diag 11-4). Twists serve adjust the string length, and so to prevent a phenomenon called made efforts are taken to give the tension is usually close, it's variations in strand tension, the string during the shot, can and increase "bow noise". By tendency is reduced or reason for adding twists to a greater the stretch on shock. While that's generally not desirable, it may help protect some bows that need a little extra cushioning, older selfbows being an example.

11-4 String twists keep the strands together, even when the bow is unstrung, and can be used to adjust the brace height.

The number of twists can vary from 10 to 50 for most bows. There's no set limit on the number of twists you can put into a string, but if the unstrung string begins to kink while twisting, it's possible that there may be too many twists. The resultant strand to strand abrasion may shorten the life span of the string.

Adding twists to a string is pretty simple, but care should be taken to twist the string in the direction that tightens, not loosens, the braid on a Flemish Splice string, or the serving on an Endless Loop string. Note that the serving on a Flemish Splice string needs to be in the same direction as the twists in the braid. Likewise, the center servings on an Endless Loop string need to go in the same direction (diag 11-5) *(Note: Owing to the way an endless loop serving is made, the loop binding servings may be in different directions. Since the center serving receives more ware and tear than the binding servings, it's best to twist the string in the direction that tightens the center serving.)*

11-5 Twisting the bowstring so that either the center serving on an Endless Loop string or the braids on a Flemish Splice are tightened, and not loosened.

Waxing the bowstring

Strings should have a very light coating or rather an impregnation, of wax. This is not only to keep moisture out (which would add weight to the string, and spray the shooter on release) but also to help keep the strands together during the shot or help prevent ballooning if only a few twists are used. It will also help prevent fraying and help to keep the twists in the string if the string is removed from the bow. I prefer beeswax or beeswax blends (diag 11-6). (Beeswax is very hard at room temperature and blending it with pitch or softer waxes can give it a more useable consistency.) A cake of beeswax should last you a lifetime, and it has a wonderful aroma! Any of the newer synthetic "waxes" will work equally well, but they don't have that characteristic beeswax aroma. Most string materials come pre-waxed, so there's really no reason to wax a new string, but with time, the wax can dry or wear off. If the string feels slightly tacky to the touch, there's enough wax. When it starts to feel dry, or the strands begin to separate when the string is loose, then an application of wax is in order.

With the bow strung, apply/rub the wax into the string material only, not the servings. Then take a piece of leather or cloth, and briskly rub the newly waxed string. This will melt the wax into the strands, giving it a more even coating, maximum protection, and a very neat look (diag 11-6b). Note that if dyed leather or colored cloth is used, the color may be transferred to the wax and string. This isn't harmful, but depending on the color may make the string less attractive. Conversely, some colored string materials, particularly the reds, can transfer some of their color to the leather or cloth. This too is not harmful, nor does it weaken the string, but may be disconcerting the first time you see it happen.

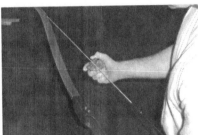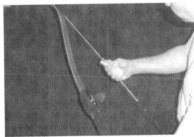

11-6a A well-used cake of beeswax and a tube of commercial synthetic wax
11-6b Waxing a bowstring: applying the wax (left), and rubbing with a piece of cloth or leather to melt the wax into the string (right)

String replacement and repair

A common question is, "How often should I replace a bowstring?" Some people say once a year; some say once every six months. The best answer is – when it needs it. Dacron and the newer fibers have very long life spans and hold up quite well. Adequate waxing should keep fraying to a minimum. If the strands of the bowstring show excessive fraying, something's wrong, and the string may have come in contact with a sharp or abrasive object, which would be cause to replace the string and determine the etiology of the cause. Also note that some string colors show fraying or stretching faster than others; a slight lightening of string color, usually near the ends of the servings, is nothing to be overly concerned about, but "whiskering" should alert you to a problem that should be addressed (diag 11-7). Excessive bowstring stretching or creeping as evidenced by a shrinking brace height is also a sign of trouble and needs immediate attention. This situation is more common with Flemish Splice strings than Endless Loop strings.

The most common areas for non-fatal string failure are the servings, both the loop servings on an Endless Loop and the center serving on either an Endless Loop or Flemish string. If the center serving or the end of a loop binding serving (the part where the loop is bound to a single bundle) begins to separate or loosen, or the tied-off end becomes unraveled, it is usually repairable by retying it. This can be done even in the field, providing, of course, that you know how to tie off a serving. The section on string making has instructions for tying off a serving (diag 11-8).

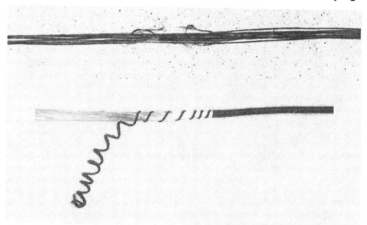

11-7 Fraying or "whiskering" on a bowstring should warn the archer that something is amiss and needs to be looked into (left).

11-8 Unraveling of a loop binding serving, see diagram 11-11 for one method of performing a field repair (right).

Center or end loop serving repair – If the tied end comes loose, just unwind the loose end a few inches and re-tie. If there is serving separation under the finger area, remove the nockset first; then remove the old serving and reserve. (If the center serving does begin to spread or separate in its midsection, under the finger area, it's usually because there was insufficient tension on the bowstring when the serving was applied or the tension on the serving jig was inconsistent.) If the nockset is a crimp-on type, the edges may be sharp and when the serving is removed, it may damage the string; remember what we said about sharp objects and strings? It's safer to remove the nockset with the bow unstrung. If it's a tie-on, you may need to cut it off with a sharp knife or razor blade. It's safer to cut it off with the additional protection of the remaining serving still in place and the bow unstrung.

Loop servings – Loop serving failure is more common than center serving failure and unfortunately more ominous. Frayed areas on the actual loop indicate an abrasive or cutting contact within the bow's string nocks (diag 11-9). *This is quite serious and needs to be attended to quickly, as it will lead only to frequent string replacement and may result in a broken bowstring, a broken bow or injured shooter.*

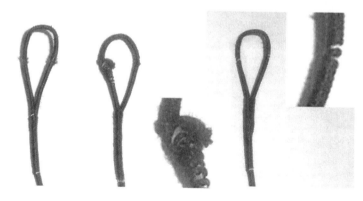

11-9 Fraying on the loop serving of an Endless Loop or Flemish Splice string indicates a sharp or cutting edge near the limb groove and needs to be addressed. The first picture shows the beginnings of loop fraying due to a rough string nock. The second picture (middle + insert) shows a likely progression if left uncorrected. The last picture (right + insert) shows serving separation on a string loop. This is not due to a rough surface, but rather to the string being served with insufficient or inconsistent tension.

The most common cause of loop fraying is a rough edge somewhere in or near the nock groove. Careful examination may reveal this and it can be remedied by careful application of either a small "rattail" file or fine sandpaper (diag 11-10). It is usually not advisable to start blindly filing or sanding a nock groove without a clear idea of what needs correction. If this route is taken, the removal of material must be done carefully so as not to render the nock grooves asymmetrical; the resulting uneven pressure may cause a limb to twist. If the finish is removed during this process, a sealer such as varnish, polyurethane or finishing oil should be applied to seal the wood and allowed to dry. If this sounds daunting, the other option is to return the bow to the manufacturer with a clear explanation of the problem. If the bow is well past warranty and the manufacturer is either unavailable or unwilling to help, then seeking out a qualified bowyer may be the only other recourse.

11-10 Cleaning up a sharp edge on a string nock with a rattail file

Sometimes the cause of the fraying may not be apparent. In addition to a sharp or jagged edge, sometimes the bend the loop makes around the nocks to the flat of the limb may be too severe; the solution is the same as the above. Lastly, it is possible that inspection may not reveal anything untoward. The worst case scenario would be an incipient limb delamination. The limb nocks look fine when examined unstrung, but when strung, and during draw, the force on the limbs is sufficient to cause a slight separation of the limb laminations and expose a sharp edge. The only way to see this is to have an experienced archer or bowyer watch the limb nocks as the bow is being drawn, and hopefully, they will be able to see slight shifting. An old trick that may help is to coat the grooves with a wax pencil, crayon or lipstick, and see if any separation occurs during the draw. While this occurrence is rare, it has happened, and the only recourse is either return the bow to the bowyer or manufacturer. If that isn't possible, then resign yourself to leave it as a wall hanging or collectable. It most certainly should not be used.

If the shank of the distal loop binding serving (the part where the loop is bound to a single bundle) begins to loosen or become untied, it can be treated as a center serving failure but may require a string-making jig to reserve. (See the string making section.) In the case of an emergency (you forgot to bring a spare string) you might be able to reverse string the bow and use it as a makeshift jig (diag 11-11).

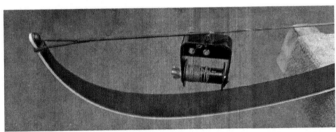

11-11 Reverse stringing a recurve bow may provide enough tension to allow you to do an emergency repair. If the end just unraveled, a quick tie-off might do the trick.

Flemish Splice strings are subject to the same problems as Endless Loop strings with regard to center servings and string nock problems. Flemish Splice strings do experience more stretching than endless loop strings, but if an excessive amount of string stretch is noticed, as evidenced by a gradually shrinking brace height, the splices need to be inspected for signs of slippage (diag 11-12). As stated above, a possible cause is insufficient twists in the string to keep the splices snug, or simply poor workmanship. While you may be able to re-braid the string, it might be safer to replace it.

11-12 A decreasing brace height may suggest loosening of the braids on a Flemish Splice string. This string is in need of replacement.

Why leaving a bow strung is *NOT* a good idea:

As we stated earlier, modern bows do not experience any ill effects from being left strung for prolonged periods of time, and neither do modern bowstrings. Still, leaving a strung bow unattended for any length of time is tantamount to leaving a loaded gun unattended.

Here are six reasons for unstringing a bow after use:

1. A strung bow is a spring under tension. If the "thing" holding it under tension fails, the spring opens forcefully and will hit anyone or anything in its way.

2. A strung bow is an open invitation to friends, guests, young, and not so young, family members to "try it out" when you're not looking. Releasing the string with or without an arrow could have dire consequences. Family members include pets that might like to taste the bowstring, especially one with a fresh application of beeswax.

3. Bows are easier to store unstrung, especially if you have more than a few.

4. Leaving a Takedown bow strung defeats the purpose of the takedown feature.

5. Bouncing a strung bow around the trunk of a car on the way to the range may make it necessary to replace the bow.

6. Finally, and most importantly: ***A strung bow is a weapon; an unstrung bow is a stick***.

Myth – Unstringing a bow will make you lose the number of twists you've added, and so, cause changes in brace height.

Fact – Since the string is usually not removed from the bow, the string can't untwist. If you have a takedown bow and do remove the string, it will not lose its twists if the string was properly waxed and not over-twisted.

Bowstring Materials

Here's a list of some of the popular string and serving materials available today.

Brownell

B-50 Dacron polyester
B-50, being a synthetic material, has excellent abrasion resistance, durability and consistency. It has a 4,460 ft-lb (foot-pounds) breaking strength and is approximately 0.018" diameter. Dacron polyester was developed in the 1950's by the Dupont Corporation and was the first synthetic bowstring material produced by the Brownell Company, also in the 1950's. (The first Dacron was called B-43, and was the precursor to B-50.) It is a durable, but heavy string, and considered soft by today's standards; it has more stretch during initial break-in and on shock than other materials. Its weight combined with its stretch on shock absorbs energy that could otherwise be used to propel the arrow and therefore does reduce arrow speed from 5 to 10 fps when compared with newer low-stretch fibers. It is the only material considered safe for ***all*** bows, including wood selfbows and vintage laminated bows. It usually provides a very quiet shot. It should also be noted that the cost of Dacron is only 20% to 25% of the newer low-stretch fibers.

D-75 – 6,800 ft-lb breaking strength and approximately .016" diameter.
D-75 THIN – 8,967 ft-lb breaking strength and approximately 0.011" diameter.

D-75 and D-75 Thin are newer and thinner Dacron polyesters. They have less stretch than B-50, and so provides a small speed advantage. I would be careful about using either of these materials on prized vintage bows or selfbows.

Fast Flight (FF) – 8,700 ft-lb breaking strength and approximately 0.015" diameter. Made from Spectra, FF exhibits minimal creep with lighter weight than Dacron and has superior strength and durability. While FF is the harshest string material available today, its minimal stretching characteristics and low weight it can produce the fastest possible arrow speeds. Bows using Fast Flight must be FF rated, or listed as FF compatible by the bowyer or manufacturer. Older bows without re-enforced tips have had limb tips sheered off and laminations split on shock; some early magnesium risers were known to fail at the pivot point. FF strings can also be noisier than "softer" materials.

Fast Flight 2000 – was actually introduced in 1998 and rated 30% stronger than FF. The same warnings apply as with regular FF.

S4 Thin – 3,831 ft-lb breaking strength and approximately .018" diameter. Similar to FF and made of Spectra and Vectran, it also shows very little stretch. It is slightly slower than FF due to its heavier weight.

Ultracam – 6,474 ft-lb breaking strength and .013" diameter. Thinnest diameter blended bowstring currently available.

TS-1 Plus – (TS-1 + Dyneema) Diameter 0.14" Lightweight, minimal creep string, introduced in 2005.

Xcel – 1/3 Vectran and 2/3 SK75 Dyneema. Released in 2006, touted as the ultimate in speed and stability. Specifications, not available at this time.

SERVING Material (Brownell)

2 FASTFLIGHT and 2 FASTFLIGHTSPECIAL Excellent abrasion resistance, 9,696 ft-lb breaking strength, 0.022" diameter and 10,080 ft-lb breaking strength and 0.018" diameter, respectively.
FASTFLIGHT.026 Black and white blend of original Fast Flight center serving. Diameter 0.026"

TCD-150 Dyneema and Carrari fibers tightly braided together to produce very low creep and high flex fatigue in an extremely strong string material.
Diameter: 0.076"

EXCELLERANT BRAIDED Dyneema and Carrari fibers tightly braided together. It is highly abrasion resistant and has virtually no creep while it offers a very soft shot.
Diameter: 0.13"

#5 POLYESTER BRAID Available in 4 lb. (approximate) spools. Waxed diameter: 0.076"; un-waxed diameter: 0.068" Color: Natural

DIAMONDBACK Braided HMPE (High Modulus Polyethylene) and polyester construction. Superior grip and durability, lies flat, will not unravel. Colors available: black, blue, gold, green, and red.

.018 7,875 ft-lb, 0.018 diameter approx. 1 lb 120 yd jig
.022 6,192 ft-lb, 0.022 diameter approx. 1 lb 93 yd jig
.026 5,327 ft-lb, 0.026 diameter approx. 1 lb 65 yd jig

.030 (breaking strength not given, questimate in the mid 4,000 ft-lb range), 0.030 diameter approx. 1 lb 45yd jig.

#4 TWISTED NYLON The original multifilament serving thread, also excellent for tying in peep sites and string silencers. 6,087 ft-lb breaking strength and 0.021" diameter, approx. 100 yd jig.

#4 SHERWOODFOREST NYLON Multiple colors of greens and browns in a single strand. Diameter .021 Jig size 90 yd.

MONOFILAMENT The original monofilament center serving has a single fiber construction and can result in a cleaner and faster release. It is recommended only for center servings, as it is not as abrasion resistant as other serving materials. Given its stiffness, if the serving does fail, it will usually unwind fairly quickly, making an emergency repair unlikely. The multifilament materials unwind much more slowly and give the user more time to stop the failure and re-tie it.

#15 11,023 ft-lb, .015 diameter, approx. 5 lb 200 yd jig.
#18 7,571 ft-lb, .018 diameter, approx. 5 lb 150 yd jig.
#21 5,676 ft-lb, .021 diameter, approx. 5 lb 100 yd jig.

BCY
String Material

B-500 Dacron very similar to B-50 in size (diameter) and strength.

450 Plus A blend of Dyneema and Vectran. Minimal stretch material, similar to FF.

452X Similar to 450 Plus, but half the size. May result in increased speed.

Dynaflight97 / Dyneema '02 Spectra. Dyneema was one of the first the first (HMPE) High Modulus Polyethylene fibers used for bowstrings. Also similar to Fast Flight; seems to be a little less harsh on the bow limbs at shock, but same cautions should apply. Dyneema '02 has been marketed as being designed especially for recurve bows. (Not quite sure of the reasoning here…)

Formula 8125 Dyneema, but with a smaller diameter.

Formula 8125 Thin – Same as Formula 8125, but 10% thinner.

STRING MAKING

While not truly necessary these days, many archers find it useful to make their own bowstrings.

Reasons include:
- A feeling of satisfaction, being able to "do it themselves"
- Just another part of the hobby, making it feel more personal
- Fun (However after several thousand strings, the fun part can wear a little thin.)
- Quality control (more of a problem with commercial strings in years past, than today)
- No waiting time for a new string, except the time it actually takes to make one, usually about a half hour for both Endless Loop and Flemish Splice strings
- Less expensive than factory or custom-made strings, especially if the archer needs to experiment with string lengths, number of strands, loop sizes, serving lengths, materials, etc.

The Endless Loop string

Fairly simple to make in theory and in practice, the only drawback to making an Endless Loop string is that a fairly large string jig is required. Several styles are available commercially, but a perfectly serviceable jig can be made for a few dollars with hand tools and basic skills.

The following is an example of a simple wooden Endless Loop string jig. If any of these terms or steps seems unfamiliar to you, perhaps purchasing a commercial jig may be a better option. Also note that there are many variations on the materials and methods that can be used to make an Endless Loop string jig. These plans are generic, but the jig can be as elaborate or as simple as your tastes and ability dictate. This one pictured in diag 11-13 was constructed using the following instructions.

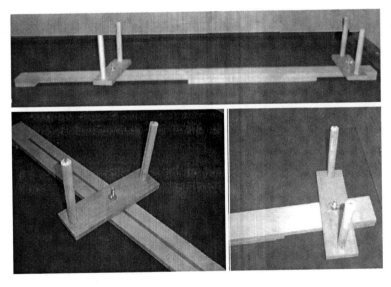

For a simple wooden jig, you'll need 12' of 1"x4" wood. (Any wood will do but the stronger the wood, the more durable the jig will be. Oak, for example, would be optimal, but if you're not used to working with it, it's a very hard, tough wood, and not the easiest to work with. Poplar is a good choice, fairly strong and readily available. Plywood is also a good option, and will make a very strong jig. Pine can also be used, however, it's the weakest of the woods mentioned.

11-13 A wooden Endless Loop string jig made by Ryan Kowalick using the following directions

Endless loop jig - raw materials

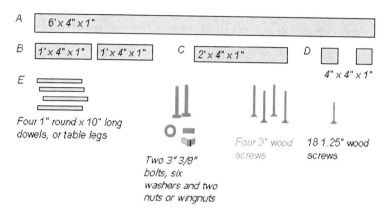

A | 6' x 4" x 1" |

B | 1' x 4" x 1" | | 1' x 4" x 1" | C | 2' x 4" x 1" | D [ ] [ ]

4" x 4" x 1"

E
Four 1" round x 10" long dowels, or table legs

Two 3" 3/8" bolts, six washers and two nuts or wingnuts

Four 3" wood screws   *18 1.25" wood screws*

11-14 Wooden Endless Loop string jig components

Four 8" to 10" 1" round dowels or commercially manufactured table legs.

Two 3/8" x 3" bolts, two nuts and six washers to fit. (Two wing-nuts if possible.)

Four 3" wood screws, and 18 1-1/4" wood screws.

Optional: wood finishes.

You'll also need a screwdriver, drill, drill bits and a countersink bit, basic wood and keyhole type saws, wrenches for the nuts and bolts, and some wood (carpenter's) glue. If you're missing any of these, the local Home Depot or Lowe's should be your first stop.

Cut the 1x4 into:

1 - 6'; 2 - 1'; 1 - 2' and 2 - 4" sections.

All measurements are approximate and this will make a jig capable of building a string for the longest bows currently on the market.

1. Take the 6' piece of 1x4 and drill two 3/8" holes along the wood's center line approximately 5" from each end, and another approximately midway between the two, centered on the board.

2. Draw tangent lines from one hole to the other and with the keyhole saw, cut a 3/8" channel from one to the other. The cut lines should be as straight and evenly spaced as possible.

3. Glue the two 4" pieces to the bottom of the 6' piece, flush with each end. Secure the pieces with four 1-1/4" wood screws. (Screw holes should be pilot drilled and countersunk as shown in the diagrams.)

4. Glue the 2' piece approximately 2" away from the 4" piece on the side without the channel. Secure it with six 1-1/4" screws. On the side without the channel, the base pieces should flank the previously drilled hole.

5. Drill 1/4" holes in both ends on the two 1' pieces about 1" from each end again along the centerline. Countersink each hole on one side of the board.

6. Drill a 3/8" hole centered on the 1' boards.

7. Drill a 1/4" receiving hole for the 3" wood screws in one end of each dowel, as close to center as possible.

8. Insert the 3" screws into the countersunk side of the 1' boards and begin to screw the dowels onto the exposed ends. Use wood glue on the mating surfaces.

9. Screw the remaining four 1-1/4" wood screws into the top of each dowel, down to the shank of the screw.

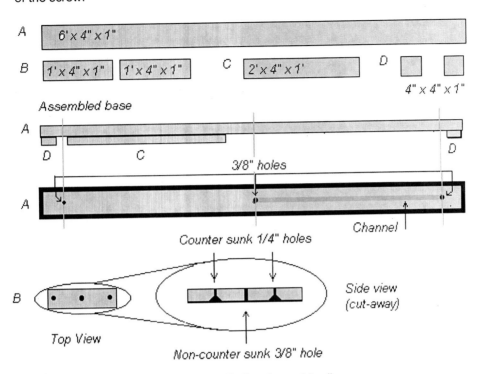

11-15 Initial construction steps for making an Endless Loop string jig

10. Final assembly – Take a 3/8" bolt and slip a washer on it. Put a bolt through the bottom of the board; place another washer on the bolt, then the 1' piece with the "goalposts" pointing up, another washer, and the nut or wing nut. Repeat for the other goal post.

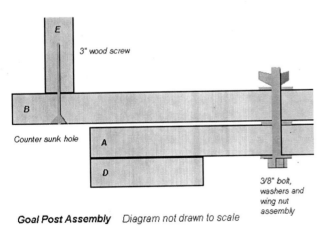

Goal Post Assembly   Diagram not drawn to scale

11-16 Close-up of Endless Loop string jig "goalpost" construction

11. You can finish the wood for protection or not; mine is at least 25 years old, looks like something the cat dragged in, and has made hundreds, if not thousands, of strings.

The above was an example of a classic wood frame Endless Loop string jig. Refer to the accompanying diagrams as a reference. By using the same principles, similar jigs can be made from angle iron, or even PVC tubing. It's really up to you and your imagination! Well, that's the jig; happily, using it is a little simpler!

Making your first 12-strand string

You'll need a spool of string material, a spool of serving material and a serving jig. You'll also need a pair of scissors or knife, either matches or glue (Fletch-tite), and string wax.

You can use an old string you're trying to replace as a template for a new string.

1. Loosen the nuts or wing nuts on the cross arms (goal posts) and turn them parallel to the main board.

2. Put each string loop on the screws atop the outermost vertical dowels and move the cross arm in the channel out so the string is taut. Slightly tighten the wing nuts.

3. Remove the string, and turn the cross arms so they are both perpendicular to the main board. Tighten the wing nuts.

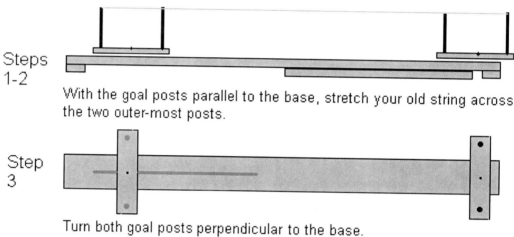

Steps 1-2

With the goal posts parallel to the base, stretch your old string across the two outer-most posts.

Step 3

Turn both goal posts perpendicular to the base.

11-17 Endless Loop string building – Steps 1 to 3

4. Stand at one end of the jig and take a spool of string material and tie it to the screw shank atop the right-hand dowel. Take the spool and bring it around the left-hand dowel screw, and then loop it clockwise around the two dowel/screws on the other end.

5. Continue looping the material around each screw until you have six turns around the screw that the thread was initially tied to. The thread should be fairly taut, but not so much as to bend the jig!

6. When the six loops are done, tie the other end of the thread to the left-hand dowel screw on the same cross arm you started on.

7. Make sure there's fairly even tension on all the stands by "strumming" the long sections. If you see a loose strand, it can usually be fixed by pulling on each side a few times, to even things out.

8. The serving jig should already be assembled with a spool of serving material. If not, assemble as described in the instructions that came with it, which are usually quite intuitive. The tension on the serving jig should be fairly taut, but still allow the serving thread to unwind freely without binding.

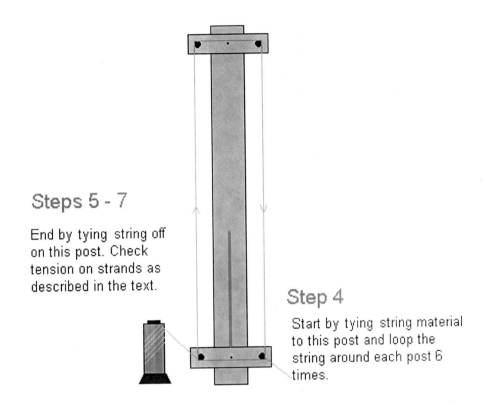

Steps 5 - 7

End by tying string off on this post. Check tension on strands as described in the text.

Step 4

Start by tying string material to this post and loop the string around each post 6 times.

11-18 Endless Loop string building – Steps 4 to 7

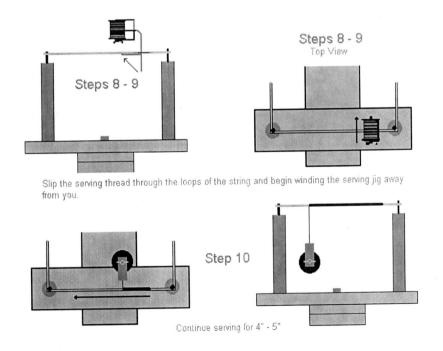

Steps 8 - 9

Steps 8 - 9
Top View

Slip the serving thread through the loops of the string and begin winding the serving jig away from you.

Step 10

Continue serving for 4" - 5"

11-19 Endless Loop string building – Steps 8 to 10

9. Starting on the end of the string jig where you started and ended the loops, slide about 2" of serving material between the string strands about 2" away from the right dowel. Loop the serving jig away from you, and start winding it around the strands. Adjust the tension on the serving jig to keep the serving coming out with some resistance. How much resistance, will be learned only from experience. As this is your first string, it's time to start getting some of that experience.

10. Continue the serving for approximately 4" to 5".

11. Tying off the serving. After the approximate length of serving has been reached, pull out about 10" to 12" of serving thread making a very large loop. Begin serving in the same direction, meaning away from you, but toward the previously served section. When you've gotten about ten loops, lay the serving jig over the left dowel top, off to the side. Hold the large loop and begin turning it around the string, so that it continues the main serving and unwinds the reverse loops. Do this so it overlaps the extended piece of serving thread. When the reverse section is completely unwound, pull the end of the serving (the part with the serving jig) taut with your right hand while pushing the far-left end toward the main serving area. Cut the serving, leaving about a 1/4" to 3/8" pigtail. This can be burned (melted) down with a match or lighter. Please refer to the diagrams; this is actually a lot easier to do than it is to describe.

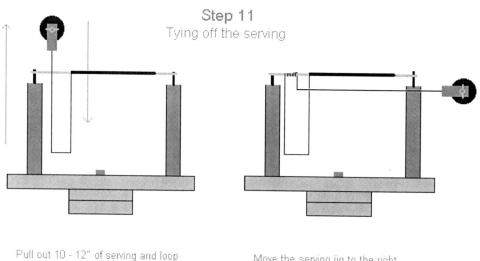

Step 11
Tying off the serving

Pull out 10 - 12" of serving and loop the jig in front of the string.

Move the serving jig to the right.

Continue serving 8 - 10 loops, away from you and through the loop, but this time to the right.

11-20 and 21 Endless Loop string building step 11, tying off the serving

12. Repeat the loop serving process on the other end of the jig.

13. Loosen the wing nuts and rotate the arms back to parallel with the main board. Slide the string around the posts so that the ends of the servings are staggered.

14. Repeat the serving process to bind the loops together. Remember that the upper string loop is usually larger than the lower. A good rule of thumb is that the upper loop should be approximately 1-1/2' to 1-3/4" in diameter and the lower about 1" to 1-1/4". The exact size will depend on the limb width of the bow for which you're making the string. Tie off each end as

before. These servings should be about 5" to 6" long for a recurve and approximately 3" for a longbow.

Step 11

Tying off the serving

continued

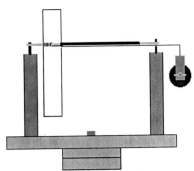

Continue to serve the string manually, from the right, overlapping the serving thread going to the jig. This will cause the reverse serving to unwind.

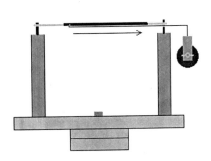

When completely unwound, pull the serving taut by grabbing the thread near the jig and the newly tied off end will come together and appear endless.

15. For exposed ends, I usually leave about 1/4" of thread sticking out, and burn it down with a match or lighter. A drop of glue can be used for added insurance. Neither the burn/melt down, nor the gluing, are actually necessary, but can add to the appearance and confidence you have in the finished string.

Step 11

Tying off the serving

continued

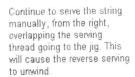

Cut the serving close to the final wrap, and burn or melt the pigtail. If you cut if off close, a drop of glue will keep it from unraveling.

Finally, cut the sting material attached to the screw shanks near the begining and end of the serving.

Step 12

Repeat the process on the other goal post.

Step 13

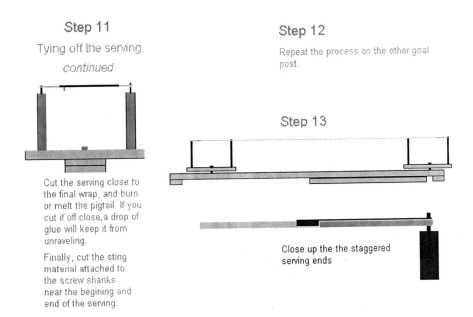

Close up the the staggered serving ends

11-22 Endless Loop string building – Steps 11 to 13 (continued)

16. Loosen the wing nuts and remove the string. (No, we didn't forget about the center serving!)

17. String the bow and check to make sure the brace height is where you want it or slightly higher. (The string will stretch.) Hold the bow with its back against your thighs, and push down on the mid/upper limb sections (diag 11-24). This should hasten the stretching. Let the bow sit for a while, if possible.

Steps 13 - 15

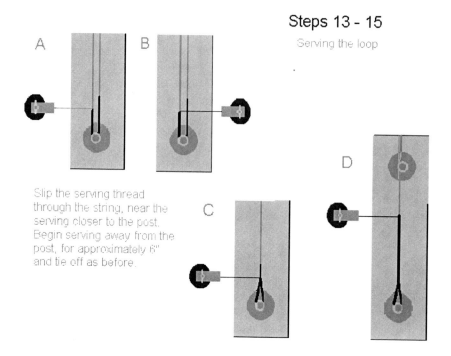

Serving the loop

A   B

Slip the serving thread through the string, near the serving closer to the post. Begin serving away from the post, for approximately 6" and tie off as before.

C

D

11-23 Endless Loop string building – Steps 13 to 15

18. If the string seems dry, a coat of wax can be applied to the string at this time, following the same procedure described earlier in this chapter. Some Endless Loop string makers like to wax their strings during construction, however most modern string materials are pre-waxed, so there really shouldn't be a need unless they seem unusually dry. We'll see in the next section that Flemish Splice strings actually do require waxing during construction.

19. Find the approximate point on the string where you would expect the nocking point to be. Start the center serving about 1-1/2" to 2" above that and continue until you're slightly past the grip on the bow, or as long as you feel is necessary. Tie off as we did for the other servings. (The reason the standard length for center servings is just below the grip is so the serving protects the string material from arm guard strikes.) We didn't put the center serving on while the string was on the jig, because the jig cannot stretch the string as the bow can. Since the center serving is usually the longest serving on the bow, if the string were to stretch under the serving, the serving would start to separate (diag 11-25).

11-24 Helping a newly made string "stretch".

20. Apply a nocking point.

Final steps
Center serving and nocking point

String the bow and stretch the string as described in the text. The center serving is created in the same way as the loop servings. It should be 7 - 8" in length. A nocking point is placed as described in the basic setup section.

11-25 Endless Loop string building – Final steps

That's how an Endless Loop string is made. Once you're used to it, the entire process should take about half an hour, start to finish. I've tried to make the directions as clear as possible, but as with most things in archery, actually being able to see the process will greatly shorten the learning curve.

If you don't have a string to use as a template, take the AMO length of the bow, subtract about 4" for a recurve and 3" for a longbow and set the outboard dowels in-line with the baseboard and that distance apart as a starting point. There will always be some trial and error when making strings. All jigs have some flex to them and what you start with lengthwise may not always be what you end up with. Also, two 66" bows may not like the same length strings. Once you've established the proper string length for a given bow and its corresponding jig settings, it's a good idea to mark the jig so you can go back to the same point the next time you need to make a string for that bow. At the very least, a record should be kept of verified string lengths, on your jig, for each bow you own.

Alternatively, when some archers have a setting for a known length bow, again we'll use our AMO 66" example, they'll mark their jigs at that point and then attach a paper tape measure to the side of the jig (diag 11-26). Then make sure the 66" mark on the tape lines up with the 66" mark on the jig. That way the jig is theoretically calibrated for AMO bows, within reason, of course. Find a method that works for you and stick with it.

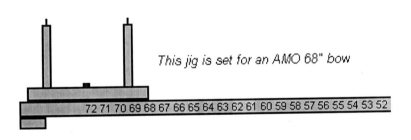

This jig is set for an AMO 68" bow

11-26 Tape measure or graduated marks on the side (or top) of an Endless Loop String jig for quick and accurate string length measurement (not drawn to scale).

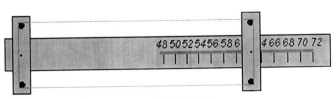

This jig is set for an AMO 64" bow

Making a Flemish Splice string

With Matt DeStefano of Native Archer Bowstrings

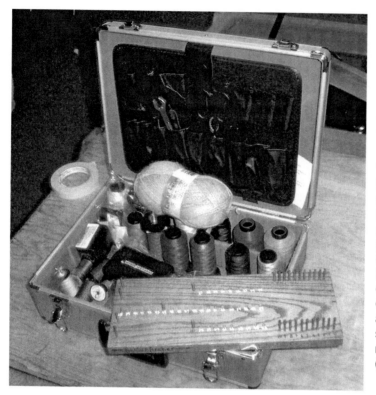

11-26 A well-stocked Flemish string maker does not need a great deal of space to transport his materials or make strings. Here we see a Flemish jig, multiple spools of string and serving materials, serving jig and all necessary tools in a fairly compact box (Native Archer Strings).

The first question should be – Do I need a jig or not? No, you don't, but it can make things a little easier and result in a neater looking string. The purpose of a Flemish jig (as opposed to an Irish jig, which is something completely different), is to help you get the correct overall string length, and to stagger the individual strands to give the splice a more tapered appearance (diag 11-26).

11-27 A very neatly braided Flemish splice string loop

In the interest of neatness, we'll start by making a Flemish jig.

The following instructions are for a fairly elaborate jig, but there are several simpler versions available, and plans can be found on several Internet sites. This one will allow you to make a string from approximately 50" to 70". If shorter strings are needed the overall length of the jig can be reduced in size and likewise additional length adjustment holes can be drilled.

One drawback to this type of Flemish string jig is that the length adjustment holes are placed to give 2" changes in string length. This is not too great an issue, as most bows are manufactured in 2" increments. Also recall that Flemish Splice strings typically have more twists than Endless Loop strings, providing greater flexibility in effective length and brace height. Lastly, as you become more familiar with the jig, you can make smaller adjustments by staggering the positions of the length adjustment pegs.

For this version, all you need is a piece of wood, approximately 6" by 32", and about 1" thick (the size really isn't critical, but the wood should be straight and free of knots) and some small, 1" or 1.5" nails or brads.

Building the Flemish Splice jig (diag 11-28)

1. Draw a line lengthwise, down the centerline of the board, and then two more lines spaced 1" apart from the centerline on each side of the centerline.

2. Start driving the nails into the two outermost lateral lines starting 1" from one end, and continuing every 3/8" so until you have 10 on each side. These are the tapering pegs.

3. Measure 26" from the first nail (closest to the end of the board) and drive four nails into the four lines as shown in the diagram.

4. Drill 20 holes at 1" intervals to accept nails on each of the two lines, 1" from center. These holes will be used for string length adjustment.

5. As with the Endless Loop jig, you can stain, paint or otherwise finish the wood as you like, or leave it unfinished.

6. You should, however, number the length adjustment holes for various string lengths. Some people like to add notes directly to the board, to remind them that a certain bow needs a certain length adjustment configuration or the number of strands needed for each weight range.

Flemish Splice String Length Jig

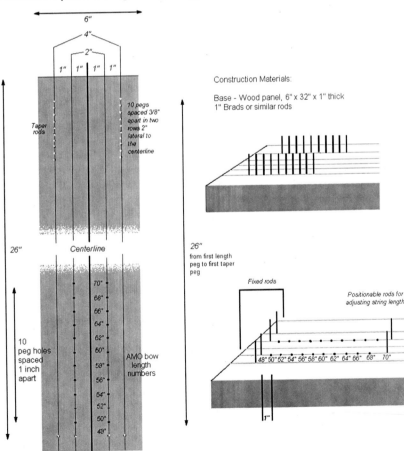

11-28 Flemish Jig design and construction (In this diagram and diagram 11-29, white dots represent pegs and black dots represent drilled holes.)

We'll use our 66" recurve model as we did in the previous Endless Loop example, but in this case the bow will have a draw weight of 70# and so we'll need a 16 strand Dacron string.

For this bow we'll need a 62" string. *(If you recall, for recurves we use a string 4" shorter than the specified AMO length of the bow. For long bows it would be 3" shorter.)* While your actual string length requirements may differ, that's usually a good estimate. And since we're using B-50, which has a tendency to stretch, we can always make length adjustments by adding twists to the string later if necessary. We'll start by making a simple two bundle / two-color string. Once the procedure is understood, three bundle / three-color stings can be made using the same process.

Since a Flemish Splice string is made from individual strands, we'll need to add approximately 8" to each end to construct the loops. That's 16" added to our required string length of 62", or a total strand length of 78".

Initial setup:

Place the jig on a stable working surface; you may clamp it to your work table using "C" clamps down if you like.
Set the pegs as required for a 66" AMO bow (or a 62" actual length string).

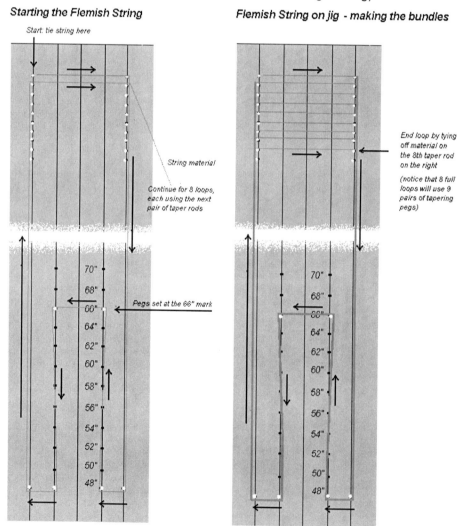

11-29. Make the first wrap on the jig (left) and complete the wraps for the first bundle (right).

Making the bundles (diag 11-29):

Tie the string material to the first peg and loop the material around each peg as shown. This will

Stacking the wraps on the Flemish jig rods will yield a neater and rounder bundle

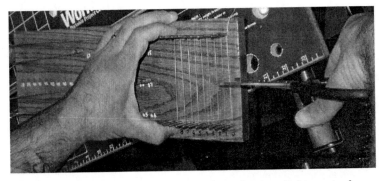

be a 16-strand string; therefore we'll make two 8-strand bundles. Hint: when wrapping the material around a peg, stacking one strand above the previous one helps to ensure a nice rounded bundle and a neater completed string (diag 11-30).

11-30 Stacking one strand on top of the previous one around each peg.

Continue looping the material around all the pegs, but using successive pairs of tapering pegs. Remember that the first set of pegs is not counted as part of the eight loops, therefore 9 pairs of tapering pegs will be used. Cut the string down the centerline of the jig as shown and discard the short "tag" ends. The staggered ends will create a tapered effect, making a neater string. End the string at the last tapering peg.

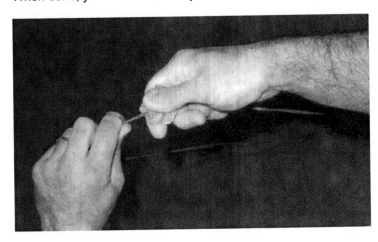

11-31 Cutting the continuous loop to make separate strands. Matt simply holds the string material on the last peg while cutting.

Remove the stands and heavily wax each end of both bundles (diag 11-32). Beeswax is an excellent choice as it is thicker and stickier than most synthetic waxes and that helps to keep the strands together. Apply a light coat of wax to both newly created bundles (diag 11-33).

When done, you'll have two fairly stiff bundles approximately 16" longer than your new bowstring!

11-32 Using beeswax to wax the ends of the bundles

Set the new bundle aside and repeat the process in its entirety with a different color Dacron. (There's absolutely no reason why the same color can't be used, but one aspect of Flemish Splice strings is that some archers find the use of multiple contrasting colors aesthetically appealing.)

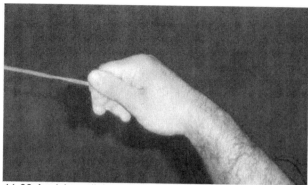

11-33 Applying a light coat of wax to both bundles (left).
11-34 Notice the gentle tapering of the bundle ends (right).

Making the first loop splice:

Hold a bundle in your left hand and twist the last 8" of the waxed end AWAY from you with your right hand. About 20 twists are usually sufficient. The more strings you make, the more of a "feel" you'll get for how may twists will work for a given number or stands (diag 11-35 and 11-36). Repeat at the opposite end and on the other bundle – going in the same direction – AWAY from you, that's important!

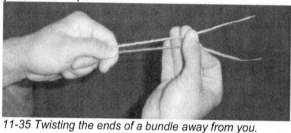
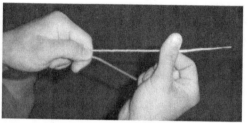

11-35 Twisting the ends of a bundle away from you.
11-36 Here's another picture of both bundles showing the ends twisted and ready for the "splice".

Take both bundles (with twisted ends) in your left hand. (Here's the tricky part for a new Flemish String maker – but as you'll see it's the same process through the procedure, so once learned, the hard part is over!) Starting about 8" from the end, twist one bundle end ONCE away from you, as you did before, and then lay that end OVER the other bundle twisting TOWARDS you. Repeat with the other bundle (diag 11-37 and 38).

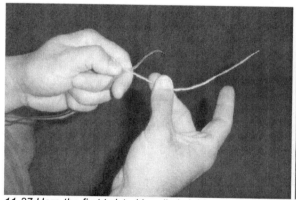

11-37 Here the first twisted bundle is laid over the second (towards you).
11-38 Repeating the process, here the second bundle receives a twist and is laid over the first.

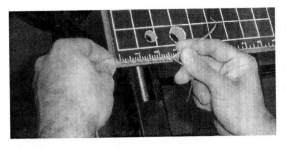

Continue the "once away / once over" splicing for approximately 2" to 3" for the bottom (smaller) loop and 3" to 4" for the upper (larger) loop. The actual size will depend on the limb width of the bow. You should have about the same 3" left "unspliced" (diag 11-39).

11-39 Checking the length of the first loop braid

Making the loop:

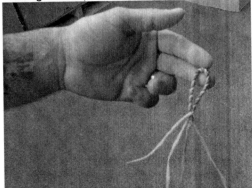

11-40 Bending the twisted portion of the bundle to create the loop

Approximately halfway down the splice, bend the splice into a loop, so the unspliced sections meet. Matching up the colors adds a touch of professionalism (diag 11-40).

The loop is again "spliced" together with the same procedure we used to braid the bundle ends (diag 11-41). Continue until the splice is complete (diag 11-42).

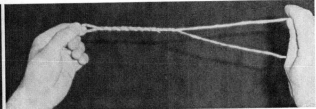

11-41 Again, create the splice by twisting a loose end once away from you and then laying it over the now combined strands (towards you).
11-42 Continue until the splice is complete (meaning you've run out of string!). Adding a few twists to the body of the string after the termination of the splice makes a very neat splice.

Carefully remove any "tag" ends with a pair of scissors and repeat the process on the other end.

As with the Endless Loop string, the upper loop should be a bit larger than the lower loop to allow the string to slide down the upper limb (diag 11-43). The actual loop sizes should be determined by the width of the upper limb so the string stays in place when the bow is unstrung.

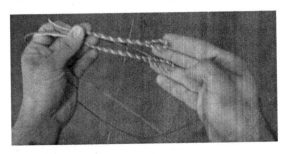

11-43 As with the Endless Loop string, you should make the upper loop slightly larger than the bottom loop.

Final steps:

Twist the string 10 – 20 times and rub in the wax to help it keep its shape; add additional wax. If necessary, we will remove any excess later.

At this point the string will need to be kept under tension. Here Matt uses a stretching jig, but the bow itself will work as well (diag 11-44). It's also a good time to confirm the string's overall length.

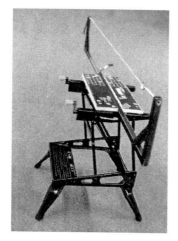

11-44 Adjustable stretching jig (left) and confirming the string length with a tape measure (right).

If the string is too long, remove the string and add more twists. If it appears too short, you can try stretching it as described earlier in this chapter. If that doesn't help, you may have to chalk this one up to a learning experience and start a new and longer one. If the string checks out, great! To finish the string, remove any excess wax by looping a piece of string material or serving around the string, pull it taut and drag it down the length of the string (diag 11-45).

To apply the center serving without the bow handy, find the midpoint on the string. In this case since we have a 62" string the midpoint is the 31" mark (diag 11-46). Measure 2" from the midpoint, toward the top loop. Continue serving until approximately 5" past the midpoint (toward the bottom loop) and tie off the serving as described in the Endless Loop section.

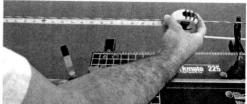

11-45 Removing excess wax with a piece of serving material
11-46 Finding the midpoint of the string for serving placement

That pretty much covers the bowstring materials, care and building. It also completes our look at archery equipment. We've seen only the tip of the iceberg, but you should now have enough information to get started, or at least you know what questions to ask when talking to a bowyer or dealer about a new bow, arrows or string. There's a list of books in the appendices that will go into greater detail if you're so inclined.

What I've tried to give you thus far is an explanation of how things are done in archery. In the next section, we'll look at a few more of the *"how's"* and try to answer a couple of the *"why's."*

Part 3

Making the Shot – Theories and Practice

Chapter 12

Aiming

It might seem strange that we've come this far and haven't discussed the subject of aiming in any significant way. If the steps in the first section were followed and the arrows are generally centered in the target then you already know how to aim. What follows is simply a detailed description of what the brain is actually doing while you're busy focusing on the center of the target. We'll also discuss various methods of aiming, noting their similarities and differences. There is no one correct way to aim an arrow; while the underlying principles of nearly all aiming methods are remarkably similar, the different approaches or mechanisms may not seem to be, at least not at first glance.

Before we discuss the various aiming mechanisms we should mention the term *eye dominance*. Just as people are right or left handed, most people are predominantly right or left-eyed and this may not coincide with their "handedness". Generally if one eye is stronger (has greater visual acuity) than the other, the stronger eye becomes the dominant eye. If the eyes are very close in visual acuity, then other factors may come into play, or there may be no demonstrable reason at all. Whatever the reason, most of us are either right or left-eye dominant.

Until recently, eye dominance has been considered a major factor in determining whether a person should be shooting a right- or left-handed bow. The theory stated that the arrow needed to be directly under the dominant eye to facilitate the aiming process. This makes logical sense but human beings are inherently an illogical species. There have been too many excellent archers, including Howard Hill and Fred Bear, who were cross-eye dominant and did quite well for themselves. I'm strongly left-eye dominant and have been known to *(occasionally)* shoot quite well right-handed.

If you're curious to see whether you are right- or left-eye dominant, there are several fairly simple ways to tell. Here's one:

1. With both eyes open point a finger at an object across the room.

2. Close your right eye; if the finger stayed in the same position relative to the object you were pointing at, you're left eye dominant.

3. If it shifted position, you're right eye dominant (diag 12-1 to 4).

Eye Dominance

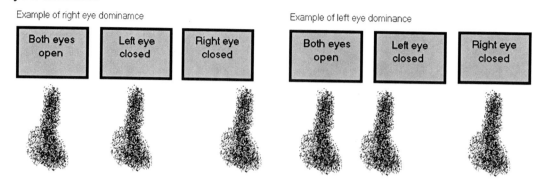

12-1 Left eye dominance and Right eye dominance (the blurry thing represents your thumb)

Cross eye dominance - visual differences

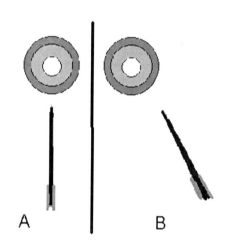

A   B

Figure A represents what a right handed, right eye dominant shooter would see if he were to "shot gun" an arrow.

Figure B represents what a right handed, left eye dominant shooter would see if he were to "shot gun" an arrow.

Clearly the initial alignment is easier for the archer depicted in Figure A, however the situation in Figure B is not insurmountable, as most of the calculations are carried out subconsciously.

12-2 Schematic representation of what a same-eye and a cross-eye dominant shooter "sees" when looking down the arrow

Got it? Good. Now forget it!

There are two exceptions that need to be mentioned. When working with new shooters, especially with children, we sometimes see that they actively try to "aim" by looking down the arrow with the eye opposite to the side they are anchoring. With this

type of cross-eye dominance, if your efforts to persuade them to focus on the target and not the arrow fail, they should consider switching hands. A good instructor should be able to pick up on that fairly quickly and suggest the change before too many bad habits develop, or the new shooter loses interest. If a new right-handed shooter is using a bow sight and the sight appears to be set up correctly but the arrows are impacting far left, it's very likely he is sighting with the wrong eye. To confirm this, tape the left eye closed with a piece of masking or Scotch tape. If that solves the problem, the shooter or instructor will need to consider switching hands.

We also need to talk about visual acuity in relation to accuracy, or potential accuracy. With all aiming methods, there's a sight picture being utilized on one level or another. As we'll see, that sight picture involves both near and far objects. In most cases, a person with better visual acuity, either native or corrected (by whatever means), will have a greater accuracy potential than someone with less. This does not mean that someone with less than 20/20 vision cannot become a good archer, however, the better the visual acuity, the greater the potential.

OK, let's talk about "aiming".

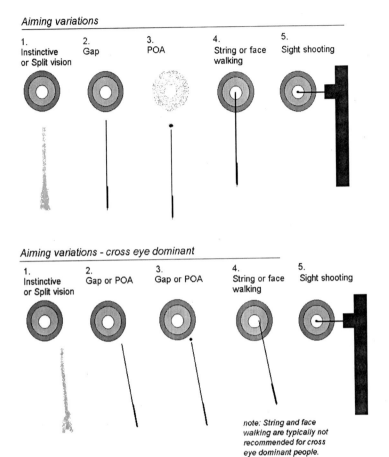

Aiming variations

1.
Instinctive
or Split vision

2.
Gap

3.
POA

4.
String or face
walking

5.
Sight shooting

Aiming variations - cross eye dominant

1.
Instinctive
or Split vision

2.
Gap or POA

3.
Gap or POA

4.
String or face
walking

5.
Sight shooting

note: String and face
walking are typically not
recommended for cross
eye dominant people.

12-3 Comparison of the various methods of aiming discussed in the following sections

Instinctive shooting

Instinctive
or Split vision

12-4 Instinctive sight picture. Notice that the arrow is visible but blurred and only in the peripheral vision.

The classical style of aiming the stickbow is called "Instinctive" shooting (diag 12-4). It's hardly instinctive by any dictionary definition, or even by any stretch of the imagination. It's been called that because to an observer, and sometimes to the archer, it seems to be happening without any **conscious** thought. To a very large extent, that may be true, but the key word is conscious, because a lot is happening on a subconscious level. Instinctive shooting is indeed a trained or learned process, actually several processes happening simultaneously.

If you recall from the Basic Shooting section, we described focusing on the target's center, the smallest part that you can see clearly, and letting the brain figure out where to point the bow. Consciously that may be all that's happening. The brain is receiving input from several sources and subconsciously interpreting the data and placing the bow arm to send the arrow to its mark.

When we focus on the center of a target, that's all we're consciously seeing, or rather paying attention to, but our brains actually see a lot more. (The retina, the part of the eye that receives incoming light waves or images, is the terminal part of second cranial nerve, so it is actually part of the brain.) We see the bow arm, the riser and the arrow superimposed on the backdrop of the target and background as part of our peripheral vision. That's the type of attention or focus we want on the mark we wish to hit. We want to keep the bullseye in focus and let everything else in the field of view become blurred. Given enough shooting, and yes, trial and error, our brains learn that for a given distance a certain "sight picture" is required to place the arrow in the bullseye (diag 12-5). Notice that a right-handed, right-eye dominant shooter will "see" the arrow nearly directly below the target's center. Only if the arrow is directly below the eye, and the bow perfectly tuned, will it be directly below dead center. A right-handed, left-eye dominant shooter will see the arrow off to the low right of the target's center, and will have to extrapolate its projection to center.

Even in a darkened room it's nearly impossible to block out the bow arm, bow, and arrow completely from our peripheral vision. If we can see the target we will be able to see the silhouette of the bow, bow arm, and arrow; that's usually enough for our brains to extrapolate the details and figure out the correct sight picture to aim the arrow (diag 12-4). In most cases, when an archer is placed in complete darkness and a laser light or dot is pointed at a backstop the resultant shots are generally not good.

12-5 Silhouette of the bow, arrow and bow arm as seen while shooting at an illuminated target in a darkened environment.

If we consider that a shooter with good basic form and properly tuned equipment should have very few left and right shots, then it follows that good left and right patterns at 10 yards should translate into good left and right patterns at any distance, relatively speaking. That makes sense as either tuning errors or form errors generally cause lateral dispersions. If the arrows are acting too stiff, they will tend to deviate to the left, and that deviation will increase with the distance. Conversely, an arrow that behaves too weak will deviate to the right. Torqueing the bow or plucking the bowstring will also give left or right arrows, respectively. Given the expected theoretical variance due to the increased distance, a 2" left or right variance at 10 yards, should be a 4" variance at 20, 8" at 40, etc (diag 12-6). That's usually not the case due to other factors influencing the arrow in flight as distance increases, but let's accept it for this discussion.

Schematic of arrow dispersion with increasing distance

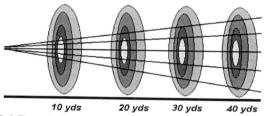

10 yds   20 yds   30 yds   40 yds

12-6 Expected group dispersion due to increasing distance

That leaves elevation as the only remaining aiming problem to solve. Experience shooting at different distances is the only answer for the instinctive shooter; the more accustomed you become shooting at a given distance, the more ingrained or subconscious the sight picture for that distance becomes. So, it follows that the more experience you have at different distances, the more sight pictures you are able consciously or subconsciously to draw on. In theory, this is quite simple; in practice, it's a little more difficult for several reasons. First it assumes we've had enough time or shooting experience to ingrain the different sight pictures in our subconscious, and second, varying terrain can easily make us think that objects are closer or farther than they really are. We have all experienced the phenomenon that things look closer outdoors than they do indoors. Without the visual references such as walls and furniture to help us gauge relative distance, our brains, both consciously (believing the distance to be different from what it actually is) and subconsciously (knowing the correct distance and still using an incorrect sight picture), can be deceived quite easily.

I recall my first outdoor International match (formerly called an outdoor PAA match). The first target was at 20 yards and being an indoor or "spot" shooter, 20 yards was a known and comfortable distance. Unfortunately, even though the distance was clearly marked and I knew exactly how far the target was, I proceeded to throw a very respectable 3" group, nowhere near the target's scoring area. Even though I knew the distance, my brain believed it was closer and aimed accordingly – three times!

Well – so much for the myth that instinctive shooters need not be concerned about judging distance! There will always be a trajectory problem to contend with. Even a high power rifle bullet, that can travel 15 times faster than a fast stickbow can throw an arrow, will have trajectory problems the shooter will need to resolve.

Here are some examples of arrow trajectories at various distances.

Example 1: Arrow launched horizontally at a target at shoulder height.

Arrow Speed (fps)	Distance (yards)	Drop (inches)
200	5	1.9
200	10	4.3
200	20	17.4
200	30	39.1
200	40	69.5
200	50	108.7

Example 2: Arrow launched to hit target center at a target 20 yards away.

Arrow speed (fps)	Distance (yards)	Drop (Inches)
200	20	0.0
200	30	13.0
200	40	34.8
200	50	65.2

It should be noted that 200 fps was used as an example; even with today's bow designs and materials, 200 fps is exceptionally fast. Most stickbows will fall into the 160 to 190 fps range, and the trajectories will be considerably more severe as the initial speed decreases.

Also note that these calculations are for a generic arrow. Due to air resistance, larger diameter shafts and arrows with larger fletching will increase the trajectory or arc; smaller diameter shafts and smaller fletching will decrease the arc. As we've seen, changing the FOC can also change the shape of the arc, or more correctly, the rate of fall.

If we return to our initial premise, that to shoot at varying distances the archer needs to have a mental image of where his bow/bow arm should be in relation to his target, it follows that the more he shoots at varying distances, the better he becomes. One way to augment the "subconscious sight picture" model used by a number of skilled archers is to visualize the flight of the arrow, before release. By having a sight picture at a given distance, and knowing the flight or arc of a given bow/arrow combination, the archer seems to know "instinctively" where to aim for each distance.

Training tip: *When learning to shoot at distances beyond the archer's normal comfort range, it's suggested that a substantial number of shots be taken at each distance to help ingrain the sight picture. A relatively new archer would not be well served by jumping from one distance to another with every arrow. He hasn't given his brain, or subconscious, enough time to store the various sight pictures. As the archer gains experience, then shooting from various distances and different angles becomes excellent practice. Since he already has his sight pictures stored, gaining the flexibility to react to shooting at different distances is a significant benefit in certain types of matches and certainly hunting situations. Additionally, the brain is very capable of calculating differences in distances, if the archer is familiar with shooting at 30 and 40 yards, he should be able quickly (subconsciously or not) to figure out where to hold for 33 or 38 yards.*

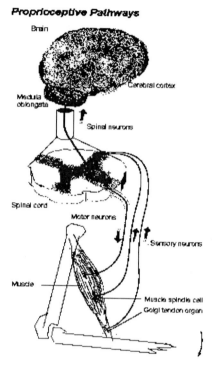

Proprioceptive Pathways

Brain

Cerebral cortex

Medula oblongata

Spinal neurons

Spinal cord

Motor neurons

Sensory neurons

Muscle

Muscle spindle cell

Golgi tendon organ

12-6 Schematic representation of the proprioceptor neural pathways

There is another variation of instinctive shooting but, quite honestly, I know or have seen very few archers actually develop it successfully. Within our joints there are specialized nerve endings called proprioceptors (diag 12-7). They tell the brain where our various body parts are at any given moment. For example, if I where to ask you where your left foot or right hand was, you wouldn't have to look at it to know. *If a person were to shoot at the same target, over the same distance with the same equipment long enough with enough attention to detail, both consciously and subconsciously, then it would be possible for the proprioceptors to give the brain enough information to repeat the entire shot sequence and hit the bullseye without actually having to see it.* In the shooting-in-the-dark scenario we described earlier, an archer shooting in a darkened space would still be able to see the silhouette of the bow arm, bow and arrow as visual reference points. So, the only way to test the proprioceptor phenomenon would be to use the laser dot we described or possibly blindfold the archer! I would very strongly advise against trying that at home!

My best guess is that most instinctive archers use about 95% visual input and 5% proprioceptive, but that's only a guess.

The instinctive aiming method has often been likened to throwing a baseball. This really isn't the best analogy, as throwing a baseball is considerably more difficult than aiming an arrow. With the arrow there are the aforementioned visual references; with the baseball there are none, so the baseball analogy would be more in line with the proprioceptive scenario. Also, I tend to think that most archers are looking for better accuracy than would be possible with a baseball. The best instinctive shooting analogy would be the simple act of shaking hands with a friend. You come face to face with someone, they extend their hand and you do the same; a second later, the hands interlock and shake – 95% visual (albeit peripheral) and 5% proprioceptive. While this too is a fairly gross example, and an archer would require greater accuracy that that of two hands meeting each other for a handshake, the neural mechanisms are the same.

The instinctive method of aiming can be quite effective at the shorter ranges. It allows for a smooth and fast shot when necessary, as in a hunting situation. It can also be a very relaxing way to shoot, for the casual archer. As with most things, there are limitations or pitfalls that must be understood and accepted, if this aiming method is chosen. For any type of precision shooting, competitive target shooting, for example, where a large number of arrows are to be fired and scored, it is probably the most difficult and least accurate or consistent method. There are no conscious or tangible reference points and the archer must totally focus on the very point he wishes to hit, relying on and trusting only his experience and the aforementioned peripheral or subconscious visual clues to "aim". *That level of attention or focus is very difficult to maintain for extended periods of time.* It can become mentally and physically exhausting. This is not to say it cannot be used very effectively, just that it requires the greatest commitment, dedication and practice; the archer truly has to trust himself, his form, and his equipment. There are very few, if any, top competitive barebow shooters who shoot purely instinctively. Those that can are truly the masters of the game.

I have been using the word "*focus*" and not concentration for a very specific reason. Concentration has the connotation of blocking out everything except the one thing that's being concentrated on (diag 12-8). That may not be the best idea in most shooting situations. While it may work at a supervised archery range, while hunting, field shooting or even just plinking in your backyard, it might be better to have an idea of what's going on around you – for safety's sake. Focus, as when focusing a camera, binoculars or telescope, brings the object of your attention into crystal clarity, while everything else remains visible but blurred. The fact that the periphery is still visible is vital, not only to your ability to aim instinctively, but to your safety and the safety of those around you. You'll be able notice if anything has gone awry, placing either you or someone else in harm's way. For example, if someone were to wander in front of your shooting position, or behind your backstop, or your dog decides he wants to play with your target, you would be able to see him and take appropriate action. That distraction, while it might not help in your shooting regimen, may be of more value to you in the long run than burning a hole in the target and ignoring everything else around you. Lastly, I've found that concentration can be considerably more taxing mentally and physically than focusing; that too can be detrimental when many arrows are required to complete a match.

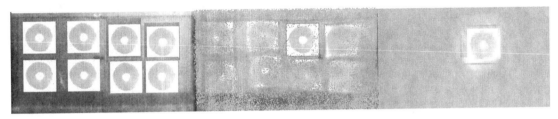

12-8 Representation of focusing on a point vs. concentrating on it. *The first picture shows a fairly standard archery range set up for an NFAA match. The second picture represents an archer's view "focusing" on his target. The third picture represents an archer "concentrating" on the same target, effectively blocking out everything else.*

When should focus on the target begin and how long should the focus last? Many instinctive shooters begin to focus the moment the target is acquired. At that point the focus is general, meaning it's on the entire target. As the draw commences the focus becomes narrower and continues to narrow on the point they wish to hit; at anchor it becomes a pinpoint. By doing this, the pinpoint focus needs only last a second or two, saving the archer unnecessary fatigue. If you try to remain focused for too long a time, despite all good intentions the focus will start to drift. When that happens there's a good chance that the arrow will go to whatever point the focus has drifted to. As we'll see, the time at anchor needs to be only long enough to set up the shot and initiate the follow-through.

There's an old saying, dating back to at least the American Revolution and possibly medieval times, "*Aim small, miss small*". The meaning is that, if you aim at a small spot, say a 1" aiming dot and miss it by an inch, the shot will still be closer to the intended point of impact than by aiming at a 16" target an missing that by an inch! As with many things, while the original intent is correct, it seems that some newly evolved "Traditional" archers, believe it's better to aim at a small mark, be it a small piece of paper, Styrofoam, leaf or soda can, rather than a full sized target. As you would expect, their shots may very well be quite close to that mark. What they are actually doing however, is training themselves to aim at the whole, albeit small, target. Because of that practice, some have never learned to "pick" a spot. Transitioning to a full size target, a foam animal in a 3D match, or a live animal in a hunting situation usually becomes disastrous, as they do exactly what they have trained themselves to do – aim at the whole target! So, instead of picking the center of the "X" in the paper target, or a shadow on the foam Styrofoam or paper deer, they aim at the whole target or whole deer, and often miss both. It's fun to see who can get closest to or hit a 1" spot at a given distance, and it can certainly help to sharpen your mechanical shooting skill or form. However, without being able to pick a spot naturally, or instinctively, on a larger target, it can, and has, put many archers at a severe disadvantage both at the target range and in the field.

While picking a spot is critical for accurate shooting, sometimes a "spot" may not readily present itself. There may be other objects near the target or bullseye that can draw our attention away from our intended mark. Even an arrow slightly off target center may draw the next arrow to it. Bowhunters are typically taught to pick a spot on their quarry; it can be a shadow or a lighter/darker patch of hair. Unfortunately, nearby objects or the animal's movements may distract them from that focus, or sometimes the "spot" just doesn't exist. A technique suggested by Jay Kidwell in his book, Instinctive Archery Insights, is to visualize a small familiar object over the point you wish to hit. The object may be a quarter, a Poker chip, or even a 1" orange aiming spot; some archers with very good imagination (and eyesight) actually use an image of an aspirin. By mentally placing that object there, you have a defined "spot" to direct your arrow. As with any technique, this one will work only as well as the effort you put into practicing it.

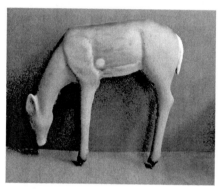

If you plan on using the imaginary spot technique, the first thing to do is look at the genuine article long enough so it becomes a concrete image in your mind. Once you know exactly what it looks like, then practice placing it on a wall, hay bale or anything. The process has to be established well before it is time to use it in earnest (diag 12-9).

12-9 Imaginary aiming spot on a foam deer target

Split vision

Instinctive
or Split vision

Closely akin to "instinctive shooting" is a method called "Split vision" (diag 12-10).

Howard Hill, probably the one name that requires little or no introduction in most Archery circles, coined the term.

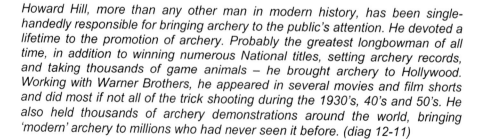

Howard Hill, more than any other man in modern history, has been single-handedly responsible for bringing archery to the public's attention. He devoted a lifetime to the promotion of archery. Probably the greatest longbowman of all time, in addition to winning numerous National titles, setting archery records, and taking thousands of game animals – he brought archery to Hollywood. Working with Warner Brothers, he appeared in several movies and film shorts and did most if not all of the trick shooting during the 1930's, 40's and 50's. He also held thousands of archery demonstrations around the world, bringing 'modern' archery to millions who had never seen it before. (diag 12-11)

With split vision the archer still focuses on the center of the target, but is more aware of the position of the arrow in his vision and conscious mind. There is a mental note made of the relative position between the arrow and target. Here, the aiming has begun to come out of the subconscious. With a conscious reference point, the focus still remains on the target, but there is now a semblance of a "device" to aim with. With this type of aiming it is more advantageous to have the arrow directly under the dominant aiming eye; while still not a necessity, the reasons for doing so should be relatively obvious.

2-11 An older Howard Hill seen shooting a reflex/deflex longbow at an archery tournament in the early 60's

Most good instinctive shooters are actually using more of a split vision approach and the actual difference between the two is really a matter of degree.

As the archer begins to move farther and farther away from the target, it should come as no surprise that the arrow will need to be aimed higher and higher to account for the trajectory. As that happens, the arrowhead will get closer and closer to the center of the target. As it does, it will come out of the peripheral vision and into the focal region of the archer's sight. There will come a point when the arrow actually overlays the center of the target. That distance is called the archer's point on or point blank range (diag 12-12). For most people using a corner of the mouth anchor that distance is typically between 40 and 60 yards. That distance will be closer if the archer's anchor point brings the arrow closer to his eye, as happens when using the middle finger to the corner of the mouth as a reference/anchor point. When shooting at that point on distance, the instinctive shooter has now become a gap shooter. As the human eye cannot focus on two objects at different distances at the same time, the arrow will still be blurred, but clear enough to be used as a reference.

Instinctive or split vision at point on distance

12-12 Instinctive or split vision sight picture at an archer's point blank range. Strangely enough, as we'll see, a gap or point of aim shooter sees the same thing at his point blank distance (above right)!

Gap Shooting

Gap

12-13 Sight picture for gap shooting

When shooting with the gap method, the relationship between the arrowhead and the target becomes an exact science (diag 12-13). Not only are you aware of the tip of the arrow, but you've made a conscious decision about where to place it in relation to the point you want to hit (diag 12-11). Here, you are actually using the arrowhead as a sight. A gap shooter will be very conscious of the distance from the tip of his arrow to the target. He will know exactly how far below and to the left or right he needs to put the tip of his arrow to hit dead center for every distance he needs to shoot. Some gap shooters actually put a mark on the target frame or ground to serve as an aiming point; that variation is hence called "Point of Aim" shooting. This is a very accurate method of shooting and is used by a number of top competitors in both target and 3D events. Be aware that any change in arrow length or even tip configuration (such as going from a target tip to a hunting head) will change the "gap" or point of aim.

An extreme variant of gap shooting, used by a few barebow indoor target shooters, is to de-tune their bows, to deliberately slow them down sufficiently so that their point on distance is 20 yards or 18 meters. Typically the shooter will use a very lightweight bow, with heavy, full-length arrows and three, four or even six large feathers. This becomes a very accurate method of sighting while still remaining within the barebow rules. It's not for everyone, and certainly would have limitations beyond 20 yards, but for a specific purpose, it's hard too beat (diag 12-14).

"Gaps" at various distances

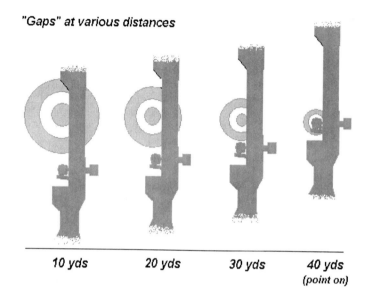

12-14 Representation of a gap shooter's sight picture from 10 to 40 yards.

10 yds   20 yds   30 yds   40 yds
                                                (point on)

.Point of Aim Shooting

POA

12-15 Sight picture for point of aim shooting

Akin to gap shooting is point of aim shooting, or POA shooting. The difference here is that the archer effectively disregards the target while shooting (12-15). The target is important only when initially setting up his *point* of aim. With gap shooting, the archer is aware of the distance between his target and the tip on his arrow. With POA that distance is clearly defined and marked or identified in some way. The archer may place a physical item on the group below the target, or use a clump of grass, stone, or area of discoloration on the target frame. Once at anchor he places the tip of arrow on that point. The POA shooter either totally disregards the target or shifts his attention back and forth between the target and the aiming point. This method is quite effective in certain types of target archery, especially those matches that are shot at a single distance and position. Taking your focus off the spot you wish to hit is a risk that must be carefully weighed before making the commitment to adopt this style of shooting.
POA shooting requires discussion as a number or archers are currently using it successfully. However, I cannot personally recommend POA shooting, as it is antithetical to our current goal, which is a sharp focus on the target we wish to hit.

A variation on POA shooting is using a part of the riser as a reference point or sight. For example, at 20 yards, the tip of the arrow may be several feet below the target, but the top arch of the sight window may be somewhere on the target or near the bullseye itself (diag 12.16). While this takes the same type of experimentation as gap and POA shooting, some shooters find this method quite easy to accept. Some barebow archers go as far as selecting a bow that has an appropriately sized sight window to facilitate this method of aiming.

Note that in certain types of competition, any markings on the face of the bow near the sight window make the bow illegal for use in the barebow classes. These marking may include the ends of laminations, decorative engraving or even very prominent grain features. The solution is to cover the markings with an opaque tape, such as black electrical tape. It is also the reason that above the arrow clickers were never allowed in many barebow classes.

12-16 Two examples of an archer using his riser as a sighting device. The left illustration shows the angle of the sight window overlays the bullseye. Unfortunately, most archers aren't quite so lucky. The second picture shows the top of the target being "bracketed" by the arch of the sight window.

String Walking and Face Walking

String or face walking

12-17 Sight picture for string or face walking

As gap shooting (or gapping) proved to be an accurate means of putting the arrow in the center of the target, the logical progression was to find a way to have the tip of the arrow in the bullseye regardless of the distance being shot (diag 12-17). As we've said, with a standard, index finger in the corner of the mouth anchor, at distances closer than the point on distance, the arrow is well below the eye. If the tip were brought to the bullseye, the arrow would sail over the target. It would be great if you did all your shooting at your point blank range, for example 47 yards, but unfortunately, that's not the case for most people. Face walking and string walking solve that problem.

Face Walking

So you need to shoot at distances other than your point blank range, do you? If you were to shift your anchor point up, closer to your eye, you'd find that your point on range would be getting closer and closer (diag 12-18). When the arrow was directly under your eye, or lateral to it, you would be at a theoretical zero trajectory distance, or very close to it! (Gravity begins to affect an arrow as soon as it leaves the bow – which is why we're calling it theoretical.)

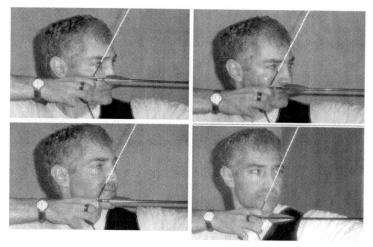

12-18 Multiple anchors for use with face walking. The closer the arrow is to the eye, the shorter the point blank range (top left picture). As the arrow is brought away from the eye, the point on distance increases.

If you were to anchor lower than the corner of your mouth, your point on range would be extended. For practical purposes, the "below the chin" anchor used by target archers with sights is about as low as most people can go. Also, since our faces are not flat, in addition to the desired vertical change, each new anchor point may impart some left or right deviation. Seeing as the archer in this case is changing his anchor to different landmarks along his face, the term for this type of shooting has been aptly named Face Walking. Its greatest benefit is using a constant sight picture for varying distances; the greatest problem is that several anchor points need to be found, remembered and mastered. This type of shooting lends itself to formal target matches, where there are limited numbers of distances, such as the 900 round (formerly called the American round) shot at 60, 50 and 40 yards, or the FITA shot at 90, 70 and 50 meters. With unknown and non-standard distances, the archer would need to have set anchor points for the major distances, for example 10, 20, 30 and 40 yards, and then hold off above or below the bullseye, to compensate for intermediate distances such as 18, 23, 36 or 48 yards.

String Walking

Following the evolutionary trail of aiming methods, if an archer wanted to maintain a constant sight picture and a constant anchor, face walking was not an option. It was discovered that if you were to place all three fingers below the arrow, called *three-under* for some strange reason (as opposed to placing the arrow between the index and middle fingers) you could maintain the same anchor point and vary the point blank range by sliding your fingers down the string and away from the arrow.

If you normally anchor with your index finger in the corner of your mouth, but have the arrow above the index finger, it's about 1/2" to 3/4" closer to your eye. From the previous section, this will naturally shorten your point on range. If you were to slide your hand down another 1/2", that would bring your point on range even closer; likewise for going 1" below the arrow and 2", until the arrow is right below the eye. Most archers who practice this form of string walking actually count the loops of serving to determine where to hold the string for various point on ranges (diag 12-19).

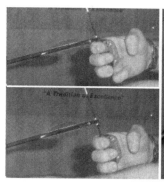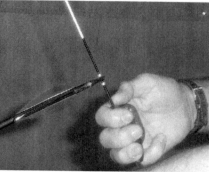

12-19 String walking positions for a far target (left top) and one at a closer distance (left bottom). This archer is actually using his thumb nail to count the wraps of serving to determine his finger placement for a given distance (right).

For hunting or casual shooting, the center serving may be marked for different distances, or multi-colored serving thread can be used. For safety, two nocking points are typically used, one above and one below the arrow. The two nocking points should be far enough apart so as not to pinch the arrow during the draw or at anchor; 1/8" farther apart than the width of the arrow nock is usually sufficient. Dual nocking points and multi-colored servings are illegal in many types of barebow or traditional competitions, so if you plan on attending one of these shoots and are using one of these methods, check the applicable rules first.

It is also not uncommon for shooters to use a combination of string walking and face walking, as well as gap. As we described in string walking, the anchor point defines the point on range or maximum effective range with the arrowhead on the bullseye. For longer distances the archer would either have to aim above the target, which many do, or to shift from string walking to face walking. It has been said that the best shooters not only understand various methods of aiming, but understand how and when to use each. In the final analysis the only thing that matters in competition or when afield is where the arrows land.

A final note about face walking and string walking: Both techniques are designed to turn the arrow into a sight. By modifying the position of the anchor point or arrow's nock on the string relative to the drawing hand, you are effectively changing the draw length and power stroke and possibly the tiller of the bow. This by definition changes the speed of the arrow and has an effect on the point of impact. How much of an effect that has, in relation to the changes imparted by changing the distance from the arrow to the eye, is minor but measurable and given the number of variables, will be different for each archer. Therefore, when determining the specific anchor or hand position on the string for a given distance, only trial and error can determine the final result.

The string as part of the sight picture

The question often arises whether the bowstring can or should be utilized as part of the barebow sighting mechanism. Some very experienced archers line up the bowstring with the inner edge of the sight window or center it on the upper limb as a means of confirming sight picture alignment and a correct anchor. Although the bowstring will be very blurred, it can be a benefit to those with years of experience who demand a very high level of precision. For new shooters the answer is an emphatic "no". It adds to the workload that the new shooter needs to accomplish while at anchor and may take the focus away from more important aspects of the shot. Therefore it can become more of a detriment than a benefit. For beginning and intermediate level archers it is better to develop a consistent anchor and rely on that for sight picture alignment.

Bow Sights

Sight shooting

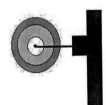

12-20 Sight picture for a sight shooter

Long before there was formalized gapping, string walking or face walking, there were bow sights (diag 12-20). A sight is nothing more than a reference point attached to the bow that can be calibrated to have the archer's line of sight coincide with the arrow's path at the bullseye (diag 12-21).

12-21 This diagram shows how the archer's line of sight, through the bow sight coincides with the trajectory of the arrow at the bullseye of the target.

A very simple sight can be made from a toothpick or pin and a piece of masking tape (diag 12-22). If the sight is to become a permanent fixture on the bow, numerous commercial versions are available. (I have even seen several homemade sights that rival some of their commercial counterparts.) These devices range from simple tape-on or screw-on sight bars with single or multiple adjustable pins (diag 12-23), to separate sight mounts that attach to the back (diag 12-24), face (diag 12-25), or side (diag 12-26) of the bow. Most new risers and all Olympic risers have predrilled holes, ready to accept side mounted sights (diag 12-22).

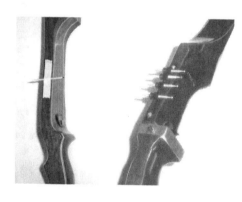

12-22 Toothpick sight on a Hoyt Pro Medalist (left) and screw or tape on bow sight (right), such as this Merrill Heart Shot hunting sight on the author's Ben Pearson Silencer TD, were quite popular from the 1970's to the present day.

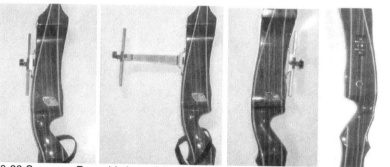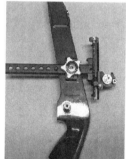

12-23 Screw-on Reynolds bow sight (c1970) on back of riser (left to right). The following picture shows the optional extension.
12-24 Screw-on Reynolds bow sight, c1970 on face of riser
12-25 Screw-on Check-it bow sight bracket on side of a riser
12-26 Side mounted bow sight on an Olympic T/D riser

The sighting device itself may be a simple pin as we described earlier or a multiple pin sight. With multiple pins, a separate pin is used for each distance the archer wishes to shoot, as seen wit the Merrill Heart Shot hunting sight 12-18). An aperture sight (diag 12-27 and 28) or in some cases a magnifying lens (diag 12-28) can reduce the archer's workload. Most stickbow target competitions do not allow "scopes", so we have to choose between a pin and aperture sight. Pin sights were quite popular in the early days of modern archery and are still used quite often.

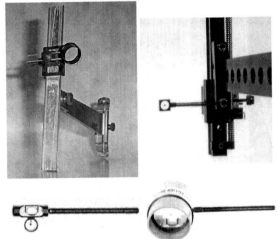

12-27 *Target style aperture sight from the 1970 (Reynolds Bowsight –top left)*
12-28 *(Spigarelli aperture on a Check-it sight extension, (top right)*
12-29 *A more common type of aperture sight (bottom left)*
12-30 *Magnifying sight or "scope", both with integral levels (bottom right)*

As we'll see later, with a pin, the archer needs to decide whether to focus on pin or the target. With an aperture sight, it's recommended to look through the "hole" and focus on the target. This is more natural for most people and is why the aperture has become the sighting device of choice for most target archers today. In either case he will have to determine how much of the target he will allow to be obscured by the pin or how much of the bullseye he wishes to see through the aperture.

Sight set up and configuration

To set up a simple sight, attach it to the bow by the appropriate means (as discussed in the Basic Shooting section). Measure the distance from the corner of the archer's mouth to the center of his eye, usually about three to four inches. Position the end of the sight "pin" that distance above and in line or slightly to the left of the arrow, as it sits on the rest. This doesn't have to be exact, as we'll have to adjust it by actually using it. Again, starting at a close range (10 yards), hold the pin center on the bullseye, anchor normally and let a few arrows fly. They should be grouped somewhere on the target.

To correct the sight settings for a given distance, if the arrows are grouping high, move the sight UP; if they are going low, move the sight DOWN; if left, then LEFT; and right, RIGHT. An easy way to remember this is that the sight always follows the arrow (diag 12-31).

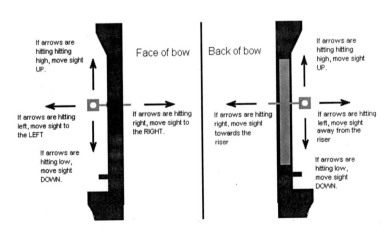

12-31 *Sight corrections shown both from the archer's viewpoint and while looking at the back of the bow.*

An interesting comparison to rifle shooting is that while a bow sight is analogous to the front sight on a rifle, using face or string walking is effectively the same as adjusting the rifle's rear sight.

Once the arrows are grouped near the center, move back to 15 or 20 yards, and fire a few more shots. It's natural for the arrows to be low at 20 yards, due to their trajectory. Move the sight pin DOWN to compensate. There should not be a significant change in windage (horizontal variation) as you move back if you were centered at the closer distance and the bow was tuned properly. Repeat for any other distances you will need to shoot. You should notice several things; the farther back you go, the amount the sight has to move, for each additional 10 yards, will be progressively greater. If you recall the arrow drop/trajectory table we used earlier, it showed that the longer the arrow was in flight, the faster it falls, following what's called in Geometry a *parabolic arc*. You will eventually reach a point where the sight pin will overlap the arrow on the rest. That's the point on or point blank range we are talking about with gap shooting, and it can become a real problem when having to shoot at longer distances with a sight (diag 12-32). For that reason, most sight shooters generally do not use a "corner of the mouth" anchor. They will shift their anchor to below the chin or side of the chin anchor, more properly called a "reference point" (diag 12-33). The greater the distance the arrow is from the eye, the greater the distance the sight can be lowered on the sight bar to extend the shooting range.

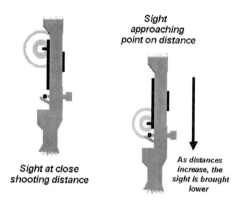

Sight
approaching
point on distance

**Sight at close
shooting distance**

As distances
increase, the
sight is brought
lower

12-32 As the archer approaches his point on or point blank range, the sight will begin to overlap the arrow. Notice the similarity to what happens to a gap or POA shooter (left).

12-33 Below the chin anchor used by most sight shooters. This allows for longer distances than the corner of the mouth anchor (below).

For some archers, even with a low anchor the sight may coincide with the arrow, or go below it to reach certain distances. In that case, the only remaining option is to "sight" not on the bullseye, but on a point above it. It may be the top of the target's outer ring, target frame or even an object behind that target such as a tree or patch of grass.

With a low anchor, depending on the type of shooting and specific rules, a peep sight and/or kisser button may be placed on the string (diag 12-34 and 12-35). The peep sight gives the shooter a rear aperture to help confirm the line-up to the target, very similar to how a rear aperture sight is used on a target rifle. The kisser button, a flat plastic disc attached to the string and touched between the lips at full draw, helps to ensure a reproducible anchor and string alignment. It cannot be stressed strongly enough – the peep sight and kisser buttons are only aids to confirm the proper anchor has been reached.

It must be remembered that the use of a peep sight or kisser button cannot take the place of, or lessen the importance of, a solid anchor.

(I strongly recommend beginning sight shooters to use the corner of the mouth anchor before attempting the low or below the chin anchor. The former provides a more consistent and solid anchor, which promotes the development of proper shooting form. Once the archer is demonstrating proper form then the low anchor becomes advantageous for shooting at extended ranges.)

Note that Olympic and FITA (recurve) type matches generally do not allow the use of peep sights or kisser buttons. In that case, many archers line up the string to the side of the sight window, face of the bow, or the arrow itself. As with barebow shooting, that technique adds to the workload at anchor and is best left to more experienced archers. They may also use additional reference or touch points such as placing their thumbs below their ears on the angle of their jawbones, or their little fingers on their collarbone (diag 12-36).

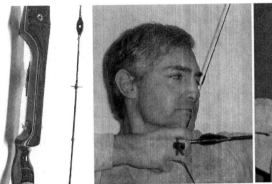

12-30 Kisser button and peep sight on string (left)
12-31 Kisser button and peep in use (middle)
12-32 Notice the additional reference points on this archer using a side of the chin anchor. The thumb is locked behind the ear and the pinky finger is touching the collarbone (right).

Placement of the sighting device on the bow

As we discussed in detail in the chapter on Olympic style tuning, the sighting device may be placed at various distances from the shooter's eye. Simply, the further the sighting device (pin or aperture) is away from the shooter's eye (the sight radius), the more precise minute sight movements can be detected. An archer who understands that those movements will be occurring, whether detectable or not, may opt to place the sight closer to his eye. By shortening the length of the sight extension bar (or reverse mounting it so that it is behind the face of the bow) one minimizes the psychological effects of seeing the sight wobble. Typically as the archer gains experience and can hold steadier, he can extend the sight radius to increase his precision somewhat.

A new sight shooter should not use a maximum sight radius, as the sight's wobble over the target face will prove disconcerting and have an adverse effect on his shooting.

Variations in sight aiming techniques

As we become older, it becomes increasingly apparent that we can't optically focus on two things at different distances at the same time. (Younger people, otherwise known as "kids", can't either, but they can switch back and forth between objects at different distances a lot faster than adults can. That may give the illusion that they can actually focus near and far at the same time.) So we have to choose what we want to bring into optical clarity – the sight or the target. If we choose an aperture sight, the decision is typically made for us, as we can look through the blurred aperture, and focus on the target. With a pin sight, we actually have more of a choice; we can keep either the pin or the target in focus, or alternate between the two. Conventional and practical wisdom dictates that we should focus on the target and let the sight blur. The obvious reason for this is that we want to hit the target and not the sight pin. More germane to our shooting is that if we were to focus on the sight pin, we would pick up on minute sight movements (bow arm movements). While this sounds like a desirable thing to do, given that the sight pin is never really still, seeing every little movement has proven to be more of a detriment than an aid to accurate shooting. Alternating between the two is of course an option, but with the number of other things going on at full draw, not the least of which is the string trying to tear itself from your fingers, adding the task of switching focus may not be the best option (diag 12-37). However, the final decision has to remain with the individual archer. The best approach we've seen is to give each method a fair chance and let the position of the arrows in the target over time be your guide.

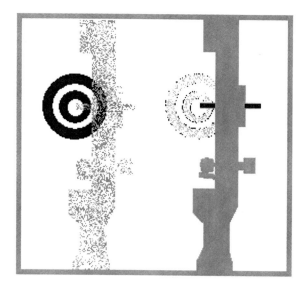

12-33 While focusing on the target is preferable, it is also possible to focus on the sight pin. It's impossible to do both at the same time.

For those of you who have been involved in competitive rifle shooting, this is the exact opposite of the standard practice in that discipline. With iron sights (rear aperture sight and front aperture or post sight) on a target rifle, shooters are usually taught to focus on the front sight and let the target blur. The reasoning is exactly the same as with a bow sight, but the desired effect is exactly the opposite. With a rifle, a steadier hold is possible and so the shooter typically wants or needs to see the minute movements in the sight. This is especially true when shooting from the prone position at long distances up to 1,000 yards. At the longer distances the rifle target appears as a dot, so there isn't really anything concrete to focus on.

The approach and consistency of sight shooting

While it's entirely possible to train the sight on the bullseye, and keep it there throughout the draw, it's more likely that most beginning and intermediate shooters will not be "on" from pre-draw to anchor. Since that's the case, it's helpful to let the sight approach the bullseye the same way every time. Some people like to bring the sight down to the bullseye from above, some like to bring it up, from below, and some from one side or another. While each style might have its devotees, and there may be reasons for using one over another, it really comes down to what is natural and reproducible for the individual. Don't be surprised if even reproducing the approach to the target is difficult in the beginning, with experience it will happen.

That being said, whether shooting barebow or freestyle (with sights), it's never advisable to draw the bow with the bow arm putting the arrow at a 45-degree or steeper angle down or up and then raise or lower the bow arm to the target. Besides being very bad form, and possibly injuring your shoulder joints, in the event of a premature release, the effects can be either embarrassing or hazardous.

Special Conditions in Regard to Aiming

Uphill and downhill shots

Whether shooting instinctively, gapping, or using a sight, there will be times when the shot is not on level ground. While a small grade can usually be ignored, as the angle becomes more severe, as would be the case when a bowhunter is shooting from a tree-stand or elevated position, several things need to be considered. They are, namely, the effect (vectoring) of gravity and the possible effect on changes in the archer's form.

First – gravity always pulls an object toward the center of the Earth, otherwise known as "straight down". Therefore, the distance from the archer to the target is not measured along the slope of the hill or line of sight, either uphill or down, but along a horizontal line (diag 12-38).

12-38 The downhill shot geometry

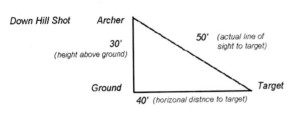

The distance to the target is actually 50' along the archer's line of sight, however gravity is only exerting its force on the arrow in flight for 40'. If the archer assumes a 50' shot, then he will shoot high. He needs to understand that the horizontal distance called the *"True Ballistic Range"* is less than the line of sight distance. It may not be necessary to employ geometric formulas, in this case *the Pythagorean Theorem*, but it is necessary for the archer to know that **the distance to the target is always measured along the horizontal**. Therefore, when not shooting on level ground, the target is actually closer than the line of sight. Usually, aiming a little low will suffice; not scientific, but it works.

What may be less intuitive, is that the same holds true for an uphill shot (diag 12-39).

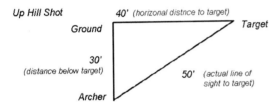

12-39 The uphill shot geometry

While the total forces on an uphill shot are slightly different than on a downhill shot, the effect of gravity is exactly the same. The correct distance to the target must be measured along the horizontal.

For those who enjoy mental gymnastics, consider the following: While gravity acts upon the arrow only for the horizontal distance it travels, note that because the arrow is traveling a longer distance than its horizontal component, it's spending more time in flight. Therefore gravity will exert its effect on the arrow for a longer period of time. In the case above, the arrow is traveling 50' and not 40', though gravity is only acting along the 40' vector. The extra time in flight equates to an increased drop. To make matters worse, on an uphill shot gravity is acting as a retardant and on a downhill shot it's acting as an accelerant as it's pulling the arrow down to earth. That increases the arrow's time in flight for an uphill shot, and decreases it for a downhill shot. For most situations, it's usually best just to recall that when shooting uphill or downhill, you generally have to "aim" lower than the true line of sight distance to the target. The best if not the only way to determine how much is by experience and that means practice.

The other factor affecting uphill and downhill shots has to do with the archer's form. Changes in elevation, whether due to terrain or distance, are made from the waist and not the shoulder or bow arm. The shoulder girdle geometry must remain constant if the arrows are to fly consistently. As the bow shoulder is slightly lower than the anchor point, assuming that your anchor is consistent, raising the bow arm will shorten your draw length and lowering the bow arm will lengthen it (diag 12-40).

This is fairly easy to see. Nock an arrow and draw your bowstring to your anchor with your bow arm parallel to the ground. Look at the tip of the arrow and its position in relation to the rest. Now, lower your bow arm 12" to 18" while keeping your shoulders parallel to the ground, and note where the tip now is in relation to the rest. Repeat the exercise, this time raising the bow arm 12" to 18". Needless to say, do not release an arrow in either of these positions. If this is too difficult due to the draw weight (this may indicate that you may be over-bowed), you can do the same exercise without the bow. Simply rest an arrow shaft on your bow hand and place the nock between your index and middle finger and bring it to your normal anchor. Then raise and lower your bow arm and note the movement of the arrow on your bow hand.

The same effects must also be considered when aiming at moving targets or shooting when the body cannot be positioned perpendicular to the target. The upper body acting as a turret pivoting about the waist handles the lateral movements or displacement of the target. A right-handed shooter attempting to compensate for lateral movements by using his arm or shoulder will shorten his draw length going from left to right and lengthen it when going from right to left.

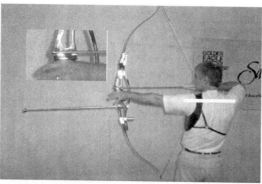

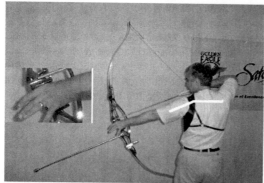
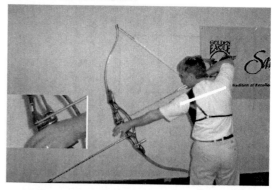

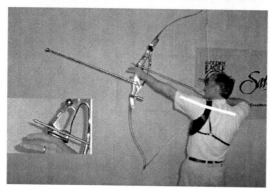
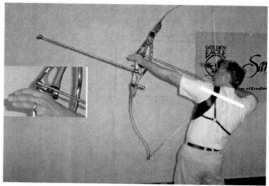

12-40 In the top picture, the archer is drawing on a target at shoulder level. Notice the position of his arrow tip in relation to the riser (insert). The left middle and lower pictures show what happens if the bow is lowered or elevated by primarily raising or lowering the bow arm. The right middle and lower pictures show that shoulder geometry and draw length are maintained when bending at the waist is used to change elevation.

Shooting with or against the wind

Unless you limit yourself to indoor shooting, sooner or later you'll have to contend with the effects of wind on the shot. Even before you release the arrow, a strong wind can have an effect on your shooting. Being buffeted by the wind can make a steady hold almost impossible. There really isn't a lot you can do to stop that from happening. Unless you're at a major match or planning to attend one and want to be prepared for any possible situation, a buffeting wind may just be enough of a reason not to shoot on a particular day.

If you decide to shoot on a windy day, there are several things to consider. An instinctive or split vision archer may be able to shoot quickly enough to minimize the apparent effects of the wind-induced swaying. For gap or sight shooters, whose hold is typically longer, that may not be an option. In those cases, consider waiting for a lull and timing your shots to coincide with that lull. An old rifleman's trick for shooting in the wind was to mount or shoulder the rifle during a gust, knowing (or hoping) that as soon as the gust passed, there would be a relative lull, giving enough time to make the shot. Either way, the only comfort you can take is knowing that every other archer out that day is having the same dilemma.

For casual shooting or hunting practice you may want to consider shooting from a kneeling or sitting position. Those positions will be more stable than standing and provide less of a sail for the wind to blow against. Also learning to find a suitable barricade such as a large tree or natural structure may prove helpful. Unfortunately, these techniques do not help on typical target matches.

If the wind isn't really buffeting you that much and you can take a reasonably solid hold on the target, even slight winds can have a serious effect on the arrow's flight and point of impact. If you recall our discussion on arrow stabilization there are several things that you can do to lessen the wind's effects. A thinner arrow will be slightly less affected by wind, as will an arrow with smaller fletching and a heavier head (greater FOC). Regardless of what you do, however, the arrow will still be affected by the wind. If shooting shorter distances is an option, that option should be taken. In the case of a hunting situation, under calm conditions an archer might feel confident with shots out to 25 yards; as the winds increase in intensity or variability, he may need to limit his effective range or comfort zone to 15 or even 10 yards.

An arrow is by definition a weather vane, and so, unlike a bullet, which will deviate in the direction the wind is blowing, an arrow will turn into the wind. When an arrow in flight is hit by a cross wind, the larger surface area of the fletching will be deflected or moved more than the thinner pile end, so the point is directed into the wind and the rest of the arrow has to follow. Naturally, the greater the distance to the target and the stronger the wind, the greater the deviation.

Basic rules of thumb for shooting in wind:

Headwind (12 o'clock orientation) – A pure headwind will slow down the arrow and yield a lower than expected point of impact. Interestingly, a true headwind may also help to stabilize an arrow faster, due to the increased air resistance on the fletching. In the real world, we rarely see perfectly aligned headwinds (diag 12-41a).

Tailwind (6 o'clock orientation) – In theory, it should slow down the arrow less than expected and so yield a higher than expected point of impact. Unfortunately, as the wind is moving in the same direction as the arrow, there will be slightly diminished stabilization; add to that the fact that just as headwinds are rarely aligned perfectly, neither are tailwinds. Therefore, tailwinds can be very unpredictable (diag 12-41b).

Crosswinds (3 o'clock or 9 o'clock orientation) – Winds coming from the right or left, will deviate the arrow in the direction the wind is coming from, as described above (diag 12-41c and diag 12-41d).

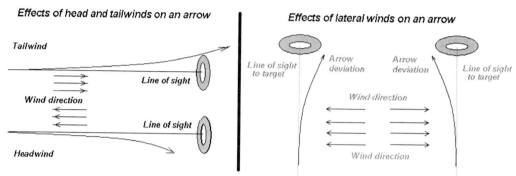

12-41a Effect of a headwind (12 o'clock) on an arrow.
12-41b Effect of a tailwind (6 o'clock) on an arrow
12-41c Effect of a right wind (3 o'clock) on an arrow
12-41d Effect of a left wind (9 o'clock) on an arrow

Compound winds – Winds coming from directions other than 12, 3, 6, or 9 o'clock. These cases need to be handled as if you were dealing with components of winds from the cardinal points. For example a wind from 2 o'clock would result in a major deviation to the right and a lesser low deviation. Typically, the crosswind component will have a greater effect than the head or tail component. Yes, it can be a guessing game.

So how do we handle this, if staying home isn't an option? You could easily assume, aim high for a headwind, low for a tailwind, and right or left for wind coming from the left or right, but the next question would be, how much? As with shooting at varying distances, the only answer is again, experience. With enough outdoor shooting, you'll develop a feel for what kind of deviation to expect at various ranges and with winds from varying directions, or you could read on...

Here's an example of what one target archer did to solve the problem:

All target matches have practice sessions before scoring begins. For major matches, usually all the competitors have access to the shooting area a day or two before the actual competition. This gives the shooters a chance to warm up and get used to the lay of the land, so to speak. On one occasion, strong and varying winds were predicted and presented. One archer, during his practice session, aimed every arrow dead center on the bullseye. Needless to say, his arrows were all over the target and honestly, the other competitors who saw this decided not to take him too seriously as a competitive threat. What they didn't notice was that with every shot, he not only noted the position of the arrow in the target, but the position of the wind flags. He now had a record matching the wind flag position relative to the degree of the arrow's deviation from center. During the matches that followed, he just checked the wind flags, and held off the appropriate amount. If I recall correctly, he won the match.

All sanctioned outdoor target matches have wind flags, and most people just think, "Ok, the wind is from 5 o'clock, I need to hold a little left and a little low". That would be a good guess but the archer in the above scenario wasn't guessing. Not all matches have pre-match days to practice, but all have practice ends at the very least. Those six, ten or twelve arrows can be very telling, if used effectively.

Light and terrain

As mentioned earlier, terrain can make objects, in this case, targets appear closer or farther away than they really are due to presence or absence of objects near the line of sight. Light may have a similar effect. Bright light may make objects appear larger, and therefore, closer (diag 12-42). This is especially critical to bowhunters shooting in early morning or late afternoons. The combination of variable lighting conditions, uneven terrain and an elevated shooting position can make a seemingly close and easy shot quite tricky for an inexperienced shooter.

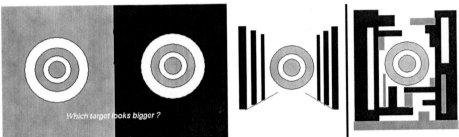

Which target looks bigger?

12-42a Effect of bright light on a target – Yes, they are both the same size, but the one on the right looks bigger and so – closer (left)!
12-42b Which target looks bigger here? (You might have to stare at these for a few seconds). This shows the effects of context or "clutter" on our perception of distance (right).

Even when the exact distance is known, sometimes our eyes can be tricked.

Rain

Shooting outdoors, whether at paper targets or bowhunting, sooner or later you may have to shoot in the rain. While a light misting might prove little more than an annoyance to the archer, it may increase the trajectory of the shot, especially at longer ranges. As the rain gets heavier, not only can the trajectory change but water may weigh down the feathers and alter the arrow's flight. As with wind conditions a bowhunter may need to shorten his effective range and a target archer may need to accept the conditions and simply do the best he can under the circumstances. If the archer has an option, curtailing the day's shooting should be considered.

Again, the only teacher is experience.

"Experience is the toughest teacher, because you take the test before you learn the lesson."

Chapter 13

Back Tension, Breathing and Related Topics

Back tension

Back tension is a common buzzword in archery discussions. Rightfully so, because without effective back tension and proper joint alignment a perfect shot would be impossible. The real question becomes, how do we develop and maintain effective back tension? We've actually covered this in the basic shooting section; we just never used the phrase "back tension". If you followed the instructions and were able to emulate the diagrams in Chapter 3, especially the anchor and follow-through positions, then your back tension and alignment had to be correct!

To draw a bow of any weight, maintain that weight at anchor, and correctly pull through the release, the major force exerted by the archer needs to come from the deep muscles of the upper back. Those muscles are the *Major and Minor Rhomboids and Trapezius*, as well as a few others we'll discuss in detail in Chapter 15. The arm and shoulder muscles simply aren't strong enough or aligned properly to make that happen efficiently. These archery "deep back" muscles are generally not used for most other activities and even when specifically exercised are not used in the same way as when drawing and shooting a bow and loosing an arrow.

Classically we were taught to use back tension by thinking about pulling the shoulder blades together during the draw and continuing to pull while at anchor. Some go as far as saying, "feel like you are crushing an egg between your shoulder blades". I have not seen this work too well with many people. Most people do not function well at athletic endeavors by trying to isolate certain muscle groups and expecting them to behave a certain way on command, especially when their *focus* needs to be elsewhere. That type of teaching usually leads to an exaggerated and uncontrolled movement or reaction instead of a natural and controlled one. In the case of archery it manifests as a flyaway release or flailing bow arm with little or no consistency. People do, however, respond well to cause and effect; in this case an effect resulting from the cause Diag 13-1).

13-1 A correct follow-through position means that back tension was maintained throughout the shot.

When we began our shooting training the first position we practiced was the follow-through, the position we should have ended in after the release. The only way to arriving at that position is to maintain back tension during, and more importantly, *after* the shot! So, by teaching ourselves the end result, we are teaching ourselves to use back tension.

Even if the action was initially artificial, meaning the new shooter forced it to happen, after a while it became the natural response and so became reflexive.

At this juncture, it may be beneficial to look more closely at how and why back tension works in shot execution. Archery coaches from several disciplines often suggest pushing the bow arm forward while at anchor as if you were trying to push the bow into the target. A way of visualizing this is to imagine you are actually holding the target up by extending the bow arm and pushing it against the target center. But what does this really do anatomically?

If you recall our initial discussion, the bow arm is fully extended, fairly straight (but not locked) during the draw, while at anchor and during follow-through. Therefore, it is safe to assume that the "push" needs to come from the shoulder joint and not the elbow. ***By pushing the bow towards the target, you are moving the shoulder joint into better or more linear alignment perpendicular to the target.*** Anatomically the upper arm bone (*humerus*) of the drawing arm is moving forward (*ventrally*) in the shoulder (*rotator cuff*) socket (diag 13--2). By doing this you can achieve increased bone support and use less muscle strength. That results in a steadier hold, cleaner release and natural follow-through.

13-2 Bow shoulder in a relaxed or slightly rearward position (left)

13-2a Bow shoulder moved forward by "pushing the bow toward the target" (right)

Bio-mechanically it's the most efficient position to execute the shot. However, it must be approached cautiously. If the humerus is thrust too far forward and the bow arm is nearly parallel with the arrow, it can place the bow arm in the path of the string, leading to an upper arm or forearm strike by the string and usually a missed shot (diag 13-4). The best practice, in my opinion, is compromise between the most bio-mechanically efficient position and the one that affords adequate clearance for the path of the bowstring.

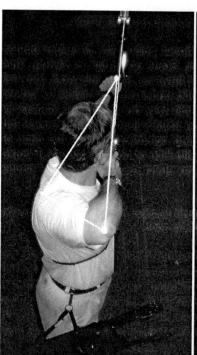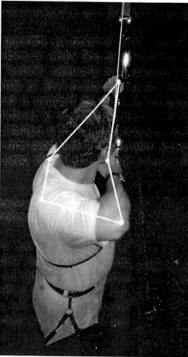

Diagram 13-3a (left) shows a bow arm and shoulders in an effective position that allows good alignment (bone support) while affording adequate string clearance.

Diagram 13-3b (right) shows a bow arm in a bio-mechanically poor or inefficient position. In addition to poor shoulder and arm alignment the head is cocked forward to meet the drawing hand.

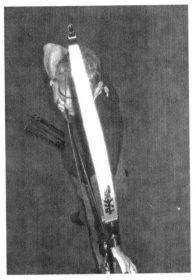

Diagram 13-4 shows an exaggerated bow arm / shoulder position. While a bio-mechanically-efficient position, it's one that can allow the bowstring to hit the bow arm. Also note that by over extending the draw, the archer has rotated his head away from the target, placing his nose as well as his arm in jeopardy!

Exercises for developing, confirming and maintaining "back tension"

Despite the fact that a good follow-through is a good indication of proper back tension, there may arise an occasion when you want to check or "work on it". At one time or another everyone's shooting falls into a slump. While this is usually more mental than physical there can be real physical causes. A common physical cause is incorrect shoulder/arm alignment or failure to maintain back tension throughout and *after* the shot. In those cases a refresher course is in order; whether the benefit is psychological or physical is irrelevant, as long as it works. In addition to rehearsing the positions in Chapter 3, I know of only two ways to exercise correct form and back tension without actually shooting, and both involve very specific devices.

In the case of a "slump" due to a form problem such as poor alignment, continuing to shoot may not be a good solution, as it may serve only to reinforce the error. Additionally, the longer a slump exists the greater the psychological toll.

The "Rigid Formaster"

Marketed by the Range-O-Matic Archery Company, the Formaster is a training device specifically designed to teach and exercise effective back tension as well as demonstrate flaws in the archer's technique. It is available from most of the larger archery retailers (diag 13-5). Very detailed instructions are given with the device for its use and correcting the problems it can diagnose.

The Formaster is basically a double nylon band that goes over (above and below) the archer's drawing elbow and a length of parachute cord that attaches to the bowstring. The length of the parachute cord is adjusted so that after release the string travels only an inch or so and therefore protects the bow from a dry fire situation. The fact that there is still forward force acting on the drawing arm and the entire system can be very revealing. *(There is also a Flexible Formaster, which uses rubber tubing in place of the parachute cord. While useable for our purposes, it is primarily designed for use with compound bows.)*

With the cord attached to the bowstring (diag 13-6), either below the nocking point, or below the position of the ring finger, the bow is drawn without an arrow to a normal anchor position (diag 13-7). When the string is released, if back tension is maintained during and after the shot, the drawing hand and arm will move rearward in a limited follow-through and the bow arm stays relatively still (diags 13-8 and 13-9). When most people first try the Formaster, the initial "shot" is a bit of a shock, literally. If back tension wasn't maintained after the release, the shooter is rewarded with a noticeable forward jerk. (For this reason, the Formaster should not be used on bows over 40#.) After a few attempts the archer quickly learns to maintain back tension throughout the release and avoid the jolt. Additionally, the Formaster can also tell the archer if he is losing tension on the bow arm, by noting its movement on release, as the bow arm will jerk to the left.

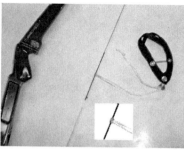

13-5 The Rigid Formaster (left)

13-6 Formaster cord can be attached to the bowstring either below the nocking point or below the position of the third finger (right).

13-7 At pre-draw with the Formaster (left),
13-8 At anchor (middle)
13-9 At follow-through (right). As can be seen, the Formaster makes practicing in your living room possible!

For pure form training a target or aiming point is not necessary, however aiming can help develop your **focus** on the center of the target while working on form. Using one can also reinforce the transition from anchor to follow-through by teaching you to keep the sight trained on the target throughout the shot sequence. I use my Formaster in conjunction with a simple sight on the bow and a simulated target a few feet away. By placing the pin on the center of the "X" in the bullseye, it's easy to notice any bow movement on release or shock.

The Formaster can also be used to train proper use of back muscles during the draw and anchor, by letting the parachute cord draw the bowstring back using only the elbow. By using the elbow and not the fingers on the string, it forces the proper use of the deep back muscles, while saving wear and tear on the fingers. Drawing and holding for a few seconds, then relaxing for a few seconds and repeating the exercise can develop both form and strength. The holding and relaxing intervals can begin at five seconds and then be lengthened, as tolerated, to a maximum of 30 or even 60 seconds (diag 13-10). This can also be done next to a mirror so the archer can get both visual and tactile input.

Forcing the follow-through. Once the basic Formaster techniques are mastered, the device can be used further to strengthen the muscles that maintain back tension during and after the release. As noted above, when the string is released the Formaster allows only a slight rearward motion of the drawing hand. As strength and technique develop, you should be able to continue *or force* the drawing hand a few inches farther back in a smooth motion after the parachute cord becomes taut (diag 3-11). This not only increases muscle strength but serves to condition muscle memory. Next we'll use an additional exercise to solidify the muscle memory.

13-10 Holding exercise using the Formaster (left). Notice that the elbow is pulling the string and not the fingers. This allows development of the back or "archery" muscles without undue wear and tear on the fingers.
13-11 Forcing the follow-through using the Formaster (right)

Suggestion for a Formaster training session (an arrow is not used in this example):

1. *Warm-ups. Attach the Formaster to the bowstring and your drawing arm as shown. Draw the bow back to the follow-through several times without touching the string. A more elaborate version of this warm-up is to use a 10 count.*
   Draw the bow (with the elbow) and hold for 1 second, relax for 9 seconds
   Repeat, but hold for 2 seconds, and relax for 8.
   Hold for 3 and relax for 7.
   Continue for 4 and 6, 5 and 5, etc. until on the last repetition you are holding for 9 seconds and relaxing (if you can call it that) for 1.

2. *Shooting practice. This is your actual "live fire" with the formaster. Draw the string to anchor with your fingers. Hold for a specified number of seconds or until you feel the alignment settle in and your focus is correct, then "release". This should be repeated at least 20 times, or until you are mildly fatigued.*

3. *Strength training. Draw the string to anchor with your fingers and hold for at least 30 seconds. This should be repeated at least 10 times. As you build up strength, you should attempt to increase the holding time to 45 or 60 seconds with a 1-minute rest between "shots". (Alternatively, you can draw the string with your elbow, if your fingers vigorously object!)*

4. *The forced follow-through exercise can be incorporated into steps two or three.*

Using resistance bands

Another technique for developing proper shooting form is derived from our initial discussion of muscle memory. As we discussed, it is very difficult to think about back tension in an abstract way (what's a trapezius?). We tend to learn and remember movements better by actually doing them, thereby developing a muscle memory as well as an image or conscious memory of the action. While not as diagnostic as the Formaster, another approach is the use of resistance bands. These are elastic or rubber bands or tubes sold in most department or fitness stores for a few

dollars (13-12). Find one with relatively light resistance or tension. Heavy tension versions can become quite uncomfortable when "released". Also, avoid the heavy coiled spring versions for the same reason, which will become evident in the next paragraph.

13-12 Rubber Exercise or Resistance bands such as these from Valeo can be purchased from most Sporting Goods stores for a few dollars or made from surgical tubing. The larger band is preferable, as the smaller one tends to slap the wrist on release!

Hold the band as shown in diag 13-13, anchoring as close to normal as possible. Focus on a point across the room and release. If you have your alignment correct, the "bow" arm should remain fairly still, and the drawing arm should snap back to the follow-through position (13-14). This is the same action as shooting a very light bow.

13-13 Practicing anchoring and releasing using rubber resistance bands.

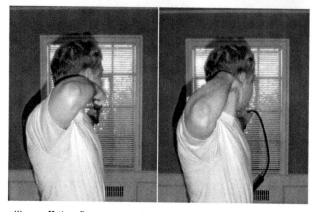

13-14 Correct anchor (left) and follow-through positions (right) using rubber resistance bands

The most obvious benefit is that this can be done almost anytime and anywhere, as it doesn't require a bow, nor is it physically demanding. By repeating this exercise, over and over, your brain will learn and remember what is supposed to happen during a real shot sequence. It will remember how the band or string should feel rolling off the fingers, and how the hand should react to the release. That memory training cannot be over-emphasized and is an advantage over the Formaster, as it lets you complete the follow-through normally. Occasionally, there will be times when real shots don't feel exactly right; we've all had that experience. Being able to recall the action of the band shooting forward and the hand snapping back may be enough to clear up a sloppy release on the shooting line. ***Having created a strong foundation to fall back on is one, arguably the best, way of overcoming that eventuality.***

Another benefit to the light rubber band method is that that since there is very little resistance, some form errors can become readily apparent. For example, the bands above and below your fingers should be in the same vertical plane (assuming you don't cant the bow). If they are not one on top of the other at anchor, odds are you will be torqueing the string on release (diag 13-15). With the force of a real bow, you may never see that, but it would have an effect on the arrow, and not necessarily a positive one.

13-15 The resistance band exercise clearly shows how the bow hand can torque the string. The picture on the right shows correct alignment, the left picture shows the misalignment or "torque" In this case the torque is made clear by placing an arrow in each grip section of the band.

While the Formaster is a worthwhile diagnostic and training tool, the fact that it only partially develops the muscle memory used in the follow-through makes it best used in conjunction with resistance band training. I use both the resistance bands and Formaster on days when I can't get to the range.

Wall push

13-16 Starting position of the wall push exercise (left)
13-17 Ending position of the wall push exercise (middle)

Another method of feeling back tension is an elbow to wall pushing exercise. To do this, stand with your side to a wall, about a foot and a half away from it. Place your drawing hand and arm in your normal anchor position and lean against the wall so that your elbow is supporting your body weight (diag 13-16). Keep your torso as straight as possible, and move your hand from the anchor position to the follow-through position (diag 13-17). The movement should push your body slightly farther away from the wall. Come back to the anchor position, and repeat it a few times. (If you find balancing difficult, you can use the corner of a room and place your back against one wall and your elbow against the perpendicular wall.) The action of pushing your body away from the wall by the movement of the elbow is very similar to the muscle contraction used in "back tension". This is not an exercise to develop the archery muscles, but one to help you understand which ones they are.

Twisting technique

13-18 Trunk twist to exaggerate the "feel" of back tension (right)

An exercise recently recommended by some coaches for people having difficulty with back tension is to take a few shots with the feet parallel to the target, instead of perpendicular to it (diag 13-18). While this is not a position anyone would want to shoot from continually, it's said that the extreme midsection twist exaggerates the sensation of back tension and gives the archer a feeling to try to emulate during a normal shot. It's also been suggested that a slightly open stance may be more conducive to engaging the back muscles properly than a neutral or closed stance. As with most things we're discussing, there's certainly no harm in trying. If it works, great! If not, just return to your normal stance, knowing that you have another tool in your arsenal should the need arise.

The "no-anchor" exercise

We said earlier that if the follow-through is correct it's safe to assume that back tension has been maintained throughout the shot. If despite the above techniques you still have a problem with a consistent follow-through the "no anchor" exercise may help.

Stand about five yards from a target and set up for a shot. Draw back slightly past your anchor position and keep your hand away from your face – do not anchor. Be careful not to pull the arrow off the rest. Hold at that floating anchor for a second or two (diag 13-19). There should be a feeling of equilibrium between the force of the string pulling forward and the force of the drawing arm pulling back. Without the lock of the anchor as a stop that balance of forces becomes more obvious. When you release the string, your drawing hand and arm should fly back cleanly. Repeat the exercise a few more times until the feeling of the reaction is established. Once you are comfortable with it try a shot from your normal anchor position. You should be able to

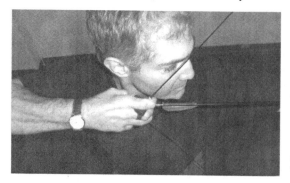

reproduce the *"fly back"* reaction of the drawing hand from anchor. Don't be surprised if the first few times you try it from anchor your hand seems to fly back in an uncontrolled or forced manor. That's to be expected and will evolve into a smooth follow-through the more you practice it.

13-19 A free-floating anchor (and release) allows you to feel the near equilibrium at full draw and the explosion that should occur on release.

To stop at anchor or keep pulling?

When I began shooting competitively in the early 1970's, the wisdom of the day was that you had to maintain a constant rearward motion of the drawing hand, even at anchor. The reasoning was that it was easier and more efficient to continue pulling, and maintain momentum, than to come to a complete stop, and have to overcome the inertia to resume the motion. The fact of the matter is, you must maintain a rearward force to oppose the forward force of the bowstring, but should the hand actually ever stop moving? This has come under considerable debate in recent years. Proponents of the constant pull methodology cite not only the inertial benefit, but that continually increasing the draw lessens the possibility of a collapse occurring should the drawing hand stop.

The classic target example of this is demonstrated by the use of a clicker. Is it better (more efficient) to continue pulling rearward once at anchor, until the clicker "clicks", or is it better to stop at anchor, settle in, and then resume pulling until the clicker clicks?

Current thinking is that the drawing hand can and should physically stop moving at anchor, but obviously not stop pulling, and then resume pulling to get through the clicker if one is being used, and continue to follow-through. It must be remembered that at anchor the amount the draw length can increase is on the order of 1/16" to 1/8", if that much. Unless the drawing hand actually moves forward the difference in measurable movement may be minimal in all but the most elite circles. I typically come to what I perceive as a stop at anchor, but as the rearward force is constantly increasing, it is hard to say whether the hand actually stops or not. As the difference may be quite subtle, you'll have to judge which method is best for you.

Breathing

Most physical activities can be enhanced or hindered by effective or counter-productive breathing, respectively, and archery is no exception. Breathing is a very natural function and it is probably safe to say we've been doing it our entire lives. Generally, if we don't think about it, our nervous system can handle it quite well by itself. Unfortunately, being a sentient species, we tend to think about it and that usually messes up the works.

We inhale by expanding the volume of our chest (thoracic) cavities. The pressure within the thoracic cavity becomes less than the external (*or ambient*) pressure, and because of that pressure gradient air rushes in and fills the lungs. The thoracic cavity expands primarily by the diaphragm (the muscle that separates the thoracic and the abdominal cavities) contracting, flattening and is assisted by the chest wall muscles raising the ribcage. We exhale by allowing the diaphragm and the chest wall muscles to relax, reducing the chest cavity's volume. That in turn increases the pressure inside the chest cavity and forces the air out (diag 13-20).

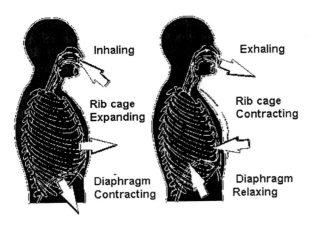

13-20 The thorax during inhalation and exhalation

When we raise the bow arm and drawing arm to start the shot sequence, that action naturally lifts the ribs and so begins to expand the chest and cause a natural inhalation. The act of drawing the bow further expands the chest wall and so the inhalation continues. Recall that while at anchor, we are still pulling against the string, and while there is little, if any, chest expansion, the logical progression is to continue inhaling, albeit at a slower rate (diag 13-21. The release is initiated by a slight relaxation of the drawing fingers. That relaxation should trigger the exhalation. Immediately after that, the back and shoulder muscles can, or should relax, and the exhalation completes. That's what should happen if we don't get in the way!

13-21 Here we see that raising that bow arm and drawing the bow expands the rib cage and initiates an inhalation. The arrows represent the direction of rib cage expansion.

From the preceding discussion, it should be clear that exhaling while at anchor may result in a partial collapse, and therefore should be avoided.

Let's do it step by step:

1. Raise the bow arm and drawing arm	Inhalation	Shoulder muscles
2. Draw the string to anchor	Inhalation	Shoulder and back muscles
3. Anchor and hold	Inhalation	Back muscles
4. Relaxation of the string fingers	Inhalation	Back muscles
5. Release	Inhalation to Exhalation	Relaxation of the drawing forearm (finger) muscles and maintenance of back muscle tension
6. Follow-through	Exhalation	Relaxation of back muscles (must be after the release)

There are several caveats to consider. The timing of the relaxation of the fingertips must precede the relaxation of the back muscles, or else a collapse of the drawing arm and shoulder will occur at the worst possible time. This is not as simple as it sounds, as our nervous system generally wants us to act as a single unit or at least as a unit in concert. When the fingers begin to relax, so does the back. This is where training with devices like the Formaster or rubber bands can pay off. There is a bit of reprogramming involved, but it's necessary reprogramming if your shots are to be released and followed through cleanly. Happily, if we don't let our higher brain centers get in the way this may actually happen quite naturally.

Some people hold their breath during the shot. This usually had its origin from the time they began shooting and the excitement or anticipation caused them to tighten up and not breathe. Holding your breath is generally not a good idea, as it leads to a shortage of oxygen to the brain, which can blur the vision and make you less steady. That generally does not make the shot any better. Exhaling on the draw is another variation, probably based on the premise that when lifting a heavy weight, you exhale on the lift/contraction to assist in the lifting process. While the assumption may be correct, the end result isn't, for two reasons. First, as we have demonstrated, the act of drawing the bow expands the chest, and so causes an inhalation, whereas the exhalation is a tightening of the chest wall. Second, once you're at anchor, the "lift" isn't over and you may well be short of air to continue the shot.

Holding at anchor and the "feeling" of the shot

How long you need to hold at anchor is based on several factors. We'll assume that you're not over-bowed and can hold steady at anchor as long as it takes to make the shot. Some archers hold for a fraction of a second, and some hold for as long as eight to ten seconds. Which is right? Well, both and neither, as several things need to happen during the hold at anchor.

Confirmation of correct anchor point/reference points
Confirmation of proper lines of tension/alignment in relation to the target
Confirmation and focus on the intended point you wish to hit or settling the sight on the bull
Visualization of the arrow in flight, hitting the target's center
Visualization of the follow-through position

It may sound like a lot to think about and for a new shooter it may well be! With proper form and practice, the anchor and alignment should become subconscious, as should the understanding of the follow-through action. They become part of the archer's feeling of the shot. The archer knows when the shot feels right and knows if the shot will hit the bullseye before the release ever happens. As the archer gains experience, he'll be able to recognize that feeling, correct the problem or let the arrow down and start over. The best archers will never release an arrow that doesn't feel right or one that they know will not go exactly where they intend it to go.

This needs to be repeated: *If anything about the shot doesn't feel right, don't release the arrow – it will miss.*

Even if it doesn't miss, an arrow in the bullseye by luck is not a good shot. That knowledge is probably the most important difference between a good or adequate shooter and a true archer or champion.

So how long should you hold at anchor? The only real answer is, as long as it takes to accomplish the above tasks. There is a simple exercise that can tell you what your maximum mental holding time should be. Pick a small object across the room, a highlight on a picture, light switch, anything. Focus on it, and see how long you can maintain focus. Maintaining focus means not drifting to a nearby point, not blurring, but keeping it as the only point clearly in focus. The first time most people try this, they're surprised at how quickly they break focus, usually a few seconds at best. Yes, with practice, the time you can maintain focus will increase. The analogy is clear; you can only hold on a target as long as you can maintain focus on it. Once the focus is broken or shifts, the arrow will either go to the new point of focus or strike a random point on the target.

Chapter 14

Variations in Technique

Whuen we began our journey into the world of archery, we made the rules very specific and allowed little room for variation. That was necessary to develop good shooting form and a strong foundation. While most top archers share the same fundamentals and technique their physical differences and idiosyncrasies will dictate variations in form. Those variations will remain bio-mechanically sound and can be called the archer's individual style. The following is a brief review of some variations and their implications.

Stance

The neutral stance, feet approximately shoulder width apart and both heels in line with the target's center, works well for most people (diag 14-1A). It's solid and reproducible. Some who require additional string clearance may chose to use an "open" stance, where the rear foot is brought forward 4" to 10" (diag 14-1B). As discussed in the last chapter, an open stance may have the added advantage of enhancing the engagement of the deep-back archery muscles. Bringing the rear foot back a few inches is called a closed stance (diag 14-1C). While it does reduce string clearance, some people believe it helps to align the upper body for the shot. Interestingly, it seems that a lot of shooters who use severe cants favor a closed stance. Whether neutral, open or closed, target archers will shoot standing fairly upright with knees straight (but not locked). For string clearance, a slight forward bend at the waist is sometimes used (diag 14-2).

14-1a-c Neutral, open and closed stances. The horizontal line bisects the centerline of the target.

14-2 A slight bend at the waist may provide better string clearance

Which stance should you use?

Use whichever one works best for you. Most people will gravitate toward one stance or another over time; their bodies will find the most comfortable and reproducible position and always return to it. I use a classic neutral stance, but I tend to stand slightly to the right of the target's centerline, so the stance is effectively closed.

The natural point of aim

One technique taken from rifle competitors can work quite well with intermediate level archers. Stand neutral to your target's center and with your eyes closed, draw and anchor normally, but don't release. Open your eyes and see if your natural tendency is to point to the left or right of center. This technique is naturally easier for someone with a sight on their bow, but even a barebow shooter can get a good idea by simply shot-gunning or looking right down the arrow. If your "natural point of aim" is to the left of the target's center you may need to close your stance a bit and if it's to the right of center, open it up (diag 14-3). This of course assumes that your basic form and alignment are correct and reproducible; that's why it's used only on intermediate or advanced level shooters and not beginners.

Determining your natural point of aim

14-3 Determining your natural point of aim

| Stance is correct | Stance needs to be opened | Stance needs to be closed |

Whether neutral, open or closed, the feet should remain approximately shoulder width apart. Placing them close together reduces your base or platform and can make you less steady. (You'll have to use more effort, both muscular and neural, to steady yourself.) Conversely, widening your stance may appear to increase your base, but by doing so requires added muscular effort to support the body, and that too will decrease steadiness as the day wears on. As long as the extremes are avoided, there is room for variety in the exact width of the stance. Similarly, the knees should be straight, but not locked for the same reason as the bow arm should be straight but not locked. A locked leg expends muscle energy needlessly and makes the whole system rigid and unstable. Locking a joint also increases wear and tear on the joint itself, which over time may lead to injury.

Recently, some shooters have adopted a bent-kneed, hunched-over posture that should be avoided. I have no idea where this came from or why, and it is only mentioned as an example of what not to do (diag 14-4a). Both bending the knees and hunching place undue strain on the lower back and force increased use of the larger leg muscles. The former can result in, or exacerbate, lower back pain over time, and the latter will simply tire the leg muscles needlessly. While the leg and hip muscles do form the foundation for the shot, they are not necessary for shot execution. From a pure shooting perspective, the hunched-over posture is almost impossible to reproduce and results in a loss of consistency. Shot to shot consistency has been our primary goal throughout our journey and still is!

Another variant is what can only be called a forward leaning or *"hood ornament"* stance (diag 14-4b). Some new shooters may believe this to be a more aggressive posture or that it may get them closer to the target. In reality all it does is make the base unstable and the position forced.

To put this even more simply, we want to make the shot by doing as little work as possible. Anything that will add stress to the system should be avoided at all costs.

14-4a The hunched-over crouched stance

14-4b The forward leaning or "hood ornament" stance

Both stances are examples of what NOT to do!!!

"Other" stances

What I've demonstrated thus far are the basic postures for target archery. In some situations, such as field, hunting or causal shooting, you may wish to try shooting from kneeling or sitting positions. Shooting while kneeling or sitting can be a natural transition from the basic standing or upright stance once that stance has been mastered. The most important thing to remember when changing shooting positions is that the shoulder geometry must retain the same alignment as when standing. If the shoulder geometry changes, so will your draw length and follow-through due to changes in the lines of tension at anchor. Those changes are usually enough to cause a miss at targets within your normal comfort range.

One way to confirm that shoulder geometry hasn't changed is to attach a temporary clicker to the bow. If the shoulder alignment has changed, then getting through the clicker will either be more difficult or you'll pull through sooner than expected.

In the kneeling position (diag 14-5a), we see that the lower limb of the bow is outside the high or *"bow"* leg. This provides excellent clearance and helps to maintain shoulder geometry. When sitting (diag 14-5b), the same theory applies. In both situations, it's common but not vital to cant the bow.

Both kneeling and sitting will restrict your range of motion; therefore it is vital that you practice these positions at relatively close range before trying to use them during a match or on a hunting trip. If you recall, uphill and downhill shots require that elevation be achieved by bending at the waist and not simply lifting the bow arm. While kneeling and more so when sitting, your base is firmly rooted and any left to right variation, in addition to up and down, must come from the waist and not the upper body or shoulders.

14-5 In the kneeling (left) and sitting positions (right), notice that the shoulder geometry/alignment remains the same as when standing.

Bow arm

While most people believe that a steady bow arm will compensate for a number of shooting errors, the bow arm itself is at the mercy of the shooter's overall form and alignment.

Elbow rotation

The elbow of the bow arm should be straight, but not locked, and the tip of the elbow needs to be rotated as far clockwise (as seen from the shooter's perspective) as is comfortable (diag 14-6). Most archers find that a clockwise rotation with the elbow between the eight o'clock and nine o'clock position the most comfortable. There have been a number of top archers who do shoot with a locked arm and also some who have a noticeable bend in their elbows.

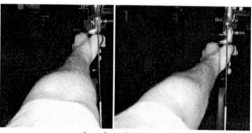

14-6 Notice how rotating the elbow of the bow arm clockwise increases string clearance

The caveats are that a locked bow arm will be more rigid than one which is not locked, and will turn the shoulder joint into a fulcrum with a very long lever arm. That means it will be harder to steady during the hold and on release. The locking of any joint, especially one under pressure can also lead to wear and tear injuries on the joint and surrounding soft tissue. This is clearly not an advisable practice, but needs to be mentioned as an alternative for those desiring to try it.

A bent elbow will of course shorten the draw length, which may not be desirable as it can add another inconsistency. Some archers who shoot with a bent elbow use a clicker to confirm their draw length, or in the case of those shooting a compound bow have stops built into the bow which pre-determines their draw length. Compound bow shooters also typically hold less weight at anchor, which lessens the pressure on the elbow joint. Stickbow shooters don't have the advantage of built-in draw stops. Also remember that with the elbow in a bent position, the extensor muscles (*triceps*) need to do more work to keep the arm extended, while the flexors (*biceps*) need to work harder as skeletal stabilizers (diag 14-7).

14-7 Using a bent bow arm, the triceps muscles of the upper arm have to do more work than is necessary. That leads to early fatigue and inconsistencies due to changes in draw length.

I have seen very few people shoot with their elbows rotated downward (counterclockwise) without striking their arms or arm guards. While it may be possible, that's one experiment I personally wouldn't try. *Experiment and see what effects different positions have on you and your shooting, but please do so cautiously.*

Canting the bow

If you are using a sight, either as a training tool or a permanent fixture, you have no option; the bow will need to remain vertical. Instinctive or gap shooting allows the use of canting or tilting the upper limb slightly to the right, for a right-handed shooter (diag 14-8). Like most aspects of archery, to cant or not to cant is a personal choice. While a vertical bow position is fairly easy to reproduce and generally better suited to most new shooters, canting does have some advantages. The most often cited is that it gets the riser out of your line of sight to the target.

For some people, canting also improves the bow hand to drawing hand alignment. Given the anchoring methods we discussed, it's possible that the natural position of the string hand is not vertical, but slightly tilted. Canting the bow may allow the bow, bowstring and drawing hand to be in the same plane, resulting in less torque and a cleaner release. A natural cant, usually about 10 degrees off vertical, or with the upper limb in the 1 o'clock position, usually works well. Over-canting the bow beyond 10 to 15 degrees can lead to the same problem as holding the bow vertically, creating a misalignment between the bow and the drawing hand and again, torqueing the bowstring. If that misalignment occurs, then the archer will be forcing the drawing hand into an awkward position and making a clean release almost impossible (diag 14-9). It also follows that over-canting may lead to bending at the waist more than necessary and we've established that that's not a good thing to do. It's best to experiment and find the most comfortable and efficient position for your shooting style, then practice until that position happens without conscious thought.

14-8 While the bow is canted, the alignment described in previous chapters must be maintained (left).

14-9 Bow hand / bow string misalignment resulting in considerable string twisting or "torque" (right).

There are two ways the bow may be canted. The first and most obvious is simply to apply a slight clockwise rotation to the wrist of the bow arm. The second method is to keep the bow in line with the upper torso and bend slightly at the waist. While not a true cant, it has a similar appearance and yields a similar benefit (diag 14-10). With the latter, the upper torso should remain fairly straight and not hunch over. The two actions need not be mutually exclusive. Most archers who cant the bow use a combination of the two. *It is critical to remember that if the bow is canted by either or both methods, the geometry of the shoulder girdle at anchor and follow-through must remain consistent with the basic form we earlier demonstrated for a vertical bow.* If you allow the shoulder geometry to change as you cant the bow, the draw length may shorten. As canting may in itself add a slight variable to your form, the change in draw length can complicate the matter further. It's not an insurmountable obstacle, just something that needs to be considered.

If you decide to try canting the bow, in addition to making sure the degree of cant is consistent, be aware that the arrow will usually strike to the right of where it would have hit if the bow were held vertically. That's because the arrow is above the pivot point of the system, which in this case is the wrist or forearm of the bow arm. If you're shooting instinctively, you'll quickly make the adjustments subconsciously. If using gap or a point of aim, the relative position of the arrowhead to the bullseye or the aiming point will need to be adjusted accordingly.

A variation on a theme: I've seen some target archers who apparently "reverse cant" the bow, meaning the upper limb tip is tilted to the left instead of being held vertically. Most target archers shoot with an open bow hand allowing the bow to float between the thumb and forefinger. While generally a good practice, if the drawing hand is rotated slightly counter-clockwise, the bowstring will experience torque and the bow itself will follow and be reverse canted! (diag 14-11)

14-10 Canting the bow: Vertical bow (left), slightly rotating the forearm (middle) and leaning the entire upper body forward (right). Notice that the shoulder alignment remains constant in each variation.
14-11 Reverse cant of the bow due to torqueing the bowstring (far right)

Bow grip

There are three schools of thought on how to hold the bow. The first is an open grip (diag 14-12a), followed by a relaxed grip (diag 14-12b), and lastly, a firmer grip similar to a firm handshake (diag 14-12c). An open grip, meaning the fingers are completely open and not holding the bow at all, requires the use of a bow, wrist or finger sling. An open grip prevents torque and allows the reaction of the bow to occur without interference, and usually results in the cleanest shot. The relaxed grip is very similar to the open grip, but the fingers are loosely curled around the grip. A sling of some type is also recommended, but clearly not as necessary as with a fully open grip. The firm grip usually does not require a sling. With a firm grip, it is possible that it may get firmer and firmer as the day's shooting goes on, and what may have been an acceptable grip at the beginning of a shooting session may turn into a death grip by the end of the day (diag 14-12d). It is also possible that as the grip on the bow gets stronger, the tension in the hand progresses to the entire bow arm and possibly the shoulder. The more rigid the bow arm and shoulder get, the harder it is to keep the bow steady. As we stated at the beginning, it's impossible to steady a bow by muscle strength alone.

14-12 Grip variations from left to right: a. Open grip, b. relaxed grip, c. firm grip and d. a white-knuckled death-grip

Bow hand wrist positions

While the bow should always be held with its grip just deep to the mound of the thumb (the belly of the muscle just central to the thumb) and along the lifeline, the wrist may be held in three basic positions. The design of the grip will have a lot to do with how the bow is held, and so may be a factor in which bow you choose; within each style there are still options (diag 14-13).

14-13 Low grip (with leather wrapping - left), Medium (middle) and high (right) bow grip configurations on a Bear magnesium T/D riser

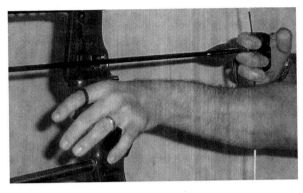

14-14a High bow hand position with only the web of the thumb and index finger making contact

The high grip may lengthen the draw as the wrist is fully extended and it may reduce torque as there's minimal bow to hand contact. It also gives the best possible alignment of force through the bones of the bow arm (diag 14-14a). However, it may be uncomfortable or difficult to maintain during an extended shooting session, especially with heavier bows and bows without specific high grip risers. It's also difficult, if not impossible, to use on a straight-risered longbow. Once favored by a great many top shooters, it seems to be falling out of favor for the above reasons.

14-14b Low bow hand position with heel pressure on grip

The low grip is just the opposite. The grip is closer to vertical and more of the hand rests on the bow. The main advantage is that it's solid (diag 14-14b). It can be used on any bow type, including straight-risered longbows and recurves with high grip risers. Once established, it really can't change, and that's a big plus for extended shooting sessions such as target matches. It does change wrist alignment, will shorten the draw somewhat, and can lead to "heeling" the bow. Heeling means exerting increased pressure from the heel of the hand and pushing the bow upward on release. Not only is it bad form, but it will also usually result in a low arrow, as the bow is rising while the arrow is leaving the bow and still attached to the string. That raises the tail of the arrow and pushes the tip down.

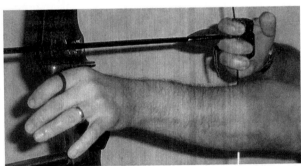

14-14c Medium or intermediate hand position

The medium grip is, as you would think, a midway point between the high and low grips (diag 14-14c). It allows good alignment, a solid and comfortable position that shouldn't change throughout a long shooting event, and should reduce the tendency to heel the bow. The only problem, if any, with a medium grip, is that depending on the grip design of the bow, it may not be as reproducible as the more extreme high or low grips.

An additional variation of the high grip used by some target archers is to rotate the bowhand to an angle of up to 45 degrees from the axis of the grip (diag 14-14d). This may reduce torque and is believed more reproducible for some people. This may be valuable on some bows, especially those that are very critical to bow hand torque. Additionally, it may improve arm alignment and allow an additional degree of elbow rotation, which will give the archer better string clearance.

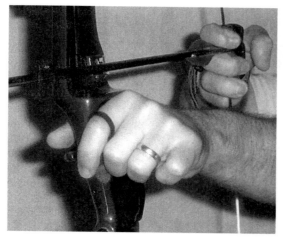

14-14d Olympic variation on the high wrist position – this position provides minimal hand to bow contact and should reduce inadvertent torqueing.

There's no best grip for all archers and all bows. It's very possible that an archer may use a high grip on some bows, a medium grip on others and a low grip on different bows. Many archers have been known to change grips as they progress through their shooting careers. This is one case where there really is no right or wrong answer. You find what works best for you and you stick with it until it stops working; then you start experimenting again.

Drawing the bow

There are two main variants in drawing the bow – the set bow arm and the swing draw. We began with what maybe called a set or "pre-set" bow arm, meaning the bow is raised towards the target and the string is drawn back in line with the intended flight path of the arrow. This not only allows for a pre-aim, beginning the aiming process before the draw and anchor, but also allows for a more efficient draw. By raising the bow arm before initiating the draw, the shoulder joint of the bow arm can be seated into a solid position and the drawing shoulder is better aligned to directly transfer the force of the back muscles to where they need to be to bend the bow. (The only force vectors about the shoulders are in direct opposition to each other.) When done properly, there is minimal shoulder strength necessary, and therefore less chance of injury.

The opposite of the set draw is the swing draw. The bow begins low at the shooter's side and the draw initiates as the bow is raised to target level. While this may provide for a quicker shot, it's not as efficient as the set arm draw, less consistent and potentially more harmful.

Using the swing draw, the bow shoulder is initially forced upward in its socket, and may not return to the seated position at anchor. The drawing arm is initially pulling the bowstring at an upward angle instead of a lateral one. That hinders an efficient transfer of force from the back muscles and recruits shoulder muscles that should not be used in the draw. Combining the force vectors exerted on both shoulders, the shooter may find himself in a hunched position at full draw. That position not only makes efficient shoulder alignment impossible, but also may overstress the joints and lead to injury.

Of equal concern for those choosing a swing draw, is that there's a strong possibility of releasing the arrow while the bow is in motion, making consistent accuracy impossible. That alone is reason enough to forego the swing draw. Further, it's been my experience that most people adopting the swing draw method also have a tendency to snap shoot (releasing before anchor or not achieving a consistent anchor). Snap shooting combined with a bow arm that may be in motion at the instant of release does not bode well for accuracy.

Despite all the negative features of the swing draw it can and has been used successfully in certain situations, particularly those situations where speed is required, such as some types of demonstration or trick shooting or some traditional competitions where there are timed events. In those cases the archer needs to understand the mechanics of the swing draw and practice the procedure sufficiently to minimize the risks. Needless to say, first attempts should be carried out with a bow light enough to mitigate the aforementioned risks.

Finally there are some shooters who begin with the bow elevated above target level and the arrow angled upwards, then lower the bow into alignment with the target. While more common with new, and typically, over-bowed compound shooters, some stickbow shooters have adopted the same practice, unfortunately for the same reason – being over-bowed. As we'll see when we discuss the horse draw procedure in the chapter on fitness, it does recruit additional muscles to assist in the draw, but should not be considered a long term procedure as it is an indication that something is amiss.

With all the possible drawing angles and contortions some shooters find necessary, it's my fervent belief that the simplest is still the best. Set the bow arm towards the target and draw straight back!

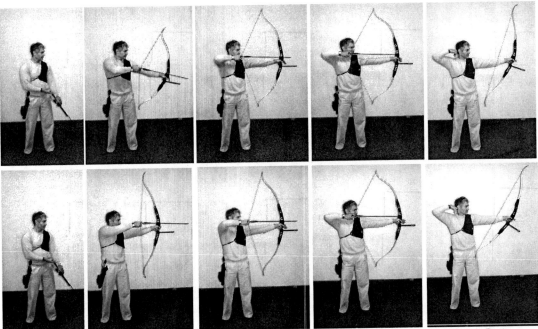

Diag 14-15 Top row shows a swing draw where the bow is drawn as it's raised to target level. Bottom row shows a conventional straight arm draw. The beginning and ending pictures are nearly identical.

Anchor points

So far we have only discussed the basic index finger in the corner of the mouth anchor. While it is probably best for most archers, we are all built differently and so it may not be the best for everyone. The number of anchoring variations can be as different as the differences in people's faces.

The basic anchor originates by putting the string into or deep to the first finger joint (that part really isn't negotiable); the tip of the index finger touches the corner of the mouth and the web of the thumb and index finger are anchored below the jawbone (diag 14-16). This is pretty natural for most people and does work well, but may not be optimal for everyone. Some people can touch the index finger to their eyetooth (canine tooth) (diag 14-16a); some people are more comfortable with the tip of their middle finger in the corner of their mouth, or on their canine tooth and the index finger under their cheekbone (diag 14-16b). Some just use the index finger on the cheekbone by itself. I recall some archers used to extend their thumbs and anchor them under their ears against the back (angle) of the jawbone (diag 14-16c), a little uncomfortable for me, but does work for some. Some very high anchors are also used, with the arrow right next to the eye (diag 14-16d); very good for sighting down the arrow, but not very good if a nock breaks or a brass nockset flies off. Each of these anchors has advantages and disadvantages. As long as they are reproducible for the shooter, and safe, then they're fine. If shooting inconsistencies appear and can be traced back to a faulty, inconsistent or floating anchor, then that needs to be corrected or a new anchor position found.

14-16 Standard anchor position we learned earlier

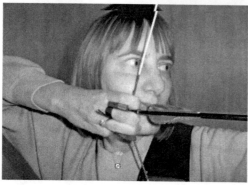
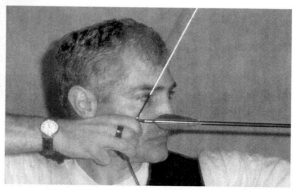

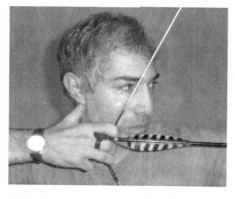
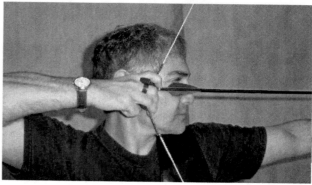

14-16a Anchor/reference point with the index finger on the canine tooth (left)
14-16b Anchoring with the ridge of the index finger under the cheekbone (in this case using a three finger under grip (right)
14-16c Anchoring with the thumb behind the ear (left)
14-16d High anchor with arrow level with the eye. While this is practiced in some circles, it is not recommended for obvious safety reasons (right).

The below the chin anchor was discussed in the sight shooting section, and is a special case. Those folks with a Kirk Douglas cleft in their chins have a definite advantage (diag 14-17). Those that don't, and even some that do, don't really call it an anchor point, as it doesn't have the same solid contact that the side of the face anchor does. It's more appropriately called a reference point. Many archers using the below the chin method also have additional reference points. The thumb behind the jawbone, possibly their little finger on their collarbone, whatever serves to make the "anchor" reproducible.

14-17 Below the chin anchor used by Olympic-style target archers. Notice the string reference point on the tip of the nose.

Lastly, there is one other requirement of an anchor point we have not yet discussed. The position of the anchor must allow the drawing elbow to rotate sufficiently rearward to allow the forearm to be in-line with the arrow, or nearly so if we expect the follow-through to occur naturally (diag 14-18). The described anchors work well for most people, but as we're all built a little differently, some experimentation may be required. Sometimes shifting the anchor rearward a small amount may make the difference between efficient lines of tension and poor or non-existent ones. The most common occurrence related to insufficient rearward rotation of the elbow is the drawing hand coming away form the face, resulting in a "pluck".

14-18 The anchor position must allow adequate rotation of the drawing elbow to yield proper shoulder alignment. As can be seen here, the drawing elbow is in line with the arrow in the left picture, but not on the right.

Some archers do not or cannot get their elbows back far enough to line them up with the arrow and still shoot quite well. If your particular build doesn't allow this (assuming you're not over-bowed), you'll have to pay even closer attention to the follow-through to effect a clean release. With some luck, as your shooting skills develop, your shoulder joint may loosen enough to allow a solid anchor and correct alignment.

Anchoring before anchoring

The following is an advanced technique for use by those with established form and utilizing a below-the-chin anchor.

As can be imagined, the target-style or below-the-chin anchor doesn't have the stability of the side-of-face anchor due to the diminished bone on bone contact. It may also make adequate rotation of the drawing elbow difficult, as it may be farther forward on the face than the side-of-face anchor. One way of minimizing the problem is to fully draw to anchor before making hand to face contact.

If you recall the initial "big-bird" exercise from section one we used to learn basic form, a variant of that can be used to pre-set the anchor.

With the bow arm preset, the string is drawn back until the archer feels his forearm line up with the arrow. At that point he should also feel the drawing shoulder blade settling into a locked position. If the archer's form is correct, his drawing hand should be very close to his anchor position. Aligning the anchor should then be a simple matter and the follow-through will be completed as usual.

The drawing fingers and hand – *The Deep Hook*

We emphasized earlier that the bowstring needs to be in the crease of the first joint from the fingertip (diag 14-19 and 14-20) and not on the pads of the fingertips. This really isn't a debatable option. The "deep hook", as it's called, has several important benefits:

1. Provides a stronger, more controlled grip on the string

2. Allows the back (or dorsal aspect) of the drawing hand to be relaxed and straight

3. Reduces the ballooning effect of the fingertips that happens when a shallower fingertip grip is used

4. The deep hook results in a more solid and controlled anchor, a cleaner and possibly faster release.

5. Not often mentioned, but critical to accurate shooting is that a deep hook provides very consistent finger placement on the string. The finger tip grip can have greater variation which will not only affect the release, but will also result in small changes in draw length.

Deep hook vs fingertip grip

Deep hook

Fingertip grip

14-19 and 14-20 Deep hook vs. a fingertip grip Ballooning of the fingertips caused by a fingertip grip

Theoretically, we'd like the string to be in the first crease of all three drawing fingers and have each finger carrying an equal share of the workload. In practice this isn't always possible, so again we see room for variation. The first thing that should become apparent is that the drawing fingers are not all of the same length. At the very least, that would mean that the longest or middle finger might need to bend or curl more than the index or ring finger. Some archers draw the bulk of the weight with their middle and ring fingers, typically about 85%, and the remaining 15% with their index finger, which acts as a reference point for the anchor (diag 14-21). The opposite is also used; the index and middle fingers carry most of the draw weight and the ring finger just contacts the string to stabilize the hand (diag 14-22).

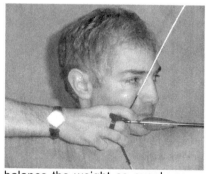 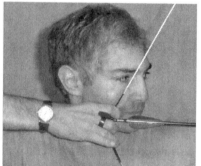

14-21 Drawing with the middle and ring fingers doing 85% of the work (left)

14-22 Drawing with the index and middle and using the ring finger to stabilize the hand (right)

With new shooters, it's always best to try to balance the weight as evenly as possible on all three fingers. As the shooter develops into an archer, the exact style of the grip will evolve. The only caveat is that whichever grip is used must meet the aforementioned criteria.

Lastly, the fingers should be nearly perpendicular to the string from initial placement through the draw, anchor and release. While a slight downward angle may not adversely affect the shot, too severe an angle may result in arrow pinch and a faulty release.

Release

If you recall our earlier discussions, the "release" doesn't really exist as an entity unto itself. It's what happens between the anchor and follow-through. In reality, "something" does happen, albeit a result, rather than an action, and several variations of that result are possible.

There used to be some debate concerning the merits of a dead or static release versus a pull-through or dynamic release (diag 14-23 and 14-24). With a dead release, the drawing hand appears to stay glued to the face in the same position, before and after the string leaves. Unfortunately this really isn't possible. The fingers of the drawing hand and the string form the trigger mechanism or "sear" holding the force of the bow and the force of the archer's muscles in balance (actually the latter should be winning, albeit slightly). When the trigger sear disengages and the string rushes forward, there needs to be an equal and opposite reaction with the drawing hand. As the arrow and string weigh considerably less than the drawing arm and shoulder, the latter will have considerably less movement, but still must move to some degree.

14-23 Dynamic (right) vs. 14-24 static or dead release (left)

People who believe they have a dead release and occasionally shoot well, actually do move their hand back slightly and are, in fact, using extraneous muscle tension (typically shoulder and biceps) to keep the hand "glued" to the face and prevent it from moving back. That muscle effort is not necessary and possibly detrimental to making a good shot, and should be avoided. The other possibly is that they have learned to time the release so perfectly that the collapse (of back tension) occurs a fraction of a second after the string is gone. While possible, it does seem to be a very risky way to maintain consistency. Conversely, people who believe they have a dead release and shoot poorly, are, in fact, collapsing before the string has cleared the fingers, and that collapse is by definition inconsistent.

The pull through release is more efficient, as the archer doesn't get in the way of what should naturally happen. A pull through release is very strongly recommended, as it requires the least effort on the archer's part, and that gives greater consistency and precision.

Exactly how far back the drawing hand should move is not carved in stone. In the earlier section, we described a full dynamic release, where the drawing hand ends up either on the neck or behind the head. While that does indicate an unhindered reaction, it need not be that extreme. As long as the hand moves rearward to some degree, it's a safe bet that adequate back tension was maintained as long as was necessary.

When teaching compound bow shooters, I use a technique that drives home the point of a dynamic release quite effectively. Once the shooter has his basic form down, I place them at five yards from the bales and have them draw on a target. As soon as a solid anchor is achieved, I have them close their eyes and keep their fingers off the release aid's trigger. While instructing them to maintain tension against the stops (meaning the point where the string cannot be draw back any farther), I activate trigger. The release is a total surprise, the drawing hand snaps directly back and the bow jumps forward in their hand. The feeling is very different from what most are used to. If they can recall that explosion, they never forget what a good release should feel like.

That technique can't be used with a stickbow shooter drawing the string with his fingers. However, if a stickbow shooter is having difficulty with the release/follow-through, I may borrow a release aid for them to use and they usually get the surprise of their archery lives!

Three fingers under

In addition to the split finger (index finger above the arrow, middle and ring fingers below), also called the Mediterranean hold or release, some archers favor putting all three fingers under the arrow (diag 14-25). By using the same anchor point, this has the advantage of moving the arrow closer to the eye; some believe shooting "three-under" provides a more precise sight picture and possibly a cleaner release. Additionally, some believe that their bows actually perform better with that hold. One clear advantage of shooting "three-under" is that it becomes virtually impossible to twist or torque the arrow off the string.

On the downside, there is less control of the arrow during the draw and anchor, and a slightly greater possibility of injury should a nock break or nockset come loose. Many archers who shoot "three-under" use two nocksets, one above and one below the arrow's nock to prevent the arrow from sliding on the string and ensure consistent arrow placement. This type of string hold is very common, almost necessary, with the string walking or face walking methods of aiming. Volumes have been written on the advantages of one style over another. The only thing that can be said with some certainty is that when changing from a split finger grip to three-under the bow will have to be retuned. Typically a slight raising of the nocking point is all that is required. Some custom bowyers actually ask their clients which method they use, and balance (tiller) the limbs accordingly. This is typically not necessary as most bows can be shot either way with only a nocking point adjustment. The only exception to this might be some bows with very short limbs, due to the decreased limb lever arm, which may exaggerate the effects of tiller.

14-25 The Mediterranean vs. the 3-under string grip using the same anchor point

Snap shooting

We discussed snap shooting earlier as an example of "bad form". The cause may be the archer being over-bowed, target panic (which will be discussed at length in Chapter 16) or simply that the shooter wants or thinks he needs to shoot quickly for some reason. No matter the cause, it can be one of the most devastating maladies that can plague an archer, especially if it gets to a point where he has no choice but to snap shoot. It is not a shooting option for serious shooters and only mentioned in this section because some people mistakenly believe that it is a valid style of shooting.

There's a difference between shooting quickly and snap shooting. The former implies that proper shoulder alignment has been reached and the anchor is both solid and consistent. The latter, true snap shooting, means that the anchor has become a "touch point" and not a true anchor. Using the example of the index finger touching the corner of the mouth, if you recall, that's actually a reference point, the true anchor is the web of the thumb and index finger "anchored" under the jaw. With snap shooting, the shooter tries to "hit" the touch point believing that he has anchored.

The problem with the touch point being used in place of a true anchor and the resultant snap shot is that the shooter can never be sure whether the string was released before, at or past the touch point or whether the aforementioned shoulder alignment was ever achieved. Without proper lines of tension, plucking, collapsing with the drawing hand, and flailing the bow arm become more prevalent. To make matters worse, we have seen that even with a solid anchor, it's possible to vary the draw length by several inches. While this may not be a problem if the shooter limits himself to very close range shooting or accepts fairly large groups, as shooting distances increase and/or the required group size gets smaller, those inconsistencies begin to take a toll on accuracy.

If quick shooting is something you wish to learn, then the best practice is to start off slowly as described in the first section on this book and gradually increase the tempo as each aspect is mastered. That way a quick shot is possible without loss of form.

If an archer ever finds himself not being able to lock into a solid anchor or hold as long as he wants, he needs to quickly reassess what he is doing and take corrective measures. Once snap shooting becomes ingrained, it is a very, very difficult habit to break. To put it simply: Snap shooting is NOT a variation, it's a mistake!

While some archers believe that snap shooting may be cured by "hunkering down" or pure "intestinal fortitude", typically the harder the effort to correct the problem, the worse it gets. Two time-proven methods for curing snap shooting are the use of a clicker and the no-fire drills, which are discussed elsewhere in this book.

Drawing elbow

We stated that keeping the drawing forearm, and so the elbow, in line with the arrow is part of proper or efficient form. In that position, the lines of tension from bowhand to the drawing elbow form a nearly straight line (diag 14-26). On release the drawing hand should snap straight back. Pretty simple, but if you look at pictures of top target shooters, you'll see that some have their drawing elbows pretty high. In addition to losing clean lines of tension, the biggest disadvantage is that it can cause increased pressure on the ring finger of the drawing hand. Indeed, when there's abnormal callous formation on the ring finger, a high elbow is often but not always at fault. A high elbow may also lead to hunching of the shoulders, which also disrupts efficient lines of tension. A *slightly* raised elbow will typically be tolerated fairly well, however there comes a point where it is clearly counterproductive. Years ago, this was a fairly common practice, and given some of the people who still use it, a high drawing elbow must work. For new shooters it should be approached with caution.

14-26 Drawing elbow in line with the arrow vs. angled upwards

Special Considerations for people shooting a "classic longbow"

We discussed earlier that a recurve has several advantages over a longbow for a new shooter. Most people with an interest in classical archery, however, at one time or another may feel a need or desire to try a longbow. While the principles of shooting either bow are very similar, there are a few variations that need to be considered.

Note that we are talking about the classic "D" shaped or "Hill" style longbow, with a relatively straight grip, mildly reflexed limbs and a typical length of 66" to 70". Current longbow variants may be quite short, have reflexed/deflexed limbs, pistol grips and sight windows very similar to recurves. Some even have weighted risers for added stability or carbon foam limbs for increased performance. Those types of bows are virtually indistinguishable from modern recurves and may be regarded as such.

The first thing that you'll notice with a classic longbow is the lightness of the bow in your hand. While a great feature for carrying the bow, the lack of mass and so inertia may detract from the stability of the shot, especially at the higher draw weights. The design of the bow can add or replace that stability and make up for the loss of inertia; a lot of archers appreciate a little heft in the hand to help steady the aim and absorb vibration on shock.

The real difference between shooting a recurve and a longbow is the grip. A straight grip longbow riser doesn't fit the hand as well as a contoured pistol grip. The edge or face of the grip will still be resting along your lifeline, but by necessity you'll be using more of a low grip. Howard Hill stated that the straight grip should be held as if you were holding a heavy suitcase, meaning the fingers should be comfortably wrapped around the grip but not squeezing or strangling it – still pretty good advice. It will also become apparent that a very relaxed or open bow hand will be impossible. Without the rearward projection of the shelf, an open grip will allow the bow to slip from your hand on release.

Given the longbow's short brace height or fistmele, keeping the grip centered along the lifeline and the elbow of the bow arm rotated clockwise becomes of greater importance to keep the lower forearm out of the path of the bow string. A slightly open stance may also help protect the bow arm, but there is room for variation.

Most longbowmen shoot with a slight cant. There are several reasons for this. First, without an arrow rest, slightly canting the bow helps keep the arrow on the narrow shelf before the draw has progressed to uncurl the fingers sufficiently to begin pushing the arrow into the riser. As most longbows of this design do not have true sight windows, the cant gets the riser out of the archer's line of sight and thus provides a better view of the target. As with the recurve the bow arm should be fully extended (but not locked) at the elbow and pointed toward the target prior to commencing the draw.

14-27 Canting a longbow; notice the low, but relaxed grip.

The drawing arm and hand should follow the same procedure as previously described for a recurve. Aiming methods can vary as much as with any other type of bow. Comparing competitive longbow archers and FITA /Olympic archers, you might be hard pressed to notice any significant differences in form!

Chapter 15

Physical Fitness

*A*nything that makes you stronger or healthier will make you a better archer. From the preceding chapters, we have seen that becoming a proficient or successful archer requires both physical and mental training and discipline. This chapter will discuss the physical part.

Basic rules of physical fitness apply. To perform well at any activity we need proper exercise, a balanced diet and adequate rest – requirements that are easily neglected in today's hectic culture. Archery may not require the same level of conditioning as football or gymnastics, but the better physical condition you're in, the better you'll perform. If you've been sedentary for any length of time, a medical check up would be a good idea as there will be some physical effort involved. Discussing with your doctor that you are planning to take up archery may not be a bad thing; just don't be surprised if he has no comment either way or just says, "Take it slow at first, and build up gradually". As generic as that may sound, it is actually pretty good advice. Archery can become addictive, so it's very easy to overdo it and strain or injure yourself. Some muscle soreness is to be expected but we want to try to keep it to a minimum and avoid more serious injury.

The first thing to consider is your definition of archery. Many archers with access to indoor ranges are quite happy to shoot indoor leagues and matches, or just shoot casually at whatever distances their ranges will allow. The basic indoor NFAA match consists of two ends of five arrows each for practice, followed by 12 ends of five arrows for record, totaling 70 arrows. Add to that walking 20 yards each way, 14 times. That's 560 yards or about a third of a mile. Total time expenditure – about one to one-and-a-half hours. There's really not a lot of physical exertion involved, unless you've decided to shoot a very heavy bow or are shooting at a very high level of competition. The former may turn the match into a weight lifting session and the latter requires sustained focus that can be as physically demanding as it is mentally taxing.

Outdoor target shooting generally involves more arrows, up to 144 for record on FITA type matches, and considerably more walking as the distances go out to 90 meters (98 yards). There's also the additional stress of sunlight, heat or cold, and wind to contend with. Field and 3D courses have fewer arrows than a FITA match, usually 112 plus practice for a field match and as few as 30 or 40 for a 3D shoot. In addition to the actual shooting, there's weather and uneven terrain that must be negotiated. Some clubs hold outdoor winter leagues or matches, called Snowflake leagues, so dealing with sub-freezing temperatures can also be part of the agenda. A bow hunter may experience the same adverse weather conditions, and may need to make a shot after sitting or standing still for several hours. If he harvests game, he'll need to track the animal and move the carcass from the field to his vehicle or camp. While a bow hunter may shoot fewer arrows during any given session, the draw weight of his bow may be considerably higher than that of a target or casual archer. Conversely, a serious target archer may hold the string at anchor for considerably longer than a bow hunter. Each scenario requires a different type of "fitness".

Most people's first concern is the physical strength required to draw the bow. That's a very real concern, as the muscles used to draw a bow and release an arrow correctly aren't used in the same way for anything else. ***The best way to develop the archery muscles is to practice archery.*** While shooting may not technically be considered a gym type workout session, it's hard to deny certain similarities. Assuming you've chosen a bow within your physical capabilities, the more you shoot with it, the more the archery muscles are exercised and developed. The caveat here is, as with any physical endeavor, not to over-train, or "overdo" it. Typical signs of over-training are muscle fatigue, increased difficulty coming to or holding at full draw, and unsteadiness at anchor. An early warning sign is loss of accuracy or precision; basically you're not shooting as well as you did when you started the session. For a serious shooter, that's the first indication to stop shooting. While that seems like a fairly simple statement, it's one of the toughest things for a lot of archers to do. As archery can be quite addictive, meaning that we want to continue shooting, because we enjoy it, we always want to shoot "just one more end" or "just one more arrow". It's also human nature that when something starts going wrong, we want to try to fix it. So, if we notice our shooting starting to deteriorate, we try to correct the problem. While it is always nice to end a session on a high note, or a good end, sometimes when things aren't going well the best course of action is to stop. Continuing to practice once fatigue has set in will do little more than frustrate the shooter and reinforce the errors that caused the problem in the first place. While it's possible to rest for an hour and resume shooting, it's usually better to call it quits for the day, rest and let the body heal. With this approach shooting errors due to fatigue may be forgotten and the muscles are given time to strengthen. The next session can serve as a fresh start and should last slightly longer than the previous one.

There are a few exercises that can help with archery muscle conditioning when not at the range. Before we discuss supplementary exercises, it's important to remember that while archery shouldn't be a weight training session, we need to consider the similarities and use them to our advantage. Since we are in fact exercising muscles, we can take a lesson from successful weight lifters. When muscles are exercised, two things happen.

First – blood rushes to and engorges the muscles being exercised. That excess blood in the muscle tissue during and right after a workout, gives us that "pumped" feeling and appearance.

Second – during strenuous exercise, muscle fibers are microscopically torn, and it's that tearing and the subsequent healing, thanks in part to the increased blood flow and nutrients it carries, that makes the muscles grow larger and stronger (diag 15-1).

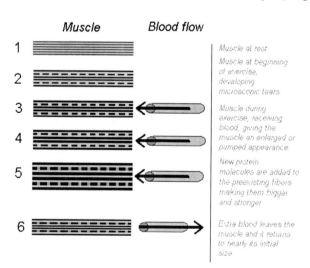

15-1 Schematic of muscle development. The total number of muscle fibers doesn't significantly increase due to exercise, rather the individual fibers get larger due to the increased blood flow and addition of protein molecules.

The muscles actually develop during the resting period after the exercise session, not during the exercise, although the "pump" you get might make you think otherwise.

What this means in terms of archery practice, is that for most beginning and intermediate shooters, shooting every day may not be as beneficial as it might seem, or as we'd like to believe. *A good shooting session that ends in mild fatigue followed by a day or two of rest will develop the archery muscles faster and better than shooting every day.* Even elite archers, who do practice every day, limit their actual shooting time so as not to tear their muscles more than is necessary and allow for adequate rest. At that level, it can be assumed that what's being exercised most is correct form, technique and focus, not merely muscles.

Exercises to assist in developing or increasing the strength of the archery muscles

In addition to the Formaster and resistance band exercises, described in a previous chapter, there are a few basic exercises that are safe and effective, when shooting is impossible.

Important note: If you use the bow to exercise at home with a nocked arrow, be sure it's pointed in a safe direction, both for other people and for property. Also, recall the discussion about not dry-firing a bow.

The simplest exercise is simply to draw the bow (with or without the Formaster). Using an arrow is preferable, as it will more closely simulate the actual shot and actually helps with alignment (diag 15-2). Weigh the risks of drawing with a nocked arrow versus without one in your particular situation. Draw the bow to your normal anchor and hold it there for 5 seconds and let it down. While at full draw, pay particular attention to the feel of your hand on the bow, the position of your fingers on the string, your drawing hand on your face and even the way you feel your back muscles contracting. Sounds like a lot, but by doing this you're not only building muscle strength, you're also learning the details of the shot and reinforcing proper form. It also makes the 5 seconds go by faster. Repeat this as many times as possible until mild fatigue sets in. Not being able to hold your bow at full draw for 5 seconds, at least 10 times, may be an indication that you're over-bowed. In that case, reduce the amount of time to three seconds, and build up as your strength increases. The goal of the exercise is to be able to hold at full draw, without tremor for a minimum of 30 seconds, repeated at least 10 times. This may sound daunting, and in the beginning it is, but the benefits will be very apparent, when you realize that you are pulling more and more of your arrows from the bullseye. *While this exercise is quite familiar to many target archers, it will also benefit bowhunters (who may use bows with heavier weights) by giving greater control during shot execution.*

15-2 Drawing a bow for strength training

A few words of caution: It's been recommended in several places that to accelerate the strength gains, an alternative to this exercise would be to over-draw the bow to increase its effective draw weight, thus making the normal draw feel easier. If you recall our initial training session we showed that the natural position of the drawing hand and arm is not at anchor, but indeed further back in the follow-through position. We needed to modify, or relearn that part, so the anchor became the natural and reproducible position. By exercising an "over-draw" position, you could negate the work that has been done to make the anchor position natural and consistent. An "over-draw" position also changes the alignment of the shoulder girdle and may lead to further form problems. For example, it may lead to over-drawing the string and then creeping forward into your anchor position. By doing that you begin to relax your back tension and may facilitate a collapse on release. Over-drawing some bows is not advisable, as some types of bows do have draw limits, and overdrawing them can lead to a hazardous condition or equipment failure.

Some people have advocated a very slow draw, or partial draw exercise. An example of that would be to draw the bow slowly to 1/2 or 1/3 draw, stopping at those positions for a few seconds, then continuing to anchor; repeat the exercise, stopping at the 1/2 draw position while the arrow is being brought back down. Not only can this disrupt the timing of the draw we've been trying to solidify, but actually be harmful to the shoulder joint, also known as the rotator cuff muscles, which we'll be discussing shortly.

Given the dynamics of the shoulder joint, it's at its weakest, most unstable, and most susceptible to injury during the draw. It is imperative that during these exercises, as when taking a real shot, the draw be accomplished in one smooth and uninterrupted motion terminating in a solid anchor. Stopping the break-down phase at the halfway point or deliberately breaking-down too slowly, not only imparts the same risks as stopping during the draw to anchor but simulates what weight lifters call a "negative rep" or an eccentric contraction. While it may enhance muscle development it increases the possibility of shoulder joint injury. Most knowledgeable weight lifters have stopped using negative reps in their routines for that reason.

Some target bows are actually quite heavy in mass weight when outfitted with sights and multiple stabilizers. Keeping the bow arm elevated and steady may become problematic. A good weight training exercise for this is the lateral deltoid raise, and you don't even need weights to do it. A plastic milk or juice container or a bucket filled with water will work quite well. Stand holding the container at your side, then lift your arm laterally to shoulder level. Your palm will either be vertical or horizontal, depending on the container you use. If you do use dumbbells, holding your hand or palm vertically will better emulate the position of the bow when at anchor. You can do this exercise with both arms at the same time or individually, although both at the same time helps to keep the body balanced (diag 15-3). With this exercise it's best to raise the weight and maintain the position until you're mildly fatigued. Repeating the single action several times better simulates holding the bow on the target than doing multiple sets of the exercise.

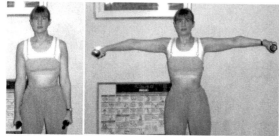

15-3 Lateral deltoid raises using dumbells

The "Little John" Exercise

In Howard Pyle's book, _The Merry Adventures of Robinhood_ it is recounted how Little John loosed three arrows without lowering his bow arm between shots. Not only was that the _"stuff that legends are made of"_ but also an excellent exercise to develop bow arm and shoulder strength especially with youngsters.

When teaching youngsters who may not have the shoulder strength to hold the physical weight of the bow on target for a sufficient amount of time, I have them stand about ten yards form the target, snap an arrow on the string, raise their bow, draw, anchor, aim and follow-through. Then while holding their bow arm towards the target (_not returning it to the resting position_) repeat the process. After a few shots, the bow shoulder begins to fatigue and they are given a chance to rest and recoup their strength. The exercise is repeated several more times. It becomes a game to see how many arrows they can loose before they can no longer hold the bow on target. After a few sessions, shooting a single arrow becomes remarkably easy.

The same exercise can be used with adults who are struggling with the physical weight of the bow. In addition to extending the amount of time the bow can be held on target, it may also increase the archer's steadiness. As with the lateral deltoid raises, some shoulder soreness may be expected until the muscles are conditioned to support the additional weight.

The "Archery Muscles" – Anatomy for the archer

First and foremost: There are no specific weight training exercises for the archery muscles. If we consider the primary "archery muscles" to be the deep muscles of the upper back, specifically the *Major and Minor Rhomboids, Lower Trapezius, and Latisimus Dorsi muscles,* there certainly are weight lifting exercises that can be used to develop these muscles. Those exercises do not use the muscles in the same way that shooting a bow does. It's the brute force versus finesse principle. During the shot sequence the *Rear Deltoids, Upper Trapezius* and deeper muscles around the shoulder joint and shoulder blade, making up the rotator cuff act to raise and stabilize the joint. The *Lateral Deltoids* are used to raise the bow, as previously discussed. The *Triceps* of the bow arm keeps the elbow extended and is stabilized by the *Biceps and Brachialis muscles* (diag 15-6). These muscle groups are used on both sides of the body, but slightly differently, given the actions they perform.

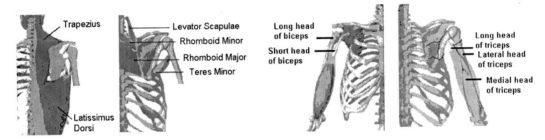

Diagrams 15-4 and 15-5 Archery muscles, superficial and deep views (left two pictures)
15-6 Arm muscles used while shooting the bow: front view of biceps (third picture) and rear view of triceps (far right)

The muscles and tendons that comprise the shoulder's rotator cuff are: the *Supraspinatus, Infraspinatus, Subscapularis, and Teres Minor* muscles and combine to form a cuff over the end of the bone of the upper arm (*Humerus*), effectively creating a socket for it (diag 15-7). These muscles lift and rotate the arm and provide stability during the draw and at anchor. As the socket in this case is made of soft tissue it can be prone to injury. The greatest risk to the rotator cuff is during the draw, usually the first part of the draw, when the socket or joint is in its least stable position.

(One of the reasons compound bow shooters may be at greater risk when drawing heavy bows is that their maximum weight needs to be overcome when their shoulder joint is in its weakest position.)

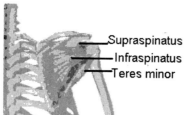

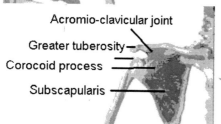

Suprapinatus

Infraspinatus

Teres minor

Acromio-clavicular joint

Greater tuberosity

Corocoid process

Subscapularis

Points of pain suggesting rotator cuff injury

15-7 Rotator cuff complex viewed from the back (left)

15-8 Pain at these points may indicate a rotator cuff injury and should be taken seriously (right)

Summary of the upper body muscles and how they relate to archery

Muscle	Origin	Insertion	Function	Relation to archery
Rhomboids Major and minor	Thoracic spinal column	Medial aspect of scapula	Draw the humerus rearward toward the centerline of the back	Primary drawing muscles. These are the muscles referred to when you hear the expression "squeezing your shoulder blades together"
Trapezius (upper part)	Base of skull	Upper spinal column	Raises the scapula (shoulder blade)	Minimal, except to stabilize the shoulder blades
Trapezius (lower part)	Cervical and thoracic spinal column	Scapula (shoulder blade)	Adducts the scapula (brings them together) Lowermost aspects draw the scapula downward	Brings and holds the shoulder blades together during the draw, anchor and follow-through
Latisimus Dorsi	Upper / dorsal part of the humerus (upper arm bone)	Spinal column and upper rim of pelvis	Pulls the upper arm downward	May assist in drawing, but should be considered a stabilizer for the drawing and bow arms by providing downward pressure and preventing "hunching".
Teres Major	Lateral edge of the scapula	Medial aspect of the humerus	Helps stabilize the shoulder joint and draw the humerus rearward	Assists in the draw, hold and follow-through
Rotator Cuff (Teres Minor, Infraspinatus, Supraspinatus and Subscapularus)	Various (see diagram 15-7)	Various (see diagram 15-7)	Forms the shoulder socket for the humerus and stabilizes its external rotation	Stabilizes the upper arm in the shoulder socket. If unbalanced forces are repeatedly applied, one or more of the rotator cuff muscles can be injured

Deltoids (Anterior, lateral and posterior)	Anterior and lateral deltoids originate on the clavicle (collar bone) and the posterior head on the scapula	Proximal humerus	Raise the upper arm anteriorly, laterally and posteriorly (respectively)	Anterior and lateral heads raise the bow and drawing arms and the posterior head assists in the draw
Triceps	Long head originates on the scapula, lateral and medial heads on the humerus	The three heads of the triceps join to form one tendon and attach to the ulna (large forearm bone)	Extends the forearm and to a very small degree draws the upper arm downward (Long head only)	Keeps the bow arm from collapsing at the elbow joint
Biceps (Biceps Brachii) Long and short heads	Long and short heads originate on the scapula	Long and short heads attach to the radius (smaller forearm bone)	Flexes (bends) the forearm at the elbow joint and rotates the forearm outward (called supination)	Stabilizes the elbow joint and triceps. The biceps should NOT be used to keep the drawing hand against the face

If pain is experienced in the front part of the shoulder joint (diag 15-8), it may possibly indicate a rotator cuff injury, or the beginnings of one. While it's most common on the side of the drawing shoulder, damage may occur in the bow shoulder. In either case the archer needs seriously to reevaluate his draw weight, and more importantly, his form. While rest and limited exercising of the affected muscles is the only real treatment, it is one potential injury that necessitates a trip to the doctor – preferably one with experience in Sports Medicine followed by a few sessions with a Physical Therapist trained in rehabilitating sports injuries.

While the most prudent course of action if shoulder pain develops is rest and medical attention, if the archer insists on shooting with shoulder pain, there is a way of working around it temporarily. The following is provided as a means of preventing further injury and not a solution to an existing problem or treatment thereof.
The horse bow draw

The horse bow draw most likely originated with Asian cultures that needed a way to draw heavy bows while riding a horse. The purpose of the exercise is to recruit additional muscles not normally used to assist in the drawing of the bow, or more correctly, giving secondary muscles more responsibility, thereby easing the pressure on the primary muscles and potentially injured ones.

1. *Stand with your feet slightly further apart than the normal shoulder width (diag 15-9A).*
2. *Engage the arrow and string as usual (diag 15-9B).*
3. *Instead of bringing the bow arm directly in line with the target, bring it and the drawing arm about 45 degrees above parallel to the ground. The arrow must still be parallel to the ground (diag 15-9C)).*
4. *Draw the bow back and down to anchor (diag 15-9D and diag15-9E). Release and follow-through normally.*

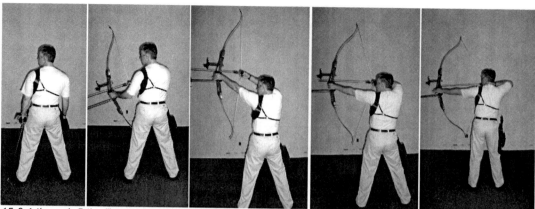

15-9 1 through 5 the "horse draw" technique

By drawing from above the normal pre-draw position you will be using the large back muscles, the Latisimus Dorsi, to a greater extent and taking some of the pressure off the shoulder muscles. It bears repeating – while this may allow someone to shoot a few extra arrows it cannot be considered a long-term fix. Ultimately, medical attention must be sought.

As I stated in the beginning of this chapter: Anything that makes you stronger and healthier will make you a better archer. Are frequent trips to the gym, weight room or aerobics class necessary to excel in archery? That's not an easy question to answer. They certainly won't hurt, and most, if not all, of the more competitive archers have a fairly strong all around strength/aerobic training regimen and also adhere to a balanced diet, as do all elite athletes. The word necessary, however, makes it difficult to answer easily. The "best" possible answer, and one that I wholeheartedly agree with, would be a resounding *yes!* – However, there are simply too many fine archers who do nothing more than just "shoot".

If a plan of physical training is undertaken it needs to be well rounded and not archery specific. While it's clear that the back, shoulder and arm muscles, comprising the "power unit", do most of the actual work in archery, the other muscle groups need to be developed in concert with the primary archery muscles. The chest muscles oppose and stabilize the actions of the back muscles; the abdominal and lower back muscles maintain our posture and alignment; the buttocks and leg muscles form the foundation, creating the "base unit" to keep us steady. If the legs allow us to be unsteady at anchor, by definition the bow will be unsteady and the shot faulty. A weak link in any of these groups will ultimately weaken the whole shot process. Likewise the heart and lungs need to be up to the task of supplying nutrients and oxygen to the brain and muscles, so some aerobic work should be included. It is beyond the scope of this book to describe a full training regimen for all body types and levels of fitness. The final decision remains with the archer as to what he needs to attain his individual goals.

Last, and by no means least, is adequate hydration. It might seem obvious that if you plan on shooting outdoor matches in the hot sun, perspiration can lead to dehydration. Less obvious is that during indoor matches or practice sessions, even in air-conditioned ranges, continuous shooting may dehydrate you. Some people are outwardly more susceptible to this than others, but everyone is affected by it. If you find yourself tiring prematurely or getting mentally "cloudy", a possible reason may be dehydration, and with a little planning, an easy one to remedy.

A brief thought on draw weights…

There's a bell shaped curve to an archer's accuracy in regards to draw weight. There is a certain weight range where it just feels right. The draw is unforced; the string is comfortable to hold and gently pulls away from our fingers. Above that weight and the bow starts to become a challenge to draw, difficult to anchor and the release becomes unsure. Go too light and the string doesn't have sufficient force to free itself from our fingers. Strangely enough, the more experienced the archer the greater and lesser draw weight he can shoot accurately!

Warming up before a shooting session

There's a general consensus that "warming up" is a good idea before any athletic activity. *Archery is considered an athletic activity, so it would seem logical that some warm-up exercises should be in order.* This too is a personal matter; the warm-ups may be as simple or as elaborate as the individual believes he needs and may be dependent on the general physical condition of the archer. Particular issues the archer may have, such as specific tightness in a given muscle group, may need to be addressed as part of the warm-up session. Generally, for most people a few simple neck and shoulder stretches are sufficient.

As the head needs to be rotated as close as possible to 90 degrees to face the target, some limbering of the neck muscles before shooting may be helpful. Head rotations and simply turning the head far to the right and left with slight force is usually adequate.

A few simple warm-up exercises:

Head rotations – Let the head fall forward, with the chin as close to the chest as it will naturally go. Let it hang there for a few seconds and then begin rolling it to the right shoulder, then back, left shoulder and then front again. Repeat in the opposite direction. For some people, this may reveal some tightness or "creaking", so go slow and don't force any of the movements as the weight of the head provides enough force (diag 15-10).

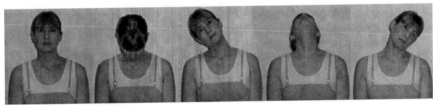

15-10 Head rotations

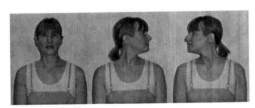

Head turns – As the name implies means keeping the head level and turning it as far as it will go to the left and right and holding it in each position for a few seconds (diag 15-11).

15-11 Head turns

Shoulder /arm rotations (diag 15-12)– are accomplished by holding your arms straight out to the sides, with palms facing forward and moving them in a circular motion, first clockwise, then counterclockwise, beginning with small circles and making them as large as comfort will allow (diag 15-12). A variation of this would be to begin again with your arms out at shoulder height and

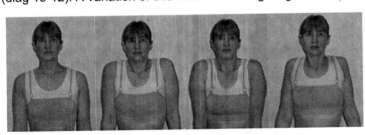

instead of describing circles, bring them forward and cross in front of your chest in a hug, and then as far back as they will go.

15-12 Shoulder/arm rotations and variation

Stretches need only be repeated a few times. Some archers include toe touches and trunk twists as part of their regimen; they're kind of like chicken soup, they couldn't hurt! An added benefit of a warm-up routine, one that is often overlooked, is that it helps to prepare the archer mentally for the shooting session. Having a set routine can formalize the activity and establish a boundary between shooting time and other matters of day to day life; more about this in the next chapter. People will decide, usually through trial and error, what works best for them and yes, doing nothing at all is also an option.

An additional stretching exercise you may find beneficial:

This is a stretch I use during my normal exercise routine. While an excellent torso stretch, with a slight modification it can also improve your shooting. For this stretching exercise, you'll need a pole or rod about 6' long. A broomstick may work in a pinch.

Stand with your feet roughly shoulder width apart and place the center of the pole behind your neck with your hands near each end as in the illustration. Attempt to roll it down your back as far as is comfortable. If you haven't "stretched-out" for some time, don't be surprised if the pole doesn't travel too far down your back at first. Roll it up and down a few times and let it rest just behind your shoulders.

Keeping your upper back straight, bend forward at the waist as far as is comfortable and hold that position for a count of 20. *Do not bounce; just hold that position.* If that becomes painful you may want to reduce the count to 10. Return to the starting position.

Turn your head to the left and look over your left shoulder (if you're a right-handed archer, if you're left handed, look over the right shoulder). Twist to the left (counter-clockwise if viewed from the top) at the waist as far as is comfortable and hold for a 20 count, keeping your head turned to the left. Smoothly rotate to the right (clockwise) as far as comfortable also for a 20 count, again while keeping your head turned over your left shoulder.

Return to center and this time bend at the waist to the left, as if you were shooting downhill for a 20 count and then bend to the right, as if you were shooting uphill; hold for a 20 count and come back to center.

Lastly, turn your head back to center and arch your back rearward and hold for a 20 count. Return to center and repeat as many times as you can. I find three to four cycles sufficient to limber up the spine.

Let's examine this stretch a little more closely. Except for the forward bend which stretches the lower back and hamstrings (rear thigh muscles) notice that we are in, or close to, our follow-through position for most of the exercise. In addition to stretching out the lower back, oblique abdominal muscles and hips, you are re-enforcing the proper shoulder geometry you learned earlier. By repeating this exercise often, you will not only gain flexibility, but also get accustomed to shooting at various angles without sacrificing form.

Please remember that if this stretching exercise is painful or if you feel dizzy while stretching, slowly back off from the position you are in and stop the exercise.

15-13a Place a long pole behind your head and gently roll it down your back as far as is comfortable and repeat several times.

15-13b Stand with feet about shoulder width apart and bend forward from the waist.

15-13c Return to the original position, but bend your right arm and look over your left shoulder. Twist from the waist as far as comfortable to the right and then

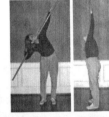

15-13d This time bend at the waist as if you were taking a downhill shot, then bend the opposite way simulating an uphill shot (left).to the left, then return to center.

15-13e Finally, return to the original position with both arms extended and head forward. Arch your back as far as comfortable while maintaining your balance (right).

Cooling down after the shooting session

While common in weight lifting and aerobic circles, in all honestly, I've never seen anyone do a specific cool down routine after a shooting session. That doesn't mean that is necessarily a bad idea, only that it may not have caught on – yet. A very simple cool down regimen could simply be the same exercises or stretches we discussed earlier. While never proven clinically, they may help some archers, especially if there is some muscle tightness after a shooting session and like chicken soup, it couldn't hurt.

Preventing fatigue at the end of a match (or shooting session)

If you're getting fatigued before the end of a match or before you actually want to stop shooting *(now there's a concept – "wanting" to stop shooting),* there really isn't much you can do when it happens. It has to be taken care of before it happens. Naturally, being in adequate physical and emotional shape is a big part, as is having adequate nutrition, hydration and rest. If we can assume the above has been taken care of to the best of your ability and as circumstances allow, then your training needs to be modified to increase your shooting endurance.

One simple approach is to "over train for the event", which is different from over-training as discussed earlier. Here, you attempt to make the norm greater than the necessity. It's easier than it sounds. For example, if you typically shoot an indoor NFAA round, 60 arrows for record, shot in 12 ends of five arrows each, you may practice by shooting six or seven arrows per end and try to shoot two full matches back to back. (You can even keep score by marking the sixth and/or seventh arrows, and disregarding them when scoring.) By shooting more than the required number of ends, you'll not only be used to shooting more arrows per end, but the actual match may seem to finish early, and more importantly, before fatigue sets it.

Some of my old shooting buddies and I had a habit of shooting the scheduled match at our local range, then re-shooting it afterwards – *usually several times!* While the main reason was that we simply enjoyed shooting, we never had a problem with fatigue during the regular match.

An alternative and less time consuming exercise would be to shoot a specific match during a practice session with more than the required arrows. For example: The standard indoor NFAA match is made up of twelve ends of five arrows each. A practice "match" may be twelve ends of six or seven arrows. Simply mark the additional arrows with a felt pen and don't include them while scoring!

Working out (exercising) and shooting – sleep / caffeine / medication, etc.

It may seem obvious, but trying to have an effective practice session or shoot a winning score after an exhaustive weight lifting or aerobic workout may not be the best idea – for most people anyway. Nor will it be beneficial to shoot when you are sleep deprived. (Actually there have been a few accounts to the contrary, and we'll discuss that in the next chapter on mental training, but for this discussion, and for the majority of people, it's generally not a good idea.) Nor is it a good idea or sometimes, even possible, to shoot well with a hangover, or while recovering from an illness. People respond to caffeine, nicotine, and similar stimulants differently. In the shooting sports, typically the more relaxed you are, the better the shooting; therefore they are probably best avoided before any serious training sessions or matches. *There are always exceptions to every rule; some people cannot shoot well without a cup of coffee and a cigarette. While that may not be typically recommended, it is just another case of the archer knowing what works for him or her.* Just remember that after the nicotine high, there may well be a rebound low, so the only way of truly knowing how you will react is by relying on our old friend, experience. Any use of prescription medications and possible regimen changes should be discussed with your doctor before undertaking any physical activity, and needless to say, no weapon should be handled when under the influence – those are the standard legal disclaimers.

The use of performance enhancing, stimulant or depressant drugs is illegal in most sanctioned competitions and just generally a bad idea. They are only mentioned here as a warning of something not to do.

Some additional thoughts…

Some people are just natural athletes. They seem to excel at whatever physical activity they do. There's certainly a genetic component for this, including natural muscle strength, good vision and eye-hand coordination. People involved in any sports activity, be it baseball, football, tennis, golf and any of the martial arts or shooting sports tend to pick up new endeavors quicker and become proficient faster than those without prior athletic training. In addition to the genetic component, each previous activity, once mastered, acts as a building block for future endeavors. This is not coincidental. Most sporting activities, while differing in actual techniques, have the same core principles. These include the ability to center one's energy, focus on the task at hand and leave extraneous thoughts and actions to the side. They also require the athlete to act reflexively to accomplish that task. The term "reflexively" is quite important. As we've seen with our archery training, there's nothing reflexive about it. *(Reflexive in a medical sense means that an action is innate and happens without higher brain involvement.)* In the beginning of our training, everything we did was very deliberate, and we repeated the exercises hundreds and thousands of times before it *appeared* reflexive. That's exactly what most elite athletes do to accomplish their specific goals. During their training, they have repeated the same series of tasks, correctly, enough times that during the competition or performance it appears effortless or reflexive. The physical tasks are committed to the subconscious, allowing the conscious mind to focus on the goal, in our case – the center of the target.

Chapter 16

Archery – the Mental Game

Recently there has been a plethora of books written on the mental aspects of sports activities, and for good reason. There are only minor differences in high-end equipment, and most top athletes are privy to similar or similarly effective physical training regimens. The deciding factor besides luck (which is always a factor) is the mindset of the competitor. Any archer wishing to improve his or her game can use the same strategies that an Olympic gold medallist uses to perform at his best.

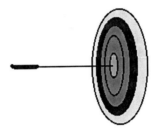

Part 1 – The Goal

The first thing to consider when developing a mental strategy is to determine the immediate goal or short-term end result. In the beginning, the goal may be synonymous with the reason we decided to take up archery. It is safe to say that we all thought shooting a bow and arrow would be fun, or we wanted to be able to shoot them well enough to accomplish a specific task, such as attaining a given score in a match or hunting successfully. That may have been a starting point but now we need to look deeper if we are to succeed or reach that goal. All goals are relative as to where we are at present and what it is we wish to achieve, or what we can realistically achieve from our current position. From there we can determine where we ultimately want to be. When we reach one goal, either the journey has ended or a new leg has begun.

We have come full circle. When you began reading this book, I asked the question, *"Why are you interested in taking up archery?"* The answers were anything from: it looked like fun, to spending more time outdoors or with my family; gaining additional hunting time, to becoming a National, International or Olympic champion. Hopefully, with a better understanding of what archery is really about, we now have gained a better idea of where we want this "new" activity to take us.

If you choose to be a casual or backyard archer, that's great; archery is a wonderful way to relax, spend time with family and friends or just spend time alone to gather our thoughts and reflect on the meaning of life. If you are content with your shooting ability, then a goal has been achieved and you need look no further. But if we choose to go beyond that, we need to set a new goal. It may be a higher score at a local match or just for our own records; increased accuracy at greater distances or a greater degree of confidence when we draw a bow and loose an arrow in the field be it at a leaf or a deer. If that's the case, then a new goal is necessary and must be chosen carefully.

Short term vs. long term goals

We can create a goal very easily; it can be a certain score on an NFAA target, a Field course, or a certain size group at a given distance. The goal needs to be concrete and attainable. For a new shooter, averaging 180 or 200 on an indoor NFAA 20-yard target, setting a short-term goal of 280 would be unreasonable. It's not to say that it will never happen, but it would take so long that most people would lose interest well before that goal was achieved or even approached. That can have a negative impact on the individual's frame of mind and lead to a loss of interest in the endeavor or possibly an early withdrawal from the activity altogether. A more reasonable short-term goal would be a score of 210 or 220. That's within the reach of most new shooters, given proper instruction and a few months of practice. Once that goal is achieved, a new goal of perhaps a 230 can be set, again, then 250, and so on. Reaching these short-term goals paves the way to the long-term goal of a 280 score or even a perfect 300. Each time a goal is reached there's positive reinforcement, a feeling of accomplishment and that spurs us on to create the next goal and then achieve it.

It will be noticed that going from 200 to 230 is easier and takes less time than going from 230 to 250, and going from 250 to 260 is more difficult still. This is simply because the higher the goals, in this case the higher the score, the fewer mistakes are allowed for the goal to be achieved. For barebow shooters (those not using a sighting device) in the higher ranks, going from a 270 to a 275 or 280, may take considerably longer than going from 200 to 270. That's why they call 300 a "Perfect" score – there are no mistakes allowed. At the time of this printing, I know of no one who has shot a perfect 300 with a recurve or longbow in the barebow classes. The same holds true for shooting at longer distances. Minor form errors may not be evident at shorter ranges, but as the distance to the target increases those minor form errors become glaring mistakes.

To illustrate this type of goal system, when I was competing, the NFAA used classifications for their indoor 300 matches; the score "brackets" for the barebow classes were as follows:

Archer 0 –189   (D – class, bronze medals)
Bowman 190 – 209   (C – class, silver medals)
Expert B 210 – 249   (B – class, gold medals)
Expert A 250 – 279   (A – class, gold medals)
Expert AA 280 – 300   (AA – class, gold medals)

(The NFAA indoor match is shot at 20 yards, and is comprised of 12 ends of 5 arrows each on the blue 40cm target with a white bullseye. Scoring is 5 points for a bullseye, followed by four, three, two and one for each shot in each consecutive ring. There are typically two practice ends, also of five arrows each, prior to scoring.) It should come as no surprise that there were very few people in the AA class.

In a sense, the goals were predefined for a lot of us, and were set so they were attainable. Getting "upped in class" became a sign of achievement; we wanted to get the gold medals for winning a match. It may have seemed trivial, but on some level it really wasn't. It gave shooters a mental advantage, for two reasons. First, knowing that they were shooting only against others of relatively equal ability, and had a fair chance of winning, and second, they had an attainable goal to strive for, reaching the next level.

Interestingly during that era, the NFAA recognized only three shooting styles, or divisions, based on equipment.

- Barebow – any bow without sights or release aids
- Freestyle – any bow with sights, but no release aids
- Unlimited Freestyle – any bow using a release aid, with or without sights; there were no restrictions on bow or arrow materials or configurations

In effect, the equipment played no part in the classification schema. You shot against people using your particular style or method of shooting and more importantly, at your skill level – very simple and very effective.

The JOAD (Junior Olympic Archery Development) program, designed to get youngsters involved in archery under the supervision of experienced shooters, had the same methodology, and it still does. Anyone joining the program started at the lowest level, which meant shooting at a very large target, and they worked their way up through the ranks, by shooting qualifying scores at progressively smaller targets. Setting attainable goals and achieving them is one of the most powerful incentives in athletic competition, and in life. The JOAD program is still alive and well, and has been the starting point for a number of top archers.

The Payoff

To understand how a goal works, we need to understand the concept of the payoff. For a goal to be achieved, the payoff or reward needs to be sufficient to warrant the effort required for achieving the goal.

If you are content with your shooting as a form of relaxation and are satisfied with your level of accuracy, then setting a goal, for example, shooting a better score or tighter group, may not have much meaning to you. Or rather achieving that goal doesn't have a sufficient payoff to warrant the additional effort required for shooting the higher score. More so than the goal needing to be tangible and achievable, the payoff needs to be real and important to you.

I was recently at a management seminar and the question came up, "Why do you want to get a promotion?" The standard answers were given, such as, to make more money, for more responsibility, for the prestige of a better title, and so on. While that's the way most of us approach our goals, it's not really an effective motivator, as the reasons are too general, vague, and most importantly, there's no tangible or meaningful payoff.

Using the above as an example, consider the following:

I need a promotion to make more money
vs.
I need a promotion to make $XXX more per year so I can afford a mortgage on a particular size house my family needs.

I need a promotion to get more responsibility
vs.
I need more responsibility or authority, to make XXX happen within the company.

I need a promotion because I want a new, more impressive title
vs.
I need the title of XXX, so I can do more and work my way up to the position of Vice President within 5 years.

XXX in each case has a well-defined goal with either an amount or "thing" attached to it.

In the above cases, the first statement in each pair is vague and lacks a defined payoff. There's no urgency to make it, whatever "it" is, happen, so the payoff doesn't warrant the effort. The second statement has meaning and urgency to the person saying it.

In the first example, the person may be expecting a new addition to the family, and a new, larger house isn't a luxury that would be nice to have, but a necessity, and the time frame is somewhat urgent. Notice the use of the phrase "...on a particular size house my family **needs**".

In the second example, there may be a project that the person truly believes in, is vitally important to him for some reason, and that he needs to be part of or possibly in charge of. It may also mean that he believes that successfully completing that particular project will lead to further advancement. In this case, we have an example of the employee setting a short-term goal, in order to prepare for a long-term goal. That leads us into the third example.

In the third case, it is clear that the person has a long-term goal in mind, and is utilizing one or more short-term goals to achieve the payoff. That scenario may be the most similar to those goals and payoffs we're dealing with in archery. We may not be seriously planning a trip to the Olympics or the FITA World Championships, but there is a level of expertise we'd like to have. For a very real archery example, it wouldn't be the first time an archer set a goal of out-shooting a long time "friend" or adversary. That may not seem like much to someone on the outside, but I'd be willing to bet that type of friendly competition has spurred more than one archer on his road to future greatness.

If we are to achieve a goal in archery, to get to the next level, there has to be a reason or a payoff attached to it. As our ability improves, more and more effort is required to progress. Once the individual person can determine what payoff will justify the required effort, then the goal has meaning and can be achieved.

The final question that must be asked, in relation to goals, is what happens when a goal is achieved, and a new goal isn't needed or wanted? If we are comfortable with the status quo, that's fine, but most people need or want to keep the challenge alive, to have something to work on; without that, the activity may become a pastime, or worse, boring. I'll challenge you to think about that for a while.

Part 2 – The Plan

Once the above "payoff" has been recognized, and the desire to achieve a new goal established, the next step is the creation of a plan to accomplish that goal.

The first step is fairly easy; by following the instructions outlined in the previous chapters, the physical, or rather mechanical aspects of archery need to be learned, practiced and mastered. As with most physical endeavors, repetition plays a key role. Once the physical actions are learned, the repetition commits them to memory, both to intellectual and muscle memory; to a casual observer, as we discussed in the previous chapter, they appear reflexive. Without that level of physical training, the mental aspect, while not totally useless, does lose a great deal of value.

Clearly, if one aspect of the fundamentals is troublesome, or inconsistent, then a goal (to correct the problem or inconsistency) has been established, and an appropriate plan needs to be devised. If, for example, you don't always come back to the same follow-through position, and so have an inconsistent release, the goal is to make it consistent, and the plan may include daily drills with resistance bands to augment actual range time. Further, a certain amount of range time may need to be devoted to "blank bale shooting" to focus on the follow-through. Likewise, if your anchor is inconsistent, practicing the anchor in front of a mirror, combined with "no-fire" drills may be an appropriate plan.

With regard to the above, you may need to ascertain exactly how much range time you will need to accomplish the goals you've set. It may be two, two-hour sessions a week, two, two-hour sessions plus several additional hours on weekends or a one-hour session each day. You may also need additional "study" time at home to supplement range time. Clearly, the higher your level of shooting, and the higher your goals, the more time you'll have to devote to it. Not only do you have to consider the amount of time you want to devote to it, but the amount of time you can devote to it. That is a very real concern with school, work and family obligations. A realistic understanding of the time requirements of the goals you are setting for yourself needs to be balanced against the value of the payoffs.

The mindset of the champion

One of the key tenets of becoming a champion is to believe, beyond a shadow of a doubt, that you are a champion. You don't think you are going to repeatedly place arrow after arrow in the bullseye, you know you are; you expect to. That belief doesn't come from daydreaming or wishing for it, it comes from hours, days, months and years of rehearsing the actions that will get you to that point. You know you will hit the bullseye every time, because you have hit the bullseye every time in the past. You know that if you follow a certain process, as you have done thousands of times before, the end result will be the same as it has been thousands of times before. It will be the arrow landing in the bullseye or X ring of the target you are shooting.

Most elite competitors in any field will have very similar skill sets and tools at their disposal. All have the requisite physical strength, eyesight, and disposition to be the best; their equipment is usually not a factor, as most competition level equipment is more than capable of taking its user to the top. The man or woman who wins is usually the one who believes most that they will indeed win. Or put another way, if you are competing to win, and don't believe inside that you will win, then you can't. It's that simple. (Yes, luck can always play a part, and that can't be denied, but even luck has a habit of favoring the best-trained and best mentally prepared competitor.)

This bears repeating. **Confidence can't be hollow; it's based on hard work, maximum effort and experience.** There's a very big difference between being boastful about being the best, and knowing deep down that you are the best. The person who knows that he or she will win, more often than not, will win. Winning can mean anything from leaving the range or field with a feeling of accomplishment, knowing you shot to your potential, or walking away with a trophy or gold medal, or even being able to fill your freezer with meat.

We have discussed a great many details on the mechanics of archery, both regarding the equipment and the techniques or form we use to direct the arrow to its mark. Those techniques are the foundation we need to perform the work of making the shot. We have also just discussed the confidence that comes from that work and goes along with being successful. Now let's add a few mental exercises to enhance the process.

Mental rehearsal

The old saying, *"Practice Makes Perfect"*, is not exactly accurate. **"Perfect Practice Makes Perfect Shooting"** is a more accurate concept. We've gone over a lot of techniques to make a "perfect" shot, and if we were able to do those steps correctly every time, then every arrow would go exactly where we wanted it to go. That's the ultimate goal, the end game, but even with all the details we've discussed in the preceding chapters, most of us aren't quite there yet. Let's see if we can bridge the gap to the next level.

The following assumes that you are at a stage where you understand your correct shooting form and can routinely hit the target, or rather, the center of the target, and your equipment is tuned to at least your level of shooting.

Mentally rehearsing the shot

Right now, sit in a comfortable chair, relax and without moving any body parts, go through an entire shot sequence. Start with taking an arrow from the quiver, nocking it, drawing the string to anchor, releasing and following through to the point where you see the arrow hitting the center of the target. You may want to repeat it a few times. OK, put the book down and try it!

How did it go, pretty well? What level of detail were you able to recall? Most people can mentally conjure only the gross features of an activity without actually doing it. Try visualizing it again.

- Think about your stance in relation to the target, the position of your feet.

- Recall the length of the arrow coming out of the quiver, the color of the shaft and the fletching.

- Recall the manipulation of the nock between your thumb and forefinger and its snap onto the string.

- Recall the placement of your fingers on the string, the exact position of your fingers, including the amount they curl around the string and possibly what the tab looks like under the string.

- Recall the feel of the tab or glove as you begin to apply drawing pressure.

Getting the idea?

- When did you first acquire the target and from what direction?

- How did you raise your bow arm?

- What was the position of your bow hand on the grip?

- What does your hand feel like against your face at anchor?

- What, if anything, did you do to release the string?

- Exactly where did your drawing hand end up after the shot?

We're not done yet.

- At anchor, did you notice the relationship of the bow, arrow or bow arm in your peripheral vision?

- Did you feel any tension in either arm during the draw, and at anchor, and if so, what kind of tension and where was it?

- Were you aware of the muscles in your back, during and after release?

- How were you breathing during the shot?

- What happened to your bow and bow arm at release and during follow-through?

- Did you "see" where that arrow landed in the target? (For this exercise, the arrow should have landed in the center of the X ring.)

- Finally, how did you lower your bow back to the resting position?

Try it again, and try to recall as many details as possible. Don't be surprised if you can't remember all of them the first few times. If you are in a position to shoot the bow, take a few shots. Shoot the same way you normally do, but instead of focusing on the center of the target, pay close attention to the details of the shot. Put the bow down and mentally rehearse the process again. You should have been more conscious about the details of the shot. Repeat actually shooting the bow, and then mentally rehearse it a few more times. Each time, you should be able to add more details to the process. This technique not only commits the shot sequence to memory (to your brain, you're actually shooting, even though you're only thinking about it), but has been proven to stimulate the brain cells required to perform the specific task and certain memory cells. So effectively you're not only becoming a better archer, but you may actually be getting a littler smarter!

After a few back and forth sessions, you should be able to recreate the entire sequence (or at least most of it) in your mind. The process for each "mental" shot, in the beginning, will take considerably longer than an actual shot sequence, but after a while will take exactly the same amount of time as a live shot. What should be obvious now, is that by this exercise we have accomplished two things. First, we should be more aware of the nuances of the shot sequence, and second, *we have given ourselves the opportunity to practice anytime, anywhere, with or without a bow, arrow or target!*

It's imperative that when you begin this exercise, you strive to codify the smallest detail, and bring the so-called reflexive actions into consciousness. See how they work together, and how one flows into the next. Just as we built a physical foundation in Chapter 2 on Basic Shooting Form, this will build, or enhance the mental foundation. As you continue this exercise, you will modify it to reflect the points that are critical for you personally to make a perfect shot. You'll develop your own mental shot sequence, or checklist, of the points that are required for you to ensure a perfect shot. Once that happens, you will have attained "Perfect Practice" and then, "Perfect Practice does Make Perfect".

An example of the initial critical points for one archer may be:

1. Foot placement in relation to the firing line and target
2. Initial hand placement on the riser
3. Nock engagement to string
4. Initial position of the fingers on string
5. Target acquisition
6. Feel of pressure on bow hand and drawing hand as the draw commences
7. Shoulder/back alignment during draw
8. Feel of drawing hand against the face at anchor
9. Confirmation of bow hand pressure at full draw
10. Confirmation of shoulder/back alignment
11. Focus on target center acquisition
12. Mental image of follow-through position
13. Visualization of arrow in target center
14. Confirmation of follow-through and recovery

After some experience is gained, the critical points may be reduced to:

1. Foot placement in relation to the firing line and target
2. Initial hand placement on the riser
3. Initial position of the fingers on string
4. Target acquisition
5. Feel of drawing hand against the face at anchor
6. Confirmation of shoulder/back alignment
7. Focus on target center acquisition

8. Visualization of arrow in target center
9. Correct follow-through position

The above examples are clearly for an archer in a target situation. The same theory applies to a bowhunting situation. This is a scenario a good friend of mine uses when deer hunting:

1. First sighting of a deer (and the rush of adrenaline)
2. Maintain deep and steady breathing
3. Stop. Do nothing until calm
4. If the game is within range slowly and quietly nock an arrow
5. Confirm a relaxed grip on the bow
6. Deliberately place fingers on the bowstring
7. Continue to evaluate the shot / path of arrow
8. Reposition body for best aspect to target
9. Pick or create a specific aiming point
10. Re-evaluate the path of the arrow and make any adjustments necessary
11. Carefully draw, lock into anchor and confirm the "spot" or point to place the arrow
12. See the path of the arrow to the spot on the deer
13. Follow-through
14. Confirm hit and take note of the direction the deer moved
15. Relax and wait

This bowhunter is demonstrating his experience as an archer and hunter. Every move he made or didn't make was for a purpose. He knew what his reactions would be in a given situation and confirmed his vital points before taking the shot. If something changed, the deer moved behind a tree or branch, he would reposition himself to allow a clear path for his arrow, or he would let the shot pass.

Either way, there's a lot to think about, no doubt. If you recall from in the aiming section, we discussed what happens during the hold at anchor. As we said, it's not simply aiming; the elite shooters are going through a checklist to ensure a perfect shot. Some of the items on the checklist may be conscious, some subconscious, but they all happen – every time. If something doesn't feel "right", you quickly become aware of it, and you will not loose a bad arrow. Recall that earlier we said that a perfect score means no mistakes? *If something feels wrong, and you realize it, and let the shot down, it's not a mistake because the shot never happened.* You can restart it from the beginning and make it right. Having a checklist is a way of letting you know when to let down. The sequence of critical points may be slightly different from archer to archer, but once understood, your number of good shots will begin to increase exponentially. Still too much to think about? Read on.

The next step: Occasionally we see some fine archers shooting quite quickly, touching anchor and releasing without hesitation, or holding for very short periods of time. Assuming that a consistent anchor is reached, we might ask ourselves, "How can they be going through a checklist in so short a time?" Well, they are, and it's possible for several reasons. With experience many of the checks can be handled on a subconscious level and the number of items in their sequence may be slightly different than what we described. While most of the points we illustrated are necessary, they need not be done in the given order. For example, it's quite possible that the bow hand and finger position check take place during the draw, as does initial target acquisition. Also, several checks may occur simultaneously. The combinations are truly infinite. It may also become a *negative checklist*, meaning that with enough experience, only problems are brought into the conscious mind, as "red flags" so to speak. It must be stressed, however, that those successfully using that style of rapid shooting have been practicing that way for years or decades, so while it's certainly possible to shoot very quickly, it's not recommended for beginning or intermediate level shooters. It truly is a case of trying to run before you can walk.

When bad shots happen to good people

With all the discussions so far, it would seem pretty simple to make every shot perfect, or nearly so. Unfortunately, that's not the case in the real world. We all make mistakes and occasionally miss the bullseye, or even the whole target. If you've developed a sound shooting foundation, as previously outlined, and you throw a bad shot, the best thing to do is forget it. Yes, just forget it, as if it never happened. Go back to your shot sequence and take the next shot. What we have been striving for throughout this book is to teach and reinforce a consistent pattern of executing a good shot. If the foundation has been firmly rooted and well developed, then a mistake is simply your body reminding you that you're human. Deal with it and forget it, and continue making good shots. Trying to overanalyze a mistake, especially on the shooting line, can only reinforce the mistake. For example, if you missed because you broke focus on the target before the release and you think about breaking focus, it's very possible that you'll be establishing that function as the norm, rather than the correct function of maintaining focus throughout the shot sequence. It can also start letting negative thoughts into your consciousness, and that can also set a foundation for subsequent misses. It's the exact opposite of what we discussed in the previous section. If the miss was simply human error, let it go and the next shot should be fine.

Back to basics

If during a practice session things start to deteriorate and despite all good thoughts and intentions, shots are frequently missing some degree of reflection or analysis is required. For a reasonably seasoned shooter, the first things to consider are outside factors. A quick equipment check is in order. Did the nocking point move? Is the sight or rest loose or set incorrectly? Did the plunger freeze or "jam" in the forward or retracted position? Am I using the right arrows for this bow? Doing this not only confirms that the equipment is intact and correct, or reveals a malfunction or change, but it is causing you to stop what you are doing and start over. That alone may solve the problem. Once equipment problems are ruled out, then things that are physically or emotionally distracting need to be considered and addressed. Naturally, illness and lack of adequate nutrition or sleep (more on this later) can take a toll on your performance. Unfortunately, there's usually not a lot you can do to change the condition you're body is in at any given moment. If you're dealing with a practice or casual shooting session, the best course of action is usually to call it quits for the day, and get the food or rest you need and relax. If you're at a match, you'll need a plan B, which we'll get to in a moment. If it's a casual match, and for whatever reason, leaving isn't a good option, then just relaxing and accepting the fact that this won't be your best score may be a viable solution that may alleviate part of the problem. Yes, it's possible that some people can and do rally to overcome physical or emotional deterrents, and only you will know if that works for you by experiencing it. Usually, the more training and shooting you have under your belt, the greater the chance of overcoming that type of adversity. Again, you need to be honest with yourself as to the best course of action for a given situation.

Emotional stress can affect your performance the same way physical stress can. Well-trained and seasoned individuals can actually use shooting, or any athletic endeavor, to override external emotional stresses. That's one reason we used the term "focused" in relation to our shooting. By focusing our attention on the task at hand, it can or should push other thoughts to the background, even if just for the few seconds of the shot, and so allow us to perform to the level of our ability. That level of focus comes only after serious amounts of training and lots of experience and is one of the things that defines a true champion.

Consider the mental rehearsal we discussed in the last section. Once learned, the entire shot sequence may take only a few seconds. If focus can be maintained for those few seconds, the arrow will reach its mark, and the external thoughts cannot enter the consciousness and disrupt the shot. That's why we have gone through the steps in such exhausting detail. That detail is the technique we, or rather our brains, use to focus. Simple? Yes. Easy? No. But that's how it works!

Sometimes we're not dealing with an isolated bad shot, and there's no apparent physical or emotional stress at play. When shots are not hitting where they are supposed to, and we've confirmed that the equipment isn't at fault, we may need to do some self (shooting) analysis. This is when we need go back to basics, literally. Set up your target at a comfortable distance, 10 yards, 10 feet, or 5 feet, it doesn't matter, and review the basic form training we discussed in Chapter 3. One of the best exercises to diagnose and remedy subtle form problems is the "watch the tip of the arrow" exercise we discussed in several previous chapters. Most physical shooting errors are due to some subtle change in form, incorrect shoulder alignment, or lines of tension causing "something" untoward to happen at the moment of release. Even something as simple as a slight change in foot position or slight difference in anchor placement can result in an errant shot or group. Reviewing Chapter 4 on Common Shooting Errors may shed some light on what needs to be addressed. Sometimes, however, the cause may not be apparent to the shooter; that's why it is imperative that another archer, who can see things objectively, observe the archer having problems. Hopefully, any specific form errors will be detected, and the appropriate corrective measures taken. Sometimes the above strategy may reveal the symptom but not the cause; remember this chapter is on the Mental Game.

To cover all the bases

*While uncommon, the possibility of a "hidden" equipment failure must be considered. If you are completing your mental checklist successfully and you are certain that you are doing everything in your shot sequence correctly (that's where knowing your true capability comes into play), then your equipment may be to blame. A slight shift in the nocking point can easily be checked with a bow square, as can a change in brace height. Similarly, a loose sight or rest should be easily identified by visual or tactile inspection. A faulty cushion plunger may be identified by pushing it in and releasing it a few times with your finger and checking for any pressure or binding. Less common is invisible or early limb delamination, where the internal structure of the limb is beginning to separate. The first symptom can be arrows **repeatedly** not going where they are aimed. That occurrence although very rare may have to be considered if all else appears in order. If you honestly believe the bow itself may be at fault, then you'll need to replace it and see if the problem resolves. If this happens during a match or hunting trip and you don't have a back-up bow, your only recourse would be to readjust your aim to compensate for the deviation. **If you do so, proceed with caution, as an early delamination may progress to a frank failure without further warning.**

Target Panic

This term came about or became popular with sight shooters. It was usually manifested by not being able to hold the sight pin or aperture on the bullseye, releasing before the pin was on the bullseye or before the anchor was reached. A particularly troublesome variant was not being able to release the arrow when the sight was centered. While that's certainly a symptom of target panic, it's not a complete definition. Target panic is, in its broadest sense, not being able to control the execution of the shot, assuming the archer is not over-bowed and can draw and anchor comfortably. The underlying psychological cause is always the same – a lack or loss of confidence. The following paragraphs provide exercises that will not only restore the archer's confidence, but will reinforce efficient shooting form. Restored confidence and improved shooting form will work synergistically to get the archer back on course.

Symptoms of Target Panic

- Short drawing – releasing before anchor
- Snap shooting – releasing before a consistent anchor and shoulder alignment are established
- Releasing immediately on target acquisition – as above

- Collapsing – loss of back tension prior to or during the release
- Inability to release the arrow – cannot let the fingers relax enough to allow the string to escape cleanly

Classically, the underlying mental cause of all of the above symptoms has been attributed to the fear of missing the bullseye, or the entire target and it becoming a self-fulfilling prophesy; the result is exactly what is most feared, a bad shot. Emotionally, we, being human, want the next shot to be better, so we try harder, and we, also being human, fall deeper into the panic mode of fearing a miss. If repeated long enough, that symptom becomes the norm.

Depending on the temperament of the archer, target panic, once established, may be the greatest challenge he or she will ever have to face in their archery career. Countless documents have been written about the causes and cures for target panic and some have worked better than others. The following method, while time consuming, has been the most effective, in my experience. Understand that this method is not a foolproof recipe, and that each part may have to be repeated until the desired learning objective has been achieved. In fact, these exercises need to be performed in place of actual shooting and not in addition too shooting. Also, we must assume that the archer is not over-bowed, and actually does know correct form and how to execute the shot.

First, the archer needs to realize that he can indeed anchor and hold the string at full draw and not be required to release. This can be accomplished by drawing the bow either at an empty bale or at something that the archer does not wish to shoot. A brick wall comes to mind, as that would serve only to destroy the arrow, and given the price of arrows, that may be enough of a deterrent. While at anchor, the archer should confirm the exact position on the drawing hand, bow arm, and lines of tension; in other words, he should go through the checklist from the previous section. This holding exercise needs to be repeated enough times that the archer is convinced that the physical aspects of the draw and hold are still within his or her capabilities. For this exercise, obviously no shots are released. The exercise needs to be repeated almost to the point where the archer can no longer tolerate doing it and is convinced, "That's not the problem". If the exercise is being observed by a coach or partner, the coach should notice whether the target panic victim approaches or holds the bow or string any differently when he knows he is not going to release the arrow, as opposed to when he is going to actually fire. It's very possible that when the archer knows he will not be able to loose the arrow, he takes a deeper or firmer grip on the string or anchors slightly differently. While usually not the cause of all the symptoms of target panic, that can very well be a contributing factor and well worth watching for.

After the target panic victim is convinced that he or she can hold and anchor, and that at anchor the alignment is correct, it's time to loose an arrow. This again needs to be done at an empty bale, where there is nothing to "aim" at. As the bale is fairly close, it should also be a single arrow shoot and retrieve exercise; that way the first arrow will not become an aiming point for the next arrow. This removes the "target" from the target panic and also helps preserve expensive arrows. If there is evidence of target panic with this, then the exercise should be repeated with the eyes closed. Once clean shots are achieved, repeat with the eyes open. Again this needs to be repeated until the archer believes, "That's not the problem". A word of caution – if you need to try the closed eye technique, you should not draw and anchor with the eyes closed and then open them and try to release. By doing so, it's very possible that the act of opening the eyes and acquiring the target or bale may trigger the release.

To further reinforce the ability to hold and release in a controlled fashion, the next step requires a shooting partner or coach. Move back to a safe shooting distance. Here the archer will actually release an arrow, but not until after the coach says, "Fire". The archer will draw, anchor, aim, and go through his personal checklist from the last section, and when the "fire" command is given, the shot is released. If the drawing hand follows through properly, great; unfortunately, it may not the first time. If after several attempts, the archer still cannot demonstrate a clean follow-through, then repeat the last step and return to this one during the next shooting session. If this part has been successful, then the archer should be able to return to the shooting line. A minor variation is to have the partner randomly alternate between the fire command and saying "down", meaning not to release the arrow. By doing that, the target panic victim has no way of knowing whether the fire command will be given or not, and must assume that he will not be allowed to release the arrow.

The purpose of this exercise is to let the victim experience or "feel" what a good or clean shot feels like. Once they get that feeling down, they have something to reproduce when firing in earnest.

Two other exercises that have been quite successful for treating target panic are our old friend the "watch the arrow" exercise and the use of a clicker, both described in the first section of this book. The "watch the arrow" exercise shifts the attention from the target to the arrow, and so removes the target from "target panic". That exercise needs to be practiced at the end of every shooting session, and any time the symptoms of target panic appear.

If the above exercises do not control target panic after two or three months of serious practice then the odds are very good that they will not succeed and the only remaining option is a clicker. The clicker forces the archer to reach a given draw length and hold as he "breaks the clicker".

Unfortunately, once an archer has had target panic, there's always a chance that it may return in one form or another. Hopefully, he now has tools in his arsenal with which to re-program his "computer" and restore his confidence. Happily, the converse is also true, once target panic has been beaten the foundation has been laid to beat it again, should it come back. It is usually not necessary to go through the entire sequence, once the foundation has been established. Some archers, myself included, run a few "no-fire" drills before the first real shot of each shooting session. If something doesn't feel right during a session repeating the no-fire drill will set things right in short order!

Can you let down?

A very subtle manifestation of target panic is being at anchor and knowing there is something wrong with the shot and not being able to let down and start over. It could be the shoulder alignment feeling off, the anchor being not quite right, or just the "feel" of the shot being "wrong". It may be something as simple as losing focus on the target for a moment. Once the anchor is reached, or in some cases, before it's reached, the release process, or "launch sequence" has already begun, and you are committed to releasing the arrow. Unfortunately, most archers suffer from this variant of target panic and don't even realize it. (They may just believe that they "should" be able to correct a bad feeling shot, during the draw or at anchor.) While it may not be a real problem for the casual shooter, a serious target archer can and will lose points unless he has trained himself to let down on call. You'll rarely hear a top archer say, "I knew I shouldn't have released that one."

The only way of preparing for that event, which will happen, is to rehearse letting down. During a practice session, you can randomly choose to let down on several arrows. If that is too difficult to do, and it may be, you can use an external stimulus to trigger a let down. That stimulus can be a shooting partner randomly saying, "Don't fire", or a given environmental sound such as a door closing, a phone ringing, anything that doesn't happen too frequently. Whatever you decide on, practice it, so you know you can do it when something "just doesn't feel right". It's a worthwhile skill, and may indeed mean the difference between winning and losing a match or taking what will be a poor shot at game.

Over-thinking

Another malady that plagues some archers is that they over-think themselves into missing. This can have two variations: over-thinking equipment and over-thinking technique. Over-thinking the equipment, also known as equipment envy, is described in the next section. The other variant is over-tuning the equipment to make it even more perfect. Well-tuned equipment can certainly be a joy to shoot and will increase your accuracy. But as we've seen in the chapters on tuning, it need not take a terribly long time to tune, and for most archers, the basics can be accomplished fairly quickly. The advanced tuning generally happens over time, and certainly should not be attempted all at once or by beginning shooters. To put it very simply, tuning to reduce your group size by 1/2" doesn't mean a lot if your basic group size is 8". Similarly, tuning for a perfect shot at 90 meters is of little value if all of your shooting is at 20 yards or closer. Will the former in the previous examples be better tuned? Yes, but will a benefit be derived from such tuning in the cases given? No. The best way to think of this, is that **you can only tune as well as you can shoot**.

Another variant is trying to tune the wrong thing. For example, if you are experiencing poor arrow flight, and are trying to tune the bow to improve the flight pattern, it would be wise to be sure that a poor or inconsistent release really isn't at fault. Similarly, trying to improve an arrow flight by tuning the nocking point position would be useless if you're experiencing fish-tailing (side to side) flights, or using arrows of incorrect spine.

Another over-thinking situation is worrying about technique when you should be shooting. This may sound strange, in light of what we have just discussed, and although not as common as the equipment variant, it does happen. **It's very difficult, if not impossible to focus on the target and on shooting form at the same time.** That's why we place such great emphasis on form in the beginning. Your correct form must be firmly ingrained into the subconscious, so that when it becomes time to actually shoot at a target, our consciousness focuses solely on the point we wish to hit and the form or technique appears reflexive. Sometimes it's necessary to "just shoot". This doesn't contradict the checklist mechanism previously described; as the archer develops, most of the checklist becomes subconscious, and the remaining parts that remain in the realm of consciousness are, or should be, over by the time the focus has shifted to the target.

Another possible "archer's paradox"

In Chapter 15 on Physical Fitness, we discussed the need for adequate nutrition and rest. While not an advisable exercise, and not one to be tried deliberately, it's been documented that some people, especially those who are over-thinking, or rather outwitting, themselves, may perform better when tired, exhausted or even sleep deprived. While seemingly counterintuitive, if we consider that the brain has capacity to do only a limited number of things at a given time, when somewhat resource depleted it should be able to do only the one task in priority, in this case – shooting the bow. Simply put, it doesn't have the resources to go through the extended thought process – it just shoots! In that case the shot may actually be (somewhat) reflexive!

A similar exercise that can be deliberately tried is a speed round. Here, the goal is to shoot as high a score as possible, using correct form, with an unlimited number of arrows in a limited time period, usually 30 or 60 seconds. The timekeeper also acts as an umpire and disqualifies the shooter if there is a serious breach of form, meaning failure to lock in at anchor, flailing or jerking the bow arm, or simply an uncontrolled shot. The purpose of the exercise is not to throw as many arrows as possible randomly into and around the target, but to shoot as many "good" bullseyes as quickly as possible. The mechanism is somewhat similar to shooting in an exhausted or sleep deprived state; as the brain can only focus on one thing at a time, the action in priority is shooting, not thinking. Most shooters enjoy speed rounds as a diversion from the usual disciplined regimen of regular target shooting, not knowing that it's actually reprogramming their brains and making them better archers.

Equipment envy

It is very common today to place too great an emphasis on the equipment or the degree of tuning. With our highly technological and information saturated society there is a strong tendency to believe you have to have the latest and greatest equipment to be successful. Not only this year's model, but next year's model is required to be competitive, or you may feel you must have the exact same equipment that a given pro or superstar uses (a notion fostered by some manufacturers and their ad agencies). Similarly, the equipment must be tuned to very exacting parameters to be at all usable. In reality, for the vast majority of shooters, nothing can be farther from the truth.

First, we'd like to believe the "Pros" have based their selection of equipment on years of experience of what works for them, for their style of shooting and their physical capabilities. More often the case, they are being supported or sponsored by one or more archery manufacturers, and will always be shooting that company's latest and greatest. Secondly the "Pros" got to be "Pros" not by the name or logo on their equipment, but by their innate ability, skill, training and determination. The best shooters will probably win with whatever equipment they shoot, as long as they have had the time familiarize themselves with it and to set it up properly for their shooting style and needs. Finding equipment that's comfortable for you, that performs to your satisfaction and shooting it to the best of your ability will take you considerably farther than getting "next year's model". The simple truth is, most good equipment designed and manufactured in the last 40 years is more than capable of outperforming any archer alive today.

Does this mean you should not be experimenting with new ideas and equipment? Certainly not! There might be a variation out there that will work better for you, either in hardware – your bow, arrows and accessories, or software – your shooting style. *When experimenting, make one, and only one, change at a time and evaluate it over several shooting sessions.*

Your scores and your comfort level should dictate the value of the change:

- A transient change in your scores, either better or worse, means nothing and may just be what has been called the "New Toy Syndrome".

- If your scores show a consistent improvement over time, then the change had a positive effect.

- If your scores show a consistent degradation over time, then the change had a negative effect.

- If your scores remain the same over time, but you feel more comfortable or confident with your shooting, the change had a positive effect.

- If your scores remain the same over time, but you feel less comfortable or confident with your shooting, the change had a negative effect.

Plan B

Otherwise known as the *"what if"* scenario. There are simple mechanical examples, such as what to do if a string or rest breaks or a nockset comes loose. Easy, right? You should have a spare pre-stretched and nocked string and spare rest with you. Most elite athletes have a "Plan B" for shooting problems as well. Despite outward appearances, elite athletes are human, and being such, things can go awry. A broken string or rest will usually cause the elite athlete little more than a raised eyebrow. When shots start missing during an important match like the Olympic games or the FITA World or NFAA Championships (or final match at a local league), and there's no equipment malfunction, what do you do? You go to *Plan B*.

Everyone's plan B or backup plan will be different. It has to be as concrete and rehearsed as everything else we've discussed has been. Simply saying hunker down and work harder or concentrate more won't do it, and actually might make things worse. As we've seen, "working harder" can be more of a detriment than a benefit. Usually when shots start missing during competition, it means something has changed or gone wrong with the shooter's mindset. It may be as simple as forgetting a subtle step in the shot sequence, or as serious as a breakdown in the ability to focus. Plan B is your recovery system. It can be stopping for a moment and clearing your mind by using a quick meditation exercise, or hearing a familiar song in your mind, if that's what works for you. It can be "going back to basics", or changing the tempo of the shot sequence. It typically involves a change of some sort – a break in the action, if you will. It is individual, and must be thought out and rehearsed prior to the competition.

A very simple example for some barebow shooters may be simply changing from a vertical bow to a canted one, or vice versa. One thing I've done in the past was to use a forced cant. Typically, I shoot more accurately with a vertical bow; if things are going wrong, I may draw vertically, cant to about 10 degrees and then release. The extra action of canting forces me to have the extra time to confirm proper a line-up. Naturally, that's not an option for a sight shooter, and might not work for anyone else, but it's one of my "Plan Bs". Another simple example is to do a quick DON'T FIRE drill, if time permits. Go through a full shot sequence or two but don't release. Then when all checks out, repeat the sequence and release.

Warm-up exercises

The simple warm up drill we discussed in the last chapter, if formalized, can serve as a boundary between shooting time and non-shooting time, otherwise known as "everything else". Every athlete has something that establishes such a boundary. It may be simply walking into the range or out on the field, and taking a breath to clear the mind; it may be the stretching exercises we demonstrated, or a combination of several things, as long as it's a real break point to the archer. You're probably doing something like that already, and may not be calling it that. In my competitive days, in addition to a few very basic stretches, I would take three NO FIRE "shots" before loosing my first arrow. That put me in the right mind frame and re-established the shot sequence, and more importantly confirmed the fact that I was in control of the shot. The first loosed arrow hit exactly where it was aimed.

Triggers

No, we're not talking about mechanical release aids but psychological or emotional triggers. We all have them and some work for us and some work against us. If you've ever heard someone say that they can shoot really well in their own backyards or when there are only a few people (usually close friends) at the range, but completely fall apart when "other people" are watching, those "other people" are triggers. Conversely, some people claim to shoot poorly when alone and really start to "show off" when they have an audience. The latter is an example of a positive trigger and one that most of us wish we had; the former is a negative trigger and unfortunately more common and troublesome.

A trigger, for our purposes, is an external stimulus that while having no direct physical contact, does elicit a very real psychological effect that manifests itself by shot placement, or a lack thereof.

Dealing with triggers is not easy. First the trigger or triggers needs to be identified and the effect of the trigger understood before it can be dealt with. The trigger may be a certain person watching you, a coach, a competitor or someone you like (and are trying to impress) or dislike (and trying to impress even more). It may be that formal (or even informal) matches or just "keeping score" are triggers. Some people do their best under pressure and some people fall apart or "crack" under pressure. If you can identify the stimuli, or the "pressure" that works for you and those that work against you, you've completed step one – the easy part.

Next you need to understand what it is about that stimulus that affects you.

- Does shooting a match force you to worry about missing the bullseye or the entire target and by worrying about it, do you do the very thing you're afraid of doing?

- Does wanting to win or out-shoot another person make you try harder and over-work or over-think the shot?

- Do you think more about beating some other person than you do about making the shot?

- Does turning in a bad score make you feel embarrassed that others might think you're a poor shooter?

- Does a bad shot or a few bad shots put you in a downward spiral that you can't recover from?

The above examples have a common thread. The "score" has taken precedence over the shot and the archer lacks the honest confidence in himself that he can make the shot or shots to live up to his self-perceived potential. The solution is simple in theory, but not so simple in practice.

The first step is to acknowledge exactly how good you are and accept that as your current level. You may certainly strive to become better, but thinking you're a 280 NFAA indoor shooter, when you know you're a 220 shooter isn't doing you any good. Better to know where you stand and work on making it better than to lie to others and indirectly to yourself about where you think you are or should be. (Remember the goal setting exercise, earlier in this chapter?) Knowing what to expect and what you are really capable of lets you deal with the occasional less-than-perfect shot, and recover quickly. Even the guy who just shot a perfect NFAA 300 probably had at least one arrow that was just "touching" the edge of the bull!

If having a certain person or people watch you makes you shoot poorly (failing to come to anchor, release prematurely, collapse or whatever the symptom) you might have to ask yourself what your feelings are toward that person which allows that stimulus to have such an effect on you. The standard old coach's response was to "just put it out of your head". That may have been good advice at one time, but again, it's easier said than done. A better approach is to acknowledge the situation and figure out how to deal with it. The solution will be a personal one to you, and there are no pat answers. A simple example: if you're comfortable shooting only around friends, either make sure you have only friends around you when you shoot, or assume that the people around you are your friends and want to see you succeed. Even with fierce competition, that's actually the case more often than not. Certainly making friends with a person, who initially intimidated you will go a long way toward turning a negative trigger into a positive one.

Consider that a great athlete doesn't want you, even as his competitor, to fail, he expects to win. He doesn't care how you're doing; he's thinking about how he's doing! That may sound like a subtle difference, but it cuts to the heart of the matter. If you concern yourself with the task you have at hand, you'll be able to shoot to your potential.

We can take an example of this from competitive rifle shooters. It is said that a beginning shooter is concerned about his overall score; an intermediate shooter is concerned about his score on a particular end and an expert shooter is concerned only about a single shot.

On the other hand, if you have positive triggers, you probably didn't need to read this section at all! The people who just "show off" are those who truly know how well they shoot and are secure in their ability. They take the external stimuli and feed off them, as in working with the high of an adrenaline rush. The old coach's advice to "just block out external stimuli" may work for some folks to one degree or another but sooner or later the external stimuli may break through the synthetic blockade. A better way of handling it would be to accept the external stimuli as part and parcel of the overall experience. Them your mind can gate (block) out the insignificant ones, while using the others to your advantage. The din of spectators may become white or background noises and ignored, while the scrutiny of the officials or your competitors may spur you on to do even better.

The "secret" to making a good shot

By now it should be pretty clear that there really are no secrets to good shooting. It boils down to a solid foundation in shooting technique, good, well-tuned equipment and a confident mental affect. As an archer travels or evolves through his shooting career those three factors should combine to allow the archer to perform at his best when necessary.

If you were to watch any top-level archer shoot, one thing would become very apparent. Champion archers, like champion golfers, tennis players or any other elite athletes will appear very relaxed during the critical moments of their game and their actions appear effortless. Their hearts are pounding, sweat is streaming down their faces and there may be physical exhaustion setting in, but that is all secondary – they remain in control of the action being performed. There's almost a serenity that takes over before and during the critical moments of play. It might seem strange to think about relaxing while holding a 50# bow at anchor, focusing on a target 90 meters away. There's a nasty 10 mph crosswind buffeting you while thousands of people are watching and taking pictures and your adrenaline is pumping, but that's exactly what a champion archer needs to do – and does.

Being able to relax also prevents extraneous muscle activity from getting in the way of the shot. That's why earlier we discussed never using muscle tension or locking any joint while shooting. Relaxing lets you and the equipment do exactly what you and it are supposed to do!

Being able to "relax" comes from the three factors I stated above: confidence, technique and equipment, in that order. Most of us will not be competing in the Olympics or FITA World Matches, but we might compete in regional or league shoots. We may be trying to best an old friend or score a hit on a trophy game animal. **The pressure we feel is not due to the event, but rather to our anticipation of the event.** Being able to "relax" during the shot process, which is a learned skill, will allow you to use the techniques you've learned and exploit the equipment you've tuned. Being confident in your technique and equipment will allow you to relax and that will make the shot appear effortless.

The "secret" is that you don't need to wait for a shot at an Olympic title or a trophy buck to experience relaxing through the adrenaline rush. Once your form begins to solidify spend some time relaxing at anchor. Hold a second or two longer than usual and feel the process. Find the equilibrium between the string pulling forward, its weight on your fingers and the draw of your back countering it. As bizarre as that may sound, the sooner you begin incorporating that into your practice sessions, the sooner you'll be able to get in "the zone" as athletes call it. The moment of relaxation before the sear disengages and the arrow flies to its mark. As you practice, find the equilibrium, enjoy the sight picture and relax!

To sum it up, making your best shot, means doing so by doing as little work as possible!

Teaching and Coaching

Sooner or later someone will ask you for advice, or you'll be in a position to offer it. They may ask a question as simple as which way to move a sight to change the arrow's point of impact, something more complicated like, "Which arrow should I be using" or possibly as open ended as, "How do you aim a bow and arrow?" How you deal with those questions may have a profound impact on a new shooter. An instructor or coach's syllabus is beyond the scope of this book, but there are several principles than can help to make the interaction a positive one for all parties involved.

Understand the question being asked

Using one of the examples above: If someone asks, "Which way do I move the sight to make my arrows hit higher?" The real question could be, "Which way do I adjust my sight to raise the point of impact", or "How do I physically move the sight pin on a new sight I just bought". You could easily have answered the question by saying "move the sight down". A better answer could be "loosen the screw on the back of the sight pin and move it in the direction the arrows are going" – you can always later add "if the arrows are hitting high, move the sight up; if left, move the sight to the left". Instead of giving him merely a factual answer, you covered more bases and gave him a principle that he can remember and hopefully use in the future. In the case of, "Which arrow should I be using", does he mean an 1816 versus a 1916, or Carbon versus aluminum? From there you can see whether the person would like more information and may be really asking "why" instead of "what". "How do you aim that thing?" is really wide open, and you have to evaluate what's going on and answer the question at the appropriate level for the questioner. He may be asking how YOU aim your shots or what should he be doing to aim his.

Another example may be someone asking a question about arrow flight or point of impact. He may be expecting an answer regarding arrow spine or bow tuning, when in fact you, acting as an observer, may see that his bow arm isn't steady or he may be collapsing on the release. The shooter knows something is wrong, but can't see the whole picture; hopefully, you can.

Use of the KISS (Keep It Simple, Stupid) principle

There are long and short answers to everything. As with the example we just used, answer the question asked with meaningful information. Clearly, going into various aiming methods and the differences between one sight and another would be inappropriate, unless of course the guy came back with follow-up questions. It's pretty much a common sense approach.

Patience and pacing

Some people pick up on things faster than others. Both extremes can be problematic. When teaching, you'll need patience with people who don't pick up things as quickly as others, or as quickly as you would like; that's when you'll need to slow down and make sure what you're saying has been digested. Knowing when to press on with an issue and when to let it go is a necessary, but learned, teaching skill. On the other hand, some people just soak up new information and ideas like a sponge; while that sounds great, the teacher may be tempted to do a brain-dump. Archery is, after all, a physical activity, and the motor skills are not learned as quickly as some intellectual facts are assimilated. Sometimes it is necessary to hold back a little and really give things a chance to settle in, to avoid undue strain both physically and mentally.

Don't do a brain-dump

Similarly, if you take on the responsibility of teaching a new person how to shoot, it's best not to do a brain-dump and tell them everything you know about archery in the first hour at the range. As we've demonstrated in the early chapters of this book, start with basic safely precautions, give a brief overview of the equipment, and then introduce one technique at a time. Don't throw the prospective archer into overload. As you see the person grasping one concept, and using it correctly, introduce another. There are no recommended time frames you have to follow. One of the hardest things for a new "coach" to do is to know when to hold back information or tell the shooter he's had enough for one day. We all get excited about what we're doing and the prospect of getting someone new to experience what we have experienced. It gets difficult to remember that what we've experienced took months or years to amass, and we shouldn't try to condense that down to a few minutes or hours.

We have covered a great deal of information thus far and all of it will become valuable at one time or another. A good teacher or coach will know when to employ specific techniques or exercises and when to exclude them. The question then becomes "What does this archer need to correct a specific error or to enhance a specific skill and when should it be presented?"

Encouragement and Praise

While encouragement and praise should be a part of every training session, it must be honest and directly related to what has taken place. The instructor must find something positive about the student's experience, encourage and praise that, and be very specific. Hollow praise is easily detected, becomes worthless, and leads to a lack of confidence in the instructor. Telling a new shooter that was a "great shot" may sound like a good thing to say, but for a beginner, there were probably so many things going on during that "great shot", that the phrase may become meaningless. A better approach would be to comment on the specific point you're working on, or something about the shot that really was great. Saying something like, "Solid anchor, that time" or "Perfect follow-through, now do it again" has much more meaning, due to its specificity, than simply saying, "Great shot".

Working with kids

That's probably a misnomer as in some ways, a novice in any activity might be considered a "kid". However, it should be remembered that children are a special case. They usually have shorter attention spans than adults do and may not follow instructions correctly the first or second time they are given. Also they may not have the physical coordination to accomplish the tasks at all the first time out. If they don't, concentrate on safety and let them play. As muscle strength, coordination and interest develop, you can gradually begin introducing new concepts. Children between 11 and 12 years old can usually grasp the concepts and begin shooting properly. Younger than that, it's more of a game to them, and perhaps it should be. Those ages are of course only guidelines, and it is up to the coach to sense when the child is ready to begin practicing in earnest. The excitement that kids exhibit by simply letting an arrow fly is incredible while the excitement of actually hitting the target (anywhere on the target) has a greater intensity than repeatedly hitting the bullseye has for more seasoned shooters. It would be a terrible mistake to rob them of that experience. After all, that's how most of us got started.

This is the basic method I use when getting "kids" of any age started.

Teaching

1. Make it clear, in the beginning, that there are no options regarding safety. In that regard, it's a "follow the range rules or go home" scenario. That might sound harsh, but we are dealing with weapons, and safety is always the first, sometimes sole concern. Discuss range rules, especially when it's permissible to shoot and when it's not. Make it clear that those rules are not negotiable.

2. Once those guidelines have been established, quickly go over the parts of the bow and arrow and basic nomenclature. Discuss only pertinent details.

3. Next, demonstrate the fundamentals of holding the bow, arrow/string and drawing. But do it at a level they can understand.

4. Start out close. We have 10 yard shooting points off to the side of our regular range. That's usually close enough for most kids, regardless of age.

5. Begin attempting to develop an anchor of some sort. For children, the anchor is usually the most difficult part to learn. Whether it's the fear of getting the arrow or string close to their faces or just being a new position they are not accustomed to, if you can get them to a reasonable anchor by the end of the first session you're off to an excellent start.

(Note that some younger kids will insist on drawing back to their ears, or chest, as soon as you look away. If that happens, they're not ready to get into real "shooting" yet. As long as they are obeying range protocols, let them have fun. When they come to you and want to "shoot better", then they are ready to start learning.)

6. Once there is a semblance of an anchor, the next step is to start "shooting". For the first shot, I tell them to "anchor" and not let go of the arrow until I tell them to do so. That's where a light bow really pays off. I tell them to raise or lower their bow arm so that the arrow doesn't fly over the target or bounce off the floor. Most people are surprised how low they have to "aim". After a few attempts most people get the hang of it, and as we said, some do take longer than others.

7. From there, you basically follow the chapters in the book, adding one component or technique at a time, as their desire and proficiency dictates.

8. For older kids with a little experience under their belts, it also advisable to stick to the fundamentals until they appear to be firmly rooted. It makes no sense to let someone start experimenting before the foundations are established.

9. Basic equipment tuning can take place as skills develop.

Coaching – a brief overview

There is a delineation of when teaching ends and coaching begins, but it's a gray area in most cases. Teaching implies a new beginning, and a learning of the fundamentals. Coaching implies that the basics have been taught and are being used successfully and more advanced topics are being handled. As that happens, the caliber of questions the archer is asking should reflect a level of understanding and not simply curiosity. The new archer should be making logical assumptions and suggestions as to his form and the functioning of his equipment. The "my way or the highway" approach is no longer necessary, nor advisable. By this time, the shooter or archer's individual style has begun to emerge. The coach now needs to work with the archer to develop that style to hone the fundamentals to the archer's physical and mental make-up. Here it becomes critical that the coach let the archer explore variations in technique, and act as an observer to see what the archer can't. The coach needs to understand "form", not only from a textbook perspective, but its underlying ergonomics and bio-mechanics. That way he can see if the choices or style the archer is using will ultimately be beneficial or detrimental. At the end of the day, what we have shown are only guidelines. Every situation is different and a coach needs to see and accept those differences for what they are.

A few additional thoughts

We have discussed, and dissected each facet of shot execution as separate entities in considerable detail. We also mentioned that as the archer develops, in addition to mastering the individual steps, there comes a point where a flow develops from one step to the next. As that is happening teaching has evolved to coaching. The coach needs to take a step back, and not look at the draw or the anchor or the follow-through as isolated pieces. He needs to see the entire shot sequence from beginning to end and ensure that the archer is smoothly transitioning from one function to the next. ***The final step, the follow-through, can only happen correctly if all the previous steps were successfully completed. That's the big picture!***

There may come a time when the archer's ability and desire surpasses the coach's knowledge. At that point, the coach needs to accept the fact that his student now needs to move on and seek more sophisticated instruction. At a local or club level that may be as simple as finding a better or more experienced archer to work with the student, or possibly an archery professional. Seeking out a regional or national level coach or team may be required if the developing archer desires to continue at higher levels. The greatest accomplishment an instructor or coach can achieve is to have someone he's worked with develop into a true champion (on several levels).

A closing note

Archery is practiced today primarily for enjoyment; long gone are the days when the bow was a weapon of war or the only means of putting meat on the table. That may seem like an obvious statement, but it's one that people sometimes forget. The ideas or implications of archery as "Fun" can have as many definitions as there are people shooting bows and arrows. It can range from simply being outdoors, loosing an arrow, watching it fly through the air, and hearing its unmistakable whistling sound to being a means of spending quiet time with friends sharing a common interest or a brotherhood rooted in something almost as old as history itself. Indeed it may be a way for some people to relive a part of the past that bears a special interest or meaning for them. For others it can be the thrill and challenge of competition, whether at a local, national, Olympic, or World level. Whatever the reason, it's something we "want" to do. As with most things that are worth doing, there is a price to pay; the price may be time, effort or the dedication required for achieving a desired level of proficiency. What must be remembered is that when it stops being fun, when the man or woman does not want to string and draw a bow or go to the range and loose a well aimed arrow, if they no longer look forward to it, it's time to give it a rest. The rest may be temporary until the drive or desire returns, or may be permanent, replaced by another more appealing interest. While that may be difficult for some archers to fathom it can and does happen. It's far healthier to let go of something for which the desire no longer burns within us, than to persist in doing it half-heartedly.

Part 4

Memories and Musings

Chapter 17

The Golden Era of Archery

No, this has nothing to do with the Middle Ages. In the US, and possibly around the world, the golden age of archery had its beginnings in the 1950's and was in full swing by the 1960's and 1970's. Archery returned as an Olympic event in 1972, and with the US winning gold medals in both men's and women's events, archery became increasingly popular in schools, colleges and on a grassroots level. It seemed like archery was the fastest growing sport in the United States and for good reason – it was! Local ranges sprang up everywhere, both commercial and private, and high schools and colleges were teaching and practicing archery. Even urban areas had indoor ranges. Some used converted bowling alleys or warehouses; anything with enough space would suffice. My original local range was a converted theater in the basement of an apartment building. Except for the space requirements, an indoor archery range required relatively little expenditure to function; adequate lighting, heating, air conditioning (sometimes) and rest rooms were about all it took from a physical standpoint. The range would need adequate insurance and the building would have to meet local ordinances with regard to adequate exits and capacity planning. From a financial perspective the club or range had to make sure that the income from dues or fees exceeded their expenditures.

Some clubs were much more elaborate, with Pro Shops, lunch counters and lounges for the members to relax in after a match. Our range even had a wet bar and pool table in the back! Many of the local clubs acted more like extended family groups than simply shooting ranges. There was always the usual cadre of people who did the lion's share of the management and/or maintenance, but everyone pitched in.

With the emergence of so many clubs, organized competition, or "matches" became popular. These were either weekly club shoots or leagues similar to bowling leagues; some even used handicapping systems borrowed from bowling leagues. Inter-club leagues and matches were also common. The sense of camaraderie mixed with friendly (and occasionally, not so friendly) competition gave the budding and veteran archers a strong desire to become better shooters.

Also of note during the Golden Era of Archery was the *Teela-Wooket Archery Camp*, originally in Roxbury, Vermont and managed by Mrs. Myrtle Miller, a champion archer dating back to the 1930's and a major proponent of archery education. Mrs. Miller was instrumental in developing junior and senior college level archery syllabuses. TWAC (yes, pronounced *"twack"*) was one of the major centers responsible for coach and instructor training and certification during that time. They later moved their headquarters to New Jersey, and the name was mercifully changed to *The World Archery Center*, but the acronym stayed the same.

The archery manufacturers were in their glory; the major companies were receiving raw materials by the trainloads and were producing hundreds of thousands of bows per year. Many of those bows survive today and shoot as well as their current counterparts. The basic bow riser geometry and limb design by Earl Hoyt Jr. in the 1950's and 60's is still evident in today's top Olympic target bows; only the materials have changed.

Before the compound bow appeared around in the late 1960s at the US Nationals, stickbows, primarily recurves, ruled. Bowyers strove to make them faster, more stable and more aesthetically appealing, if not fanciful. Target bows had evolved to have massive wood risers for inertial stability (and appearance) and long thin limbs for speed and smoothness of draw. Metal-risered bows became popular with target shooters, and several companies introduced metal risers for hunting bows, citing their superior strength and rigidity. Elevated rests, stabilizers, sights and even rudimentary release aids were popular and all of the major archery manufacturers offered their own version of each, or at least bought the rights to re-label another manufacturer's devices.

The only arrows being used by serious archers were aluminum or occasionally fiberglass; wood arrows, usually Port Oxford (*also called Port Orford*) cedar were used only by beginners or those who could not afford "real" arrows. This is not to say that during that period, archery was all function and no form. Some fletchers crafted arrows, including wooden arrows, which were works of art. Fine-lined crests and spliced feathers were often seen (but less often shot), and carried in hand-tooled leather quivers.

By 1972, the compound bow had made a significant impact on the archery market. When they first appeared they were heavy, unwieldy monsters that afforded only modest gains in speed and small reductions in holding weight (typically 20 to 30 fps per given draw weight and 35 to 50% let-off.) Those who tried them didn't really think of them as being that different from the stickbows they previously shot. They were just a little faster, a little easier to hold at anchor and a little heavier to physically hold on the target, pretty much the direction a number of stickbows were going anyway. By the mid 1970's, it was quite common to see equal numbers of archers on a shooting line with hunting bows, target style recurves and both target and hunting style compounds. Each group had sight shooters and barebow shooters. While there was always some kidding between the groups, each archer respected the other's skills and for the most part knew, when all was said and done, it was the better archer and not the equipment that won.

As compound bow technology advanced, the compounds got faster and shorter; the latter made the use of fingers as a means of drawing and releasing the bowstring impossible. Release aids became more popular and more complex. For a while, except for some small pockets of stalwart stickbow shooters it appeared that compounds had completely replaced the recurves and longbows.

Interestingly, in the late 1970's and early 1980's, some pro shops and sporting goods stores were doing all they could to get rid of whatever remaining recurves they had in stock. For stickbow shooters this was a windfall. I was lucky enough to buy several top-of-the-line recurve bows for about a quarter of their previous market price (including a brand new *Hoyt Pro Medalist Super Hunter* for $50); I had no reason to complain about the compound bow revolution!

As archery continued to evolve, the distance between the compound shooters and the remaining stickbow archers increased, in more ways than one. As let-off percentages and speed increased the compound bow became more sophisticated and the differentials in target scores and successful bow hunts widened. However, by the middle to late 1980's, a strange thing began happening. The die-hard stickbow guys were still there and some of the compound shooters started picking up their stickbows again. Possibly because the compounds had gotten too complicated or too easy to shoot or just didn't feel right for some people, there began a resurgence of stickbow archery.

Small mom and pop custom bowyers were springing up and getting deluged with orders. Some of the larger manufacturers saw what was happening and the term "Traditional Archery" was coined.

These companies reintroduced stickbows to their catalogues. Not only recurves, but also longbows, because of their simplicity and more rustic appearance, had a newfound appeal. There was a "Traditional" rebellion against the high-tech world of compound bows and related paraphernalia. Compound shooters, many of whom had never seen, much less shot a stickbow believed that accuracy was impossible with such primitive devices, without the use of sights, mechanical rests or release aids. The new "Traditionalists" rejected almost anything technological, because it wasn't "Traditional", even if what they were rejecting had been part of archery long before the things they were rebelling against appeared. The Traditional rebellion went as far as people going beyond "traditional", whatever that actually meant, and embraced a more primitive style of archery. Primitive archery meant trying to reproduce not only the bows and arrows of Native Americans and early Asian and European cultures, but trying to reproduce the construction methods and shooting techniques as well.

That's the full spectrum of archery we have today. Bows and arrows made with stone knives and native woods to high-tech bows with more moving parts than some cars from the 1960's! Which one is right for you? Only you can answer that question, and that is not the purpose of this book.

What I have tried to do here is give someone with an interest in <u>Shooting the Stickbow</u> the information they need to get started on a long and enjoyable journey. That road can have many twists, bends and detours, but few dead-ends. The road you travel in archery is personal and a matter of choice.

***Just remember that no matter what equipment you choose
– it's still just two sticks and a string. Have fun and good luck!***

The Comanche Bowman Archery Range in Brooklyn, NY c1978

Buying vintage bows:

What to look for / watch out for when buying a used or vintage bow

Basically you look for the same things in a used or vintage bow that you would look for in a new bow. The bow itself has to appeal to you on some level; if it doesn't, there's no reason to look at it in the first place. It has to be something you'll enjoy shooting. Bows built in the Golden Age of archery were made to be shot, and with very few exceptions they should shoot about as well today as the day they were made unless they were pretty badly abused. Of course we're talking about laminated bows. Wooden selfbows from the 1960's and 50's or earlier should always be considered suspect. Wood, no matter how well sealed or finished, can dry out; small natural defects can become big natural defects and result in failure. Examine old selfbows very carefully and draw them slowly and in small increments to confirm their integrity. Any abnormal (non-symmetrical) arching or bending or any cracking noises should be reason enough to retire the bow.

Also produced in the 1950's and early 1960's were bows with metal limbs and/or risers. *Usually made from aluminum alloys, these bows with metal limbs should not be shot or even strung under any circumstances.* While a novel idea for that era, metal fatigue quickly set in and limb failure, occasionally causing injury to the shooter, resulted. Most of these metal-limbed bows were recalled or otherwise taken off the market. Some, however, survived and are seen at auctions or garage/yard sales. Purchase one only if you plan on using it as a decorative wall hanging.

We'll take it for granted that we're limiting ourselves to laminated bows, made from the middle to late 1960's to the present day. It's quite possible to find very good bows at yard sales, garage sales, or estate sales, at very attractive prices – sometimes unbelievably low prices.

Things to look for not only does the bow have to appeal to you, the bow has to be useable by you. Remember we mentioned the two words to keep in mind when buying your first bow – cheap and light. A 1970 Bear Super Kodiak in excellent condition for $25 might be great find, but if it has a draw weight of 70# it might not be your best choice for a first bow. If you did find one like that, and at that price, you might want to grab it anyway as it can easily be resold for 10 to 20 times the price you paid for it! Likewise a wonderful old right-handed Hoyt Pro Medalist would be a wonderful find, unless of course you are left-handed! (Honestly, if I found a left-hand Hoyt Pro Medalist for $25, I would probably buy it and give it to a left-handed friend!)

There's use and there's *abuse*

An old bow that has seen considerable time in the field or on the range can show a lot scratches, dents, chips or "dings". These usually will not affect the bow's performance or life span one bit and most can be cleaned up quite easily, if you're so inclined. Naturally, if the bow appears to have been run over by a truck, or chewed on by the family dog, you may want to pass it by.

Of greater concern are cracks, splits and areas of delamination (separations of glue joints), missing pieces, and possibly twisted limbs.

Stress cracks are vertical lines in the fiberglass of the limbs, usually, but not always, near the fade out areas, or closer to the riser (diag 17-1). While these may be common (I have heard some people say that these cracks are "normal" for older bows, and should pose no problems) I would not buy a bow with any cracks in the fiberglass anywhere in the working parts of the limbs. If a bow I've owned for some time develops a stress crack, my first inclination would be to make it a display piece. If, for some reason, I felt I had to use it, I would mark the ends of the crack or overlay the crack with a piece of masking tape and check it frequently for signs of the crack traveling (getting longer). The longer the crack remains the same size, the safer the bow should be to shoot. The difference is that with a bow I own – I should know when the crack first appeared, its initial size, and can make a safe guess as to the outcome. Some people recommend gluing the cracks with some type of cyano-acrylate glue (Crazy-Glue), but such repairs are best left in the hands of a skilled bowyer.

Horizontal cracks in the limb fiberglass are always a showstopper. Examine the cracks carefully; if they appear to be only in the finish, they are harmless. Any horizontal cracks in the fiberglass itself mean the bow should not be strung (diag 17-2).

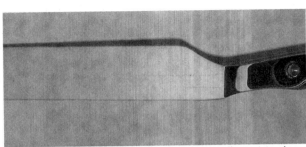

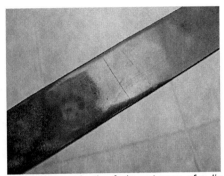

17-1 Two stress cracks in the fiberglass adjacent to riser and a faint one in the fade out area of a limb. These require close attention and if they appear to lengthen, the bow must be retired (left).
17-2 Horizontal crack in a fiberglass limb

Very mild hazing (lightening) in the fade out area

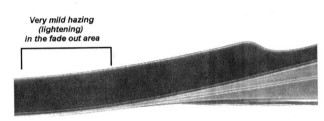

Glass silvering or "crazing" is typical on well-used dark colored fiberglass limbs, and while typically harmless, should be watched for signs of progression to frank stress cracks (diag 17-3).

17-3 Crazing just distal to the fade outs is typical on older bows and not necessarily cause for concern.

Separations and delaminations are exactly that, glue joints that have or are beginning to come apart. Under no circumstances should you try to shoot a bow with any evidence of impending or frank delamination. A greater problem is that many times the separations are hairline and cannot be seen with the naked eye. Worst case is when a delamination begins at the bow tip and involves the string nocks. When the bow is unstrung, the separation may be virtually invisible, but when placed under pressure, a slight separation occurs. Not only can this progress to a total limb failure, but before that happens, the separation can form a sharp or jagged edge that can sever the string loop.

In diagram 17-4, we have the beginnings of fiberglass separation from the wood core near the string nock. While prudent to retire this bow, it may in fact be repairable. The following is a technique I've used on a few bows with good results. You'll have to decide if it's worth the risk to the bow and possibly you!

1. Clean the area as best you can.
2. Apply thin or standard viscosity cyano-acrylate (Crazy Glue) to both sides of the separation, getting as much between the halves as possible.
3. Clamp the parts together. In diagram 17-4 (center), I'm using a hemostat, available at most surgical supply or fishing tackle shops, but any type of appropriately sized clamp will work.
4. Allow the glue to cure at least overnight, but longer is preferable.
5. Apply a coat of thick or "gap-filling" Crazy Glue over the edges of the separation. Clamping may not be required for this step, but it couldn't hurt!
6. Allow the new layer to cure; again longer is better.
7. Sand the hardened thick Crazy Glue with fine sandpaper.
8. Apply a coat of finish to seal the repair. I use Tru-oil, which will be discussed in a later section.

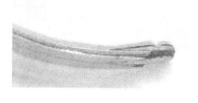

17-4 Beginnings of a limb delamination. The "belly" fiberglass is pulling away from the maple core (left). One method of repair, as described in the text, (middle) and the finished repair (right).

While rare, a total limb delamination can occur (diag 17-5).

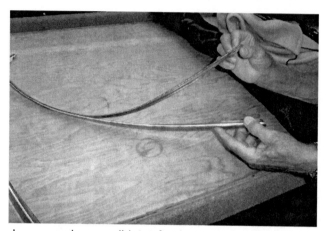

17-5 A nearly full-length limb delamination in a new takedown bow. While rare, it does happen. Happily the bowyer replaced the entire bow in a matter of days.

The best you can do with a used bow is to give it the best visual inspection you can, and ultimately trust your intuition. The most common reason for a delamination, other than poorly constructed or "dry" glue joints is exposure to extreme heat for extended periods of time. Bows that are stored in hot attics or left in car trunks on hot days are prime candidates for these types of failures. Some people have recommended filling the separations with glue and clamping the limb together. This practice needs to be avoided at all costs, as the possibility of limb failure and injury is still too great and as with stress cracks, their repair needs to be left to those with the appropriate skills and experience.

Broken or missing parts can also be problematic. Naturally, 1/4" of wood missing from the back of the arrow shelf is a little less troublesome than 1/4" of wood or overlay missing from the string nock area. Again, use your common sense to decide.

Fiberglass splintering anywhere on the limb, while it may or may not be a sign of impending failure, may present a potentially hazardous condition. Fiberglass splinters are quite sharp and quite small and very painful if they find their way under your skin. Some people can and do sand these away, and retouch the bow with finish, but unless you are very comfortable working with fiberglass, splintering is a good reason to pass on a bow. I spent a few hours, some years ago, removing fiberglass splinters from my thumb, after a few fibers came loose from a bow I was trying to repair. *Experience is a wonderful teacher!*

Twisted limbs are typically caused by exposure to excessive heat or storing a bow vertically against a wall, resting on one end (diag 17-6). Limb twists may not be a reason to pass on an otherwise good bow, for several reasons. First, more than one Olympic champion has competed and won with twisted limbs (bow limbs, that is; I can't speak for any physical issues the individual shooters may have had). Unless the twist is severe enough to allow the string to come off the side of the limb and doesn't appear to be progressing it usually won't affect the shootability or accuracy of the bow. Second, most limbs can be "untwisted".

17-6 Twisted limb on the author's Hoyt 5PM. The first picture shows a slight twist to the left while unstrung. Once strung (right) the twist is more obvious. This bow is perfectly safe to shoot and typically makes the author look good!

Fixing or "bumping" a twisted limb

With the bow unstrung, the procedure is to twist or "bump" the limb in the opposite direction of the initial twist (diag 17-6). This may have to be repeated several times until the limb remembers the correct position. Some stubborn twists can be coaxed back into shape by gentle heating with hot tap water or heat from a hair dryer during the bumping process. Again, several attempts may be required to convince the limb to return to straight.

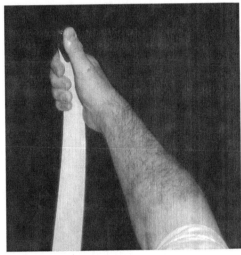

17-7 "Bumping" a limb to correct a twist, as described in the preceding text.

Another, albeit less common, reason for limbs twisting is uneven string nock cuts. If the nocks are not symmetrical the force of the string can twist the limb. This should be more common with new bows than with vintage ones as it would have been detected earlier on and remedied, one way or another. The only remedy for this is to reshape the nocks with a small circular or "rattail" file. As before, if the thought of filing down part of a bow troubles you, it should be left to the professionals, or you should pass on the bow.

Interestingly, some Olympic/FITA type risers have been known to be less than straight, making the limbs appear twisted to an untrained eye. This prompted the manufacturers to build lateral limb adjustment mechanisms into some of the higher-end risers' coupling mechanisms. (This was more evident before manufacturers understood stress relieving aluminum risers.) While not recommended, the lateral adjustments could also be used to correct recalcitrant limb twist and therefore cover a multitude of sins.)

I have a prized rosewood-risered Hoyt Pro Medalist target bow from the early 1970's, with a slight twist in the lower limb that has resisted all attempts at remediation. The bow, despite the twist, has no difficulty forgiving any flaws in my form and places arrow after arrow in the bullseye, and will probably continue to do so for many years to come.

eBay

Today the most common place to find used archery equipment, not only bows, but arrows, quivers and just about anything else, is eBay. As we said, most bows from the Golden Age of archery were made to be shot, and so a great many are still around to be used by the next generation or generations of archers. The popularity of eBay coupled with the number of vintage bows still in existence has made a number of excellent bows available at exceptional prices. Some vintage bows can be purchased for slightly more than the original retail price; that's a bargain considering the inflation we've experienced over the last 30 to 40 years. Naturally, bows with collector value will draw a higher selling price than the more common models, but a lot of the more common models will perform as well and sometimes better than the "collectibles" at a fraction of the cost.

Basic eBay considerations

1. Know what you're buying, if possible. Very rarely with there be only one offering of a particular model. If you decide to go the eBay route, start looking over the offerings and find one that suits your fancy. Check for similar items over a few weeks or months, if you have the time. If you have access to more experienced archers, ask them about the models you're considering. The final auction prices are usually fairly consistent; the more times that model is listed, the lower the subsequent prices – simple supply and demand.

2. Ask the seller questions. Often the seller is an archer or has some knowledge of the item he's selling, but many times they don't. They may have bought the item at an estate or garage sale, and know only what's written on the bow. Ask very specific questions and be very clear in your statements. "*Are there any stress cracks*", may not mean anything to someone who has only seen a bow (any bow) for the first time a few days before they opened the auction. However, asking – "*Are there any cracks or long vertical lines on the flat parts of the limbs*", might give you a better answer, as you have given the seller something specific and understandable to identify. If you are uncomfortable with the reply or get no reply at all, it's probably safer to pass on that auction.

3. Understand that eBay is a blind auction no matter how well the seller describes the item. You cannot personally inspect the item before you bid on it. If that's bothersome, then eBay isn't going to work for you.

4. Most auctions state the item is being sold "as is". That means once you've won it, and paid for it, it's yours unless the item was seriously misrepresented. Some sellers, especially if you have communication with them before the auction will offer a buy back or refund option. Those are rare, but are the safest, as you have a way out if you're not satisfied. If you use a credit card to pay for your purchase you may have other options for disputing the charge, however you should confirm your rights with your credit card company first.

5. Check feedback references: If the seller has more than 2 to 3% negative feedback replies, echoing the same sentiment, especially if they are recent, pass on the item unless you are willing to take the risk.

6. Bid only what you feel the bow is worth to you.

7. As a courtesy to your fellow bidders and the seller, don't bid on an item you don't intend to buy.

My personal experience with eBay has been very favorable. Most people I've dealt with have been very honest and have tried to make a fair transaction. Use the same common sense approach you would with any purchase and you might walk away with a good bow at a good price and a good experience.

Now for the downside: With the increasing popularity of "traditional archery" and the proliferation of the Internet, the rules of supply and demand can work against the vintage bow buyer. As more people realize that the older bows shoot every bit as well as their new counterparts and some of the old-timers who have been out of archery for a while return to the sport, the older bows are becoming more in demand. Therefore the prices may go up. As for current production bows on eBay, most of the people bidding on them already know the retail or street price of the item, so the eBay winning prices are only a few dollars less than the store or mail order price, if that much.

There are other on-line auctions for archery equipment, and a check of any of the standard search engines, such as Google (www.google.com), should yield a few. Many archery web sites have "Trading" forums, where members buy, sell and trade their used equipment (see appendix C).

As has been discussed before, if an older bow, or one of undetermined age or manufacture is chosen, a new string made of B-50 Dacron should be obtained. Dacron will be safe for any bow, and mandatory for older "vintage" ones.

Refinishing an old bow

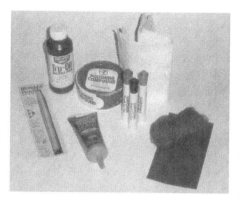

17-8 Collection of things you'll need for most touch-ups and refinishing jobs.

Quick tutorials for making old bows look new

The amount of time and effort you want to spend on a bow to enhance its appearance depends on how important its appearance is to you. Some folks take great pride in keeping their equipment in pristine condition. Others regard the bow as a tool, to be kept in good functional condition and could care less about its appearance. I'm of the feeling that while scratches and dings may add character to a bow, bows generally look better when cared for both functionally and aesthetically. The following paragraphs are the steps I take to rejuvenate a tired bow.

Finished wood bows
Bows with gloss finishes can be treated like fine wood furniture.
If there is nothing seriously wrong with the bow, wiping it with a damp cloth to remove surface dust or dirt, followed by air drying and an application of furniture polish such as Pledge, is usually sufficient. Slightly more protective and longer lasting would be a coat of paste floor wax, followed by buffing with a soft cloth.

For minor surface scratches and surface wear and tear, light rubbing with fine white polishing compound (available at auto supply stores) also followed by a coat of paste wax has been known to work miracles. For deeper scratches in wood, sometimes furniture touch-up markers can work. Guardsman has a set of three markers that can match a multitude of colors and grains. Cover the scratch with the marker and quickly wipe off the excess (diag 7-9).

17-9 All that's needed to rejuvenate most tired looking bows is a can of polishing compound, paste floor wax, paper towels and a little time (left). Wood touch-up markers by Guardsman (right)

Matte finished bows should be wiped down with a damp cloth. The use of any furniture polish may leave a glossy residue. Scratches can be camouflaged with furniture markers as above.

Here's an example of an old Damon-Howatt Del Rey target bow from the early 1970's I recently purchased on eBay. The bow was structurally sound and in good general condition. It did, however, show the effects of considerable use and long term storage (diag 17-10a). The arrow rest, clicker, strike plate and leather saddle were showing their age and were removed (diag 17-10b).

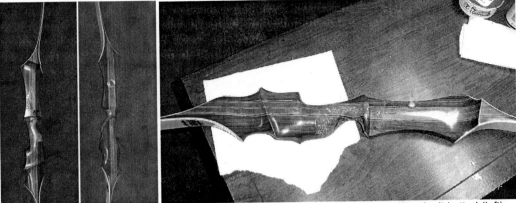

17-10a Damon Howatt Del Rey Target bow – direct from eBay. Not bad, but we'll make it better! (left)
17-10b Del Ray with lots of glue residue to be removed (right)

The glue residue was removed with Orange-Glo furniture cleaner and a bit of elbow grease. The entire bow was then rubbed out with polishing compound and a coat of Minwax dark floor wax was applied. Except for the sight and clicker mounts, which I decided to leave on, as they appeared professionally installed, the bow now looks about as it did when it left the Damon-Howatt plant in Yakima, Washington, in the 1970's. The total time invested was approximately two hours (diag 17-11).

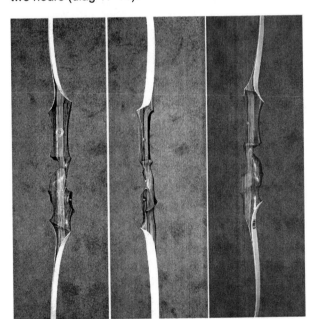

17-11 Del Ray fully restored to near factory-like condition.

If there are serious scratches, dings or scrapes, you have several options. You may be able to refinish the bow yourself, if you're familiar with woodworking, or you could send it out to a professional bowyer for refinishing. Most charge between $100 and $200 for a complete refinishing job, depending on the type of finish you want. Typically a high gloss finish will be more expensive than a matte finish, due to the amount of work and care required to achieve a mirror-like finish. As always, if you plan on going that route, get references first. Being able to see the bowyer's work first hand is always a plus.

If you plan on trying it yourself, this is a method I've used successfully.

You'll need a few sheets of 200, 400 and 600 grit wet and dry sandpaper, some rags or paper towels, a bottle of Beechwood Casey's Truoil (available at most gun shops and sporting goods stores), paste floor wax, and a little time.

If the bow has multiple problem areas, it's best to do one at a time. Start with the lightest grit sandpaper that will effectively remove the scratches or blemishes. Keep the sandpaper wet, to prevent clogging of the abrasive surface and ease cleaning of both the paper and the bow. Usually, 400 grit is sufficient, but really deep problems may require 200. Sand out the defects, and smooth out the area with the finer grits. I generally sand in the direction of the wood grain. If you reach bare wood, feather or taper the area as best you can. It won't be perfect, but the other option is to strip the entire riser or bow, followed by a full refinishing. You may be able to remove the finish between two lines of demarcation, such as a lamination line or joint. That way the line becomes a break point and the change from the new to the old finish less apparent. Once you've smoothed an area, wipe it clean and let it dry. Apply the Truoil with a lint-free cloth or cotton applicator (Q-tip). The Truoil is self-leveling, so it's pretty hard to mess this up. If you did have to go down to bare wood, apply the Truoil a little more heavily, as it will have to soak in and fill the pores. Let it dry for 24 hours. Lightly wet sand the area with 600 grit paper and apply another coat of Truoil. Repeat the process, using progressively lighter coats, until the pores are filled and the desired finish is achieved. Usually three to four coats will be enough but the more coats you apply, the deeper the finish, and the more protective. When you're happy with the results, go on the next area (diag 17-12).

17-12 Spot refinishing; This bow had a 1/2" area of it's original finish scraped off, near the front of the sight window. Feathering the finish with steel wool and several coats of Truoil have restored it to a near new condition.

Truoil is not the toughest finish you can use but it's practically foolproof, can be touched up easily, and gives an excellent finish. Its natural finish is glossy, but if a dull or more matte finish is desired, lightly rubbing the bow with 0000 steel wool will yield the desired effect. Another option is using Beechwood Casey's Stock Sheen. Again, if after dulling the finish, you decide you liked the gloss finish better, a very light reapplication of Truoil, usually rubbed in with your finger tips will restore the gloss – foolproof! When done, let the bow cure for about a week and apply a light coat of paste wax to protect your work.

Note that since Truoil is an "oil", it may interact with some woods that have an abundance of natural oils, especially if they were not fully dried first. This is particularly true with some of the more exotic woods. As with any finishing process, when in doubt, test it on a small area first. If it doesn't dry to the touch in 24 hours, it's not an appropriate finish for that wood and one of the synthetics may be a better choice.

If you decide that you need or want to refinish the entire bow yourself, then the same principles apply. Start by sanding the entire riser down to the wood (diag 17-13). With fiberglass limbs, I would just smooth out the existing finish and apply a new finish over it. Truoil is more than adequate for both the wood riser and fiberglass limbs, but if you are doing the whole bow, you may want to consider a more durable finish such as Polyurethane or Spar varnish. The urethanes and varnishes can be brushed on, but are typically sprayed on for the best results (17-14). They are much more durable than the oil finishes, but more difficult to apply evenly. If you have experience with these, or know someone who does, it's certainly a viable option.

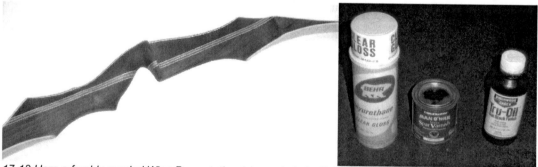

17-13 Here a freshly sanded Wing Presentation 1 is ready to be finished (left).
17-14 Polyurethane and Spar Varnish provide the most durable finishes. Truoil, while not as durable can yield excellent results, especially for first-time refinishers (right).

If there are decals (manufacturers' logos) or writing (serial numbers, draw weight, length or an inscription form the manufacturer) on the limbs or riser you wish to preserve, simply sand around them. You'll have to "feather" or taper the old finish around the decals or inscription to have it blend into the new finish as cleanly as possible. The blend may not be perfect, but the more time you spend feathering the old finish, the better it will look.

If the decals are peeling or damaged, you may need to sand them off completely. There are several dealers on the Internet who carry reproduced decals for some of the more common bow lines. They may be found through Internet searches or by visiting some of the archery web sites listed in the appendix.

Unwanted sight screw holes

Many vintage bows were equipped with screw-on bow sights by their original owners, not necessarily a bad thing, especially if you plan on using the sight that came with the bow. However, if you don't plan using it or it has already been removed, it might not be so great. In either case you're now left with two or more holes you may not need.

Note: While screw holes in the riser may diminish the collector value of a specific bow, they are nothing to be concerned about with regard to the bow's shootability. Screw holes in the limbs or near the fade-outs, however, are of greater concern as they may lead to limb splitting. While not a complete showstopper, caution should be exercised before using the bow. I would be very careful about shooting a bow in that condition.

To repair screw holes, you may simply opt to purchase new brass round head screws of the appropriate size and screw them in (17-15a). Not only will that provide a neat appearance, but it will leave you the option to reattach the sight later if you so desire.

The other option is to fill them with wood filler or *"Plastic Wood"* available at most hardware stores and do a "spot refinish". Clean out the holes as best you can and force the wood filler into the holes leaving a slight bump over the opening. Allow the filler to dry over night, and then lightly sand it flush to the surface. Careful application of matching wood stain or furniture touch-up markers followed by a drop of Tru-oil or other finish will make the holes all but disappear (diag 17-15b).

17-15a Brass screws make unused screw holes look neat (left).
17-15b screw hole on the face of a riser can be filled with plastic wood filler. A little work with a furniture touch up marker will make this all but disappear (right).

Metal risers

For magnesium-risered bows that have a few chips in them, it's usually best just to leave them as character marks. You can certainly use touch-up paint if you can match the color close enough for your liking. For primary colors, a felt tip pen can usually camouflage the offending marks. I have refinished several magnesium risers simply by removing any detachable parts and using a paste type paint remover following the directions on the container. Once completely cleaned the riser can be sprayed with a coat of primer and then the color of your choice. Automotive spray paints and touch-up paints are available in hundreds of colors, and a truly personalized bow can

be made for very little time and effort (diag 17-16). If you decide to do this, please read all the directions and cautions on the paint containers carefully and understand them before beginning, especially those concerning proper ventilation. Most aerosol spray paint fumes are toxic if inhaled for any length of time. Two additional notes: Make sure the primer and paint(s) are compatible and be careful if you sand or file magnesium risers. Powdered magnesium is quite flammable.

17-16 Bear "C" magnesium riser, refinished with Rust-oleum spray primer and gloss white paint.

Aluminum risers are generally anodized or powder coated (with a low temperature process), not painted, and that's best left to the professionals. While they can be painted, care is needed during surface preparation to ensure proper adhesion.

The following pages show pictures of bows and a few arrows my collection that were popular during the Golden Age of Archery, specifically from the mid 1960's to the mid 1980's.

BOWS

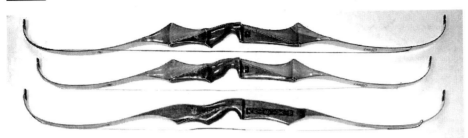

17-17a Bear Archery target bows. Tamerlane HC-300 in 70" length and a rare 63" field model (top and middle) and Tarter in 66" length (bottom).

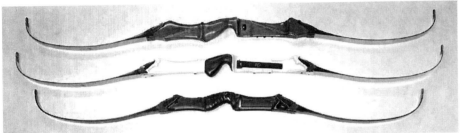

17-17b Bear Takedown Archery bows. "C" Riser wood and magnesium bows in 70" lengths (top and middle) and "B" riser Hunting / Field bow in 64" length (bottom).

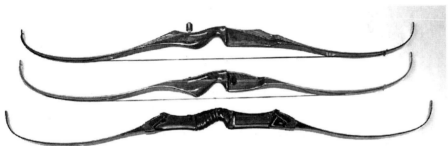

17-17c Bear Archery hunting bows. Super Kodiak (top) and Kodiak Hunter (middle). The 64" Magnesium-risered T/D bow easily fits into the hunting category as well as the target category!

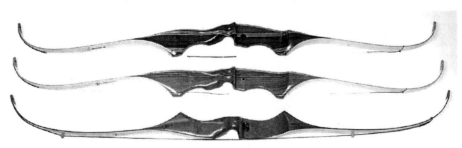

17-18a Ben Pearson target bows. Lord Mercury (top), Lord Sovereign (middle) and Javelina (bottom). These are all 66" models.

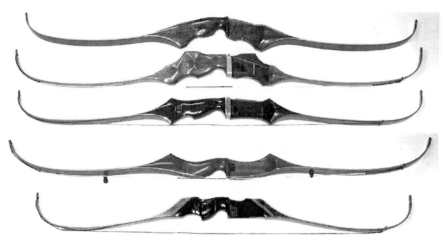

17-18b Ben Pearson Hunting bows. (top to bottom) Mercury Hunter, Marauder T/D, Silencer T/D, Javelina and Raider. Note that Ben Pearson and several other manufacturers used light colored fiberglass on bows under a given weight (40# for Ben Pearson) and dark colored fiberglass for bows over that weight.

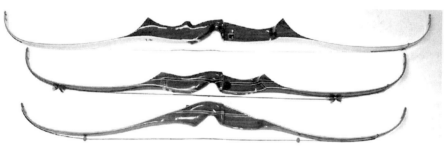

17-19 Browning bows (top to bottom) Monarch target bow, Explorer II and Cobra II hunting bows.

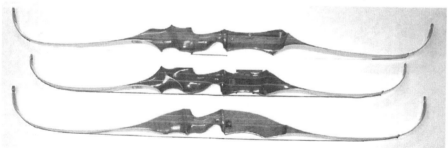

17-20a Damon Howatt/Martin target bows. Del Rey in 70" and 62" (field bow) lengths (top and middle) and Monterey in 66". Damon Howatt Archery merged with Martin Archery in 1976. While most of their recurve bows now carry the Martin name, they are still individually hand-made in the same Yakima, Washington Damon Howatt plant, by many of the same people.

17-20b Damon Howatt Hunter c1975 and Martin Hunter c1995. Martin Lynx T/D bow in 66" length (The Lynx is a compound riser fitted with recurve limbs.

17-21 Herter's target bows. Sitka (top) and CV-17 Match (bottom).

17-22 Howard Hill and Hill style longbows. (top to bottom) Hill Redman with Yew core, Tembo, Big Five with bamboo cores. Ben Pearson Pro Staff 5000. Jeffery Tradition and the R/D Trophy.

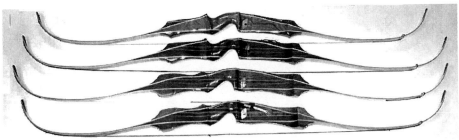

17-23 Hoyt target bows. (top to bottom) 3PM, 4PM, 5PM and 6PM.

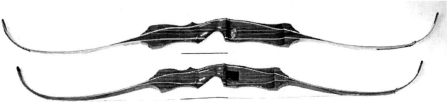

17-24 Hoyt 70" 5PM Target bow (top) vs. 62" 5PM Pro Hunter hunting bow. The only differences between the two bows, other than the length are the glass color (white for target and green for hunting) and that this particular Hunter model was ordered without an adjustable rest.

17-25 Wing Archery target bows. (top to bottom) Presentation II T/D, Presentation I, White Wing and Swift Wing.

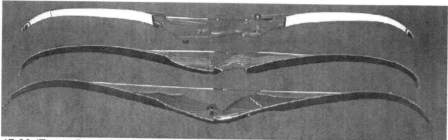

17-26 (Top to Bottom) Black Widow model 1225 c1968, Jack Howard Gamemaster Jet c1974 and Gazelle c1975. (The Gazelle was one of a few bows made by Bob Morse a friend of the author. The Gazelle was also made in the 1970's.)

ARROWS

17-27 Bear Magnum aluminum arrows

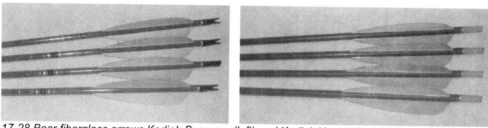

17-28 Bear fiberglass arrows Kodiak Supreme (left) and Kodiak Hunter (right)

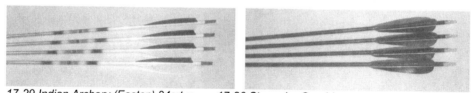

17-29 Indian Archery (Easton) 24srt-x   17-30 Stemmler Graphlex arrows

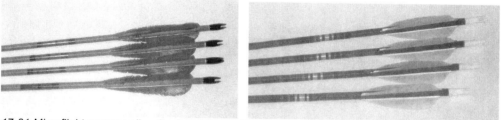

17-31 Microflight arrows yellow (top) and Bear Microflight green target arrows (bottom)

ARROW RESTS Past and present

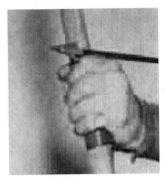

The idea of an arrow rest is not new, although the materials have changed over the years (diag 17-32). After a while it became apparent that a more consistent and less painful alternative was warranted. (Shooting an arrow resting on your knuckle typically led to feather cuts as the arrow flew by.) A simple shelf could be cut into or glued onto the riser (diag 17-33).

17-32 The first arrow rest

Some bows had a grip section that was larger in diameter than the main body of the bow, and acted as a shelf (diag 17-34). This was and is still common with one-piece fiberglass youth bows. As early as the 1950's, archers became creative in the use of arrow rests. A number of bows appeared with shelves above the grip area; these were typically covered with pieces of leather or natural or synthetic fur or even Velcro and fondly referred to as "rugs" (diag 17-35).

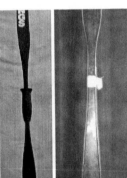

17-33 Narrow shelf on a Howard Hill longbow (left)
17-34 Solid fiberglass bow with grip "rest" and an old ambidextrous laminated bow with an arrow "shelf" fabricated from a piece of Styrofoam and masking tape (middle two).
17-35 A Velcro "rug" on a relatively flat shelf (Browning Explorer II). While functional, not the best configuration possible. Unless the arrow angle is very steep (high nocking point), there'll be too much arrow to shelf contact right).

Soon after, archers realized that while perfectly functional, the "shelf" could be improved upon. A radiused (curved) shelf gave less arrow-to-bow contact and so, cleaner and faster arrow flight. To improve on this, some archers placed a wooden match stick or similar item under both the "rug" and strike plate. This produced a high point and reduced the arrow to bow contact (diag 17-36).

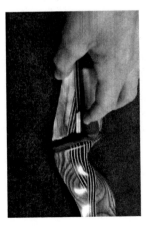

17-36 A properly radiused shelf on a SKY Sky Hawk hunting bow. If you look closely you'll see there is a slight "bump" under both the rug and strike plate to minimize arrow contact (left). Two match sticks positioned under the strike plate (right).

The problem with a shelf, radiused or flat, in addition to more arrow contact than necessary, was that there was no "give" to absorb variations in finger pressure at release. Several innovative ideas arose, both commercial and home-brewed.

Some of the more popular commercially available and homemade rests included:

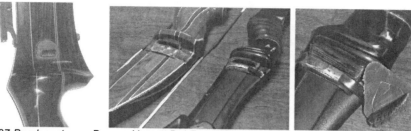

17-37 Brush rest on a Damon Howatt Del Rey (left)
17-38 Home-made feather rests: on a Jack Howard Gamemaster Jet and a Bear "B" magnesium-risered T/D bow (middle). Note that for this to work, a right handed archer needed right wing feathers and a left handed archer need left wing feathers, so the curvature of the feathers held the arrow in place on the rest.
17-39 Close-up of the feather rest (right).

Probably one of the most efficient and best shooting rests were the original Hoyt Pro rests. (diag 17-40) The Hoyt Pro rest is no longer being manufactured, but close approximations are the Hoyt Super Rest and Neet Pro rest (diag 17-41).

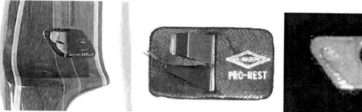

17-40 Original Hoyt Pro Rest on a 4PM Pro Medalist (left)
17-41 Neet Pro Rest and Hoyt Super Rest (middle and right)

A similar idea was the Bear Weather or J-2 rest, which incorporated some of the same features, but was a one-piece affair and made from a thicker rubber-like plastic (diag 17-42). Several other manufacturers released similar designs.

Soon after, the idea of less arrow contact became increasingly important, and the Flipper rest and Springy rests were designed and patented (diag 17-43 and diag 17-44). The flipper rests could be shot with or without an additional plunger button, originally called a Burger Button after Olympic archer and National champion Vic Burger (diag 17-45). That idea has remained virtually unchanged over the last 40 years. The flipper rests of today are more adjustable and the "Burger" buttons more refined and precision engineered than those of the 60's and 70's, but the theory remains the same (diag 17-46).

17-42 Bear J-2 rest (left)
17-43 The Springy rest is screwed into the cushion plunger bushing (middle)
17-44 Flipper II rest on a custom hunting bow and Bear Magnetic rest on a Bear Tamerlane (right two pictures)

17-45 Original "Berger Button" cushion plunger
17-46 Current style cushion plunger (Cartel)

A more recent innovation is the NAP Centershot Flipper rest. The body of the rest screws into the cushion plunger bushing and uses a flipper rest head with a built-in, non-adjustable, pressure plate. The degree of center shot is adjusted by simply turning the body of the rest clockwise or counterclockwise, and repositioning the head (diag 17-47).

Variations on the theme are the single and dual pronged or forked rests. They attach to the riser, usually through the cushion plunger hole, and have horizontal and vertical pressure arms to keep the arrow in place and yield to shooter indiscretions (diag 17-48).

17-47 NAP Centershot flipper rest on a Hoyt Radian riser (left)
17-48 Olympic style rest (Cavalier Free Flyte Elite on a Hoyt Aerotec riser) is basically a very tunable flipper rest (right).

Arrow rests need not be store bought. In addition to the feather rest, brush rests were easily made from old (or not so old) toothbrushes (diag 17-49). Some archers even made finger type rests from plastic material such as plastic milk cartons or other plastic containers (diag 17-50).

17-49 Toothbrush rest made from a worn toothbrush and held in place with double-sided tape. The rest is used in conjunction with a regular strike plate. This type of rest can also be mounted horizontally with the arrow lying on the side of the bristles (left).
17-50 Homemade plastic "finger" type rest made from a sample credit card and double sided tape. This is a left-handed rest and even has a "pressure" flap (right).

Chapter 18

The Life and Legacy of Earl Hoyt Jr., the Father of Modern Olympic Archery
(edited by Harold Rowland)

18-1 Earl and Ann Weber-Hoyt in Las Vegas, 1972.
Photo provided by www.archeryhistory.com

Saxton Pope, Howard Hill, Fred Bear and Ben Pearson are but a few of the men who come to mind when we think of the pioneers of archery in the twentieth century. But to serious target archers, Earl Hoyt, Jr. is the name that stands above all others. Although I've alluded to Hoyt's accomplishments throughout this book, his contributions to our sport warrant a section devoted to his legacy.

Earl Hoyt, Jr. was born in St. Louis, Missouri on June 23, 1911. Sometime during his early years, so the story goes, young Earl bought an arrowhead from a schoolmate and was intrigued by the whole idea of "*archery*". Around 1925 Earl fashioned his first bow from a piece of hickory, using the guidelines in the *Boy Scout Handbook*. It was an inauspicious start for young Earl as that bow and the next failed; neither would return to their original shape after being strung.

The only U.S. magazine in circulation at that time was *Ye Sylvan Archer*, published in Corvallis, Oregon. Not only did it contain articles by top archers and bowyers of the day, but provided sources for bow-making materials and reference books. Earl was thus able to obtain a yew stave and a copy of Saxton Pope's *Hunting with the Bow and Arrow*. Following Pope's instructions, Earl produced his first successful bow. Year's later advertisements for the Hoyt Archery Company would themselves appear in the same magazine (first for custom arrows and thereafter the first Hoyt bows).

In the 1930's, in addition to going to school and working for his father's construction company Earl ran a part-time archery business. But Earl had another interest that competed for his time; music was the other passion in his life and he played banjo and guitar solos at a local radio station. His performances were well received and at the prompting of a station manager, he acquired the more phonetic moniker "Eddie Lake". He subsequently put together a 12-piece ensemble, "Eddie Lake and his Orchestra" whose live performances became quite popular in the St. Louis area. But the "draw" of archery just became too great – by 1938 Earl was, despite his affection for music, designing, building and marketing bows through his own company, if only on a small scale. Coincidentally, Errol Flynn appeared in the classic *Adventures of Robin Hood* that same year and Earl's calling to the world of archery was secured.

Earl Jr. continued his education in Engineering at Washington University and eventually took a position at Curtis-Wright Aircraft (later McDonnell Aircraft). Earl Sr.'s construction company was hurt during World War II and eventually closed, but he kept the archery business alive until his son left McDonnell Aircraft in 1946 to run the Hoyt Archery Company full-time. There were a few lean years but by 1950 business was improving.

The driving principle at Hoyt Archery was unyielding product quality and design. To that end, new bow designs were a priority as were the machines necessary to manufacture them efficiently. Earl's engineering background served him well as he perfected and patented both the riser and limb geometry that has been used for the majority of Olympic-style target bows since the early 1960's. He was one of the first bowyers to use bi-directional limb tapers, meaning that the limbs tapered from the fade-out to the tip in both width and thickness. He also added a slight reflex to the limb roots and dynamically balanced the upper and lower limbs. That combination, along with a slightly deflexed riser, remains the standard today. Hoyt amassed a total of eight archery patents and licensed those patents to numerous companies.

His flagship target bow, the Pro Medalist, appeared in 1961; that bow and its subsequent revisions have won more gold medals than all other target bows combined. Hoyt's top-of-the-line hunting bow during the 1960's and 70's, the *Pro Medalist Super Hunter*, was virtually identical to his famous target bow, just shortened to 62" and given green limbs and higher draw weights.

The Hoyt Archery Company became one of the premier names in the archery industry. Earl remained president of the company until it was sold to CML in 1978. He stayed with CML as Vice President in charge of Research and Development and all-around public relations. Easton Archery bought the CML property in 1983 and retained Earl in his previous position. In 1989, Earl left Easton and opened SKY Archery. Building on his previous designs, he produced a number of superb target and hunting bows under the SKY name. He also designed and produced several longbows, which are now being sold by Mathews Archery.

During all this time Earl's interest was not simply designing and building bows, but shooting them – he had won several state and regional titles from the 1940's through the 1960's. Naturally, Hoyt spent a lot of time with the top archers of the day to learn more about what they required to meet the needs of championship competition. During this time he met Ann Weber. She had also won several state and sectional titles as well as three national championships. Their relationship became more than professional and the two married in 1971, but not before she had become a World Archery Champion and had added three additional national titles to her resume in both freestyle and barebow divisions. Ann's run of Championships spanned twenty years, an unparalleled feat in the archery community and she was honored by induction into the archery hall of fame in 1972. Earl Hoyt, Jr., whom many believe to be the greatest bowyer, and Ann Weber, perhaps the greatest archer, spent 30 years together until Earl's death in 2001.

In addition to developing the standard for "target" (now referred to as "Olympic") recurves and the methods to produce them, Hoyt was active in all things related to archery. Some of those activities included:

- Serving as Secretary (1940) and President (1941) of the St. Louis Archery Club

- Giving numerous Archery Demonstrations and lectures

- Serving as a member of the Board of Governors of the National Archery Association (1952 to 1954)

- Serving on the Board of Governors of the Southern Archery Association, Missouri Bowhunters, St. Louis Bowhunters, Midwestern Archery Association, and the Board of Field Governors of the NFAA (National Field Archery Association)

- Serving as President of the Archery Manufacturers' and Dealers Association of America (AMADA), later changed to the Archery Manufacturers' Organization (AMO) and more recently the ATA (Archery Trade Association)

- Receipt of the Maurice Thompson Medal of Honor at his induction banquet to the Archery Hall of Fame (1977).

Ann Weber Hoyt dedicated 65 years to the advancement of archery. She shot in over 70 NAA (National Archery Association) Championships, more than any other woman in the organization's history, and was active in the various aspects of the archery industry. Ann Weber Hoyt passed away in April of 2008 after a protracted illness.

Her accomplishments included:

- Winning NAA Championships (1940, 46, 47, 52, 53 and 55)

- Becoming the only woman to win both National Target and Field Championships (1955)

- Winning the International Field Archery Championship (1959)

- Winning the World Archery Championship (1959)

- Managing the US Olympic Archery Team (1984)

- Receiving the NAA's Thompson Medal of Honor (1984)

- Receiving the NAA's JOAD (Junior Olympic Archery Development) Award (1993)

A brief history of Hoyt bows.

- 1931 – At age 20, Earl Hoyt along with his father, Earl Sr., launched the Hoyt Archery Co., a part-time business producing custom wood arrows. Their first ad ran in Oregon's Ye Sylvan Archer.

  - 1938 – Earl Hoyt began designing and building bows.

  - 1939 – Hoyt bows first advertised in Ye Sylvan Archer.

  - 1942 – During the war years, Earl Jr. worked as an engineer

  - 1946 – Earl Hoyt left his engineering position at McDonnell Aircraft and founded the Hoyt Archery Co.

- 1951 – Incorporated the deflex-reflex limb design. Deflex added stability to the bow, while reflex increased performance.

- 1956 – Hoyt Archery developed and patented the first "pistol grip" bow handle and first dynamically balanced limbs on the Hoyt Pro Olympian. Later, a full pistol grip with thumb rest was developed to give the archer a more relaxed interface with the bow.

- 1961 – First wooden Pro Medalist with "Torque stabilizers" introduced with serial numbers PM-*xxxx* (diag 18-2), followed by the series 2, 2PM-*xxxx*, and continued through the early 1970's with the 6PM series.

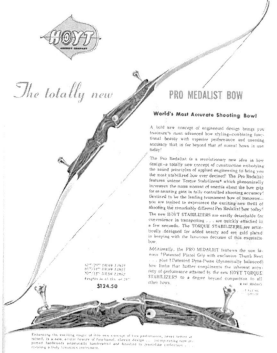

18-2 *Ad for the first (wood) Hoyt Pro Medalist. Notice the price; it may not seem like much today, but this was in 1963!*

- In subsequent years, he patented the "Torque Flight Compensator" and the first truly adjustable arrow rest, called the Micro-Adjustable arrow rest (diag 18-3). It became standard on all Pro Medalist models.

18-3 *The Hoyt Micro-Adjustable rest mechanism (disassembled).*

- The most familiar Pro Medalist design took shape in the 3rd series (3PM-*xxxx*) and Hoyt added additional riser laminations through the classic 5PM-*xxxx* series in the early 1970's. Exotic imported hardwoods were used, and the bows of that era truly were the best of the breed (diag 18-4). I have several Rosewood-risered 4 and 5 series Pro Medalists, whose limbs have turned a cream color with age, adding to the richness of their appearance, and they are indeed prized possessions.

18-4 *The Hoyt Pro Medalist 5PM series, this one with a rare Rosewood riser*

- 1972 – Due to the increasing cost of exotic hardwoods, the 6PM sported resin-impregnated riser woods, and to some, lost some of its classic appeal. Nevertheless, the 6PM series bows shot as well and possibly better than their predecessors did.
- The wooden Pro Medalist series was discontinued in 1973.
- 1972 – First Pro Medalist magnesium T/D (Take/Down) introduced (diag 18-5). These metal-risered bows maintained the same riser geometry and patented limb design as the original wooden PMs.

18-5a First Hoyt Pro Medalist T/D (pinstriped by the author); compare the overall geometry to the 5PM in 18-4

18-5b The above Hoyt T/D (top) compared to the T/D4 / Gold Medalist (middle) and later Radian (bottom).

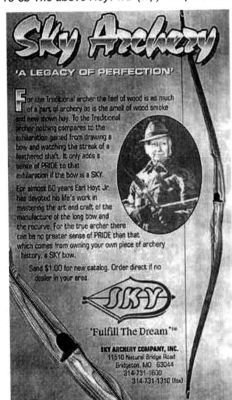

18-6 SKY Archery add

- 1976 – T/D2 was introduced.

- 1978 – Hoyt Archery merged with CML

- 1980 – T/D3 was introduced. There were also T/D2b and T/D3b with various interim improvements. While these bows shot well, the use of different proprietary limb couplings proved troublesome to some archers.

- 1983 – Easton Aluminum purchased Hoyt Archery and subsequently changed the name to Hoyt/USA.

- 1989 – Earl Hoyt created SKY Archery, and maintained the tradition of excellence in recurve and longbow design through his death in 2001. His wife Ann Weber-Hoyt managed SKY Archery through July 2003, when the company was sold to Mathews Archery. (diag 18-6)

- T/D4 (the original Gold Medalist) appeared in the in 1983 and was well represented in the 1984 Olympics. With the advent of Fast Flight strings, some T/D4s suffered from breakage at the throat of the riser grip. Hoyt Archery used high-speed film analysis to locate the failure points and soon after corrected the problem. A new heavier/thicker-gripped riser was later released.

- Subsequent Gold Medalists have retained the thick grip and have remained virtually unchanged since 1992. The heavy I-beam lower riser construction yielded a very rigid riser, resulting in increased speed, especially when coupled with carbon limbs. All of Hoyt

Archery's T/D bows to this point were made from magnesium. Current models have a crinkled finish, as opposed to the earlier smooth glossy paint (diag 18-7) The Gold Medalist is slated to be discontinued in 2007, truly the end of an era.

18-7 The original gloss black finish (top) and more recent crinkled finish (bottom).

- With the advent of the Gold Medalist riser Hoyt Archery introduced and patented the ILF (International Limb Fitting) design, which is now the standard for most Olympics bows in current production (diag 18-8 and 18-9).

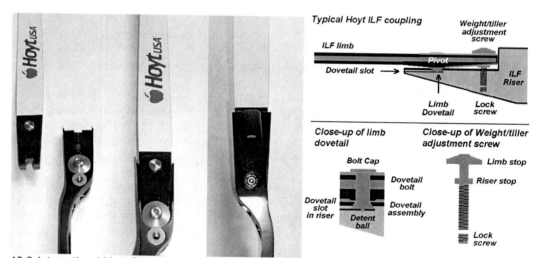

18-8 International Limb Fittings: Apart (left), assembled (middle) and assembled face view (right) on a Hoyt Radian riser and Gold Medalist wood core limbs.
18-9 Schematic of ILF tiller adjustment

- 1993/1994 – Hoyt Archery released the all aluminum Radian riser. Lighter in mass weight, it allowed the archer to customize the balance of the bow better through the use of additional stabilizers. The Radian risers had a much smaller grip area than the Gold Medalists and were a welcome improvement for small-handed archers, such as myself. The Radian did have issues with alignment and straightness that the archer needed to be aware of, but none of which were life threatening. Some people also noted increased harmonic vibration over the earlier Gold Medalist risers. Despite these early design issues, many archers still feel that the Radian riser was one of the best Hoyt Archery ever produced and in some circles considered a collectable.

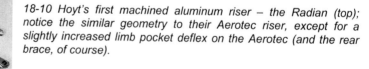

18-10 Hoyt's first machined aluminum riser – the Radian (top); notice the similar geometry to their Aerotec riser, except for a slightly increased limb pocket deflex on the Aerotec (and the rear brace, of course).

- Subsequent riser revisions of that basic design included the Avalon which came with the first limb alignment mechanism, as a way of negating the effects of riser twisting. Some Avelon risers had structural problems and Hoyt later introduced the Avalon-Plus with the appropriate correction. The subsequent Elan and Matrix risers maintained a similar geometry.

- In the middle 1990's, Hoyt designed the Tec-style riser for their compound bows. Given their previous aluminum riser's softness, they were prone to flexing, which while not a showstopper, it didn't help the performance or the feel of the bow, and some archers noticed low-frequency vibrations. To solve this problem, they introduced the AXIS recurve riser. The AXIS is a massive piece of aluminum, with a rear saber grip or flying buttress type strap. This strap or "strut" stiffened the riser without adding too much additional weight to an already weighty riser. The only downside to the AXIS riser was that its limb attaching/centering mechanism used thumbscrews and didn't allow for the standardized ILFs (diag 18-11). Their later Aerotec is of a similar configuration to the AXIS (although slightly less massive), and retains the same type of limb centering adjustments, but incorporated ILFs (diag 18-13). (Note that the Axis limb coupling hardware could easily be changed to ILF hardware, and for a time Hoyt Archery supplied the conversion kits with their limbs.

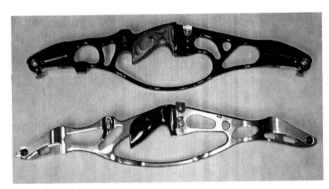

18-11 The Hoyt Axis (above) and Aerotec (left) risers

18-12 Axis (proprietary) limb fittings showing (left to right) adjustment bolt, spacer rings, thumb screw for limb attachment, spacer rings and bolt end cap. This system allowed for lateral limb displacement to compensate for riser twists (lower left).

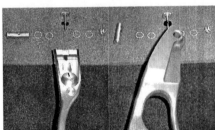  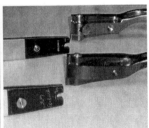

18-13 The Hoyt Aerotec riser used a similar dowel mechanism for lateral limb adjustment, but replaced the thumb screw with an ILF socket (back view left, face view right).

- In 2005, Hoyt introduced the Helix riser, basically an Aerotec, with a flexible insert to dampen or "arrest" vibration further (diag 18-14a and b). They also introduced a lower-priced magnesium TEC riser called the Eclipse, which only lasted one year. (diag 18-15)

18-14a The Hoyt Helix riser with vibration dampener below the grip.

18-14b The Hoyt Helix riser with G3 limbs

18-15 The Hoyt Eclipse riser was only produced in 2006.

- Hoyt Archery also, throughout the years, developed and improved on the carbon/wood and carbon foam limbs, which remarkably bear similar design features to the original Hoyt limb designs of 40+ years prior. Most other limb manufactures use the Hoyt patent for limb design.

- Sadly, 2006 marked the end of an era for Hoyt/USA archery. The 2007 catalog showed only two target risers, the Helix and a new entry, the Nexus. Both aimed at the high-end market. The Aerotec and even the venerable Gold Medalist became part of archery history.

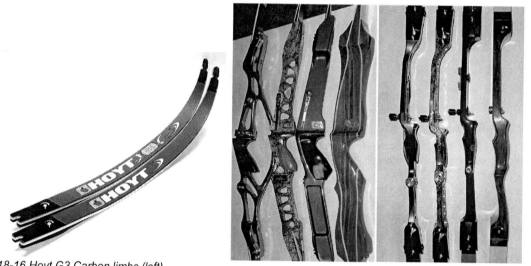

18-16 Hoyt G3 Carbon limbs (left)
18-17 Comparison of Hoyt bows through the years: Left to right, Aerotec, Radian, Gold Medalist, Pro Medalist 5PM (right)

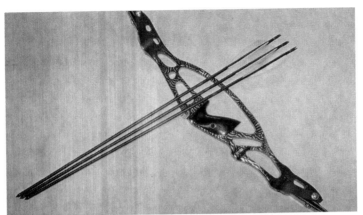

18-18 A particularly patriotic Aerotec Riser
and matching X7 arrows in a red, white and blue pattern.

Appendices

Appendix A

Math, measurements and standards

For those so inclined, here is a review of the formulas discussed in the preceding chapters and a few others that may hold interest for some.

Basic Formulas and Conventions

Draw weight at a given draw length:
Most bows are marked at a draw length of 28".
A 28" draw length means 28" from a point perpendicular to the bowstring to a point 1.75" past the deepest part of the throat of the bow's grip. For all intents and purposes, that means the back of the arrow shelf (see next section on AMO standards).

So, you have a bow that's marked 50#@28", and you draw exactly 28", so you should have a bow with a draw weight of 50#, right? Maybe not. First, there's a possibility that the bowyer's scale was slightly off; it happens more often than you'd think. Second, here are the current AMO standards for bow weights:

Bows weighing 19 – 20 – 21 lbs. will be marked 20 lbs.
Bows weighing 22 – 23 lbs. will be marked 20X lbs.
Bows weighing 24 – 25 – 26 lbs. will be marked 25 lbs.
Bows weighing 27 – 28 lbs. will be marked 25X lbs.
Bows weighing 29 – 30 – 31 lbs. will be marked 30 lbs.
Etc.

Get the idea?

What makes matters worse is that when dealing with vintage bows, some manufacturers had their own methods…

Ben Pearson used the "x" system to represent pounds above or below the marked draw weight.

Example:
A Ben Pearson bow marked xx20#@ 28" would have a draw weight of 18#; x20# would be 19#, while 20x#xwould be 21# and 20xx#, would be 22#. Likewise, xx25# would be 23#. Some manufacturers who used an "x" system on the bow, wrote the true draw weight under the arrow rest or strike plate. Might be worth a look.

If you don't have exactly a 28" draw, you would use the formula we discussed earlier:

Marked draw weight @ 28" / 20 = the amount of weight to add or subtract for each inch above or below 28".

Example:
A bow marked 30#@28", drawn to 29.5" would weigh 32.25#.

30# / 20 = 1.5#
1.5# x 1.5" = 2.25#
30 + #2.25 = 32.25#

If you're wondering where the "divided by 20" came from, it was assumed that 8" was a fairly standard brace height, therefore, the actual drawing length was 20 inches, and the bow had to go from 0# at the resting brace height to the stated weight in 20 inches. If you wanted to be technically correct, the formula would be:

Marked draw weight @ 28" / (28 – the brace height) = the amount of weight to add or subtract for each inch above or below 28". Therefore, using the above example,

A bow marked 30#@28", with a 6" brace height, drawn to 29.5" would weigh 32.25#.

30#/ (28" - 6") = 30# / 22 = 1.36#
1.36# x 1.5" = 2.04#
30# + 2.25# = 32.04#

The above assumes a linear draw-force curve, meaning a bow that gets steadily heavier the farther it's drawn. Happily, most new and intermediate archers need not be overly concerned about an additional pound or two, above or below the stated draw weight. Most pro shop or personal bow scales won't accurately pick up small differences either, and the small difference in speed can easily be handled by tuning. As we've seen, more advanced archers with Olympic type bows can adjust their draw weight by a few pounds to fine-tune their equipment to their needs.

Arrow weight

The best way to determine arrow weight is with an electronic "grain" scale. They are quite inexpensive these days and very accurate. There are also handheld "balance" type scales that, if used properly, can also give accurate results. If those aren't available, it's possible to use the manufacturer's weight for the raw shaft, multiplying the grains per inch value by the shaft length, then adding the weight of the head, inserts and fletching. To that add approximately 20 grains for glues and paints (if any). If you recall, three 5" feathers weigh approximately 10 grains.

FOC

To determine the Front Of Center percentage: use (BPL - OAL/2)/OAL = FOC

Where: BPL = Balance Point Length (measured from nock groove to balance point of complete shaft)
OAL = Overall Length of arrow measured from nock groove to back of head or point (BOP)

Example:

A 28" arrow with a balance point 21" from the nock groove will have a FOC of 25%.

(BPL - OAL/2)/OAL = FOC
(18" – 28"/2)/28" = FOC
(18" – 14")/28" = FOC
FOC = 4"/28" = 25%

Arrow spine

Only static spine can be measured. AMO uses the deflection caused by a 2# weight placed on the center of an arrow shaft, supported on posts placed 26" apart. Easton measures their static spine using a 1.94# weight placed in the center of a shaft supported on 28" centers. (Go figure.) Dynamic spine can only be determined empirically, as shaft length, head weight, fletching, bow characteristics and shooting style must be factored in.

Converting Easton's shaft deflection in inches to actual draw weight at a 28" draw length.

28/deflection of shaft in inches = approximate draw weight (at 28").

Example(s)

An 1816 deflects 0.756"
28/0.756" = 37.04#
A 1916 deflects 0.623"
28/0.623" = 45#

A 2016 deflects 0.531"
28/0.531" = 52.7#

As previously stated, these conversion are only approximations, but can serve as a quick check when choosing arrows.

Kinetic Energy

Kinetic energy is the energy contained in a moving object. It is a way to begin to understand the efficiency of a bow and arrow combination or compare one combination to another.

The basic formula is:

$KE = \frac{1}{2}MV^2$
KE = Kinetic Energy
M = Mass of the arrow
V^2 = Velocity of the arrow at a given moment, squared (VxV)

Seems pretty easy, huh? We'll need to do a little work first, and we'll need a calculator.

Here's why: The MASS of the arrow isn't the weight in grains that we're accustomed to seeing.

1. "Mass" (of anything) is a measurement of the amount of matter something contains, while "weight" is the measurement of the pull of gravity on the "mass" of an object. Weight = mass x the acceleration of gravity, or 32.2 feet per second^2.

2. Therefore, to get the "mass" of an arrow for this equation to work, we'll need to divide its weight by the acceleration (force) of gravity, which is approximately 32.2 feet/sec/sec.

3. Since KE is typically given in foot-pounds and not foot-grains, we'll need to convert grains to pounds as well. Since there are 7000 grains in a pound, we'll again have to divide the grain weight by 7000.

So for our equation to make sense, we'll have to divide the grain weight of the arrow by 32.2, and then again by 7000. Since the equation states that we are using ½M, the entire value is halved, and so we, once again, divide the number by 2.

To make life easier, if we simply multiply 7000 x 32.2 x 2, we get 450800, and can use that as a conversion or "fudge" factor.

Example:
A 400 grain arrow ("fudge" factor x M) launched at a speed (V) of 180 feet per second
$KE = \frac{1}{2}MV^2$
$KE = \frac{1}{2}(400gr) /7000 /32.2) \times (180\ fps)^2 =$
$KE = (200 /32.2 /7000) \times 32,400 = 28.75$ foot-pounds

Or
KE = Arrow weight in grains x speed in fps squared / 450800
KE = 400 x 180^2 / 450800 = 28.75 foot-pounds

If we increase the arrow weight to 500 grains, the speed will drop by a given amount, let's assume 20 fps.

KE = ½MV^2
KE = ½(500gr) /7000 / 32.2 x (160 fps)^2
KE = 28.39 foot-pounds

Or
KE = 500 x 160^2 / 450800 = 28.39 foot-pounds

In this case using a heavier arrow did not significantly change the KE of the system.

If you have access to a chronograph, you can use different arrows and determine the KE values for your bow for each arrow. Remember the KE you calculate is only valid for the instant the arrow is traveling at the speed used in the calculation. As the arrow decelerates, it loses KE. That's why KE is a valid way of comparing one bow/arrow's performance against another.

Momentum

Momentum is a property of a MASS in MOTION. In archery it is a way of determining the force an arrow will have on impact with a target, or how long it will take an object (the target) to stop the arrow's motion. In Physics, the letter P represents momentum.

The basic formula is:

P = MV

P = Momentum of an object
M = The mass of the object
V = The velocity of the object at a given time

Example:
We'll use the same arrow (400 grain) as we did in the first KE example above, but this time, we'll assume it hit a target at 180 fps.

P = MV
P = (400 / 7000 / 32.2)(180)
P = 0.319 ft-lb/second

Note that with momentum, mass and velocity have equal weight in the equation.

Using the arrow from the second KE example (500 grains and traveling at 160 fps) we get:

P = MV
P = (500 / 7000 / 32.2)(160)
P = 0.355 ft-lb/second

Here we see that while KE didn't show a significant change with arrow weight, momentum showed a change of over 10%. Also note that momentum is a "vector" quantity, meaning not only does it have a force, but a direction. That vector should be in the same direction as the arrow is traveling.

What does this mean? Quite honestly, not much; some bowhunters are overly concerned with the KE and P numbers to maximize the depth of penetration of their hunting arrows, but by these simple equations, we can see that the difference is minor.

Bow Efficiency

This is a function of the force required to bend the limbs to a given draw length relative to the kinetic energy of the arrow at launch. Or, put another way, how much of the energy the archer puts into bending the bow is actually ending up in the arrow. As we stated in the chapter on building a virtual bow, the weight of the limbs, their internal friction, as well as the weight of the string and anything on it also dissipates energy. Energy is also utilized in flexing the arrow during paradox. How much energy doesn't make it to the arrow depends on the bow design and materials used.

Total Energy in has to equal total energy out. Therefore, if we know the total energy in (Et), and know how much energy the arrow has leaving the bow (KE), then KE / Et = Bow efficiency.

If we use again the first KE example above, let's say we have a 50# bow that can launch a 400 grain arrow at a speed of 180 feet per second. The KE is 28.74 fps.

KE / Draw weight at anchor = Efficiency
28.74 / 50# = 57.84%

Using the second KE example, with a 500 grain arrow, launched at 160 feet per second, giving us a KE of 28.39.

KE / Draw weight at anchor = Efficiency
28.39 / 50# = 56.78%
A slight loss of efficiency

Hypothetically, if we had a 50# bow launching a 300 grain arrow at 200 feet per second, that would give us a KE of 26.62 [½(300) / 7000 / 32.2 x 200^2 = 26.62]

Efficiency 26.62 / 50# = 53.24%
A greater loss of efficiency
Momentum = 0.1331

What would happen if we increased the weight of the arrow to 600 grains, and it launched at 140 feet per second?

KE = ½(600) / 7000 / 32.2 x140^2 = 26.1
Efficiency = 26.1 / 50# = 52.20%
Momentum = 0.3727

It should be apparent, that with our hypothetical bow, changing arrow weights will have little effect KE and so, efficiency, but considerable effect on momentum.

As an example of a fairly efficient bow, these are the figures for one of my Olympic bows:

Bow – Hoyt Gold Medalist, Carbon Plus limbs 48# @ 29", using a 366 grain arrow.

KE = ½(366gr) / 7000 / 32.2 x $(215fps)^2$ = 37.56
P = (366 / 7000 / 32.2)(215) = 0.3491
Efficiency = 37.56 / 48# = 78.19%

Technical note: The energy of a given bow is defined by the area under its force/draw curve (for example, the curves shown for a generic recurve and compound in Chapter 8). While that would give the most accurate representation, drawing the curve and calculating the area below it can be quite time consuming and for practical purposes yields remarkably similar results to the KE/Et value.

AMO/ATA standards pertaining to stickbows

We have previously spoken of the AMO/ATA (Archery Manufacturers' Organization, now called the Archery Trade Association) standards; while the full and most current documentation is available on their web site, www.archerytrade.org, let's look at the salient features pertaining to shooting a stickbow. Note that even though the name changed from AMO to ATA years ago, most people still refer to it as AMO and AMO standards. Old habits are hard to break!

The following is an overview of the current AMO/ATA standards that relate to stickbow archery.

BOW LENGTH STANDARD

AMO/ATA bow length is defined as 3" longer than a bowstring made to a given length, based on an AMO/ATA Bowstring Master.

For example, a 63" string matching an AMO Bowstring Master will be designated as AMO 66" string and yield the bowyer's recommended brace height for an AMO 66" bow.

The AMO Bowstring Master is a "string" made of a specified length of 1/16" 7 x 7 galvanized (Mil-C-1511) or stainless (Mil-C-5424) steel aircraft cable of 480 lb. test. A full Bowstring Master Set consists of 25 strings ranging in length for 48" to 72", in 1" increments.

BOWSTRING LENGTH STANDARDS

Bowstring length will be designated by placing the string loops over 1/4" diameter steel pins. Endless loop strings will remain untwisted. Flemish splice strings are exempt from twist limitations. Length measurements are taken from the outside of the top steel pin to the outside of the bottom steel pin after 20 seconds at load.

All eight and ten strand Dacron strings are measured under 50# +/- 1# of tension load. All other strings are measured under 100# +/- 1# of tension load.

Author's note: Not sure how many amateur string makers and even professional string makers have the equipment to stretch a string to AMO specs or have full Bowstring Master sets.

SPINE SELECTION CHARTS

Draw Length is the distance, at archer's full draw, from nocking point on string to the pivot point of the grip plus 1-3/4 inches.

All production bows are weighed and marked at 28" draw length; custom bows may be marked at a draw length specified by the customer.

To determine draw weights at draw lengths other than 28", use the formula given in the first part of this appendix.

AMO WOODEN ARROW SPINE DEFLECTION VALUES

Note: The spine recommendations shown here serve as a basic guide for wooden arrow spine determination. The best spine for a particular need may not always correspond with the charts.

+ DEFLECTION	Spine Letter *
1.20 to 1.00	A
1.00 to .85	B
.85 to .75	C
.75 to .65	D
.65 to .58	E
.58 to .52	F
.52 to .47	G
.47 to .43	H
.43 to .40	I
.40 to .37	J
.37 to .35	K

+ Deflection is measured in inches with shaft supported on 26" centers and depressed with a two-pound weight.
* AMO spine symbol designation.

AMO WOOD ARROW SPINE SELECTION CHARTS

FIELD & HUNTING ARROWS

Bow wt. @ draw length	*Arrow Length								
	24	25	26	27	28	29	30	31	32
20-25	A	A	A	A	B	B	C	D	E
25-30	A	A	A	B	C	D	D	E	F
30-35	A	A	C	D	E	F	G	H	I
35-40	A	B	C	D	E	F	G	H	I
40-45	B	C	D	E	F	G	H	I	J
45-50	C	D	E	F	G	H	I	J	K
50-55	D	E	F	G	H	I	J	K	
55-60	E	F	G	H	I	J	K		
60-65	E	G	H	I	J	K			
65-70	F	G	I	J	K				

TARGET ARROWS

Bow wt. @ draw length	*Arrow Length								
	24	25	26	27	28	29	30	31	32
20-25	A	A	A	A	A	B	B	C	D
25-30	A	A	A	A	B	C	D	D	E
30-35	A	A	A	B	C	D	E	E	F
35-40	A	A	B	C	D	E	F	G	H
40-45	A	B	C	D	E	F	G	H	I
45-50	B	C	D	E	F	G	H	I	J
50-55	C	D	E	F	G	H	I	J	K
55-60	D	E	F	G	H	I	J	K	
60-65	D	E	G	H	I	J	K		
65-70	E	F	G	I	J	K			

* For all practical purposes, arrow length and draw length may be considered the same.

AMO BOW SIGHT & ACCESSORY MOUNTING HOLES STANDARD

Two holes located on the outside of the bow (sight) window are 10-24 threaded holes spaced 1.312" +- .010" center to center. Minimum thread depth shall be .250". Mounting holes in sights or other side mounting accessories should conform to these dimensions. A line through the axis of the holes shall be parallel to the bowstring.

AMO STABILIZER & ACCESSORY MOUNTING HOLE STANDARD

All threaded holes or inserts (other than the AMO Bow Sight and Accessory Mounting Holes Standard) that are used to mount stabilizer weights, or accessory items (such as bow quivers, fish reels, etc.) shall be 5/16" - 24 threaded holes. Minimum thread depth shall be 9/16".

AMO STABILIZER ROD STANDARD

The Stabilizer stud that mates with the stabilizer mounting hole (base end) shall be 5/16" - 24 thread with a length of 1/2" +- 1/16". The stud to which the stabilizer weight attaches (outer end) shall be 1/4" - 20 thread with a length of 3/8" +- 1/16".

All stud sizes have been determined to provide adequate support for their respective accessories.

PIVOT POINT

The point at which True Draw Length and Manufacturer's Draw Length and Draw Weight are determined. For all practical purposes, it's the deepest part of the grip.

AMO DRAW LENGTH STANDARD

For Manufacturers

Draw length is a specified distance, or the distance at the archer's full draw, from the nocking point on the string to the pivot point of the bow plus 1-3/4". Draw length from pivot point shall be designed at DLPP and is called TRUE DRAW LENGTH.

EXAMPLE: 26-1/4" DLPP plus 1-3/4" is the equivalent of 28" draw.

For Dealers and General Use

For practical reasons, draw length is the distance, at the archer's full draw, from the nocking point on the string to the back of the bow at the arrow rest.

AMO BOW WEIGHT STANDARD

Bow weight is the force required to draw the nocking point of the bow string a given distance from the pivot point of the bow.

For the purpose of uniform bow weight designation, bow weight is the force required to draw the bow string 26-1/4" from the pivot point. This weight will be marked on the bow as being taken at a draw length of 28".

AMO BROADHEAD & FIELD ARROW FLETCHING RECOMMENDATION

1. Fletching for three vane arrows
    a) Length 5" minimum
    b) Square inches 1.9 minimum
    c) Height 5/8" maximum

2. Fletching for four vane arrows
    a) Length 4" minimum
    b) Square inches 1.4 minimum
    c) Height 5/8" maximum

3. Fletching shall be spiraled with the limits of one revolution in 2-1/2 feet to one revolution in 6 feet.

4. Compliance with other AMO arrow standards, such as arrow length, tapers, adapters, etc.

AMO ARROW LENGTH STANDARDS

AMO Arrow Length—the length from the bottom of the nock slot forward to the designated point near the front or leading end of the arrow assembly. The designated point varies to accommodate the different designs because of the differences in arrow point design and attachment.

1. For arrows incorporating interchangeable point system inserts and other point or adapter types that insert into the open forward end of the arrow shaft, the designated point is the front end of the arrow shaft, often referred to the "cut length" or BOP (Back Of Point length).

2. For arrows having the front end of the shaft tapered or swaged, the designated point is the most forward extension of the full diameter of the shaft.

3. For arrows incorporating outserts, the designated point is 3/4" forward of the rearward end of the outsert

4. For arrows using heads that have integral cylindrical sockets incorporated within the basic head configuration, the designated point is the rearward end of the socket.

AMO ARROW SPEED STANDARD

- The bow must have a maximum draw weight of 60# at a draw length of 30 inches
- Arrow must have a weight of 540 grains (9 grains per pound of draw weight)
- The chronograph is set to detect the initial speed of the arrow as it leaves the bow

Author's note: The above should be used by manufacturers for advertising an AMO/ATA feet per second number. For practical purposes an arrow weighing 9 grains per pound of draw weight and shot from a consistent draw length is sufficient for comparing one bow to another.

Appendix B
Bowstring and arrow references

Bowstrings

Recommended strands per draw weight:

Draw weight	B-50	Fast Flight	S4	450/450+ /8125
#20 – 25	10	14	7	10
#25 – 35	10	16	8	12
#35 – 45	12	18	9	14
#45 – 55	14	20	10	16
#55 – 65	14	22	10	18
#65 – 80+	16	22	11	18

Given the high breaking strength of the newer materials such as Fast Flight, S4, and 450/8125, matching the number of strands to draw weight is not as important as with B-50. Some string makers use 14 strands of 450/450+/8125 or 18 strands of Fast Flight for all draw weights. The center serving diameters are typically adjusted by the diameter of the serving thread used, or by adding extra strands of material under the center serving.

ARROWS

Arrow Spine Charts

Aluminum arrow spine chart used in the text of this book:

The first vertical row shows the actual draw weight at your draw length. The top row is the BOP (Back of Point or length of the arrow from the nock groove to the back of the head) arrow length you will be using. In each cell is the arrow size given nominal pile weights and fletching. Note that this chart differs slightly from the chart in Chapter 1. Here we are assuming that your arrow length will be close to your draw length. As always, these are recommended only as starting points. These recommendations do not imply that additional tuning will not be necessary.

weight at your draw length	Arrow length 25"	Arrow length 26"	Arrow length 27"	Arrow length 28"	Arrow length 29"	Arrow length 30"	Arrow length 31"
30#	1616	1616	1616	1616	1716	1816	1816
35#	1616	1616	1716	1716	1816	1816	1916
40#	1616	1716	1716	1816	1816	1916	1916
45#	1716	1716	1816	1916	1916	2016	2016
50#	1716	1816	1916	1916	2016	2016	2018/2114
55#	1816	1916	1916	2016	2016/2114	2018/2114	2018/2114
60#	1916	1916	2016	2016/2114	2018/2114	2018/2114	2020/2117
65#	1916	2016	2018/2114	2018/2114	2020/2117	2020/2117	2117
70#	2016	2018/2114	2018/2114	2020/2117	2020/2117	2117	2216
75#	2018	2018/2114	2020/2117	2020/2117	2117	2216	2219
80#	2018/2114	2020/2117	2020/2117	2117	2216	2219	2219

The following is an excerpt from an old (1976) Easton Arrow chart. It is provided as a historical reference.

Some arrows are no longer being produced (of particular note is the absence of the thicker walled shafts). Since this chart was released, Easton introduced the 11 and 12/1000" wall thickness shafts as well as 23, 24, 25, 26 and 27/64" OD shafts.

Bow Weight	24"	25"	26"	27"	28"	29"	30"
15-20#	1413	1416	1516	1616	1618	1618 1713	1716 1813
20-25#	1416	1516	1518	1614 1616	1616 1618 1713	1716 1813	1718 1814
25-30#	1516	1518	1518 1614	1616 1618 1713	1714 1716 1813	1716 1718 1814	1816 1913
30-35#	1516	1518 1614	1616 1618 1713	1618 1714 1716	1716 1718 1814	1816 1913	1818 1914
35-40#	1518 1614	1616 1713	1618 1714	1716 1718 1813 1814	1718 1816 1913	1818 1914	1820 1916 2013 2014
40-45#	1616	1618 1714	1716 1718 1813	1716 1816 1913	1818 1914	1820 1916 2013 2014	1918 2016
45-50#	1618 1714	1716 1813	1718 1814 1816 1913	1818 1914	1818 1916 2013	1820 1918 2014 2016	1920 2114 2016
50-55#	----	1718 1814 1816	1816 1818 1913	1818 1916 2013	1820 1918 2014 2016	1920 2016 2114	2018 2020 2115 2213
55-60#	----	1816 1818	1818 1914 1916	1820 1918 2014 2016 2114	1920 2016 2018 2114 2115 2213	2018 2020 2115 2117 2213	2020 2117 2216

The next chart shows the current Easton arrow specifications.

Aluminum Spine / Weight Table

The following is an example of data complied from the current EASTON Arrow Selector software. Data is for a 29" raw arrow shaft, unless otherwise noted.

For arrows other than the listed 29" lengths, add or subtract the number in the grain/inch column for every inch above or below 29" to determine raw shaft weight. For total arrow weight, add the pile weight, and approximately 20-25 grains for feathers, nocks, glue and paint (if any).

Shaft Size	Spine (inches)	Weight (grains)	Weight (gr/in)	Shaft Size	Spine (inches)	Weight (grains)	Weight (gr/in)
1214	2.501	142 - 24"	5.92	2112	0.590	244	8.41
				2113	0.540	270	9.31
1413	2.036	153 - 26"	5.88	2114	0.510	286	9.86
1416	1.684	194 - 27"	7.19	2115	0.461	312	10.76
				2117	0.400	349	12.03
1512	1.554	157 - 27"	5.81				
1514	1.370	184 - 27"	6.81	2212	0.505	256	8.83
1516	1.403	197 - 27"	7.30	2213	0.460	285	9.93
				2214	0.430	302	10.41
1612	1.298	170 - 27"	6.30	2215	0.420	309	10.66
1614	1.153	208 - 27"	7.70	2216	0.375	349	12.03
1616	1.079	227 - 27"	8.41	2219	0.337	399	13.76
1712	1.099	181 - 27"	6.70	2311	0.450	242	8.36
1713	1.044	200 - 27"	7.41	2312	0.423	275	9.48
1714	0.963	219 - 27"	8.11	2314	0.390	309	10.66
1716	0.880	261 - 29"	9.00	2315	0.340	338	11.66
				2317	0.297	385	13.28
1813	0.874	228	7.86				
1814	0.799	249	8.57	2412	0.402	280	9.66
1816	0.756	269	9.28	2413	0.365	302	10.41
				2419	0.268	422	14.56
1912	0.776	220	7.59				
1913	0.733	242	8.34	2511	0.348	233	8.1
1914	0.658	269	9.28	2512	0.321	298	10.28
1916	0.623	291	10.03	2514	0.305	329	11.34
2012	0.680	232	8.35	2612	0.285	280	9.68
2013	0.610	261	9.00	2613	0.265	333	11.48
2014	0.579	277	9.55				
2016	0.531	306	10.55	2712	0.260	275	9.5
2018	0.464	356	12.28				
2020	0.426	391	13.48				

The 2007 Easton catalog introduced a new version of their Gamegetter XX75 shafts. Now sporting a black anodized finish, the shafts are available in four sizes, based on their carbon arrow nomenclature.

Size	Old designation	Actual spine
500	2016	0.531"
400	2117	0.400"
340	2315	0.340"
300	2317	0.297"

Easton Aluminum / Carbon Composite Arrow selection chart

For target archers who require the performance of composite arrows. Easton's arrow selection guide can be a little daunting. Hopefully this will simplify things.

The first table is a grid comparing your ARROW length (horizontal axis) to the draw weight of your bow at YOUR DRAW LENGTH (vertical axis), not at 28".

First find the box that intersects your arrow length and actual draw weight.
Second match the designation in that box to the corresponding box on the second table.

	23"	24"	25"	26"	27"	28"	29"	30"	31"	32"
17-23#					T1	T2	T3			
24-29#				T1	T2	T3	T4	T5		
30-35#			T1	T2	T3	T4	T5	T6	T7	
36-40#		T1	T2	T3	T4	T5	T6	T7	T8	T9
41-45#	T1	T2	T3	T4	T5	T6	T7	T8	T9	T10
46-50#	T2	T3	T4	T5	T6	T7	T8	T9	T10	T11
51-55#	T3	T4	T5	T6	T7	T8	T9	T10	T11	T12
56-60#	T4	T5	T6	T7	T8	T9	T10	T11	T12	T13
61-65#	T5	T6	T7	T8	T9	T10	T11	T12	T13	T13
66-70#	T6	T7	T8	T9	T10	T11	T12	T13	T13	
71-76#	T7	T8	T9	T10	T11	T12	T13	T13		

Table 1

T1	T2	T3	T4
ACE 1000 X10 1000 NAV 1000 ACC 2L-04, 2-04	ACE 850 X10 830 NAV 880 ACC 2-04	ACE 780 X10 750 NAV 810 ACC 3X-04, 3L-04	ACE 920 X10 700 NAV 710 ACC 3L-04, 3-04
T5 ACE 670 X10 650 NAV 660 ACC 3-04	**T6** ACE 620 X10 600 NAV 610 ACC 3L-18	**T7** ACE 570 X10 550 NAV 610 ACC 3-18, 3-28	**T8** ACE 520 X10 500 NAV 540 ACC 3-28, 3-39
T9 ACE 470 X10 450 NAV 480 ACC 3-39	**T10** ACE 430 X10 410 NAV 480 ACC 3L-18	**T11** ACE 400 X10 380 NAV – n/a ACC 3-49, 3-60	**T12** ACE 370 X10 - n/a NAV - n/a ACC 3-60, 3-71
T13 ACE - n/a X10 - n/a NAV - n/a ACC 3-71			

Table 2 (n/a – not available)
Example: If your bow is 42# at your draw, and you use a 29" arrow, that would show a T7 designation. T7 means you could use 570 ACE, 550 X10, 610 Navigator or a 3-18 or 3-28 ACC.

As always, these are only Easton's recommendations and can serve as a starting point; your mileage may vary!

Current Offerings

<u>Aluminum Arrows</u>

Standard abbreviations and nomenclature used:

<u>psi</u> (pounds per square inch) – a measurement of the tensile or breaking strength of a substance. It's basically the amount of force required to pull something apart.

<u>Trueness</u> - .00X" is the maximum deviation from perfect straightness in one direction. Therefore a shaft that has 0.002" deviation may actually be .004" off true, if there are bends in directions 180 degrees apart.

<u>Weight tolerance</u> – percentage a shaft may deviate from the stated weight in grains per inch.

Easton

Shaft	Alloy	PSI	Trueness	Weight tolerance	Color	Comments
Trooper	Fiber-glass	N/A	N/A	N/A	Black	Fiberglass youth shaft. Uses external nocks and piles
Scout	5086	58,000	N/A	N/A	Silver	1618 Youth shaft. Uses external nocks and piles
Genesis	7075	85,000	.006"	+/- 2	Hard anodized blue	1820 Youth shaft. Note, this shaft is spined to approximately 50#, makes a great adult arrow. Conventional nocks
Blues	7075	85,000	.002	+/- 2	Hard anodized blue/silver	Excellent "advanced" youth or JOAD arrow. Conventional nocks
Jazz	7075	85,000	.005"	+/- 2	Hard anodized purple/silver	Excellent "advanced" youth or JOAD arrow. Conventional nocks
Stalker	5086	58,000	N/A	N/A	Gold finish and Fall Camo	Lower psi ratings and weight/straightness tolerances. Conventional nocks
XX75 Legacy	7075-T9	95,000	+/- .002"	+/- 1%	wood grain finish	Conventional nocks
XX75 Gamegetter	7075-T9	96,000	+/-003"	1 1/4%	Green, but with a better anodization process than the originals.) and Gamegetter II Three-color hard anodized Camo pattern. These were replaced by a new version with a black anodized finish in 2007.	Conventional nocks New black shafts come in four sizes: 500 (2016). 400 (2117), 340 (2315), 300 (2317)
XX75 Camo Hunter	7075-T9	96,000	+/- .002"	1%	Hard-anodized four-tone black, brown, dark green & light green camo pattern.	Conventional nocks
XX75 Platinum Plus	7075-T9	96,000	+/- .002"	1%	Hard anodized aluminum silver, reminiscent of the original Easton aluminum arrows.	G nocks When the Platinum Plus arrows were first release they came with conventional nocks

XX75 Mossy Break-Up & Realtree Hardwoods	7075-T9	95,000	+/- .002"	1%	Natural Oak hard anodized pattern and Green PermaGraphic camo pattern	Super uni-bushing nocks
NEX75	7075-T9	95,000	+/- .002"	1%	PermaGraphic Realtree HD Green camo	Hidden Insert Technology (HIT)
XX78 Superslam	7078-T9	100,000	+/- .0015"	1%	Hard-anodized, forest Perma-Graphic pattern	Internal-fit Super nocks
X7 Eclipse	7078-T9	105,000	+/- .001"	¾ %	Hard anodized black	Super G, Uni-bushing or Super Uni-bushing nocks.
X7 Cobalt	7078-T9	105,000	+/- .001"	¾ %	Hard anodized blue	Super Swage internal nock system for use with Super Nocks or 3D Super Nocks.

Carbon Arrows

Carbon Shafts and Carbon/aluminum composites

Given the large number of carbon arrows currently available, and the frequency of modifications or updates, it would be impossible to list every arrow and their relative spine recommendations. Below is a sampling of some of the manufacturers at the time of this printing. Carbon arrow manufacturers' web sites are provided later in this Appendix and their spine recommendations can be found there.

Easton

Shaft	Trueness	Weight tolerance	Color	Available sizes	Comments
Carbon Connekt			Smooth black, matte finish.	One size to 40#	Easton's Youth carbon arrow.
CARBON EXCEL	+/- .005"	+/- 5.0	Smooth black, matte finish.	500, 400, 340	Easton's economy grade carbon arrow. Multi-layer wrapped carbon fibers. They use internal-fit Super Nocks and one-size inserts and points fit all Excel shaft sizes.
LIGHT SPEED	+/- .005"	+/- 2.0	Same as Carbon Excel	Same as Carbon Excel	Same as Carbon Excel
C2 Carbon Epic and Realtree HD	+/- .005"	+/- 2.0	Black, micro-smooth finish & camouflage patterns	500, 400 and 340, 300	Same as Carbon Excel, but with added sizes for heavier bows
Redline	+/- .004	+/- 1.5	Black micro-smooth finish	100, 900, 780, 690, 600, 520, 460, 410, 360	High strength C2 carbon composite fibers
FAT BOYS	+/- .005"	+/- 2.0	Smooth back matte finish	500, 400, 340	Lightweight carbon line-cutters.
ST AXIS	+/- .005"	+/- 2.0	Black micro-smooth finish	500, 400, 340, 300	Ultra-small diameter with HIT (Hidden Insert Technology). Internal-fit "X" Nock. One size HIT Insert fits all ST Axis shafts

Beman

Beman Archery is a division of Easton Archery.
Beman's high-end hunting arrows employ MFX carbon composite and HIT (Hidden Insert Technology, patented by Easton) for accurate broadhead alignment.

Shaft	Trueness	Weight tolerance	Color	Available sizes	Comments
MAX 4 and Black Max	+/-.003"	+/-2.0	MAX 4 has Advantage PhotoFusion™ camouflage finish, and Black Max are black	500, 400, 340, 300	Direct-fit "X" Nock (HIT Technology)
ICS Carbon Camo Hunter and Classic)	+/-.003"	+/-2.0	PhotoFusion™ graphics. The Camo Hunter uses a Mossy Oak® Break-Up® camo and the Classic, a Wood Grain pattern.	500, 400, 340, 300	C2 carbon composite arrows. Direct-fit Super Nock / CM Inserts
Hunter Elite	+/-.001"	+/-2.0	Smooth black finish	500, 400, 340, 300	CB inserts or "G" nocks
Hunter Junior	N/A	+/-2.0 grains	Smooth black finish	For bows up to 40#. Available in 26" and 28" lengths	Arrows for the younger shooter. Factory fletched
9.3	+/-.006"	+/-2.0 grains	Smooth black finish	500, 400, 340	Large diameter "line-cutter" shafts RPS inserts, one piece piles and super UNI-Bushings
Venture	+/- .006	+/-2.0	Black micro smooth finish	500, 400, 340, 300	Uses ACC –60 points and CB inserts
ICS Energy	+/-.006	+/-1.5	Black micro smooth finish	780, 690, 600, 520, 460, 410, 360	UNI-Bushings
Carbon Flash	N/A	N/A	Smooth black finish	1000, 900, 750, 630, 570	Pultruded arrows. Beman's economy arrow with small diameter, uses over-nocks and piles.

Blackhawk

Shaft	Trueness	Weight tolerance	Color	Available sizes	Comments
Vapor 23 Speed	Sold in matched dozens with a +/- .0025 straightness tolerance	+/- 2 tolerance per dozen and +/- .75 Newton spine variance	Black finish	Available in two sizes 5000 & 4000. Large OD .358" diameter shaft designed as line-cutters for competitive shooters.	Duramax high modulus carbon construction. Sold in matched dozen bundles only.
Vapor Speed 2000	+/- 0025"		Black finish	2000s (19/64 OD)	
ACA Vapor Black Pro	+/- .003" +/- .003"	+/- 2.5 tolerance per dozen	Black finish	5000, 4000, 3000, 2000	ICS design accepts standard UNI-bushing components
Vapor Carbon wood and Camo			Carbon wood and Camo finishes	5000, 4000, 3000	
JETS	+/- .003"	+/- 2.5 tolerance per dozen	Black finish	5000, 4000, 3000	
V-Maxx	+/- .003"		Realtree, wood grain and Black finish	5000, 4000, 3000	Designed for fixed-blade broadheads, allowing for maximum helical fletching and rest clearance.

PSE CARBON FORCE

Shaft	Trueness	Weight tolerance	Color	Available sizes	Comments
Competition Pro	+/-.001"	+/- 1 per dozen	Black or Camo finish	400, 300, 200, 100	Uses universal internal components
Extreme	+/-.003	+/- 1 per dozen			
Dominator	+/-.006		Black finish	400, 300, 200	Hunting shaft, same composition as above.
Dominator Camo	+/-.006		Camo finish	300, 200	
Equalizer	+/- .003"		Black finish	2300	23/64th line-cutters; 8.2 grains per inch and .410 spine deflection
XLS Hunter	+/- .005".		Black finish		
Radial X-Weave Pro	+/- .001	+/- 1 per dozen	Black finish	300, 200, 100	
Radial X-Weave Predator	+/-.003"	+/- 5	Carbon black finish	300, 200,100	manufactured on CNC machinery
Radial X-Weave Stealth Hunter	+/-.006"		Carbon black finish	300, 200,100	manufactured on CNC machinery

GOLDTIP

Shaft	Trueness	Weight tolerance	Color	Available sizes	Comments
Expedition	+/- .006"	+/- 2	Black and Camo finish	3555, 5575, 7595	Economy Hunting shaft
Pro Hunters and camo	+/- .001"	1	Black and Camo finish		
XT Hunters and camo	+/- .003	+/- 2 grains per dozen	Black and Camo finish		
Expedition Hunter & camo	+/- .006"	+/- 2	Smooth, black and Camo finish		
Traditional Hunters	+/- .006	+/- 2	Wood grain finish		
Traditional XT Hunter	+/- .003	+/- 2	Wood grain finish		
Big Game Camo 100+	+/- .005"	N/A	Black finish	spined for approximately 75-110 pounds of draw weight	10.6 grains per inch (10.5 on the camouflage model)
Falcon Youth Arrows	+/-.006"	+/- 5		Spined as a 35/55 shaft	Raw shafts are 26" long
Lightning Youth and camo	+/-.006"	N/A		Maximum length 28" and maximum weight 35#	Same as the Falcon Youth arrows.

All of the above Gold Tip arrows accept any type of screw-in broadhead and 5/16" field tips.

Shaft	Trueness	Weight tolerance	Color	Available sizes	Comments
30x Pro	+/- .001"	+/- 1	Black	150	26/64 shaft (2 grades available)
30x	+/- .003"	+/- 2			
UltraLite Series 22 Pro	+/- .001"	+/- 1	Black		large diameter (FITA legal at a .338")
UltraLite Series 22	+/- 005"	+/- 5	Black		large diameter (FITA legal at a .338" 7.3 grains / inch
Ultralight X-Cutter Pro	+/- .001".	+/- 1	Black	One spine and 2 grades	Line cutter 25/64" outside diameter 8.0 grains per inch
UltraLite X-Cutter	+/- .005".	+/- 5	Black	One spine and 2 grades	Line cutter 25/64" outside diameter 8.0 grains / inch
UltraLite Entrada	+/- .006"	+/- 2	Black	300, 400, 500 and 600	Entry level Line cutter shafts
Ultralight Pro	+/- .001"	1 grain per dozen	Black finish	300, 400, 500 and 600	Target arrows
Ultralight (XT)	+/- 003"	+/- 2	Black finish	300, 400, 500 and 600	Target arrows

Aluminum/Carbon Composites

The final category of carbon arrows is hybrids, composed of both aluminum and carbon. Aluminum/carbon composite technology combines the precision and straightness of aluminum with the stiffness, durability and speed achieved with carbon.

EASTON
Hunting/General

Shaft	Trueness	Weight tolerance	Color	Available sizes	Comments
ACC	± .003"	± 0.5	Black, micro-smooth finish	2-00, 3L-00, 3-00, 2L-04, 2-04, 3X-04, 3L-04, 3-04, 3L-18, 3-18, 3-28, 3-29, 3-49, 3-39, 3-49, 3-60, 3-71	High-strength carbon fiber bonded to a precision 7075 aluminum core tube. UNI-bushings
SUPER SLIM	± .002"	± 0.5		500, 400, 340, 300	
AC Kinetic	±.003"	± 1.5	Camo	500, 400, 300	General purpose Hunting/Target composite arrow.
Full Metal Jacket	±.003"	± 2	Low glare hard anodized diamond pattern	500, 400, 340, 300	Thick walled carbon core + 7075 aluminum alloy. HIT

Target

Shaft	Trueness	Weight tolerance	Color	Available sizes	Comments
AC Navigator	± .0025"	± 1.0	Polished black carbon finish	1000, 880, 810, 710, 660, 610, 540, 480, 430	ACE insert + screw-in head, ACE or Navigator Stainless Steel weight adjustable head or one-piece bullet point. ACE or Navigator pin or "G" nocks.
A/C/C	±.003"	±0.5		2-00, 3L-00, 3-00, 2L-04, 2-04, 3X-04, 3L-04, 3-04, 3L-18, 3-18, 3-28, 3-29, 3-49, 3-39, 3-49, 3-60, 3-71	ACC one piece bullet point, NIBBs. ½ out inserts and aluminum inserts. ACE "G" nocks, and Uni-bushings.
A/C/E	± .002"	± 0.5		1400, 1250, 1100, 1000, 920, 850, 780, 720, 670, 620, 570, 520, 470, 430, 400, 370.	Barreled shaft. ACE insert + screw-in head, ACE Stainless Steel weight adjustable head or one-piece bullet point.
X10	± .002"	± 0.0015		1000, 900, 830, 750, 700, 650, 600, 550, 500, 450, 410, 380	Barreled shaft. Tungsten or Stainless Steel points, with break off weight adjustment. Pin nocks.

ACE

X10 and A/C/E are designed for outdoor target and Olympic-style competition. Their small diameter reduces wind drift and aerodynamic drag. Easton's barreled design produces a stiffer shaft with lighter ends that create a higher natural frequency of vibration for better clearance. High-strength carbon fiber bonded to a precision 7075 aluminum core tube.

X10s hold more current FITA world records than all other arrows combined.
Current price tag with weight adjustable heads at the time of this printing: $350 – $500 per dozen.

Beman

Shaft	Trueness	Weight tolerance	Color	Available sizes	Comments
Matrix	+/- .003		Black	460	Outer carbon layer with aluminum core

Blackhawk

Shaft	Trueness	Weight tolerance	Color	Available sizes	Comments
Vapor CAA	+/- .0025	+/- 2	Gray	3710, 3600, 3490, 3390, 3280	Outer carbon layer with aluminum core

Arrow manufacturer's websites:

Easton
www.eastonarchery.com – Provides a downloadable interactive Shaft Selector.

Beman
www.beman.com - Provides an interactive arrow selector on their website.

BlackHawk
www.blackhawkarchery.com – Provides shaft reference charts.

PSE CarbonForce
www.pse-archery.com – Provides spine information on each arrow type.

CarbonExpress
www.carbonexpressarrows.com – Provides an interactive arrow selector on their website.

Gold Tip
www.goldtip.com – Provides interactive arrow building information online.

Fiberglass Shafts

This data is for historical reference, as fiberglass shafts are no longer being produced commercially in significant quantities.

Microflight Fiberglass Shafts

Bow Weight @ draw length	23"	24"	25"	26"	27"	28"	29"	30"	31"
20-25#	0	0	0	1	2	3	4	5	6
25-30#	0	0	1	2	3	4	5	6	7
30-35#	0	1	2	3	4	5	6	7	8
35-40#	1	2	3	4	5	6	7	8	9
40-45#	1	2	3	4	6	7	8	9	10
45-50#	2	3	4	5	6	7	8	9	10
50-55#		4	5	6	7	8	9	10	11
55-60#		5	6	7	8	9	10	11	11
60-65#			7	8	9	10	11	11	12
65-70#			8	9	10	10	11	12	12
70-75#				10	10	11	12	12	12

Gordon Plastics Fiberglass shafts
The numbers in the cells intersecting the shaft and draw lengths are the recommended draw weights.

Shaft Size	24"	25"	26"	27"	28"	29"	30"	31"	32"
A-20	40	33	28	23					
B-25	50	43	37	32	27				
C-30			42	39	32	27			
D-35			50	43	37	33	30	26	
E-40			55	48	42	37	33	31	27
F-45			60	55	47	43	38	34	31
G-50			67	60	53	48	43	39	35
H-55			73	64	57	52	47	43	38
I-60				73	62	55	50	46	42
J-65				83	67	61	55	51	46

Wooden arrow spine charts are given in the AMO/ATA section of appendix A.

Graphlex Graphite Shafts

These are also presented for historical reference only.
Standard shafts were color-coded by the color of the GRAPHLEX logo.

Draw weight	27"	28"	29"	30"	31"	32"
40#	Green	Green	Green	Black	Black	Black
50#	Green	Black	Black	Black	Black	Black
60#	Black	Black	Black	Yellow	Yellow	Red
70#	Black	Yellow	Red	Red	Red	Red

GRAPHLEX XT Hunting Shaft Selection Chart

Bow Weight	26"	27"	28"	29"	30"	31:"	32"	33"	34"
40-44#			16-5	16-5	16-5 17-6	17-6	17-8		
45-49#		16-5	16-5	16-5 17-6	17-6	17-8	18-8		
50-54#		16-5	16-5	17-6	17-8	18-8	18-8		19-8
55-59#	16-5	16-5	17-6	17-8	18-8	18-8	18-8		19-8
60-64#	17-6	17-6	17-8	18-8	18-8	18-8	18-8 19-8	19-8	19-8
65-69#	17-6	17-8	18-8	18-8	18-8	18-8	19-8	19-8	18-8 19-12
70-74#	17-6	18-8	18-8	18-8	18-8	19-8	19-8	19-8	19-12
75-79#	17-8	18-8	18-8	18-8	18-8 19-8	19-8	19-8	19-8	19-12
80-84#	17-8	18-8	18-8	19-8	19-8	19-8	19-12	10-12	
85-89#	18-8	18-8	18-8	19-8	19-8	19-12	19-12	19-12	
90-94#	18-8	18-8 19-8	19-8	19-8	19-12	19-12	19-12		
95-100#	19-8	19-8	19-8	19-8 19-12	19-12	19-12	19-12		

GRAPHLEX XT Specifications

Arrow Size	O.D.	I.D.	Wall	Gr/inch	Gr.WNI	Gr.WCS	Deflect	Alum Comp
16-5	.298	.250	.024	10.2	20	13	.520	1916
17-6	.315	.265	.025	10.9	20	16	.400	2016
17-8	.320	.265	.0275	11.9	20	16	.350	2018
18-8	.335	.281	.027	12.3	22	21	.310	2117
19-8	.350	.297	.0265	13.2	27	25	.270	2219
19-12	.356	.297	.0295	14.1	27	25	.210	2317

Arrow size   = Manufacturers number
O.D.   = Outside Diameter
I.D.   = Inside Diameter
Wall   = Wall Thickness
Gr/Inch   = Grains per Inch of shaft material
Gr.WNI   = Grain Weight Nock Insert
Gr. CS   = Grain Weight Converta-Sleeve
Deflect.   = Deflection (spine) measured at 26" centers using a 2# weight.
Alum Comp   = Comparable Aluminum Arrow size. Note that Easton currently uses a 1.94 pound weight with 28" centers, hence the discrepancy between the spines and aluminum arrow sizes.

Appendix C

Resources

Websites

General
The <u>Shooting the Stickbow</u> website
www.shootingthestickbow.com
The author's website for this book.

The Archer's Reference
www.archersreference.pwp.blueyonder.co.uk – Excellent document in pdf (Adobe Acrobat) format providing a comprehensive view of Olympic/FITA archery techniques and equipment.

Archery Archives
www.archeryarchives.com – Compilation of archery catalogs and information dating back to the 1950s. One of the best historical references on the web.

Archery History
www.archeryhistory.com – Wonderful site with ads and pictures of various milestones in recent archery history.

www.bowjackson.com – Archery site with detailed hunting information and several useful archery calculators.

www.lmariana.com/traj.htm – Excellent arrow drop, FOC and energy calculators.

Texas Archery Association
www.texasarchery.org – Website with numerous articles on various aspects of archery, including tuning, schedules of events and JOAD/FITA news.

Traditional Classifieds
Women Outdoors
http://65-242-99-131.hagenhosting.com/cgi-bin/classifieds.cgi – Site run By Delores Farmer, providing free classified ads for all types of archery equipment. Archers usually sell the stuff here, so they do know what they are selling.

Note that most of the larger archery forums also have classified listings for various archery products for sale, trade, or from people wanting to buy.

Arrow manufacturers' websites are listed in Appendix B.

Archery equipment (bow) manufacturers
The following are the larger, off-the-shelf, archery manufacturers:
AIM – www.Aimarchery.com (Archery International Marketing) As the name implies AIM is an archery marketing co-operative comprised of the following companies: Internature, Cartel, Samick, Aurora and G-Bow
Bear Archery – www.fredbear.net
Black Widow Archery – www.blackwidowbows.net
Howard Hill (Longbows) – www.howardhillarchery.com
Hoyt Archery - www.hoytusa.com
Martin Archery (including Damon-Howatt) – www.martinarchery.com
Mathews Archery – www.mathewsinc.com

Samick Archery – www.samicksports.com
PSE Archery – www.pse-archery.com
Win & Win – www.win-archery.com

The following are smaller or custom bowyers:

Bob Lee Archery – www.bobleearchery.com (Bob Lee was the designer or the original Wing Archery bow in the 1960's and 70's.)
Border – www.borderarchery.com
Checkmate Archery – Bows available through several dealers – they do not have a web site.
DAS-Kinetic – www.kineticbows.com
O.L. Adcock – www.bowmaker.net
Quinn's Archery – www.quinnsarchery.com

There are hundreds, if not thousands, of bowyers in the US and overseas today; to list all would be impossible.

Archery Dealers/Distributors
3Rivers Archery – www.3riversarchery.com
Alternative Sporting services - www.altservices.co.uk (UK based)
eBay – (yes, EBAY !!!) – www.ebay.com
Cabela's Sporting Goods – www.cabelas.com
FS Discount Archery – www.fsdiscountarchery.com
Lancaster Archery – www.lancasterarchery.com
Quick's Archery – www.Quicks.com (UK based)

Bow Building Supplies and Accessories
Bingham Archery Products – www.binghamproducts.com

Archery Forums
Internet archery discussion forums and chat rooms can be excellent sources of information and entertainment. It may, however, be difficult for a newcomer to know the difference. Some well-known and respected archers visit these web sites and offer suggestions or insights into issues other shooters might have; unfortunately these sites are also open to anyone with a computer and an Internet connection. Usually, someone new to one or more of these sites would be better off "lurking" (viewing, and not posting or even registering) for a while before posting a question, a response or taking anyone's advice too seriously. Lurking will give you an idea of the flavor of the site, how, or how well, it's moderated, who the seasoned contributors and real archers are, and whose opinions are of lesser or dubious value.

Archery Forum
www.archery-forum.com/index.php
Australia based target archery forum.

Archery Talk
www.archerytalk.com
Large archery forum, dealing with multiple aspects of target archery and bowhunting.

"The Leatherwall"
www.stickbow.com
Part of a larger Archery board (www.bowsite.com), this forum deals with Traditional Archery, hunting and bow making.

Sagittarius Archery board
http://sagittarius.student.utwente.nl/bb/
International Archery forum dealing with Olympic/FITA style shooting.

Stickbow Target Archery Forum (STAF)
http://staf.trinitylongbowmen.com/cgi-bin/ultimatebb.cgi
Archery site dealing with various forms of target archery – particularly aimed at longbow fanciers.

www.Tradgang.com
Web site/forum dealing primarily with traditional/primitive archery and hunting.

www.Tradtalk.com
Archery site including forums, online pro shop and photo-gallery. This site is quite progressive and discusses topics considered "untraditional" on several other sites.

Archery Organizations
AMO Archery Manufacturers' Organization – see ATA

ATA **Archery Trade Association (formerly AMO)**
www.archerytrade.org

IBO **International Bowhunters Organization**
www.ibo.net

FITA **International Archery Federation** (Federation Internationale de Tir a L'Arc)
www.archery.org

NAA **National Archery Association**
www.usaarchery.org

NFAA **National Field Archery Association**
www.nfaa-archery.org

IFAA **International Field Archery Association**
www.ifaa-archery.com

PBS **Professional Bowhunter's Society**
www.bowsite.com/pbs

Books

Archery - C.J. Longman and Col. H. Walrond (1894), Badminton Library of Sports and Pastimes. Edited by His Grace The Duke of Beauford, assisted by Alfred E. T. Watson

The Archer's Bible, by Fred Bear, et al. Main Street Books; Revised edition (May 6, 1980)

Archery Anatomy, by Ray Axford, Souvenir Press (November 1, 1996)

Archery in Earnest, by Roy Matthews, Trafalgar Square Publishing (February 1, 1998)

Archery Handbook, by Edmund H. Burke, Fawcett Paperbacks, Second Printing 1956

Archery, Shot Execution, by Larry Skinner

Bow and Arrow's Archer's Digest, Edited by Jack Lewis, Digest Books 1971

Bow and Arrow: The Comprehensive Guide to Equipment, Technique and Competition, Larry Wise, Stackpole Books; 1st edition (April 1, 1992)

Fred Bear's World of Archery, by Fred Bear, et al. Doubleday; 1st edition (January 1, 1979)

Become the Arrow, by Byron Ferguson, Target Communications Corporation (September 1, 1994)

Beginner's Guide to Traditional Archery, by Brian J Sorrells, Stackpole Books (2004)

Fundamentals of Recurve Archery, by Ruth Rowe, Quintessential Productions; Illustrated edition (October 31, 2001)

The Grey Goose Wind, by E. G. Heath, Osprey Publications, 1971

Hitting 'em like Howard Hill, by John Schulz

Hunting the Hard Way, by Howard Hill, Northumberland Press. 1956

Instinctive Archery Insights, by Jay Kidwell (April 30, 2004)

Instinctive Shooting & Instinctive Shooting II, G. Fred Asbell, Cowles Magazines, Inc (January 1, 1993)

Longbow, Robert Hardy, Distributed by Lyons & Burford 3rd edition (January 1, 1992)

Peak Performance Archery, by Al Henderson, Blue Oak Pr (March 1, 1988)

Precision Archery, by Steve Ruiz and Claudia Stevenson (editors), Human Kinetics Publishers (October 1, 2003)

Traditional Archery, Sam Fadala, Stackpole Books; 1st edition (June 1, 1999)

Traditional Bowyers of America, by Dan Bartalan, Envisage Unlimited (December 1, 1989)

Traditional Bowyer's Bible, volumes 1, 2 and 3; various authors (Jim Hamm Editor), The Lyons Press

The Simple Art of Winning, by Rick McKinney, Leo Planning, Inc. Tokyo, Japan (1996).
Total Archery, by Ki Sik Lee and Robert de Bondt, Samick Sports

With Winning in Mind by Lanny Anderson, Bookpartners (November 1, 1996)

Zen in the Art of Archery, by Eugen Herrigel, Vintage (January 26, 1999) - (several publications)

Note: I am neither recommending nor advising against any of these books. I do advise that both the new and experienced archers read as much as possible, avail themselves of as many theories and opinions as possible, and thereafter formulate their own.

Appendix D
FAQs (Frequently Asked Questions)

Q. Where can I find a range or archery club?
A. *Start with the Yellow or White Pages. Most clubs or ranges are listed. Try local sporting goods stores that sell archery equipment; they should know where it's being used. You can also try Internet searches on "Archery Club, <your state or province>".*

Q. Is my vintage bow safe to shoot?
A. *Depends on what you mean by vintage. Laminated bows from the 1960's and 70's, if showing no signs of failure or damage, yes. Older selfbows need to be inspected very carefully and any metal-limbed bow should be considered a wall hanging.*

Q. How much is my <vintage> bow worth?
A. *No idea – The monetary value of any object is determined by what someone is willing to pay for it. Sentimental value really can't be assessed, except by the owner or prospective owner. The best way to find out the market value of a given bow is to do several eBay searches on similar models over several weeks and note the final prices.*

Q. What brace height should I use for my <fill in the blank> bow?
A. *If your bow has an AMO length on it, buying an AMO string of the same length should give you the manufacturer's recommended brace height. Other than that, longbow brace heights can range anywhere from 6" to 8", recurves 64" and under usually 7" to 8.5", and recurves over 66", 8" to 9.5" or as much as 12". Beyond that, it has to remain trial and error, depending on the string material, type of arrow and shooting style.*

Q. What's the greatest factor in making a bow shoot fast(er)?
A. *Use the lightest arrow possible. However, the arrow must be of sufficient weight to handle the energy of the bow. Most modern bows can handle arrows weighing eight to ten grains per pound of draw weight. Some target bows can handle arrows as light as seven grains per pound and most vintage bows should be in the nine to ten pound range as a minimum. Going below those values is tantamount to dry-firing the bow and will ultimately result in limb or riser failure. If in doubt, contact the manufacturer or bowyer for his recommendations. If that's not possible, stay in the nine to ten grains per pound range.*

Q. Who makes the best <fill in the blank> bow?
A. *Anyone attempting to answer that question simply hasn't tried enough bows to venture an opinion. There's a big difference between "What's the best bow" and "What's the best bow I've shot". Also, the best bow for your friend may not be the best bow for you!*

Q. What's the difference between a hunting bow and a target bow?
A. *The length, and usually the draw weight, but there is always overlap. Target bows may have additional inserts for stabilizers and target accessories like plungers and clickers. Many so-called target bows make excellent hunting bows with little modification.*

Q. Can I use a Fast Flight (FF) String on my bow?
A. *Only if the bowyer or manufacturer states that the bow is FF capable or compatible. Most bows show only a modest gain in speed (5 to 10 feet per second) when switching from B-50 Dacron to Fast Flight or similar low stretch material. Using a FF string on a bow not designed for low stretch materials can result in catastrophic failure.*

Q. I'm new to shooting stickbows, should I start with a recurve or longbow?
A. *First and foremost is what type of bow you'll be most happy with. If you're not happy or dissatisfied with it, you're not going to shoot it. Most first time shooters are better off starting with a recurve. The contoured grip and heavier mass of the riser makes consistency easier to attain.*

Typically, entry-level recurves will shoot faster and have less hand shock than entry-level longbows. Recurves are also usually easier to tune for new shooters.

Q. What is the difference between a custom and a factory or "production" bow?
A. That's not an easy question to answer, for several reasons.

There are custom bowyers who produce boilerplate bows with a few options and call them "custom" and there are "production" bow manufacturers who will customize a bow to the buyer's specifications.

Typically, a custom bow might have a better fit and finish than a factory bow, unless of course the custom bowyer was having a bad day and missed an error or two. People are human, so mistakes happen. Similarly, a factory's Quality Assurance people may also have had a bad day and just let one ship out that probably shouldn't have left the plant.

It's rare that a custom bowyer, usually a "mom and pop" type operation, will have the same R and D (Research and Development) facilities (or finances) as the major archery manufacturers, but there are exceptions.

Q. Will a custom bow shoot better than a factory bow?
A. Depends on what you mean by "shoot better". In addition to the last part of the previous answer, I think we've shown throughout this book that the equipment isn't the weakest link in the shooting system. A custom bow will not turn a mediocre shooter into a stellar performer over night. However, if the custom bow fits the shooter better, and instills more confidence than a production bow, then there might be an improvement. Remember just about all Olympic bows are "production" bows.

Q. I'm shooting carbon arrows, but they seem too light; can I stuff something into the shaft to add weight?
A. Quite a few people do, but it's a pretty bad idea, for a lot of reasons. The two main reasons for using carbon arrows in the first place are durability and speed. I think we've dispelled the durability factor in the section on arrow materials; their extreme speed is due to their low weight, compared to wood and most aluminum shafts. So, the first reason is that it negates one of the reasons that you bought carbon arrows in the first place. Second, is that almost anything you put inside an arrow will move around during the shot. That can wreak havoc with spine and FOC.

Some carbon arrow manufacturers sell weighted tubes that glue onto the back of the pile insert. While this too will soften the spine somewhat, it's a known and consistent amount, and since carbon arrows are stiffer and more resilient than other shaft materials, it's usually not too great a concern.

The best answer is always to buy the right arrows with regard to spine and weight in the first place.

Q. I get the best arrow flight from my 45# bow using 2219s an inch longer than my draw length; is this OK?
A. If you're satisfied with the performance, sure. However, it's a pretty good indication that something is very wrong with your equipment or technique (shooting or tuning technique). As we said earlier, most bows can be tuned to accept a number of different arrow spines; some will be less than optimal. If your bow seems to require an arrow that much over-spined, either the bow has been tuned too close to center shot, the brace height is way too high and/or there is something very wrong with your release and follow-through.

Q. Why is it that I can get a better release from a heavier bow than from a lighter one?
A. It usually means you have not really learned to relax your drawing hand and let the string escape cleanly. With a heavier bow, the string pulls out of your fingers faster and helps to mask

some release errors. Therefore it doesn't make your release "better"; it makes it easier. The benefits of an easier release have to be weighed against the problems that might be encountered by using too heavy a bow.

Q. I've just switched from a B-50 (Dacron) string to a Fast Flight (type) string on a FF capable bow. Will I need to buy new arrows?
A. Maybe; at the very least you'll need to retune the bow. Arrow spine is a function of limb acceleration and offset from center shot. By going to a lighter weight string limb acceleration should have increased. If your arrows were marginally weak in the first place, the new string may be enough to push them over their spine limit. You may also find that you'll need to alter the brace height to keep the bow quiet and free from hand shock.

Q. What's the difference between a left wing and right wing feather? Should a right-handed shooter use one or the other?
A. Left wing feathers come from the left side of the turkey or goose and right wing come from the right side. Either will stabilize an arrow equally well for both right and left-handed shooters. If you have a dedicated left or right-handed fletching jig, you'll have to use the corresponding feather.

Q. I've heard that shooting off the shelf is better if you're an instinctive shooter, because it gets the arrow closer to your hand. Is that true?
A. It would be true if you aimed an arrow by pointing your finger, but you don't. "Instinctive shooting" still uses the arrow as part of a larger "sight picture", so the arrow's distance from your hand is irrelevant as a means of aiming.

Q. Does a bowhunter need to tune a bow the same way a target archer does?
A. The techniques may be slightly different, but the need may be even greater. Not only does it ensure the best possible arrow flight and accuracy, but it has been demonstrated to increase arrow penetration into game by virtue of less energy being lost during paradox and on impact.

Q. Is there a difference between practicing and shooting?
*A. As I have stated **"It's very difficult, if not impossible to focus on the target and on shooting form at the same time."** That presents us with a fundamental difference between practicing and shooting.*

*When we are **practicing** we need to do so with a purpose and that purpose must be specific. We may be practicing getting our bow hand in the same position every time, our follow-through consistent, our timing pattern set or aiming technique refined. Our focus is on the specific action and not the target. When we are **shooting**, the purpose is to hit the center of the target; be it to achieve a certain score or to put meat on the table.*

Q. I always hit my anchor, sometimes only for a split second. Does that mean my form is "OK"?
A. Depends on what you'll accept as "OK". Without a solid and sustained anchor (even for a fraction of a second), there's no way of telling whether you released the string before, during or after your anchor or more accurately, your "touch point" was reached. Also, even a consistent anchor (point) doesn't guarantee that you're aligning your shoulders correctly or even reaching a full or consistent draw length.

Q. What is the secret to accurate shooting?
A. That's an easy one! Do as little work as possible. Once you understand what that means, you'll have figured out how to play this game!

Appendix E

Glossary

Aiming – Method of directing an arrow toward its intended mark.

AMO – Archery Manufacturers' Organization. Governing body, setting standards for the archery industry. Name recently changed to ATA (Archery Trade Association).

Anchor – verb. To reach full-draw and lock the hand into a defined position on the face.

Anchor – noun. Place on the archer's face where his drawing hand contacts and locks in at full draw. A "reference point" is also where part of the drawing hand touches the archer's face, but does not lock in, as the anchor does.

Aperture – Literally a "hole". Type of sight where the archer centers his target in a circular opening.

Archer's Paradox – The bending of an arrow around the riser, due to its offset from center shot, as it's being fired.

Arc – The path of an arrow in flight, technically a "parabolic arc".

Archer – Someone skilled in the use of a bow and arrow. Note the word "skilled".

Archery – The skill of shooting a bow and arrow.

Arm-guard – Leather or plastic shield used to protect the forearm of the bow arm from occasional string slaps.

Arrow – Projectile to be launched from a bow.

Arrow rest – Device added to the bow above the shelf to support the arrow during the draw, at anchor, and during the first few inches of flight.

Arrow shelf – Flat or radiused part of the riser, perpendicular to the long axis of the riser. May be covered with leather or similar material, to act as an arrow rest.

Arrowhead – The pointy end of the arrow. The part of the arrow that defines its purpose.

ATA – See "AMO".

B-50 – Dacron bowstring material.

Back (of bow) – Part of the bow that faces away from the archer.

Backstop – Area or material behind the target capable of stopping errant arrows.

Back Tension – Term describing the force maintained against the bow and bow string by the deep back muscles, while at anchor and after the shot.

Ballooning – Separation of the strands of a bowstring during the shot. Usually an indication of insufficient twists and/or wax.

Barebow – Shooting a bow without sighting devices attached.

Belly (of bow) – Part of the bow that faces the archer, also called the "face" of the bow.

Blank bale shooting – Shooting at a target butt with no target face. Used for form training.

Blunt Point – Arrowhead usually made from rubber or metal used to dispatch small game by impact or "shock".

Bow – Device, when braced by a string, which has the capability to launch an arrow.

Bowman – See "Archer".

Bow Sight – Device added to a bow, used to aim an arrow. It is calibrated to make the archer's line of sight coincide with the device at the arrow's point of impact.

Bow Square – "T" shaped tool used to measure brace heights and tiller.

Bowstring, Endless Loop – String made from one continuous strand of material and bound together by serving material. See Chapter 11.

Bowstring, Flemish Splice – String made from individual strands of material and bound together by braiding or "splicing" the ends together. See Chapter 11.

Bowyer – One who makes bows.

Brace height – The distance from the deepest part of a strung bow's grip to a point perpendicular on the string.

Braced (bow) – Strung (bow).

Bracer – Old English term for an arm-guard.

Broadhead – Specific type of arrowhead with two or more sharp edges used for hunting.

Bullseye – Center circle of a target; the highest scoring area.

Butt(s) – Target material that arrows are shot into. Bales of hay for example.

Cap Dip – Method of painting the shaftment of an arrow by dipping it into a tube filled with paint.

Cast – Distance and speed with which a bow can propel an arrow.

Center-shot – Bow with its sight window cut past the centerline. Center-shot position of the arrow means that a strung bow, when viewed from the rear (face side) and held so the string appears to bisect the upper limb, will also bisect the arrow.

Central – Anatomical term meaning closer to the center of a body or object.

Cock Feather – Odd colored feather, typically set perpendicular to the long axis of a stickbow. Also called the "Index Feather".

Compound bow – A bow using cables and eccentric pulleys (cams) to increase the mechanical advantage of the limbs.

Collapse – Forward flinch of the drawing shoulder, just prior to releasing the bowstring.

Compound bow – A bow with pulleys or cams at one or both limb tips, which increase the limb's mechanical advantage.

Creep – The technical term for the permanent elongation of a material.

Creeping – Forward movement of the drawing hand or shoulder while holding at full-draw, effectively shortening the draw prior to release.

Crest – Bands of paint at the leading edge of the shaftment, for arrow decoration or identification.

Deep hook – Placing the hand on the string so the string is seated in the crease of the first joint from the fingertip.

Deflex – Positioning of the distal ends of the riser or proximal ends of the limbs toward the shooter.

Distal – Anatomical term meaning farther away from the center of a body or object.

Draw weight – Weight, in pounds, required to pull the bowstring back to the archer's anchor point. Typically measured at 28".

Draw length – Distance measured from the deepest part of the nock's groove to a point 1.75" forward of the deepest part of the bow's grip, when the archer is at full draw. For all practical purposes, it can be measured to the back of the arrow shelf.

Elevation – 1. Sight adjustment to compensate for a high or low point of impact. 2. Amount the bow needs to be raised or lowered to hit a given mark.

End – Number of arrows shot at one time, prior to retrieval.

Endless Loop string – See Bowstring, Endless.

Face (of bow) – See "Belly (of bow)".

Face Walking – Aiming method where the archer places the tip of his arrow on the target's center and changes his anchor point to adjust for different distances.

Fast Flight – Bowstring or bowstring material made from Vectran. Very lightweight and stretch resistant.

Field point – Arrow head with a shoulder beyond the primary point, to hinder penetration into wood or similar objects.

Fistmele – See Brace height.

Fish-tailing – Visible horizontal fluctuations in an arrow's flight.

FITA - Federation Internationale de Tir a L'Arc (aka: International Archery Federation). Governing body of international target archery.

FITA round – One of several types of matches sanctioned by FITA. Typically an outdoor round, consisting of 144 arrows, 36 shot in six ends of six arrows each at 90, 70, 50, and 30 meters.

FITA bow – see Olympic bow.

Flemish Splice string – See Bowstring, Flemish Splice.

Fletcher – One who makes arrows.

Fletching – The feathers or vanes on the rear of an arrow used to stabilize it in flight.

Fletching, Helical – Feathers or vanes applied so the quill wraps around the curvature of the shaft.

Fletching, Offset – Feathers or vanes applied so the quill is at a slight angle to the long axis of the shaft.

Fletching, Straight – Feathers or vanes applied so the quill is in line with the long axis of the shaft.

FOC – see Front of Center.

Follow-through – What happens after the string is released.

Footed shaft – Wood arrow with a second piece of wood spliced to it at the leading end.

Form – Posture and position for a given activity, in this case, practicing archery.

Freestyle – Shooting style using sights. See Barebow, Unlimited Freestyle.

Front of Center – The ratio of the balance point of an arrow to its overall length.

G-nock – Small nock used on a target arrow that fits into a nock bushing.

Game – In target archery, a subdivision of a match. For example, an indoor NFAA match is comprised of 3 "games", each consisting of 4 ends of 5 arrows.

Game (animal) – Any legally hunted animal.

Gap – Aiming method where the archer places the tip of the arrow a specified distance away from the point he wishes to hit.

Glove, Shooting – Skeleton-type glove with finger stalls for the index, middle and ring fingers of the drawing hand, and straps that attach to a wristband.

Group – Relative placement or clustering of arrows in a target.

H-nock – Small nock used on a target or hunting arrow that fits into a nock bushing. Larger than a G-nock.

Hen Feathers – Two feathers of the same color, typically set 60 degrees from the bowstring.

IBO – International Bowhunters Organization. Group similar to the AMO, dealing primarily with bowhunting issues.

Index Feather – See "Cock Feather".

Instinctive shooting – Aiming method where the archer focuses on the point he wishes to hit and allows his subconscious to interpret various data inputs to direct his arrow towards that point.

Insert – Metal or plastic bushing into which an arrowhead or nock is screwed or pushed.

Judo Point – Arrowhead with small wire arms perpendicular to the arrow, designed to prevent the arrow from burying itself under brush and getting lost.

KISS – Keep It Simple, Stupid; a basic principle, germane to archery.

Kisser button – A small disk attached to the string that the archer places between his lips as a reference point to his anchor.

Lamination – The practice of gluing several similar or dissimilar materials together to increase the strength, performance or esthetics of a bow or arrow.

Limb – The working part of a bow.

Longbow – Bow which when braced contacts the string only at the string nocks.

Loose – See "Release".

Match – An archery competition.

Matt – See "Butt".

Modulus (of elasticity) – Elastic force of a substance or material. Defined as the ratio of stress (force) to the distortion the material experiences when the aforementioned force is applied. The higher the modulus, the more stress the material can withstand before it fails.

NIBB – New Improved Balanced Bullet. A type of bullet-shaped target arrowhead specifically made for each size aluminum, carbon or aluminum/carbon composite shaft to yield a FOC of 7% to 9%.

Nock – Any groove in an arrow or bow that engages the string. Arrow nocks are typically separate plastic pieces glued or pressed into the tail end of the arrow.

Nocking point – Physical device on the bowstring, that provides consistent arrow placement.

Nockset – A plastic lined metal ring, crimped onto the string as a nocking point.

No-Gluv – Rubber sleeves slid over the center serving of a bowstring, creating a nocking point and eliminating the need for a tab or glove.

Ogive - A pointed, curved surface used to form the approximately streamlined nose of a projectile.

Olympic Bow – Recurve bow designed and configured for Olympic style competition. Usually used synonymously with FITA bow, although the actual configurations may be slightly different.

Over-bowed – (Using a bow that is) too heavy for a given archer to handle correctly.

Parabolic Fletching – Feathers or vanes with a rounded trailing edge.

Peep Sight – Small aperture attached to the string, used in some types of target shooting.

Perfect – Highest possible score on a given end, game or match.

Pile – See "Arrowhead".

Piles – Hemorrhoids. (Possible symptom of being over-bowed.)
Pin nocks – Type of arrow nock used on some high-end target arrows.

Pivot Point – The deepest area of a bow's grip.

Pluck (Plucking the string) – An outward movement of the hand (away from the face) on release.

Point Of Aim – Aiming method where the archer places the tip of the arrow on a set point other than the point he wishes to hit. Once that point is established, the archer will not focus on the target at all.

Point On Distance – That distance where the arrowhead overlays the center of the bullseye while aiming.

Porpoising – Visible vertical fluctuations in an arrow's flight.

Possible – See "Perfect".

Power stroke – The distance for which the arrow is in contact with and propelled by the string.

Quiver – Device for holding arrows in a position accessible to the archer during a shooting session.

Range – Indoor or outdoor area for shooting. Also may mean distance from the shooter to the target.

Recurve – Bow, which when braced, contacts the string at the string nocks, and lies along the first several inches of the distal limb ends.

Reference Point – Point on face or neck to act as an additional locator for the anchor position.

Reflex – Positioning of the distal ends of the riser or proximal ends of the limbs away from the shooter.

Reflex – Physical reaction not involving higher brain centers.

Release – Letting go of the string, hopefully after an anchor has been reached.

Release Aid – Hand- or wrist-held triggering device to release the string.

Release, Dead – Release method where the drawing hand remains in the same position both before and after the shot.

Release, Pull-through – Also called a "Dynamic Release". Release method where the drawing hand snaps rearward after the shot.

Riser – Center part of the bow, to which the limbs are attached.

Round – See "Match".

Robinhood – Splitting a wooden arrow lengthwise. With aluminum or carbon, the second arrow flutes the first. By definition, the first arrow must be in the bullseye!

Self bow – A bow made from a single material or single piece of material.

Self nock – Arrow nock created by cutting a groove in the end of a wooden arrow, typically perpendicular to the grain.
Serving – Material wound around the bowstring either to bind the strands together or protect them.

Shaft – Tube or dowel destined to become an arrow. Also slang for arrow.

Shaftment – The last 8 to 10 or 12 inches of an arrow, towards the nock end.

Shield-cut Feather – Feathers or vanes, with a flat (perpendicular to the arrow) trailing edge. Thought to resemble an elongated medieval knight's shield, divided in half, lengthwise.

Shock – The forward motion of the bow limbs being abruptly stopped by the bowstring.

Sight – See "Bow Sight".

Sight Extension (bar) – Device used to move the sight away from the shooter's eye.

Sight, Olympic or FITA type – Target style bow sight with precision elevation and windage adjustments.

Sight, hunting – Bow sight with multiple pins or apertures that can be set for several distances. Typically, more compact than target-style sights.

Sight Radius – The distance from the shooter's eye to the sighting device.

Sight Window – Part of the riser above the arrow shelf, cut out to bring the arrow closer to center-shot, and give the archer a better view of his target.

Skirt, Target – Non-scoring area of a target face.

Snap shooting – Releasing the bowstring either before anchor or before a solid anchor is achieved.

Spine, Dynamic – Amount of actual flexing an arrow undergoes during a shot.

Spine, Static – Measurement of an arrow's stiffness.

Spent Arrow – Arrow that has lost all the energy imparted by the bow.

Split Finger – (Placing the arrow) between the index and middle fingers, in preparation for a shot.

Stance – Position of the feet in relation to the target face.

Stave – Wood billet destined to become a bow, typically a self-bow.

Stabilizer – Any weight added to a bow to increase its inertia or enhance its balance.

Stickbow – A bow with a single string attached to the end of each limb, not using pulleys or cams to increase performance.

String follow – Property of a self bow where the limbs do not return to their original position when unstrung after a shooting session.

String Keeper – Leather or plastic device used to hold a bowstring in place while the bow is unstrung.

String Walking – Aiming method where the archer places the tip of the arrow on the target's center and moves his drawing fingers down the string to adjust for different distances.

Stretch – Technical term for the recoverable elongation of a material. In archery jargon, any elongation recoverable or not.

Tab – Leather or plastic plate, covering and protecting the fingers of the drawing hand.

Take-down (bow) – Bow that comes apart in two or three pieces for easy transport, or for changing limb length or weight.

Target – Arrow receptacle. See "Matt" and "Butt".

Target Face – Paper or cardboard, typically with concentric circles used for aiming and scoring.

Target Panic – Inability to execute a controlled shot. Typical symptoms include the inability to anchor (short-drawing), hold at anchor (snap-shooting), release before being on target or the inability to release the string.

T/D – See "Take-down".

Tiller – Relative strength of the upper to lower limb, or the relative reflex or deflex of the limbs to each other.

Tip Protector – Plastic or rubber cup placed on a limb tip to protect it from being marred if left in an upright position (while strung).

Torque – Twisting action by the archer on the bow or string, generally with detrimental results.

Traditional Archery – Very broad term originating in the 1980's used to distinguish stickbows from compound bows.

Trigger – See "Release Aid".

Trigger – Psychological stimulus having a positive or negative effect on an athlete's performance.

Trigger – Roy Roger's horse. You're probably wondering why Roy Roger's horse is included in a book on Archery. In addition to carrying Roy Rogers, Trigger also carried Maid Marion (Olivia DeHaviland) in The Adventures of Robinhood with Errol Flynn (Warner Bros 1938).

Tuning – Various methods of modifying certain parameters of the bow and/or arrows for optimal efficiency.

Under-bowed – (Using a bow that is) too light for a given task.

UNI-bushing – (Universal Nock Insert) Insert that accepts UNI-bushing type push-in nocks.

Unlimited Freestlye – Shooting style that allows sights and release adds.

Vane – Plastic fletching.

Watch the Arrow Exercise – Form exercise where the shooter focuses on the tip of the arrow or face of the bow and not the target.

Windage – 1. Sight adjustment to compensate for a left or right point of impact. 2. Amount the bow needs to be held to the right or left to hit a given mark.
X-nock – Arrow nock used on some carbon arrows that fits into a nock bushing. Similar in size to an H-nock.

Zeroing – Calibrating a bow sight so that the sighting device coincides with the desired point of impact.

- Viper out.

9 781602 642447